The Linwoods

THE LINWOODS.

CHAPTER I.

Un notable exemple de la forcenée curiosité de notre nature, s'amusant se préoccuper des choses futures, comme si elle n'avoit pas assez à faire à désirer les présentes.

MONTAIGNE.

SOME two or three years before our revolutionary war, just at the close of day, two girls were seen entering Broadway through a wicket garden-gate, in the rear of a stately mansion which fronted on Broad-street, that being then the court-end of the city—the residence of unquestioned aristocracy (*sic transit gloria mundi !*), whence royal favour and European fashions were diffused through the province of New York.

The eldest of the two girls had entered upon her teens. She was robust and tall for her years, with the complexion of a Hebe, very dark hair, an eye (albeit belonging to one of the weaker sex) that looked as if she were born to empire—it might be over hearts and eyes—and the step of a young Juno. The younger could be likened neither to goddess, queen, nor anything that assumed or loved command. She was of earth's gentlest and finest mould—framed for all tender humanities, with the destiny of woman written on her meek brow. "Thou art born to love, to suffer, to obey,—to minister, and not to be ministered to." Well did she fulfil her mission ! The girls were followed by a black servant in livery. The elder pressed forward as if impelled by some powerful motive, while her companion lagged behind,—sometimes chasing a young bird, then smelling the roses that peeped through the garden paling ; now stopping to pat a good-natured mastiff, or caress a chubby child. Many a one attracted her with its broad shining face and linsey-woolsey short gown and petticoat, seated with a family group on the freshly-scoured steps of the Dutch habitations that occurred at intervals on their way. "Come, do come along, Bessie, you are stopping for everything," said her companion, impatiently. Poor Bessie, with the keenest sensibility, had, what rarely accompanies it, a general susceptibility to external impressions,—one might have fancied she had an extra set of nerves. When the girls had nearly reached St. Paul's church, their attendant remonstrated,—"Miss Isabella, you are getting quite out to the fields—missis said you were only going a turn up the Broadway."

"So I am, Jupe."

"A pretty long turn," muttered Jupiter ; and after proceeding a few paces further, he added, in a raised voice, "the sun is going down, Miss Isabella."

"That was news at twelve o'clock, Jupiter."

"But it really is nearly set now, Isabella," interposed her companion Bessie.

"Well, what if it is, Bessie ?—it is just the right time—Effie is always surest between sundown and dark."

"Mercy, Isabella ! you are not going to Effie's. It is horrid to go there after sundown—please, Isabella, don't." Isabella only replied by a "Pshaw, child !" and a laugh.

Bessie mustered her moral courage (it required it all to oppose Isabella), and, stopping short, said, "I am not sure it is right to go there at all."

"There is neither right nor wrong in the matter, Bessie,—you are always splitting hairs." Notwithstanding her bold profession, Isabella paused, and with a tremulousness of voice that indicated she was not indifferent to the cardinal points in her path of morality, she added,—"Why do you think it is not right, Bessie ?"

"Because the Bible says, that sorcery, and divination, and everything of that kind, is wicked."

"Nonsense, child ! that was in old times, you know."

Isabella's evasion might have quieted a rationalist of the present day, but not Bessie, who had been bred in the strict school of New England orthodoxy ; and she replied, "What was right and wrong in old times, is right and wrong now, Isabella."

"Don't preach, Bessie—I will venture all the harm of going to Effie's ; and you may lay the sin at my door ;" and with her usual independent, fear-nought air, she turned into a shady lane that led by a cross-cut to "Aunt Katy's garden,"—a favourite resort of the citizens for rural recreations. The Chatham-street theatre has since occupied the same spot—that theatre is now a church. Isabella quickened her pace. Bessie followed most unwillingly. "Miss Belle," cried out Jupiter, "I must detest, in your ma's name, against your succeeding farther."

"The tiresome old fool !" With this exclamation on her lips, Isabella turned round, and drawing her person up to the height of womanhood, she added, "I shall go just as far as I please, Jupe—follow me ; if anybody is scolded it shall be me, not you. I wish mama," she continued, pursuing her way, "would not send Jupe after us,—just as if we were two babies in leading-strings."

"I would not go a step further for the world, if he were not with us," said Bessie.

"And pray, what good would he do us if there were danger—such a desperate coward as he is ?"

"He is a man, Isabella."

B

"He has the form of one ;—Jupe," she called out (the spirit of mischief playing about her arch mouth), pointing to a slight elevation, called Gallows Hill, where a gibbet was standing, "Jupe, is not that the place where they hung the poor creatures who were concerned in the negro-plot ?"

"Yes, miss, sure it is the awful place :" and he mended his pace, to be as near as might be to the young ladies.

"Did not some of your relations suffer there, Jupiter ?"

"Yes, miss, two of my poster'ty—my grandmother and aunt Venus."

Isabella repressed a smile, and said, with unaffected seriousness, "It was a shocking business, Bessie—a hundred and fifty poor wretches sacrificed, I have heard papa say. Is it true, Jupe, that their ghosts walk about here, and have been seen many a time when it was so dark you could not discern your hand before your face ?"

"I dare say, Miss Belle. Them that's hung onjustly always travels."

"But how could they be seen in such darkness ?"

"'Case, miss, you know ghosts have a light in their anterior, just like lanterns."

"Have they ? I never understood it before—what a horrid cracking that gibbet makes ! Bless us ! and there is very little wind."

"That makes no distinctions, miss ; it begins as the sun goes down, and keeps it up all night. Miss Belle, stop one minute—don't go across the hill—that is right in the ghost-track ! "

"Oh don't, for pity's sake, Isabella," said Bessie, imploringly.

"Hush, Bessie, it is the shortest way, and " (in a whisper) " I want to scare Jupe. Jupe, it seems to me there is an odd hot feel in the ground here."

"There sarten is, miss, a very onhealthy feeling."

"And, my goodness ! Jupiter, don't you feel a very, very slight kind of trembling—a shake—or a roll, as if something were walking in the earth, under our feet ?"

"I do ; and it gets worser and worser, every step."

"It feels like children playing under the bed, and hitting the sacking with their heads."

"Oh, Lord, miss—yes—it goes bump, bump, against my feet."

By this time they had passed to the further side of the hill, so as to place the gibbet between them and the western sky, lighted up with one of those brilliant and transient radiations that sometimes immediately succeed the sun's setting, diffusing a crimson glow, and outlining the objects relieved against the sky with light red. Our young heroine, like all geniuses, knew how to seize a circumstance. "Oh, Jupe," she exclaimed, "look, what a line of blood is drawn round the gibbet ! "

"The Lord have marcy on us, miss ! "

"And, dear me ! I think I see a faint shadow of a man with a rope round his neck, and his head on one side—do you see, Jupe ? "

Poor Jupe did not reply. He could bear it no longer. His fear of his young mistress—his fear of a scolding at home, all were merged in the terror Isabella had conjured up by the aid of the traditionary superstitions with which his mind was previously filled ; and without attempting an answer, he fairly ran off the ground, leaving Isabella laughing, and Bessie expostulating, and confessing that she did not in the least wonder poor Jupe was scared. Once more she ventured to intreat Isabella to give up the expedition to Effie's, for this time at least, when she was interrupted and reassured by the appearance of two friends, in the persons of Isabella's brother and Jasper Meredith, returning, with their dogs and guns, from a day's sport.

"What wild-goose chase are you on, Belle, at this time of day ? " asked her brother ; " I am sure Bessie Lee has not come to Gallows hill with her own good will."

"I have made game of my goose, at any rate, and given Bessie Lee a good lesson, on what our old schoolmaster would call the potentiality of mankind—but come," she added, for though rather ashamed to confess her purpose when she knew ridicule must be braved, courage was easier to Isabella than subterfuge, "come along with us to Effie's, and I will tell you the joke I played off on Jupe." Isabella's joke seemed to her auditors a capital one, for they were at that happy age when laughter does not ask a reason to break forth from the full fountain of youthful spirits. Isabella spun out her story till they reached Effie's door, which admitted them, not to any dark laboratory of magic, but to a snug little Dutch parlour, with a nicely-sanded floor—a fireplace gay with the flowers of the season, peonies and Guelder-roses, and ornamented with storied tiles, that, if not as classic, were, as we can vouch, far more entertaining than the sculptured marble of our own luxurious days.

The pythoness Effie turned her art to good account, producing substantial comforts by her mysterious science ; and playing her cards well for this world, whatever bad dealings she might have with another. Even Bessie felt her horror of witchcraft diminished before this plump personage, with a round, good-humoured face, looking far more like the good vrow of a Dutch picture than the gaunt skinny hag who has personated the professors of the bad art from the Witch of Endor downwards. Effie's physiognomy, save an ominous contraction of her eyelids, and the keen and somewhat sinister glances that shot between them, betrayed nothing of her calling.

There were, as on all similar occasions, some initiatory ceremonies to be observed before the fortunes were told. Herbert, boylike, was penniless ; and he offered a fine brace of snipes to propitiate the oracle. They were accepted with a smile that augured well for the official response he should receive. Jasper's purse, too, was empty : and after ransacking his pockets in vain, he slipped out a gold sleeve-button, and told Effie he would redeem it the next time he came her way. Meanwhile there was a little by-talk between Isabella and Bessie ; Isabella insisting on paying the fee for her friend, and Bessie insisting that "she would have no fortune told,—that she did not believe Effie could tell it, and if she could, she would not for all the world let her." In vain Isabella ridiculed and reasoned by turns. Bessie, blushing and trembling, persisted. Effie at the same moment was shuffling a pack of cards, as black as if they had been sent up from Pluto's realms; and while she was muttering over some incomprehensible phrases, and apparently absorbed in the manipulation of her art, she heard and saw all that passed, and determined that if poor little Bessie would not acknowledge, she should feel her power.

Herbert, the most incredulous, and therefore the boldest, first came forward to confront his destiny. "A great deal of rising in the world, and but little sinking for you, Master Herbert Linwood; you are to go over the salt water, and ride foremost in the royal hunting-grounds."

"Good!—good!—go on, Effie."

"Oh what beauties of horses—a pack of hounds—High! how the steeds go—how they leap—the buck is at bay—there are you!"

"Capital, Effie!—I strike him down!"

"You are too fast, young master—I can tell no more than I see—the sport is past—the place is changed—there is a battle-field, drums, trumpets, and flags flying—Ah, there is a sign of danger—a pit yawns at your feet."

"Shocking!" cried Bessie; "pray don't listen any more, Herbert."

"Pshaw, Bessie! I shall clear the pit. Effie loves snipes too well to leave me the wrong side of that."

Effie was either offended at Herbert's intimation that her favours might be bought, or perhaps she saw his lack of faith in his laughing eye, and, determined to punish him, she declared that all was dark and misty beyond the pit; there might be a leap over it, and a smooth road beyond—she could not tell—she could only tell what she saw.

"You are a croaking raven, Effie!" exclaimed Herbert; "I'll shuffle my own fortune!" and seizing the cards, he handled them as knowingly as the sibyl herself, and ran over a jargon quite as unintelligible; and then holding them fast, out of Effie's reach, he ran on—"Ah, ha—I see the mist going off like the whiff from a Dutchman's pipe; and here's a grand castle, and parks, and pleasure-grounds; and here am I, with a fine blue-eyed lady within it." Then dashing down the cards, he turned and kissed Bessie's reddening cheek, saying, "Let others wait on fortune, Effie; I'll carve my own."

Isabella was nettled at Herbert's open contempt of Effie's seership. She would not confess or examine the amount of her faith, nor did she choose to be made to feel on how tottering a base it rested. She was exactly at that point of credulity where much depends on the sympathy of others. It is said to be essential to the success of animal magnetism, that not only the operator and the subject, but the spectators, should believe. Isabella felt she was on disenchanted ground, while Herbert, with his quizzical smile, stood charged, and aiming at her a volley of ridicule; and she proposed that those who yet had their fortunes to hear should, one after another, retire with Effie to a little inner room. But Herbert cried out, "Fair play, fair play! Dame Effie has read the riddle of my destiny to you all, and now it is but fair I should hear yours."

Bessie saw Isabella's reluctance, and she again interposed, reminding her of "mama—the coming night," &c.; and poor Isabella was fain to give up the contest for the secret conference, and hush Bessie, by telling Effie to proceed.

"Shall I tell your *fortin* and that young gentleman's together!" asked Effie, pointing to Jasper. Her manner was careless; but she cast a keen glance at Isabella, to ascertain how far she might blend their destinies.

"Oh, no, no—no partnership for me," cried Isabella; while the fire which flashed from her eye evinced that the thought of a partnership with Jasper, if disagreeable, was not indifferent to her.

"Nor for me, either, mother Effie," said Jasper; "or if there be a partnership, let it be with the pretty blue-eyed mistress of Herbert's mansion."

"Nay, master, that pretty miss does not choose her fortune told—and she's right—poor thing!" she added, with an ominous shake of the head. Bessie's heart quailed, for she both believed and feared.

"Now, shame on you, Effie!" cried Herbert; "she cannot know anything about you, Bessie; she has not even looked at your fortune yet."

"Did I say I *knew*, Master Herbert! Time must show whether I know or not."

Bessie still looked apprehensively. "Nonsense," said Herbert; "what can she know!—she never saw you before."

"True, I never saw her; but I tell you, young lad, there is such a thing as seeing the shadow of things far distant and past, and never seeing the realities, though it be they that cast the shadows." Bessie shuddered—Effie shuffled the cards. "Now just for a trial," said she: "I will tell you something about her—not of the future; for I'd be loath to overcast her sky before the time comes—but of the past."

"Pray, do not," interposed Bessie; "I don't wish you to say anything about me, past, present, or to come."

"Oh, Bessie," whispered Isabella, "let her try—there can be no harm if you do not ask her—the past is past, you know—now we have a chance to know if she really is wiser than others." Bessie again resolutely shook her head.

"Let her go on," whispered Herbert, "and see what a fool she will make of herself."

"Let her go on, dear Bessie," said Jasper, "or she will think she has made a fool of you."

Bessie feared that her timidity was folly in Jasper's eyes; and she said, "She may go on if you all wish, but I will not hear her;" and she covered her ears with her hands.

"Shall I!" asked Effie, looking at Isabella; Isabella nodded assent, and she proceeded. "She has come from a great distance—her people are well to do in the world, but no such quality as yours, Miss Isabella Linwood—she has found some things here pleasanter than she expected—some not so pleasant—the house she was born in stands on the sunny side of a hill." At each pause that Effie made, Isabella gave a nod of acquiescence to what she said; and this, or some stray words, which might easily have found their way through Bessie's little hands, excited her curiosity, and by degrees they slid down so as to oppose a very slight obstruction to Effie's voice. "Before the house," she continued, "and not so far distant but she may hear its roaring when a storm uplifts it, is the wide sea—that sea has cost the poor child dear." Bessie's heart throbbed audibly. "Since she came here she has both won love and lost it."

"There, there you are out," cried Herbert, glad of an opportunity to stop the current that was becoming too strong for poor Bessie.

"She can best tell herself whether I am right," said Effie, coolly.

"She is right—right in all," said Bessie, retreating to conceal the tears that were starting from her eyes.

Isabella neither saw nor heard this—she was only struck with what Effie delivered as a proof of her preternatural skill; and, more than ever eager to inquire into her own destiny, she took the place Bessie had vacated.

Effie saw her faith, and was determined to reward it. "Miss Isabella Linwood, you are born to walk in no common track,"—she might have read this prediction, written with an unerring hand on the girl's lofty brow, and in her eloquent eye. "You will be both served and honoured—those that have stood in king's palaces will bow down to you—but the sun does not always shine on the luckiest—you will have a dark day—trouble when you least expect it—joy when you are not looking for it." This last was one of Effie's staple prophecies, and was sure to be verified in the varied web of every individual's experience. "You have had some trouble lately, but it will soon pass away, and for ever." A safe prediction in regard to any girl of twelve years. "You'll have plenty of friends, and lots of suitors—the right one will be—"

"Oh, never mind—don't say who, Effie," cried Isabella, gaspingly.

"I was only going to say the right one will be tall and elegant, with beautiful large eyes—I can't say whether blue or black—but black, I think; for his hair is both dark and curling."

"Bravo, bravissimo, *brother* Jasper!" exclaimed Herbert; "it is your curly pate Effie sees in those black cards, beyond a doubt."

"I bow to destiny," replied Jasper, with an arch smile, that caught Isabella's eye.

"I do not," she retorted—"look again, Effie —it must not be curling hair—I despise it."

"I see but once, miss, and then clearly; but there's curling hair on more heads than one."

"I never—never should like any one with curling hair," persisted Isabella.

"It would be no difficult task for *you* to pull it straight, Miss Isabella," said the provoking Jasper. Isabella only replied by her heightened colour; and bending over the table, she begged Effie to proceed.

"There's not much more shown me, miss,— you will have some tangled ways—besetments, wonderments, and disappointments."

"Effie's version of the 'course of true love never does run smooth,'" interposed Jasper.

"But all will end well," she concluded; "your husband will be the man of your heart—he will be beautiful and rich, and great; and take you home to spend your days in merry England."

"Thank you—thank you, Effie," said Isabella, languidly. The "beauty, riches, and days spent in England" were well enough, for beauty and riches are elements in a maiden's *beau-idéal*; and England was then the earthly paradise of the patrician colonists. But she was not just now in

a humour to acquiesce in the local habitation and the name which the "dark curling hair" had given to the ideal personage.

Jasper Meredith had not even a shadow of faith in Effie; but next to being fortune's favourite, he liked to appear so; and contriving, unperceived by his companions, to slip his remaining sleeve-button into Effie's hand, he said, "Keep them both;" and added aloud, "Now for my luck, Dame Effie; and be it weal or be it woe, deliver it truly."

Effie was propitiated, and would gladly have imparted the golden tinge of Jasper's bribe to his future destiny; but the opportunity was too tempting to be resisted, to prove to him that she was mastered by a higher power: and looking very solemn, and shaking her head, she said, "There are too many dark spots here. Ah, Mr. Jasper Meredith — disappointment! — the arrow just misses the mark—the cup is filled to the brim—the hand is raised—the lips parted to receive it—then comes the slip!" She hesitated, she seemed alarmed; perhaps she was so, for it is impossible to say how far a weak mind may become the dupe of its own impostures—"Do not ask me any farther," she added.—The young people now all gathered round her. Bessie rested her elbows on the table, and her burning cheeks on her hands, and on Effie riveted her eyes, which, from their natural blue, were deepened almost to black, and absolutely glowing with the intensity of her interest.

"Go on, Effie," cried Jasper; "if fortune is cross, I'll give her wheel a turn."

"Ah, the wheel turns but too fast—a happy youth is uppermost."

"So far, so good."

"An early marriage."

"That may be weal, or may be woe," said Jasper; "weal it is," he added, in mock heroic; "but for the dread of something *after*."

"An early death!"

"For me, Effie! Heaven forefend!"

"No, not for you; for here you are again a leader on a battle-field—the dead and dying in heaps—pools of blood—there's the end on't," she concluded, shuddering, and throwing down the cards.

"What, leave me there, Effie! Oh no—death or victory!"

"It may be death, it may be victory; it is not given to me to see which."

Jasper, quite undaunted, was on the point of protesting against a destiny so uncertain, when a deep-drawn sigh from Bessie attracted the eyes of the group; they perceived the colour had faded from her cheeks, and that she was on the point of fainting. The windows were thrown open—Effie produced a cordial, and the fair girl was soon restored to a sense of her condition, which she attempted to explain, by saying, she was apt to faint even at the thought of blood!

They were now all ready, and quite willing, to bid adieu to the oracle, whose responses not having been entirely satisfactory to any one of them, they all acquiesced in Bessie's remark, that, "if it were ever so right, she did not think there was much comfort in going to a fortune-teller."

Each seemed in a more thoughtful humour

than usual, and they walked on in silence till they reached the space now the park, then a favourite play-ground for children, shaded by a few locust-trees, and here and there an elm or stunted oak. Leaning against one of these was the fine erect figure of a man, who seemed just declining from the meridian of life, past its first ripeness and perfection, but still far from the decay of age. "Ah, you runaways!" he exclaimed, on seeing the young people advancing. "Belle, your mother has been in the fidgets about you for the last hour."

"Jupiter might have told her, papa, that we were quite safe."

"Jupe, truly! he came home with a rigmarole that we could make nothing of. I assured her there was no danger, but that assurance never quieted any woman. Herbert, can you tell me what these boys are about? they seem rather to be at work than play."

"What are you about, Ned?" cried Herbert to a young acquaintance.

"Throwing up a redoubt to protect our fort;" and he pointed as he spoke to a rude structure of poles, bricks, and broken planks on an eminence, at the extremity of the unfenced ground.

"And what is your fort for, my lad!" asked Mr. Linwood.

"To keep off the British, sir."

"The British! and who are you?"

"Americans, sir!"

A loud huzzaing was heard from the fort— "What does that mean!" asked Mr. Linwood.

"The whigs are hanging a tory, sir."

"The little rebel rascals!—Herbert!—you throwing up your hat and huzzaing too!"

"Certainly, sir—I am a regular whig."

"A regular fool! put on your hat—and use it like a gentleman. This matter shall be looked into—here are the seeds of rebellion springing up in their young hot bloods—this may come to something, if it is not seen to in time. Jasper, do you hear anything of this jargon in your schools?"

"Lord bless me! yes, sir; the boys are regularly divided into whigs and tories—they have their badges and their pass-words, and I am sorry to say that the whigs are three to one."

"You are loyal then, my dear boy?"

"Certainly, sir, I owe allegiance to the country in which I was born."

"And you, my hopeful Mr. Herbert, with your huzzas, what say you for yourself?"

"I say ditto to Jasper, sir—I owe allegiance to the country in which I was born."

"Don't be a fool, Herbert—don't be a fool, even in jest—I hate a whig as I do a toad; and if my son should prove a traitor to his king and country, by George, I would cut him off for ever!"

"But, sir," said the imperturbable Herbert, "if he should choose between his king and country——"

"There is no such thing—they are the same—so no more of that."

"I am glad Herbert has his warning in time," whispered Isabella to Bessie.

"But it seems to me he is right for all," replied Bessie.

So arbitrarily do circumstances mould opinions.

Isabella seemed like one who might have been born a rebel chieftainess, Bessie as if her destiny were passive obedience.

We have thus introduced some of the *dramatis personæ* to our readers. It may seem that in their visit to Effie, they prematurely exhibited the sentiments of riper years — but what are boys and girls but the prototypes of men and women! — time and art may tinge and polish the wood, but the texture remains as nature formed it.

Bessie Lee was an exotic in New-York. The history of her being there was simply this. New England has, from the first, been a favourite school for the youth from the middle and southern states. Mr. Linwood sent Herbert (who had given him some trouble by early manifesting that love of self-direction which might have been the germ of his whiggism) to a Latin school in a country town near Boston. While there, he boarded in the family of a Colonel Lee, a respectable farmer, who had acquired his title and some military fame in the campaign of 'forty-five against the French. Herbert remained a year with the Lees, and returned the kindness he received there with a hearty and lasting affection. Here was his first experience of country life; and every one knows how delightful to childhood are its freedom, exercises, and pleasures, in harmony (felt, long before understood) with all the laws of our nature. When Herbert returned, he was eloquent in his praises of Bessie—her beauty, gaiety (*then* the excitability of her disposition sometimes appeared in extravagant spirits), her sweetness and manageableness; a feminine quality that he admired the more from having had to contend with a contrary disposition in his sister Isabella, who, in all their childish competitions, had manifested what our Shaker friends would call a *leading gift*. Isabella's curiosity being excited to see this *rara avis* of Herbert (with her the immediate consequence of an inclination was to find the means of its gratification), she asked her parents to send for Bessie to come to New-York, and go to school with her. Mrs. Linwood, a model of conjugal nonentity, gave her usual reply, "Just as your papa says, dear." Her father seldom said her nay, and Isabella thought her point gained, till he referred the decision of the matter to her aunt Archer.

"Oh dear! now I shall have to argue the matter an hour; but never mind, I can always persuade aunt at last." Mrs. Archer, as Isabella had foreboded, was opposed to the arrangement —she thought there would be positive unkindness in transplanting a little girl from her own plain frugal family, to a luxurious establishment in town, where all the refinements and elegances then known in the colony were in daily use. "It is the work of a lifetime, my dear Belle," she said, "to acquire habits of exertion and self-dependence—such habits are essential to this little country-girl—she does not know their worth, but she would be miserable without them—how will she return to her home, where they have a single servant of-all-work, after being accustomed to the twelve slaves in your house?"

"Twelve plagues, aunt! I am sure I should be

happier with one, if that one were our own dear good Rose."

" I believe you would, Belle, happier and better too ; for the energy which sometimes finds wrong channels now, would then be well employed."

" Do you see no other objection, aunt, to Bessie's coming?" asked Isabella, somewhat impatient at the episode, though she was the subject of it.

" I see none, my dear, but what relates to Bessie herself. If her happiness would on the whole be diminished by her coming, you, my dear generous Belle, would not wish it."

" No, aunt—certainly not ; but then I am sure it would not be—she will go to all the schools I go to,—that I shall make papa promise me—and she will make a great many friends—and—and—I want to have her come so much. Now don't, please don't tell papa you disapprove of it—just let me have my own way this time."

" Ah, Belle, when will that time come that you do not have your own way?"

Isabella perceived her aunt would no longer oppose her wishes. The invitation was sent to Bessie, and accepted by her parents; and the child's singular beauty and loveliness secured her friends, one of the goods Isabella had predicted. She did not suffer precisely the evil consequences Mrs. Archer rationally anticipated from her residence in New York, yet that, conspiring with events, gave the hue to her after-life. Physically and morally, she was one of those delicate structures that require a hardening process—she resembled the exquisite instrument that responds music to the gentle touches of the elements, but is broken by the first rude gust that sweeps over it. But we are anticipating.

> There is a history in all men's lives,
> Figuring the nature of the times deceased ;
> The which observed, a man may prophesy,
> With a near aim, of the main chance of things
> As yet not come to life.

CHAPTER II.

> This life, sae far's I understand,
> Is a' enchanted fairy land,
> Where pleasure is the magic wand,
> That, wielded right,
> Make hours like minutes, hand in hand,
> Dance by fu' light.—BURNS.

As soon as Mr. Linwood became aware of his son's whig tendencies, he determined, as far as possible, to counteract them ; and instead of sending him, as he had proposed, to Harvard University, into a district which he considered infected with the worst of plagues, he determined to retain him under his own vigilant eye, at the loyal literary institution in his own city. This was a bitter disappointment to Herbert.

" It is deused hard," he said to Jasper Meredith, who was just setting out for Cambridge to finish his collegiate career there, " that you, who have such a contempt for the Yankees, should go to live among them ; when I, who love and honour them from the bottom of my heart, must stay here, play the good boy, and quietly submit to this most unseasonable paternal fiat!"

" No more of my contempt for the Yankees, Hal, an' thou lovest me," replied Jasper ; " you

remember Æsop's advice to Crœsus at the Persian court?"

" No, I am sure I do not. You have the most provoking way of resting the lever by which you bring out your own knowledge on your friend's ignorance."

" Pardon me, Herbert ; I was only going to remind you of the Phrygian sage's counsel to Crœsus, to speak flattery at court, or hold his tongue. I assure you, that as long as I live among these *soi-disant* sovereigns, I shall conceal my spleen, if I do not get rid of it."

" Oh, you'll get rid of it. They need only to be seen at their homes to be admired and loved."

" Loved!"

" Yes, *loved ;* to tell you the truth, Jasper," Herbert's honest face reddened as he spoke, " it was something of this matter of loving that I have been trying for the last week to make up my mind to speak to you. You may think me fool, dunce, or what you please ; but, mark me, I am serious—you remember Bessie Lee?"

" Perfectly! I understand you—excellent!"—

" Hear me out, and then laugh as much as you like. Eliot, Bessie's brother, will be your classmate—you will naturally be friends—for he is a first-rate—and you will naturally——"

" Fall in love with his pretty sister?"

" If not forewarned, you certainly would ; for there is nothing like her this side heaven. But remember, Jasper, as you are my friend, remember, I look upon her as mine. 'I spoke first,' as the children say ; I have loved Bessie ever since I lived at Westbrook."

" Upon my soul, Herbert, you have woven a pretty bit of romance. This is the very youngest dream of love I ever heard of. Pray, how old were you when you went to live at farmer Lee's?"

" Eleven—Bessie was six. I stayed there two years ; and last year, as you know, Bessie spent with us."

" And she is now fairly entered upon her teens. You have nothing to fear from me, Herbert, depend on't. I never was particularly fond of *children*. There is not the slightest probability of my falling into an intimacy with your yeoman friend, or ever, in any stage of my existence, getting up a serious passion for a peasant girl. I have no affinities for birds of the *basse-cour*. My flight is more aspiring—'birds of a feather flock together,' my dear fellow ; and the lady of my love must be such a one as my lady aunts in England, and my eagle-eyed mother will not look down upon. So a truce to your fears, dear Herbert. Give me the letter you promised to your farmer, scholar, friend ; and, rest assured, he never shall find out that I do not think him equal in blood and breeding to the King of England, as all these Yankees fancy themselves to be."

Herbert gave the letter, but not with the best grace. He did not like Jasper's tone towards his New-England friends. He half wished he had not written the letter, and quite, that he had been more frugal in his praise of Jasper. With the letter, he gave to Jasper various love-tokens from Isabella and himself for Bessie. The young men were saying their last parting words, when Herbert suddenly exclaimed, " Oh, I forgot ! Isabella sent you a keepsake ;" and he gave Jasper a silk purse, with a dove and olive-branch prettily wrought on it.

"Oh, you savage!" exclaimed Jasper, "had you forgotten this!" He pressed it to his lips. "Dear, dear Belle! I kiss your olive-branch—we have had many a falling out, but thus will they always end." Then slipping a ring from his finger, on which was engraven a heart, transfixed by an arrow—"Beg Isabella," he said, "to wear this for my sake. It is a pretty bauble, but she'll not value it for that, nor because it has been worn by all our Capulets since the days of good Queen Bess, as my aunt, Lady Mary, assured me; but perhaps she will care for it—pshaw." He dashed off an honest tear; a servant announced that his uncle was awaiting him, and cordially embracing Herbert, they parted.

As Herbert had expected, Eliot Lee and Meredith were class-mates, but not, as he predicted, or at least not immediately, did they become friends. Their circumstances, and those habits which grow out of circumstances, were discordant. Meredith had been bred in a luxurious establishment, and was taught to regard its artificial and elaborate arrangement as essential to the production of a gentleman. He was a citizen "of no mean city," though we now look back upon New York at that period, with its some eighteen or twenty thousand inhabitants, as little more than a village. There was then, resulting from the condition of America, far more disparity between the facilities and refinements of town and country than there now is: and even now there are young citizens (and some citizens in certain illusions remain young all their lives) who look with the most self-complacent disdain on country breeding. Prior to our revolution, the distinctions of rank in the colonies were in accordance with the institutions of the old world. The coaches of the gentry were emblazoned with their family arms, and their plate with the family crest. If peers and baronets were *rara aves*, there were among the youths of Harvard, "nephews of my lord," and "sons of Sir George and Sir Harry." These were, naturally, Meredith's first associates. He was himself of the privileged order, and, connected with many a noble family in the mother country, he felt his aristocratic blood tingle in every vein. A large property, which had devolved to him on the death of his father, was chiefly vested in real estate in America; and his guardians, with the consent of his mother, who herself remained in England, had judiciously decided to educate him where it would be most advantageous for him finally to fix his residence.

The external circumstances—"the appliances and means" of the two young men, were certainly very different. Eliot Lee's parentage would not be deemed illustrious, according to any artificial code; but graduated by nature's aristocracy, (nature alone sets a seal to her patents of universal authority,) he should rank with the noble of every land; and he might claim what is now considered as the peculiar, the purest, the enduring, and, in truth, the *only* aristocracy of our own. He was a lineal descendant from one of the renowned *pilgrim fathers*, whose nobility, stamped in the principles that are regenerating mankind, will be transmitted by their sons on the Missouri and the Oregon, when the stars and garters of Europe have perished and are forgotten.

Colonel Lee, Eliot's father, was a laborious New-England farmer, of sterling sense and integrity—in the phrase of his people, "an independent, fore-handed man;" a phrase that implies a property of four or five thousand dollars over and above a good farm, unencumbered with debts, and producing rather more than its proprietor, in his frugal mode of life, has occasion to spend. Eliot's mother was a woman of sound mind, and of that quick and delicate perception of the beautiful in nature and action that is the attribute of sensibility and the proof of its existence, though the possessor, like Eliot's mother, may, from diffidence or personal awkwardness, never be able to embody it in graceful expression. She had a keen relish of English literature, and rich acquisitions in it; such as many of our ladies, who have been taught by a dozen masters, and instructed in half as many tongues, might well envy. With all this, she was an actual operator in the arduous labours that fall to the female department of a farming establishment—plain farmer Lee's plain wife. This is not an uncommon combination of character and condition in New-England. We paint from life, if not to the life;—our fault is not extravagance of colouring.

It is unnecessary to enter into the details of Eliot Lee's education. Circumstances combined to produce the happiest results—to develope his physical, intellectual, and moral powers; in short, to make him a favourable specimen of the highest order of New-England character. He had just entered on his academic studies, when his father (as our friend Effie intimated in her dark soothsaying) was lost while crossing Massachusetts' Bay during a violent thunder-storm. Fortunately, the good colonel's forecast had so well provided for his heirs, that his widow was able to maintain the respectable position of his family without recalling her son from college. There, as many of our distinguished men have done, he made his acquisitions available for his support by teaching.

Meredith and Eliot Lee were soon acknowledged to be the gifted young men of their class. Though nearly equals in capacity, Eliot, being by far the most patient and assiduous, bore off the college honours. Meredith did not lack industry—certainly not ambition; but he had not the hardihood and self-discipline that it requires to forego an attractive pursuit for a dry study: and while Eliot, denying his natural tastes, toiled by the midnight lamp over the roughest academic course, Meredith gracefully ran through the light and beaten path of belles-lettres.

They were both social—Meredith rather gay in his disposition. Both had admirable tempers; Meredith's was partly the result of early training in the goodly seemings of the world—Eliot's the gift of Heaven, and therefore the more perfect. Eliot could not exist without self-respect. The applause of society was essential to Meredith. He certainly preferred a real to a merely apparent elevation; but experience could alone decide whether he were willing to pay its price—sustained effort, and generous sacrifice. Both were endowed with personal graces. Neither man nor woman, that ever we could learn, is indifferent to these.

Before the young men had proceeded far in their collegiate career, they were friends, if that holy relation may be predicated of those who are united by accidental circumstances. That they were on a confidential footing will be seen by the following conversation. Meredith was in his room, when, on hearing a tap at his door, he answered it by saying, "Come in, Eliot, my dear fellow. My good, or your evil genius, has brought you to me at the very moment when I am steeped to the lips in trouble."

"You in trouble! why—what is the matter!"

"Diable! matter enough for song or sermon. 'Not a trouble abroad but it lights o' my shoulders'—First, here is a note from our reverend *Præses*. 'Mr. Jasper Meredith, junior class—you are fined, by the proper authority, one pound ten, for going into Boston last Thursday night to an assembly or ball, contrary to college laws—as this is the first offence of the kind reported against you, we have, though you have been guilty of a gross violation of known duty, been lenient in fixing the amount of your fine.'—Lenient, good Præses!—Take instead one pound ten ounces of my flesh. My purse is far leaner than my person, though that be rather of the Cassius order.—Now, Eliot, is not this a pretty bill for one night's sorry amusement—one pound ten, besides the price of two ball tickets, and sundry confections?"

"How, two ball tickets, Meredith!"

"Why, I gave one to the tailor's pretty sister, Sally Dunn."

"Sally Dunn!—Bravo, Meredith. Plebeian as you think my notions, I should hardly have escorted Sally Dunn to a ball."

"My service to you, Eliot!—do not fancy I have been enacting a scene fit for Hogarth's idle apprentice. Were I so absurd, do you fancy these Boston patricians would admit a tailor's sister within their *tabooed* circle!—No—no, little Sally went with company of her own cloth, and trimmings to match (in her brother's slang)—rosy milliners and journeymen tailors, to a ball got up by her compeers. I sent in to them lots of raisins and almonds, which served as a love-token for Sally and *munching* for her companions."

"You have, indeed, paid dear for your whistle, Meredith."

"Dear! you have not heard half yet. Sir knight of the shears assailed me with a whining complaint of my 'paying attention,' as he called it, to his sister Sally, and I could only get off by the gravest assurances of my profound respect for the whole Dunn concern, followed up by an order for a new vest, that being the article the youth would least mar in the making, and here is his bill—two pounds two. This is to be added to my ball expenses, fine, &c., and all, as our learned professor would say, traced to the *primum mobile*, must be charged to pretty Sally Dunn. Oh woman! woman!—ever the cause of man's folly, perplexity, misery, and destruction!"

"You are getting pathetic, Meredith."

"My dear friend, there is nothing affects a man's sensibilities like an empty purse—unless it be an empty stomach. You have not heard half my sorrows yet. Here is a bill, a yard long, from the livery-stable, and here another from Monsieur Paté et Confiture!"

"And your term-bills!"

"Oh! my term-bills I have forwarded, with the dignity of a Sir Charles Grandison, to my uncle. Now, Eliot," he continued, disbursing a few half-crowns and shillings on the table, and holding up his empty purse, and throwing into his face an expression of mock misery, "Now, Eliot, let us resolve ourselves into a committee of ways and means, and tell me by what financial legerdemain I can get affixed to these scrawls that happiest combination of words in the English language—that honeyed phrase, '*received payment in full*'—' oh, gentle shepherd, tell me where!'"

"Where deficits should always find supplies, Meredith, in a friend's purse. I have just settled the account of my pedagogue labours for the last term, and as I have no extra bills to pay, I have extra means quite at your service."

Meredith protested, and with truth, that nothing was farther from his intentions than drawing on his friend; and when Eliot persisted and counted out the amount which Meredith said would relieve his little embarrassments, he felt, and magnanimously expressed, his admiration of those 'working-day world virtues' (so he called them), industry and frugality, which secured to Eliot the tranquillity of independence, and the power of liberality. It is possible that at another time, and in another humour, he might have led the laugh against the sort of barter trade—the selling one kind or degree of knowledge to procure another, by which a Yankee youth, who is willing to live like an anchorite or a philosopher in the midst of untasted pleasures, works his passage through college.

Subsequent instances occurred of similar but temporary obligations on the part of Meredith. Temporary of course, for Meredith was too thoroughly imbued with the sentiments of a gentleman to extend a pecuniary obligation beyond the term of his necessity.

CHAPTER III.

Hear me profess sincerely—had I a dozen sons, each in my love alike, I had rather had eleven die nobly for their country, than one voluptuously surfeit out of action.

SHAKSPEAR.

THE following extracts are from a letter from Bessie Lee to her friend Isabella Linwood.

"DEAREST ISABELLA,—You must love me, or you could not endure my stupid letters—you that can write so delightfully about nothing, and have so much to write about, while I can tell nothing but what I see, and I see so little! The outward world does not much interest me. It is what I *feel* that I think of and ponder over; but I know how you detest what you call sentimental letters, so I try to avoid all such subjects. Compared with you I am a child—two years at our age makes a great difference—I am really very childish for a girl almost fourteen, and yet, and yet, Isabella, I sometimes seem to myself to have gone so far beyond childhood, that I have almost forgotten that careless, light-hearted feeling I used to have. I do not think I ever was so light-hearted as some children, and yet I was not serious—at least, not in the right way. Many a time, before I was ten years old, I have sat up in my own little room till twelve o'clock Saturday night, reading, and then slept for an hour and a half through the whole sermon the next morning.

I do believe it is the natural depravity of my heart. I never read over twice a piece of heathen poetry that moves me but I can repeat it—and yet, I never could get past ' what is effectual calling !' in the Westminster Catechism ; and I always was in disgrace on Saturday, when parson Wilson came to the school to hear us recite it :— the sight of his wig and three-cornered hat petrified me !"

———

" Jasper Meredith is here, passing the vacation with Eliot. I was frightened to death when Eliot wrote us he was coming—we live in such a homely way—only one servant ; and I remember well how he used to laugh at everything he called à-la-bourgeoise. I felt this to be a foolish, vulgar pride, and did my best to suppress it ; and since I have found there was no occasion for it, for Jasper seemed—I do not mean seemed, I think he is much more sincere than he used to be—to miss nothing, and to be delighted with being here. I do not think he realises that I am now three years older than I was in New York, for he treats me with that sort of partiality—devotion you might almost call it—that he used to there, especially when you and he had had a falling out. He has been giving me some lessons in Italian. He says I have a wonderful talent for learning languages, but it is not so : you know what hobbling work I made with the French when you and I went to poor old Mademoiselle Amand—Jasper is quite a different teacher, and I never fancied French. He has been teaching me to ride, too— we have a nice little pony, and he has a beautiful horse—so that we have the most delightful gallops over the country every day. It is very odd, though I am such a desperate coward, I never feel the least timid when I am riding with Jasper —indeed, I do not think of it. Eliot rarely finds time to go with us—when he is at home from college he has so much to do for mother—dear Eliot, he is husband, father, brother, everything to us."

———

" I had not time, while Jasper and Eliot stayed, to finish my letter, and since they went away I have been so dull !—The house seems like a tomb, I go from room to room, but the spirit is not here. Master Hale, the schoolmaster, boards with us, and gives me lessons in some branches that Eliot thinks me deficient in ; but, ah me ! where are the talents for acquisition that Jasper commended ! Did you ever know, dear Isabella, what it was to have everything affected by the departure of friends, as nature is by the absence of light—all fade into one dull uniform hue ! When Eliot and Jasper were here, all was bright and interesting, from the rising of the sun to the going down thereof—now !—ah me !

" I am shocked to find how much I have written about myself. My best respects to your father and mother, and love to Herbert. Burn this worthless scrawl without fail, dear Isabella, and believe me ever most affectionately yours,
" BESSIE LEE."

———

Jasper Meredith to Herbert Linwood.
" DEAR LINWOOD,—I have been enjoying a very pretty little episode in my college life, passing the vacation at Westbrook, with your old friends the Lees. A month in a dull little country town would once have seemed to me penance enough for my worst sin, but now it is heaven to get anywhere beyond the sound of college bells—beyond the reach of automaton tutors—periodical recitations—chapel prayers, and college rules.

" I went to the Lees with the pious intention of quizzing your rustics to the top o' my bent ; but Herbert, my dear fellow, I'll tell you a secret ; when people respect themselves, and value things according to their real intrinsic worth, it gives a shock to our artificial and worldly estimates, and makes us feel as if we stood upon a wonderfully uncertain foundation. These Lees are so strong in their simplicity—they would so disdain aping and imitating those that we (not they, be sure !) think above them—they are so sincere in all their ways— no awkward consciousness — no shame-facedness whatever about the homely details of their family affairs. By heavens, Herbert, I could not find a folly—a meanness—or even a ludicrous rusticity, at which to aim my ridicule.

" I begin to think—no, no, no ! I do not—but if there were many such families as these Lees in the world, an equality, independent of all extraneous circumstances, such as the politicians of this country are now ranting about, might subsist on the foundation of intellect and virtue.

" After all, I see it is a mere illusion. Mrs. Lee's rank, though in Westbrook she appears equal to any Roman matron, is purely local. Hallowed as she is in your boyish memory, Herbert, you must confess she would cut a sorry figure in a New York drawing-room.

" Eliot might pass current anywhere ; but then he has had the advantage of Boston society, and an intimacy with—pardon my coxcombry—your humble servant. Bessie—sweet Bessie Lee, is a gem fit to be set in a coronet. Don't be alarmed, Herbert, you are welcome to have the setting of her. There is metal, as you know, more attractive to me. Bessie is not much grown since she was in New York—she is still low in stature, and so childish in her person that I was sometimes in danger of treating her like a child—of forgetting that she had come within the charmed circle of proprieties. But, if she has still the freshness and immaturity of the unfolding rosebud—the mystical charm of woman—the divinity stirring within beams through her exquisite features. Such features ! Phidias would have copied them in his immortal marble. How in the world should such a creature, all sentiment, refinement, imagination, spring up in practical, prosaic New England ! She is a wanderer from some other star. I am writing like a lover, and not as I should to a lover. But, on my honour, Herbert, I am no lover—of little Bessie I mean. I should as soon think of being enamoured of a rose, a lily, or a violet, an exquisite sonnet, or an abstraction.

" It is an eternity since Isabella has written me a postscript—why is this ? Farewell, Linwood.

" Yours, &c.

" P.S.—One word on politics—a subject I detest, and meddle with as little as possible. There must be an outbreak—there is no avoiding it. But there can be no doubt which party will finally prevail. The mother country has soldiers, money, everything; ''tis odds beyond arithmetic.' As one of my friends said at a dinner in Boston the other day, 'the growling curs may bark for a while, but they will be whipped into submission, and wear their collars patiently for ever after.' I trust, Herbert, you are already cured of what my uncle used to call the 'boy-fever'—but if not, take my advice—be quiet, prudent, *neutral*. As long as we are called boys, we are not expected to be patriots, apostles, or martyrs. At this crisis your filial and *fraternal* duties require that you should suppress, if not renounce, the opinions you used to be so fond of blurting out on all occasions. I am no preacher—I have done—a *word* to the wise.

" M___."

We resume the extracts from Bessie's letters.

"DEAR ISABELLA,—Never say another word to me of what you hinted in your last letter : indeed, I am too young ; and besides, I never should feel easy or happy again with Jasper, if I admitted such a thought. I have had but one opinion since our visit to Effie ; not that I believed in her—at least, not much ; but I have always known who was first in his thoughts—heart—opinion ; and besides, it would be folly in me, knowing his opinions about rank, &c. Mother thinks him very proud, and somewhat vain ; and she begins not to be pleased with his frequent visits to Westbrook. She thinks—no, fears, or rather, she imagines, that Jasper and I—no, that Jasper *or* I—no, that I—it is quite too foolish to write, Isabella—mother does not realise what a wide world there is between us. I might possibly, sometimes, think he loved [this last word was carefully effaced, and cared substituted] cared for me, if he did not know you.

"How could Jasper tell you of Eliot's prejudice against you ! Jasper himself infused it, unwittingly, I am sure, by telling him that when with you, I lived but to do 'your best pleasure,—were it to fly, to swim, or dive into the fire.'—Eliot fancies that you are proud and overbearing—I insist, dear Isabella, that such as you are born to rule such weak spirits as mine ; but Eliot says he does not like absolutism in any form, and especially in woman's. Ah, how differently he would feel if he were to see you—I am sure you would like him—I am not sure even that you would not have preferred him to Jasper, had he been born and bred in Jasper's circumstances. He has more of some qualities that you particularly like, frankness and independence—and mother says (but then mother is not at all partial to Jasper) he has a thousand times more real sensibility—he does, perhaps, feel more for others. I should like to know which you would think the handsomest. Eliot is at least three inches the tallest ; and, as Jasper once said, 'cast in the heroic mould, with just enough, and not one ounce too much of mortality'—but then Jasper has such grace and symmetry—just what I fancy to be the beau-ideal of the arts. Jasper's eyes are almost too black—too piercing ; and yet they are softened by his long lashes, and his olive complexion so expressive—like that fine old portrait in your drawing-room. His mouth, too, is beautiful—it has such a defined,

chiseled look—but then do you not think that his teeth being so delicately formed, and so very, very white, is rather a defect ! I don't know how to describe it, but there is rather an uncertain expression about his mouth. Eliot's, particularly when he smiles, is truth and kindness itself—and his deep, deep blue eye, expresses everything by turns—I mean everything that should come from a pure and lofty spirit—now tender and pitiful enough for me, and now superb and fiery enough for you—but what a silly girlish letter I am writing—'Out of the abundance of the heart,' you know ! I see nobody but Jasper and Eliot, and I think only of them."

We continue the extracts from Bessie's letters. They were strictly feminine, even to their being dateless—we cannot, therefore, ascertain the precise period at which they were written, except by their occasional allusions to contemporaneous events.

"THANKS, dear Isabella, for your delightful letter by Jasper—no longer Jasper, I assure you, to his face, but Mr. Meredith—oh, I often wish the time back when I was a child, and might call him Jasper, and feel the freedom of a child. I wonder if I should dare to call you Belle now, or even Isabella ! Jasper, since his last visit at home, tells me so much of your being 'the mirror of fashion—the observed of all observers' (these are his own words—drawing-room terms, that were never heard in Westbrook but from his lips), that I feel a sort of fearful shrinking. It is not envy—I am too happy now to envy anybody in the wide world. Eliot is at home, and Jasper is passing a week here. Is it not strange they should be so intimate, when they differ so widely on political topics ! I suppose it is because Jasper does not care much about the matter ; but this indifference sometimes provokes Eliot. Jasper is very intimate with Pitcairn and Lord Percy ; and Eliot thinks they have more influence with him than the honour and interest of his country. Oh, they talk it over for hours and hours, and end, as men always do with their arguments, just where they began. Jasper insists that as long as the quarrel can be made up it is much the wisest to stand aloof, and not, 'like mad boys, to rush foremost in the first fray ;' besides, he says he is tied by a promise to his uncle that he will have nothing to do with these agitating disputes till his education is finished. Mother says (she does not always judge Jasper kindly) that it is very easy and *prudent* to bind your hands with a promise when you do not choose to lift them.

"Ah, there is a terrible storm gathering ! Those who have grown up together, lovingly interlacing their tender branches, must be torn asunder—some swept away by the current, others dispersed by the winds."

"DEAR ISABELLA,—The world seems turned upside down since I began this letter—war, *war*—what an appalling sound !—has begun—blood has been spilt, and our dear, dear Eliot—but I must tell you first how it all was. Eliot and Jasper were out shooting some miles from Cambridge, when, on coming to the road, they perceived an unusual commotion—old men and young, and even boys, all armed, in waggons, on horseback, and on foot, were coming from all points, and all hurrying onward in one direction. On inquiring into the hurly-burly, they were told that Colonel Smith had marched to Concord to destroy the military stores there ; and that our people were gathering from all quarters to oppose his return. Eliot immediately joined them, Jasper did not ; but, dear Isabella, I that know you so well, know, whatever others may think, that tories may be true and noble. There was a fight at Lexington. Our brave men had the best of it. Eliot was the first to bring us the news. With a severe wound in his arm, he came ten miles, that we might not be alarmed by any reports, knowing, as he told mother, that she was no Spartan mother, to be indifferent whether her son came home with his shield or on his shield.

"Jasper has not been to Westbrook since the battle. My mind has been in such a state of alarm since, I cannot return to my ordinary pursuits. I was reading history with the children, and the English poets with mother, but I am quite broken up.

"I do not think this horrid war should separate those who have been friends ; thank God, my dear Isabella, we of womankind are exempts—not called upon to take sides—our mission is to heal wounds, not to make them ; to keep alive and tend with vestal fidelity the fires of charity and love. My kindest remembrance to Herbert. I hope he has renounced his whiggism ; for if it must come to that, he had better fight on the wrong side (ignorantly) than break the third commandment. Write soon, dear Isabella, and let me know if this hurly-burly extends to dear, quiet New York ! In war and in peace, in all the chances and changes of this mortal life, your own
"BESSIE LEE."

Miss Linwood to Bessie Lee.

"EXEMPTS ! my little spirit of peace—your vocation it may be, my pretty dove, to sit on your perch with an olive-branch in your bill, but not mine. Oh for the glorious days of the Clorindas, when a woman might put down her womanish thoughts, and with helmet and lance in rest do battle with the bravest ! why was the loyal spirit of my race my exclusive patrimony ? Can his blood, who at his own cost raised a troop of horse for our martyr king, flow in Herbert's veins ? or his who followed the fortunes of the unhappy James ? Is my father's son a renegado—a rebel ! Yes, Bessie—my blood burns in my cheeks while I write it. Herbert, the only male scion of the Linwoods, who at his own cost raised a troop of horse—our pride—our hope—has declared himself for the rebel party—'Ichabod, Ichabod, the glory is departed,' is written on our door-posts.

"But to come down from my heroics ; we are in a desperate condition—such a scene as I have just passed through ! Judge Ellis was dining with us; Jasper Meredith was spoken of. 'In the name of Heaven, Ellis,' said my father, 'why do you suffer your nephew to remain among the rebel crew in that infected region ?'

"'I do not find,' replied the judge, glancing at Herbert, 'that any region is free from infection.'

"'True, true,' said my father ; 'but the air of the Yankee states is saturated with it. I would not let an infant breathe it, lest rebellion should break out when he came to man's estate.' I am sorry to say it, dear Bessie ; but my father traces Herbert's delinquency to his sojourn at Westbrook. I saw a tempest was brewing, and thinking to make for a quiet harbour, I put in my oar, and repeated the story you told me in your last letter of our non-combatant, Mr. Jasper. The judge was charmed. 'Ah, he's a prudent fellow !' he said ; 'he'll not commit himself !'

"'Not commit himself !' exclaimed my father ; 'by Jupiter, if he belonged to me, he should commit himself. I would rather he should jump the wrong way, than sit squat like a toad under a hedge, till he was sure which side it was most prudent to jump.' You see, Bessie, my father's words implied something like a commendation of Herbert. I ventured to look up—their eyes met—I saw a beam of pleasure flashing from them, and passing like an electric spark from one heart to another. Oh, why should this unholy quarrel tear asunder such true hearts !

"The judge's pride was touched—he is a mean wretch. 'Ah, my dear sir,' he said, 'it is very well for you, who can do it with impunity, to disregard prudential considerations ; for instance, you remain true to the king, the royal power is maintained, and your property is protected. Your son—I suppose a case—your son joins the rebels, the country is revolutionised, and your property is secured as the reward of Mr. Herbert's patriotism.'

"My father hardly heard him out. 'Now, by the Lord that made me !' he exclaimed, setting down the decanter with a force that broke it in a thousand pieces, 'I would die of starvation before I would taste a crumb of bread that was the reward of rebellion.'

"It was a frightful moment ; but my father's passion, you know, is like a whirlwind : one gust, and it is over ; and mama is like those short-stemmed flowers that lie on the earth ; no wind moves her. So, though the judge was almost as much disconcerted as the decanter, it seemed all to have blown over, while mama, as in case of any ordinary accident, was directing Jupe to remove the fragments, change the cloth, &c. But alas ! the evil genius of our house triumphed ; for even a bottle of our oldest Madeira, which is usually to my father like oil to the waves, failed to preserve tranquillity. The glasses were filled, and my father, according to his usual custom, gave 'The king—God bless him.'

"Now you must know, though he would not confess he made any sacrifice to prudence, he has for some weeks omitted to drink wine at all, on some pretext or other, such as he had a head-ach, or he had dined out the day before, or expected to the day after ; and thus Herbert has escaped the test. But now the toast was given, and Herbert's glass remained untouched, while he sat, not biting, but literally devouring his nails. I saw the judge cast a sinister look at him, and then a glance at my father. The storm was gathering on my father's brow.—'Herbert, my son,' said mama, 'you will be too late for your appointment.' Herbert moved his chair to rise, when my father called out, 'Stop, sir—no slinking away under your mother's shield—hear me—no man

who refuses to drink that toast at my table, shall
eat of my bread or drink of my wine.'

" ' Then God forgive me—for I never will drink
it—so help me Heaven ! '

" Herbert left the room by one door—my father
by another—mama stayed calmly talking to that
fixture of a judge, and I ran to my room, where,
as soon as I had got through with a comfortable
fit of crying, I sat down to write you (who are on
the enemy's side) an account of the matter.
What will come of it, Heaven only knows !

" But, my dear little gentle Bessie, I never
think of you as having anything to do with these
turbulent matters ; you are in the midst of fiery
rebel spirits, but you are too pure, too good, to
enter into their counsels, and far too just for any
self-originating prejudices, such as this horrible
one that pervades the country, and fires New
England against the legitimate rights of the
mother country over her wayward, ungrateful
child. Don't trouble your head about these
squabbles, but cling to Master Hale, your poetry,
and history : by-the-way, I laughed heartily that
you, who have done *duty—reading* so virtuously
all your life, should now come to the conclusion
'that history is dry.' I met with a note in He-
rodotus, the most picturesque of historians, the
other day that charmed me. The writer of the
note says there is no mention whatever of Cyrus
in the Persian history. If history then is mere
fiction, why may we not read romances of our
own choosing ! My instincts have not misguided
me, after all.

" So, Miss Bessie, Jasper Meredith is in high
favour with you, and the friend of your nonpareil
brother. Jasper could always be irresistible
when he chose, and he seems to have been 'i'
the vein' at Westbrook. With all our impressions (are they prejudices, Bessie !) against your
Yankee land, we thought him excessively im-
proved by his residence among you. Indeed, if
he were never to get another letter from his
worldly icicle mother, to live away from his time-
serving uncle, and never receive another impor-
tation of London coxcombries, he would be what
nature intended him—a paragon.

" I love your sisterly enthusiasm. As to my
estimation of your brother being affected by the
accidents of birth and fortune, indeed, you were
not true to your friend when you intimated that.
Certainly, the views you tell me he takes of my
character are not particularly flattering, or even
conciliating. However, I have my revenge—you
paint him *en beau*—the portrait is too beautiful
to be very like any man born and reared within
the disenchanted limits of New England. I am
writing boldly, but no offence, dear Bessie ; I do
not know your brother, and I have—yes, out with
it, with the exception of your precious little self—
I have an *antipathy* to the New Englanders—a
disloyal race, and conceited ; fancying themselves
more knowing in all matters, high and low, especially government and religion, than the rest of
the world—' all-sufficient, self-sufficient, and *insufficient.*'

" Pardon me, gentle Bessie—I am just now at
fever heat, and I could not like Gabriel if he were
whig and rebel. Ah, Herbert !—but I loved him
before I ever heard these detestable words ; and
once truly loving, especially if our hearts be knit

together by nature, I think the faults of the subject do not diminish our affection, though they
turn it from its natural sweet uses to suffering."

" DEAR BESSIE,—A week, a stormy, miserable
week has passed since I wrote the above, and it
has ended in Herbert's leaving us, and dishon-
ouring his father's name by taking a commission
in the rebel service. Papa has of course had a
horrible fit of the gout. He says he has for ever
cast Herbert out of his affections. Ah ! I am
not skilled in metaphysics, but I *know* that we
have no power whatever over our affections.
Mama takes it all patiently, and chiefly sor-
roweth that Herbert has lost caste by joining the
insurgents, whom she thinks little better than so
many Jack Cades.

" For myself, I would have poured out my
blood—every drop of it, to have kept him true to
his king and country ; but in my secret heart I
glory in him that he has honestly and boldly
clung to his opinions, to his own certain and
infinite loss. I have no heart to write more.
                          " Yours truly,
                                " ISABELLA LINWOOD.

" P.S.—You may show the last paragraph
(confidentially) to Jasper ; but don't let him
know that I wished him to see it.   I. L."

CHAPTER IV.

An' forward, though I canna *see,*
I *guess* an' *fear.*—BURNS.

THREE years passed over without any marked
change in the external condition of our young
friends. Herbert Linwood endured the hardships
of an American officer during that most suffering
period of the war, and remained true to the cause
he had adopted, without any of those opportunities of distinction which are necessary to keep
alive the fire of ordinary patriotism.

It has been seen that Eliot Lee, with most of
the young men of the country, as might be expected from the insurgent and generous spirit of
youth, espoused the popular side. It ought not
to have been expected, that when the young
country came to the muscle and vigour of manhood, it should continue to wear the leading-
strings of its childhood, or remain in the bondage
and apprenticeship of its youth. It has been
justly said, that the seeds of our revolution and
future independence were sown by the Pilgrims.
The political institutions of a people may be
inferred from their religion. Absolutism, as a
mirror, reflects the Roman Catholic faith. Whatever varieties of names were attached to the
religious sects of America, they were, with the
exception of a few Papists, all Protestants—all,
as Burke said of them, "agreed (if agreeing in
nothing else) in the communion of the spirit of
liberty—theirs was the Protestantism of the
Protestant religion—the dissidence of dissent."
It was morally certain, that, as soon as they came
to man's estate, their government would accord
with this spirit of liberty ; would harmonise with
the independent and republican spirit of the
religion of Christ, the only authority they ad-

mitted. The fires of our republic were not then kindled by a coal from the old altars of Greece and Rome, whose freest government exalted the few, and retained the many in grovelling ignorance and servitude : ours came forth invincible in the declaration of liberty to all, and equality of rights.

Such minds as Eliot Lee's, reasoning and religious, were not so much moved by the sudden impulses of enthusiasm as incited by the convictions of duty. His heart was devoted to his country, his thoughts absorbed in her struggle ; but he quenched, or rather smothered his intense desire to go forth with her champions, and remained pursuing his legal studies, near enough to his home to perform his paramount but obscure duty to his widowed mother and her young family.

Jasper Meredith's political preferences, if not proclaimed, were easily guessed. It was obvious that his tastes were aristocratic and feudal—his sympathies with the monarch, not with the people. New York was the head-quarters of the British army, and Judge Ellis, his uncle, on the pretext of keeping his nephew out of the way of the seductions of a very gay society, advised him to pursue the study of the law in New England, and thus for awhile he avoided pledging himself. He resided in Boston or its vicinity, never far from Westbrook. He had a certain *éclat* in the drawing-rooms of Boston, but he was no favourite there. A professed neutrality was, if not suspicious, most offensive in the eyes of neck-or-nothing patriots. But Meredith did not escape the whisper that his neutrality was a mere mask. His accent, which was ambitiously English, was criticised, and his elaborate dress, manufactured by London *artists*, was particularly displeasing to the sons of the Puritans, who, absorbed in great objects, were then more impatient even than usual of extra sacrifices to the graces.

The transition from Boston to Westbrook was delightful to Meredith. There was no censure of any sort, but balm for the rankling wounds of vanity ; and it must be confessed that he not only appeared better, but was better, at Westbrook than elsewhere : the best parts of his nature were called forth ; he was (if we may desecrate a technical expression) in the exercise of grace. There is a certain moral atmosphere, as propitious to moral well-being as a genial temperature is to health. Vanity has a sort of thermometer, which enables the possessor to graduate and adapt himself to the dispositions, the vanities (is there any gold in nature without this alloy !) of others. Meredith, when he wished to be so, was eminently agreeable. Those always stand in a most fortunate light who vary the monotony of a village existence, and he broke like a sunbeam through the dull atmosphere that hung over Westbrook. He brought the freshest news, he studied good Mrs. Lee's partialities and prejudices, and accommodated himself to them. He supplied to Eliot what all social beings hanker after, companionship with one of his own age, pursuits, and associations. The magnet that drew him to Westbrook was never the acknowledged attraction. Meredith was not in love with Bessie Lee. She was too spiritual a creature for one of earth's mould ; but his self-love, his ruling passion, was flattered by her. He saw and enjoyed (what,

alas ! no one else then saw) his power over her. He saw in the mutations of her cheek, in the kindling of her eye, in the changes of her voice. It was as if an angel had left his sphere to cast incense upon him. Meredith must be acquitted of a deliberate attempt to ensnare her affections. He thought not and cared not for the future. He cared only for a present selfish gratification. A ride at twilight or a walk by moonlight with this creature, all beauty, refinement, and tenderness, was a poetic passage to him—to her it was fraught with life or death.

Poor Bessie ! she should have been hardened for the changing climate of this rough world ; but by a fatal, though very common error, she had been cherished like a tropical bird, or an exotic plant. "She has such delicate health ! she is so different from my other children !" said the mother.—"She is so gentle and sensitive," said the brother. And thus, with all their sound judgment, instead of submitting her to a hardening process, it seemed an instinct with them, by every elaborate contrivance, to fence her from the ordinary trials and evils of life. Only when she was happy did they let her alone ; with Meredith she seemed happy, and they were satisfied. Bessie shared this unfounded tranquillity, arising with them partly from confidence in Meredith, and partly from the belief that she was in no danger of suffering from an unrequited love ; but Bessie's arose from the most childlike ignorance of that study, puzzling to the wisest and craftiest—the human heart. She was the most modest and unexacting of human creatures ; her gentle spirit urged no rights—asked nothing, expected nothing beyond the present moment. The worshipper was satisfied with the presence of the idol. Her residence in New York had impressed a conviction that a disparity of birth and condition was an impassable gulf. It was natural enough that she should have imbibed this opinion ; for, being a child, the aristocratic opinions of the society she was in were expressed, unmitigated by courtesy ; they sank deep into her susceptible mind—a mind too humble to aspire above any barrier that nature or society had set up.

There was another foundation of her fancied security. This was shaken by the following conversation :—Meredith was looking over an old pocket-book, when a card dropped from it at Bessie's feet : she handed it to him—he smiled as he looked at it, and held it up before her. She glanced her eye over it, and saw it was a note of the date of their visit to the soothsayer, Effie, and of Effie's prediction in relation to the "dark curling hair."

"I had totally forgotten this," said he, carelessly.

"Forgotten it !" echoed Bessie, in a tone that indicated but too truly her feelings.

"Certainly I had—and why not, pray ! "

"Oh, because—" she hesitated.

"Because what, Bessie ! "

Bessie was ashamed of her embarrassment, and faltering the more the more she tried to shake it off, said, " I did not suppose you could forget anything that concerned Isabella."

"Upon my honour, you are very much mistaken ; I have scarcely thought of Effie and her trumpery prediction since we were there."

"Why have you preserved the card, then, Jasper?" asked Bessie, in all simplicity.

Jasper's complexion was not of the blushing order, or he would have blushed as he replied, at the same time replacing the card—"Oh, Lord, I don't know! accident—the card got in here among these old memoranda and receipts, 'trivial fond records' all!"

"There preserve it," said Bessie, "and we will look at it one of these days."

"When!"

"When, as it surely will be, the prediction is verified."

"If not till then," he said, "it will never again see the light. This is the oddest fancy of yours," he added.

"Not fancy, but faith."

"Faith most unfounded. Why, Bessie, Isabella and I were always quarrelling!"

"And always making up. Do you ever quarrel now, Jasper?"

"Oh, she is still of an April temper; but I"—he looked most tenderly at Bessie—"have lived too much of late in a serene atmosphere, to bear well her fitful changes."

A long time had passed since Bessie had mentioned Isabella to Meredith. She knew not why, but she had felt a growing reluctance to advert to her friend even in thought; and she was now conscious of a thrilling sensation at the careless, cold manner in which Jasper spoke of her. It seemed as if a load had fallen off her heart. She felt like a mariner who has at length caught a glimpse of what seems distant land, and is bewildered with new sensations, and uncertain whether it be land or not. She was conscious Jasper's eye was on hers, though her own was downcast. She longed to escape from that burning glance, and was relieved by a bustle in the next room, and her two little sisters running in, one holding up a long curling tress of her own beautiful hair, and crying out—"Did not you give this to me, Bessie?"

"Is not it mine?" said the competitor.

"No, it is mine!" exclaimed Jasper, snatching it, and holding it beyond their reach.

The girls laughed, and were endeavouring to regain it, when he slipped a ring from his finger, and set it rolling on the floor, saying, "the hair is mine—the ring belongs to whoever gets it." The ring, obedient to the impulse he gave it, rolled out of the room; the children eagerly followed; he shut the door after them, and repeated, kissing the lock of hair, "It is mine—is it not!"

"Oh, no—no, Jasper!—give it to me," cried Bessie, excessively confused.

"You will not give it to me! Well—'a fair exchange is no robbery;'" and, taking the scissors from Bessie's work-box, he cut off one of his own luxuriant dark locks, and offered it to her. She shook her head.

"That is unkind—most unfriendly, Bessie." He paused a moment, and then, still holding both locks, he extended the ends to Bessie, and asked her if she could tie a true love-knot. Bessie's heart was throbbing; she was frightened at her own emotion; she was afraid of betraying it; and she tied the knot as the natural thing for her to do.

"There is but one altar for such a sacrifice as this," said Meredith, and he was putting it into his bosom, when Bessie snatched it from him, burst into tears, and left the room.

After this, there was a change in Bessie's manners—her spirits became unequal, she was nervous and restless. Meredith, in the presence of observers, was measured and cautious to the last degree in his attentions to her. When, however, they were alone together, though not a sentence might be uttered that a lawyer could have tortured into a special plea, yet his words were fraught with looks and tones which carried them to poor Bessie's heart with a power that cannot be imagined by those

Who have ceased to hear such, or ne'er heard.

It was about this period that Meredith wrote the following reply to a letter from his mother:

"You say, my dear madam, that you have heard 'certain reports about me, which you are not willing to believe, and yet cannot utterly discredit.' You say, also, 'that though you should revolt with horror from sanctioning your son in those *liaisons* that are advised by Lord Chesterfield, and others of your friends, yet you see no harm in' lover-like attentions 'to young persons in inferior stations; they serve,' you add, 'to keep alive and cultivate that delicate *finesse* so essential to the success of a man of the world, and, provided they have no immoral purpose, are quite innocent,' as the object of them must know there is an 'impassable gulf between her and her superiors in rank, and is, therefore, responsible for her mistakes.' I have been thus particular in echoing your words, that I may assure you my conduct is in conformity to their letter and spirit. Tranquillise yourself, my dear madam. There is nothing, in any little fooleries I may be indulging in, to disquiet you for a moment. The person in question is a divine little creature—quite a prodigy for this part of the world, where she lives in a seclusion almost equal to that of Prospero's isle; so that your humble servant, being scarcely more than the 'third man that e'er she saw,' it would not be to marvel at 'if he should be the first that e'er she loved;' and if I am, it is my *destiny*—my conscience is quite easy—I never have *committed* myself, nor ever shall: time and absence will soon dissipate her illusions. She is an unaspiring little person, quite aware of the gulf, as you call it, between us. She believes that even if I were lover and hero enough to play the Leander and swim it, my destiny is fixed on the other side. I have no distrust of myself, and I beg you will have none; I am saved from all responsibility as to involving the happiness of this lily of the valley, by her very clear-sighted mother, and her sage of a brother, her natural guardians.

"It is yet problematical whether, as you supposed, a certain lady's fortune will be made by the apostacy of her disinherited brother. If the rebels win the day, the property of the tories will be confiscated, or transferred to the rebel heir. But all that is in futuro—Fortune is a fickle goddess; we can only be sure of her present favours, and deserve the future by our devotion.

"With profound gratitude and affection,
          "Yours, my dear mother,
                    "J. MEREDITH.

" P.S.—My warmest thanks for the inestimable box, which escaped the sea and land harpies, and came safe to hand. The Artois buckle is a *chef-d'œuvre*, worthy the inventive genius of the royal count whose taste rules the civilised world. The scarlet frock-coat, with its unimitated (if not'inimitable) capes, ' does credit (as friend Rivington would say in one of his flash advertisements) to the most elegant operator of Leicester-fields.' I must reserve it till I go to New York, where they always take the lead in this sort of civilisation—the boys would mob me if I wore it in Boston. The umbrella,—a rare invention !—is a curiosity here. I understand they have been introduced into New York by the British officers. Novelty as it is, I venture to spread it here, as its utility commends it to these rationalists, who reason about an article of dress as they would concerning an article of faith.

" Once more, your devoted son,
" M."

Meredith's conscience was easy ! " He had not *committed himself !* "—Ah, let man beware how he wilfully or carelessly perverts and blinds God's vicegerent, conscience.

Meredith was suddenly recalled to New York, and Bessie Lee was left to ponder on the past, and weave the future of shattered faith and blighted hopes. The scales fell too late from the eyes of her mother and brother. They reproached themselves, but never poor Bessie. They hoped that time, operating on her gentle, unresisting temper, would restore her serenity. She, like a stricken deer, took refuge under the shadow of their love ; she was too affectionate, too generous, to resign herself to wretchedness without an effort. She wasted her strength in concealing the wound that rankled at her heart.

CHAPTER V.

I, considering how honour would become such a person, was pleased to let him seek danger, where he was like to find fame.—SHAKSPEARE.

ANOTHER sorrow soon overtook poor Bessie ; but now she had a right to feel, and might express all she felt, and look full in the face of her friends for sympathy, for they shared the burden with her.

In the year 1778, letters were sent by General Washington to the governors of the several states, earnestly entreating them to re-inforce the army. The urgency of this call was acknowledged by every patriotic individual ; and never did heart more joyously leap than Eliot Lee's, when his mother said to him—" My son, I have long had misgivings about keeping you at home ; but last night, after reading the general's letter, I could not sleep ; I felt for him, for the country ; my conscience told me you ought to go, Eliot ; even the images of the children, for whose sake only I have thought it right you should stay with us, rose up against me : we should pay our portion for the privileges they are to enjoy. I have made up my mind to it, and on my knees I have given you to my country. The widow's son," she continued, clearing her voice, " is something more than the widow's mite, Eliot ; but I have given you up, and now I have done with feelings—nothing is to be said or thought of but how we shall soonest and best get you ready."

Eliot was deeply affected by his mother's decision, voluntary and unasked ; but he did not express his satisfaction, his delight, till he ascertained that she had well considered the amount of the sacrifice and was willing to meet it. Then he confessed that nothing but a controlling sense of his filial duty had enabled him to endure loitering at the fireside, when his country needed the aid he withheld.

The decision made, no time was lost. Letters were obtained from the best sources to General Washington, and in less than a week Eliot was ready for his departure.

It was a transparent morning, late in autumn, in bleak, wild, fitful, poetic November. The vault of heaven was spotless ; a purple light danced over the mountain summits ; the mist was condensed in the hollows of the hills, and wound round them like drapery of silver tissue. The smokes from the village chimneys ascended through the clear atmosphere in straight columns ; the trees on the mountains, banded together, still preserved a portion of their summer wealth, though now faded to dun and dull orange, marked and set off by the surrounding evergreens. Here and there a solitary elm stood bravely up against the sky, every limb, every stem defined ; a naked form, showing the beautiful symmetry that had made its summer garments hang so gracefully. Fruits and flowers, even the hardy ones that venture on the frontiers of winter, had disappeared from the gardens ; the seeds had dropped from their cups ; the grass of the turf borders was dank and matted down ; all nature was stamped with the signet seal of autumn, *memory* and *hope*. Eliot had performed the last provident offices for his mother ; everything about her cheerful dwelling had the look of being kindly cared for. The strawberry-beds were covered, the raspberries neatly trimmed out, the earth well spaded and freshly turned ; no gate was off its hinges, no fence down, no window unglazed, no crack unstopped.

A fine black saddle-horse, well equipped, was at the door. Little Fanny Lee stood by him, patting him, and laying her head, with its shining flaxen locks, to his side—" Rover," she said, with a trembling voice, " be a good Rover—won't you ! and when the naughty regulars come, canter off with Eliot as fast as you can."

" Hey ! that's fine !" retorted her brother, a year younger than herself. " No, no, Rover, canter up to them, and over them, and never dare to canter back here if you turn tail on them, Rover."

" Oh, Sam ! how awful ; would you have Eliot killed !"

" No, indeed, but I had rather he'd come deused near it than to have him a coward."

" Don't talk so loud, Sam—Bessie will hear you."

But the young belligerent was not to be silenced. He threw open the " dwelling-room " door, to appeal to Eliot himself. The half-uttered sentence died away on his lips. He entered the apartment, Fanny followed ; they gently closed the door, drew their footstools to Eliot's feet, and quietly sat down there. How instinctive is the sympathy of children! how plain, and yet how delicate its manifestations!

Bessie was sitting beside her brother, her head on his shoulder, and crying as if her heart went out with every sob. The youngest boy, Hal, sat on Eliot's knee, with one arm around his neck, his cheek lying on Bessie's, dropping tear after tear, sighing, and half-wondering why it was so.

The good mother had arrived at that age when grief rather congeals the spirit than melts it. Her lips were compressed, her eyes tearless, and her movements tremulous. She was busying herself in the last offices, doing up parcels, taking last stitches, and performing those services that seem to have been assigned to women as safety-valves for their effervescing feelings.

A neat table was spread with ham, bread, sweetmeats, cakes, and every delicacy the house afforded—all were untasted. Not a word was heard except such broken sentences as "Come, Bessie, I will promise to be good if you will to be happy!"

"Eliot, how easy for you—how impossible for me!"

"Dear Bessie, do be firmer, for mother's sake. For ever! oh no, my dear sister, it will not be very long before I return to you; and while I am gone, you must be everything to mother."

"I! I never was good for anything, Eliot—and now——"

"Bessie, my dear child, hush—you have been —you always will be a blessing to me. Don't put any anxious thoughts into Eliot's mind—we shall do very well without him."

"Noble, disinterested mother!" trembled on Eliot's lips; but the suppressed words that might imply reproach to Bessie.

The sacred scene was now broken in upon by some well-meaning but untimely visitors. Eliot's approaching departure had created a sensation in Westbrook; the good people of that rustic place not having arrived at the refined stage in the progress of society, when emotion and fellow-feeling are not expressed, or expressed only by certain conventional forms. First entered Master Hale, with Miss Sally Ryal. Master Hale "hoped it was no intrusion;" and Miss Sally answered, "by no means; she had come to lend a helping hand, and not to intrude"—whereupon she bustled about, helped herself and her companion to chairs, and unsettled everybody else in the room. Mrs. Lee assumed a more tranquil mien: poor Bessie suppressed her sobs, and withdrew to a window, and Eliot tried to look composed and manly. The children, like springs relieved from a pressure, reverted to their natural state, dashed off their tears, and began whispering among themselves. Miss Sally produced from her work-bag a comforter for Mr. Eliot, of her own knitting, which she "trusted would keep out the cold and rheumatism:" and she was kindly showing him how to adjust it, when she spied a chain of braided hair around his neck—"Ah, ah, Mr. Eliot, a love token!" she exclaimed.

"Yes, it is," said little Fanny, who was watching her proceedings; "Bessie and I cut locks of hair from all the children's heads and mother's, and braided it for him; and I guess it will warm his bosom more than your comforter will, Miss Sally."

It was evident, from the look of ineffable tenderness Eliot turned on Fanny, that he "guessed" so too; but he nevertheless received the comforter graciously, hinting, that a lady who had been able to protect her own bosom from the most subtle enemy, must know how to defend another's from common assaults. Miss Sally hemmed, looked at Master Hale, muttered something of her not always having been invulnerable; and finally succeeded in recalling to Eliot's recollection a tradition of a love passage between Miss Sally and the pedagogue.

A little girl now came trotting in, with "grandmother's love, and a phial of her *mixture* for Mr. Eliot—good against camp-distemper and the like."

Eliot received the *mixture* as if he had all grandmother's faith in it, slipped a bright shilling into the child's hand for a keepsake, kissed her rosy cheek, and set her down with the children.

Visiters now began to throng. One man in a green old age, who had lost a leg at Bunker's Hill, came hobbling in, and clapping Eliot on the shoulder, said, "This is you, my boy! This is what I wanted to see your father's son a-doing: I'd go too, if the rascals had left me both my legs. Cheer up, widow, and thank the Lord you've got such a son to offer up to your country—the richer the gift, the better the giver, you know; but I don't wonder you feel kind o' qualmish at the thoughts of losing the lad. Come, Master Hale, can't you say something? A little bit of Greek, or Latin, or 'most anything, to keep up their *sperits* at the last gasp, as it were."

"I was just going to observe, Major Avory, to Mrs. Lee, respecting our esteemed young friend, Mr. Eliot, that I, who have known him from the beginning, as it were, having taught him his alphabet, which may be said to be the first round of the ladder of learning (which he has mounted by my help), or rather (if you will allow me, ma'am, to mend my figure) the poles that support all the rounds; having had, as I observed, a primordial acquaintance with him, I can testify that he is worthy every honourable adjective in the language, and we have every reason to hope that his future tense will be as perfect as his past."

"Wheugh!" exclaimed the major, "a pretty long march you have had through that speech!"

The good schoolmaster, quite unruffled, proceeded to offer Eliot a time-worn Virgil; and finished by expressing his hopes that "he would imitate Cæsar in maintaining his studies in the camp, and keep the scholar even-handed with the soldier."

Eliot charmed the old pedagogue, by assuring him that he should be more apt at imitating Cæsar's studies than his soldiership, and himself bestowed Virgil in his portmanteau.

A good lady now stepped forth, and seeming somewhat scandalised that, as she said, "no serious truth had been spoken at this peculiar season," she concluded a technical exhortation by giving Eliot a pair of stockings, into which she had wrought St. Paul's description of the gospel armour. "The Scripture," she feared, "did not often find its way to the camp; and she thought a passage might be blessed, as a single kernel of wheat, even sowed among tares, sometimes produced its like."

Eliot thanked her, and said " it was impossible to have too much of the best thing in the world ; but he hoped she would have less solicitude about him, when he assured her that his mother had found place for a pocket Bible in his portmanteau."

A meek-looking creature now stole up to Mrs. Lee, and putting a roll of closely-compressed lint into her hand, said, " Tuck it in with his things, *Miss* Lee. Don't let it scare you—I trust he will dress other people's wounds, not his own, with it.—My ! that will come natural to him. It's made from the shirt Mr. Eliot stripped from himself, and tore into bandages for my poor Sam, that time he was scalt. Mr. Eliot was a boy then, but he has the same heart now."

Mrs. Lee dropped a tear on the lint, as she stowed it away in the closely packed portmanteau.

" There comes crazy Anny !" exclaimed the children ; and a woman appeared at the door, scarcely past middle age, carrying in her hand a pole, on which she had tied thirteen strips of cloth of every colour, and stuck them over with white paper stars. Her face was pale and weatherworn, and her eye sunken, but brilliant with the wild flashing light that marks insanity. The moment her eye fell on Eliot, her imagination was excited—" Glory to the Lord !" she cried— " glory to the Lord ! A leader hath come forth from among my people ! Go on, Eliot Lee, and we will gird thee about with the prayers of the widow and the blessings of the childless ! This is comfort ! But you could not comfort me, Eliot Lee, though you spoke like an angel that time you was sent to me with the news the boys was shot. I remember you shed tears, and it seemed to me there was a hissing in here (she put her hand on her head) as they fell. My eyes were dry—I did not shed one tear, though the doctor bid me. I cried them all out when he (she advanced to Eliot, and lowered her voice), the grand officer in the reg'lars, you know, decoyed away my poor Susy, the prettiest and kindest creature that ever went into Westbrook meeting ; fair as Bessie Lee, and far more plump and rosy—to be sure Susy was but a servant-girl, but—" she raised her voice to a shriek, " I shall never lay down my head in peace till they are all driven into the salt sea, where my Susy was buried."

" We'll drive them all there," said Eliot, soothingly, laying his hand on her arm—" every mother's son of them, Anny—now be quiet, and go home, Anny."

" Yes, sir—thank you, sir,—yes, sir !" said she, calmed and courtesying again and again—" Oh, I forgot, Mr. Eliot !" she drew from her bosom an old rag, in which she had tied some kernels of butternuts—" give my duty to General Washington, and give him these butternut meats—it's all I have to send him—I did give him my best—they were nice boys, for all—weren't they, Bob and Pete !" And whimpering and trailing her banner after her, the poor bereft creature left the house.

A loud official rap was heard at the door, and immediately recognised as the signal of the *minister's* approach. We must claim indulgence while we linger for a moment with this reverend divine, for the race of which he was an honoured member is fast disappearing from our land. Peace be with them ! Ill would they have brooked these days of unquestioned equality of rights, of anti-monopolies, of free publishing and freer thinking, of universal suffrage, of steam-engines, rail-roads, and spinning-jennies, — all indirect contrivances to raze those fortunate eminences, by mounting which little men became great, and lorded it over their fellows : but peace be with them ! How should they have known (till it began to tremble under them) that the height on which they stood was an artificial, not a natural elevation ! They preached equality in heaven, but little thought it was the kingdom to come on earth. They were the electric chain, unconscious of the celestial fire they transmitted.

We would give them honour due ; and to them belongs the honour of having been the zealous champions of their country's cause, and of having fought bravely with the weapons of the church militant.

Our good parson Wilson was an Apollo " in little ;" being not more than five feet four in height, and perfectly well made,—a fact of which he betrayed the consciousness, by the exact adjustment of every article of his apparel, even to his long blue yarn stockings, drawn over the knee, and kept sleek by the well-turned leg, without the aid of garters. On entering Mrs. Lee's parlour, he gave his three-cornered hat, goldheaded cane, and buckskin-gloves, to little Fanny, who, with the rest of the children, had at his approach slunk into a corner (they needed not, for never was there a kinder heart than parson Wilson's, though somewhat in the position of vitality enclosed in a petrifaction), and then giving a general bow to the company, he went to the glass, took a comb from his waistcoat pocket, and smoothed his hair to an equatorial line around his forehead ; he then crossed the room to Mrs. Lee with some commonplace consolation on his lips ; but the face of the mother spoke too eloquently, and he was compelled to turn away, wipe his eyes, and clear his throat, before he could recover his official composure. " Mr. Eliot," he then began, " though a minister of the gospel of peace, I heartily approve your going forth in the present warfare, for surely it is lawful to defend that which is our own ; no man has a right to that for which he did not labour ; to cities which he built not ; to oliveyards and vineyards which he planted not."

" I don't know about olive-yards and vineyards," interposed the major, " never having seen such things ; but I'm thinking we can eat our corn and potatoes without their help that have neither planted nor gathered them."

The parson gave an acquiescent nod to the major's emendation of his text, and proceeded : " I have wished, my young friend, to strengthen you in the righteous cause in which you are taking up arms ; and, to that end, besides the prayers which I shall daily offer for you and yours at the throne of divine grace, I have made up a book for you (here he tendered a package, large enough to fill half the portmanteau of our equestrian traveller), consisting of extracts selected from three thousand eight hundred and ninety-seven sermons, preached on the Sabbaths throughout my ministry of forty-eight years, besides oc-

c

casional discourses for peace and war, thanksgivings and fasts, associations and funerals. As you will often be out of reach of preaching privileges, I have provided here a word in season for every occasion, which I trust you may find both teaching and refreshing after a weary day's service."

Eliot received the treasure with suitable expressions of gratitude. The good man continued: "I could not, my friends, do this for another; but you know that, speaking after the manner of men, we look upon this dear youth as the pride and glory of our society."

"And I'm thinking, reverend sir," said the major, with that tone of familiarity authorised by age (but stared at by the children), "I'm thinking you'll not be called on again for a like service; for after Eliot Lee is gone, there's not another what you can raly call a *man* in the parish. To begin with yourself, reverend sir; you've never been a fighting character, which I take to be, humanly speaking, a necessary part of a man; then there's myself, minus a leg; and Master Hale here, who—I respect you for all, Master Hale—never was born to be handy with a smarter weapon than a ferule; then comes blind Billy, and limping Harris, and to bring up the rear, Deacon Allen and the doctor." Here the major chuckled: "They both say they would join the army if 'twas not as it is; but they have been dreadful near-sighted since the war broke out. That's all of 'mankind,' as you may say, that's left in the bounds of Westbrook. Oh, I forgot Kisel—poor Kisel! Truly, he seems to have been made up of leavings. Kisel would not make a bad soldier either, if it were one crack and done. He is brave at a go-off, but he can't bear the sight o' blood; and if he shoots as crooked as he talks, he'd be as like to shoot himself as anybody else. But sometimes the fellow's tongue does hit the mark in a kind of providential manner. By the Lor—Jiminy, I mean! there he comes, on Granny Larkin's colt!"

The person in question now halted before Mrs. Lee's door, mounted on an unbroken, ragged, party-coloured animal, such as is called, in country phrase, "a wishing horse," evidently equipped for travelling. His bridle was compounded of alternate bits of rope and leather; a sheepskin served him for a saddle, behind which hung on either side a meal-bag, filled with all his worldly substance. His own costume was in keeping; an over-garment, made of an old blanket, a sort of long roundabout, was fastened at the waist with a wampum belt, which, tied in many a fantastical knot, dangled below his knees; his under-garments were a pair of holiday leather breeches, and yarn stockings of deep red; a conical cap, composed of alternate bits of scarlet and blue cloth, covered his head, and was drawn close over his eyebrows.—Nature had reduced his brow to the narrowest precincts; his face was concave; his eyes sparkling, and in incessant motion; his nose thin and sharp; a pale, clean-looking skin, and a mouth with more of the characteristics of the brute than the human animal, complete the portrait of Kisel, who, leaping like a cat from his horse, appeared at the door, screaming out, in a cracked voice, "Ready, Misser Eliot?"

While all were exchanging inquiring glances, and the children whispering, "Hush, Kisel—don't

you see Dr. Wilson?" Eliot, who comprehended the strange apparition at a glance, came forward and said—

"No, Kisel; I am not ready."

"Well, well—all same—Kisel can wait, and Beauty too—hey!"

"No, no, Kisel," replied Eliot, kindly taking the lad's hand, "you must not wait—you must give this up, my good fellow."

"Give it up!—Diddle me if I do—no, I told you that all the devils and angels to bargain should not stop me, no—you go, I go,—that's it, hey!"

Here Major Avery, who sat near the door, his mouth wide open with amazement, burst into a hoarse laugh, at which Kisel, his eyes flashing fire, gave him a smart switch with his riding-whip (a willow wand) over the face. The good-humoured man, deeming the poor lad no subject for resentment, passed his hand over his face as if a mosquito had stung him, saying—"Well, now, Kisel, that was not fair, my boy; I was only smiling that such a harlequin-looking thing as you should think of being waiter to Mr. Eliot. He might as well take a bat, or a woodpecker."

Eliot did not need his poor friend should be placed in this ludicrous aspect to strengthen the decision which he had already expressed to him; and drawing him aside beyond the irritation of the major's gibes, he said—"It is impossible, Kisel—I cannot consent to your going with me."

"Can't, hey! can't! can't!"—and for a few moments the poor fellow hung his head, whimpering; then suddenly elevating it he cried, "Then I go 'out consent—I go, anyhow;" and springing back to the door, he called out—"*Miss* Lee, hear me—Miss Bessie, you too, and you, parson Wilson, for I speak gospel. When I boy, all boys laugh at me, knock me here, kick there—who took my part?—Misser Eliot, hey! When they tied me to old Roan, Beauty's mother, head to tail, who licked the whole tote of 'em?—Misser Eliot. I sick, nobody care I live or die—Misser Eliot stay by me all night. When everybody laugh at me, plague me, hate me, I wish me dead, Misser Eliot talk to me, make me feel good, glad, make me warm here." He laid his hand on his bosom— "He gone, I can't live!—but I'll follow him—I'll be his dog, fetch, carry, lay down at his feet. S'pose he sick, *Miss* Lee! everybody say I good in sickness—S'pose, Miss Bessie, he lie on the ground, bleeding, horses trampling, soldiers flying, hey!—I bind him up, bring water, carry him in my arms—if he die, I die too!"

The picture Kisel rudely sketched struck the imaginations of mother and daughter. They knew his devotion to Eliot, and that in emergencies he had gleams of shrewdness that seemed supernatural. They were too much absorbed in serious emotions to be susceptible of the ludicrous; and both joined in earnestly entreating Eliot not to oppose Kisel's wishes. Dr. Wilson supported their intercession by remarking, "that it seemed quite providential he should have been able to prepare for such an expedition." The major took off the edge of this argument by communicating what he had hastily ascertained, that Kisel had bartered away his patrimony for "Granny Larkin's" wishing horse, yclept Beauty; but he added two suggestions that had much force with

Eliot, particularly the last; for if there was a virtue that had supremacy in his well-ordered character, it was humanity. "The lad, Mr. Lee," he said, "may be of use, after all. It takes a great many sorts of folks to make a world, and so to make up an army. There's a lack of hands in camp, and his may come in play. Kisel is keen at a sudden call—and besides," he added, in a lower voice to Eliot, "it's true what the *creatur* says, when you are gone he'll be good for nothing —like a vine when the tree it clung to is removed, withering on the ground. Say you'll take him, and we'll rig him out according to Gunter."

Thus beset, Eliot consented to what half an hour before had appeared to him absurd; and the major bestirring himself, from his own and Mrs. Lee's stores soon rectified Kisel's equipment in all important particulars, to suit either the honourable character of volunteer soldier or volunteer attendant on Mr. Eliot Lee. This done, nothing remained but the customary devotional service, still performed by the village pastor on all extraordinary occasions. On this, Dr. Wilson's feelings overpowered his technicalities. His prayer, sublimed by the touching language of Scripture, melted the coldest heart, and raised the most dejected. After bestowing their farewell blessing the neighbours withdrew, all treasuring in their hearts some last word of kindness from Eliot Lee, long remembered, and often referred to.

The family were now left to a sacred service more informal, and far more intensely felt. Eliot, locking his mother and sister in his arms, and the little ones gathered around him, with manly faith commended them to God their Father; and receiving their last embraces, sprang on to his horse, conscious of nothing but confused sensations of grief, till having passed far beyond the bounds of Westbrook, he heard his companion lightly singing—"I cries for nobody, and nobody cries for Kisel!"

CHAPTER VI.

I do not, brother,
Infer, as if I thought my sister's state
Secure, without all doubt or controversy;
Yet, where an equal poise of hope and fear
Does arbitrate the event, my nature is,
That I incline to hope rather than fear.—MILTON.

Eliot Lee to his Mother.

"———— Town, 1778.

"I HAVE arrived thus far, my dear mother, on my journey; and, according to my promise, am beginning the correspondence which is to soften our separation.

"My spirits have been heavy. My anxious thoughts lingered with you, brooded over dear Bessie and the little troop, and dwelt on our home affairs.

"I feared Harris would neglect the thrashing, and the wheat might not turn out as well as we hoped; that the major might forget his promise about the husking bee; that the pumpkins might freeze in the loft (pray have them brought down —I forgot it!); that the cows might fail sooner than you expected; that the sheep might torment

you. In short, dear mother, the grief of parting seemed to spread its shadows far and wide. If Master Hale could have penetrated my mental processes, he would have deemed his last admonition, to deport myself in *thought*, word, and deed, like a scholar, a soldier, and a gentleman, quite lost upon me. I was an anxious wretch, and nothing else. Poor Kisel did not serve as a tranquilliser. His light wits were throwing off their fermentation, in whistling, laughing, and soliloquising; and this, with *Beauty's* shambling gait, neither trot, canter, nor pace, but something compounded of all, irritated my nerves. Never were horse and rider better matched. Together, they make a fair *centaur;* the animal not more than half a horse, and Kisel not more than half a man. There is a ludicrous correspondence between them; neither vicious, but both unbreakable, and full of all manner of tricks.

"Our land at this moment teems with scenes of moral and poetic interest. We made our first stop at the little inn in R———. The landlord's son was just setting off to join the quota to be sent from that county. The father, a stout old man, was trying to suppress his emotion by bustling about, talking loud, whistling, hemming, and coughing. The mother, her tears dropping like rain, was standing at the fire, feeling over and over again the shirts she was airing for the knapsack. 'He's our youngest,' whispered the old man to me, 'and mammy is dreadful tender of him, poor boy!' 'Not mammy alone,' thought I, as the old man turned away to brush off his starting tears. The sisters were each putting some love-token, socks, mittens, and nutcakes, into the knapsack, which they looked hardy enough to have shouldered, while one poor girl sat with her face buried in her handkerchief, weeping most bitterly. The old man patted her on the neck— 'Come, Letty, cheer up!' said he; 'Jo may never have another chance to fight for his country, and marrying can be done any day in the year.' He turned to me with an explanatory whisper; ''Tis tough for all—Jo and Letty are published, and we were to have the wedding thanksgiving evening.'

"All this was rather too much for me to bear, in addition to the load already pressing on my heart; so without waiting for my horse to be fed, I mounted him and proceeded.

"My next stop was in H———. There the company had mustered on the green, in readiness to begin their march. Some infirm old men, a few young mothers, with babies in their arms, and all the boys in the town, had gathered for the last farewell. The soldiers were resting on their muskets, and the clergyman imploring the benediction of Heaven on their heads. 'Can England,' thought I, 'hope to subdue a country that sends forth its defenders in such a spirit, with arms of such a temper!' Oh, why does she not respect in her children the transmitted character of their fathers!

"I arrived at Mrs. Ashley's just as the family were sitting down to tea. She and the girls are in fine spirits, having recently received from the colonel accounts of some fortunate skirmishes with the British. The changed aspect of her once sumptuous tea-table at first shocked me; but my keen appetite (for the first time in my life, my dear mother, I had fasted all day) quite overcame my sensibilities; the honest pride with which my patriotic hostess told me she had converted all her table-cloths into shirts for her husband's men, and the complacency with which she commended her sage tea, magnified the virtues of her brown bread and self-sweetened sweetmeats, would have given a relish to coarser fare more coarsely served.

"I have been pondering on the character of our New-England people during my ride. The aspect of our society is quiet, and to a cursory observer, it appears tame. We seem to have the plodding, safe, *self-preserving* virtues; to be industrious, frugal, provident, and cautious; but to want the enthusiasm that gives to life all its poetry and almost all its charms. But it is not so; there is a strong under-current. Let the individual or the people be roused by a motive that approves itself to the reasoning and religious mind, a fervid energy, an all-subduing enthusiasm bursts forth, not like an accidental and transient conflagration, but operating, like the elements, to great effects, and irresistibly. This enthusiasm, this central fire, is now at its height. It not only inflames the eloquence of the orator, kindles the heart of the soldier, the beacon-lights and strong defences of our land; but it lights the temple of God, and burns on the family altar. The old man throws away his crutch; the yeoman leaves the plough in the half-turned furrow; and the loving, quiet matron like you, my dear mother, lays aside her domestic anxieties, dispenses with her household comforts, and gives the God-speed to her sons to go forth and battle it for their country. The nature of the contest in which we are engaged illustrates my idea. Its sublimity is sometimes obscured by the extravagance of party zeal. We have not been goaded to resistance by oppression, nor fretted and chafed, with bits and collars, to madness; but our sages, bold with the transmitted spirit of freedom, sown at broadcast by our pilgrim fathers, have reflected on the past and calculated the future; and coolly estimating the worth of independence and the right of self-government, are willing to hazard all in the hope of gaining all; to sacrifice themselves for the prospective good of their children. This is the dignified resolve of thinking beings, not the angry impatience of overburdened animals.

"But good-night, dear mother. After this I shall have incidents, and not reflections merely, to send you. The pine-knot, by the light of which I have written this, is just flickering its last flame. 'I cannot afford you a candle,' said my good hostess when she bade me good-night; 'we sold our tallow to purchase necessaries for the colonel's men—poor fellows, some of them are yet barefooted!'

"I shall inclose a line to Bessie—perhaps she will show it to you; but do not ask it of her. Tell dear Fan I shall remember her charge, and give the socks she knit to the first 'brave barefooted soldier' I see. Sam must feed Steady for me; and dear little Hal must continue, as he has begun, to couple brother Eliot with the 'poor soldiers' in his prayers. Again farewell, dear mother. Your little Bible is before me; my eye rests on the few lines you traced on the title-page; and as I press my lips to them, they inspire holy resolutions. God grant I may not

mistake their freshness for vigour! What I may be is uncertain; but I shall ever remain, as I am now, dearest mother,

"Your devoted son,
"ELIOT LEE."

Eliot found his letter to his sister a difficult task. He was to treat a malady, the existence of which the patient had never acknowledged to him. He wrote, effaced, and re-wrote, and finally sent the following :—

"My sweet sister Bessie, nothing has afflicted me so much in leaving home as parting from you. I am inclined to believe there can be no stronger nor tenderer affection than that of brother and sister; the sense of protection on one part, and dependence on the other; the sweet recollections of childhood; the unity of interest; and the communion of memory and hope, blend their hearts together into one existence. So it is with us— is it not, my dear sister? With me, certainly; for though, like most young men, I have had my fancies, they have passed by like the summer breeze, and left no trace of their passage. All the love, liking (I cannot find a word to express the essential volatility of the sentiment in my experience of it) that I have ever felt for all my favourites, brown and fair, does not amount to one thousandth part of the immutable affection that I bear you, my dear sister. I speak only of my own experience, Bessie, and, as I well know, against the faith of the world. I should be told that my fraternal love would pale in the fires of another passion, as does a lamp at the shining of the sun; but I don't believe a word of it—do *you*, Bessie? I am not, my dear sister, playing the inquisitor with you, but fearfully and awkwardly enough approaching a subject on which I thought it would be easier to write than to speak; but I find it cannot be easy to do that, in any mode, which may pain you.

"I have neglected the duty I owed you; and yet, perhaps, no vigilance could have prevented the natural consequence of your intercourse with one of the most fascinating men in the world. There, it is out!—and now I can write freely. I said I had neglected my duty; but I was not conscious of this till too late. The truth is, my mind has been so engrossed with political subjects, so harassed with importunate cravings, and conflicting duties, that I was for a long time unobservant of what was passing under my eye. I awoke as from a dream, and found (or feared) that my sister's happiness was at stake; that she had given, and given to one unworthy, the irrequitable boon of her affections; irrequitable, but, thank Heaven, not irrecoverable. No, I do not believe one word of all the trumpery about incurable love. I will not adopt a faith, however old and prevailing, which calls in question our moral power to achieve any conquest over ourselves. For my own part, I do not think we have any power over our affections to give or withdraw them, or even to measure their amount. This may seem a startling assertion, and contradictory of what I have said above; but it is not. The sentiment I there alluded to is generated by accidental circumstances, is half illusion, unsustained by reason, unauthorised by realities—not the immortal love infused by Heaven and sustained by truth ; but a disease very mortal and very curable, dear Bessie, believe me. Such a mind as yours, so pure, so elevated, has a self-rectifying power. You have felt the influence of the delightful qualities which M—— undoubtedly possesses ; and why should you not, for who is more susceptible to grace and refinement than yourself ! Heaven has so arranged the relations of affections and qualities, that, as I have said above, we can neither give nor withhold our love—the heart has no tenants at will. If M—— has assumed, or you have imputed to him, qualities which he does not possess, your affection will be dissipated with the illusion. But if the spell still remains unbroken, I intreat you, my dear sister, not to waste your sensibility, the precious food of life, the life of life, in moping melancholy.

　　' Attach thee firmly—'
I quote from memory—
　　　　　　' to the virtuous deeds
　　And offices of love—to love itself,
　　With all its vain and transient joys, sit loose.'

"I have long had a lurking distrust of M——. He has acted too cautious a part in politics for a sound heart. Let a man run the risk of hanging for it either way ; but if he have a spark of generosity, he will be either a whole-souled whig or a loyal tory in these times.

"I know what M—— has so often reiterated. ' He had a mother in England ; all his friends were on the royal side ; and, on the other hand, his property was here, and might depend on the favour of the rebels ; and, indeed, there was so much to be said on both sides, that a man might well pause !' There are moments in men's histories, when none but cowards or knaves, or (worse than either) cold-blooded, selfish wretches, would *pause !*

"It is possible that I misjudge him ; Heaven grant it ! All that I *know* is, that he is in New York, no longer *pausing*, but the aid of General Clinton. It is barely possible that he has written ; letters are not transmitted with any security in these times ; but why did he not speak before he went ! why, up to the very hour of his departure (as my mother says, you know I was absent), did he continue a devotion which must end in suffering and disappointment to you ! There is a vicious vanity and selfishness in this, most unmanly and detestable. Do not think, dearest Bessie, that I am anxious to prove him unworthy.—Alas, alas ! I was far too slow to believe him so ; and I now only set before you these inevitable inferences from his conduct, in the hope that your illusion will sooner vanish, and you will the sooner recover your tranquillity.

"I am writing without a ray of light, except what comes from the embers on the hearth. Perhaps you will think I am in Egyptian mental darkness. No, Bessie, I must be clear-sighted when I have nothing in view but your honour and happiness. They shall ever be my care, even more than my own. But why do I separate that which is one and indivisible ! Good-night, dear sister. Let me fancy you listening to me ; your sweet eye fixed on me ; no dejected nor averted look ; your face beaming, as I have often seen it, with the tenderness so dangerous here, so safe in heaven ; the hope so often defeated here, there ever brightening ! the joy so transient here, there enduring !— Let me see this blessed vision, and I shall sleep sweetly, and sweetly dream of home.

　　　　　　"Ever thine, Bessie,
　　　　　　　　　　"E. L."

Bessie read her brother's letter with mixed emotions. At first it called forth tenderness for him ; then she thought he judged Meredith precipitately, harshly even ; and after confirming herself in this opinion, by thinking of him over and over again in the false lights in which he had shown himself, she said, "Even Eliot allows that we can neither give nor withhold our love ; then how is Jasper to blame for not giving it to one so humble, so inferior as I am ! and how could I withhold mine !" Poor Bessie ! it is a common trick of human nature to snatch from an argument whatever coincides with our own views, and leave the rest. "If," she continued in her reflections, "he had ever made any declarations, or asked any confessions—but I gave my own heart unasked and silently." She could have recalled passionate declarations in his eye, prayers in his devotion ; but her love had the essential characteristics, of true passion ; it was humble, generous, and self-condemning.

CHAPTER VII.

Si tout le monde vous ressembloit, un roman seroit bientôt fini !—Molière.

NOVEMBER'S leaden clouds and fitful gleams of sunshine, coming like visitations of heaven-inspired thoughts, and vanishing, alas ! like illusions, harmonised with the state of Bessie's mind. She was much abroad, rambling alone over her favourite haunts, and living over the dangerous past. This was at least a present relief and solace ; and her mother, though she feared it might minister to the morbid state of her child's feelings, had not the resolution to interpose her authority to prevent it. Bessie was one evening at twilight returning homeward by a road (if road that might be called which was merely a horse-path) that communicated at the distance of a mile and a half with the main road to Boston. It led by the margin of a little brook, through a pine wood that was just now powdered over with a light snow. Meredith and Bessie had always taken their way through this sequestered wood in their walks and rides, going and returning ; not a step of it but was eloquent with some treasured word, some well-remembered emotion. Bessie had seated herself on a fallen trunk, an accustomed resting-place, and was looking at a bunch of ground pine and wild periwinkles as if she were perusing them ; the sensations of happier hours had stolen over her, the painful present and uncertain future were forgotten, when she was roused from her dreamy state by the trampling of an approaching horse. Women, most women, are cowards on instinct. Bessie cast one glance backward, and saw the horse was ridden by a person in a military dress. A stranger in this private path was rather an alarming apparition, and she started homeward with hasty steps. The rider mended his horse's pace, and was soon even with her, and in another instant had dismounted and exclaimed—"Bessie Lee !—It *is* you, Bessie—I cannot be mistaken !''

Bessie smiled at this familiar salutation, and did not refuse her hand to the stranger, who with eager cordiality offered his ; but not being in the least a woman of the world, it was plain she explored his face in vain for some recognisable feature.—"No, you do not remember me—that is evident," he said, with a tone of disappointment. "Is there not a vestige, Bessie, of your old playmate, in the whiskered, weather-beaten personage before you !''

"Herbert Linwood !'' she exclaimed, and a glow of glad recognition mounted from her heart to her cheek.

"Ah, thank you, Bessie, better late than never, but it is sad to be forgotten. You are much less changed than I, undoubtedly ; but I should have known you if nothing were unaltered save the colour of your eye ; however, I have always worn your likeness here," he gallantly added, putting his hand to his heart, "and, in truth, you are but the opening bud expanded to the flower, while I have undergone a change like the chesnut, from the tassel to the bearded husk.'' Bessie soon began to perceive familiar tones and expressions, and she consoled Herbert with the assurance that it was only her surprise, his growth, change of dress, &c., that prevented her from knowing him at once. They soon passed to mutual inquiries, by which it appeared that Herbert had come to Massachusetts on military business. The visit to Westbrook was a little episode of his own insertion. He was to return in a few weeks to West Point, where he was charmed to hear he should meet Eliot.

"I am cut off from my own family," he said, "and, really, I pine for a friend. I gather from Belle's letters that my father is more and more estranged from me. While he thought I was fighting on the losing side, and in peril of my head, his generous spirit was placable ; but since the result of our contest has become doubtful, even to him, he has waxed hotter and hotter against me ; and if we finally prevail, and prevail we must, he will never forgive me.''

"Oh, do not say so—he cannot be so unrelenting ; and if he were, Isabella can persuade him—she can do anything she pleases.''

"Yes, a pretty potent person is that sister of mine. But when my father sets his foot down, the devil—I beg your pardon, Bessie, and Belle's too—I mean his metal is of such a temper that an angel could not bend him.''

"Isabella is certainly the angel, not its opposite.''

"Why yes, she is, God bless her ! But yet, Bessie, she is pretty well spiced with humanity. If she were not, she would not be so attractive to a certain friend of ours, who is merely human.''

Bessie's heart beat quicker ; she knew, or feared she knew, what Herbert meant ; and, after a pause, full of sensation to her, she ventured to ask "if he heard often from New York.''

"Yes, we get rumours from there every day—nothing very satisfactory. Belle, in spite of her toryism, is a loving sister, and writes me as often as she can ; but as the letters run the risk of being read by friends and foes, they are about as domestic and private as if they were indited for Rivington's Gazette.''

"Then,'' said Bessie, quite boldly, for she felt a sensible relief, "you have no news to tell me !''

"No—no, nothing official,'' he replied, with a smile ; "Belle writes exultingly of Meredith having, since his return to New York, come out on the right side, as she calls it—and of my father's pleasure and pride in him, &c. Of course she says not a word of her own sentiments. I hear from an old friend of mine, who was brought in a prisoner the other day, that Meredith has been devoted to her ever since his return. They were always lovers after an April-day fashion, you know, Bessie, and I should not be surprised to hear of their engagement at any time—should you !''

Fortunately for poor Bessie, her hood sheltered the rapid mutations of her cheek ; resolution or pride she had not, but a certain sense of maidenly decorum came to her aid, and she faintly answered, "No, I should not.'' If this were a slight departure from truth, every woman (every young one) will forgive her, for it was a case of self-preservation. Linwood was so absorbed in the happiness of being near her, of having her arm in his, that he scarcely noticed how that arm trembled, and how her voice faltered. He afterwards recalled it.

Herbert's visit to the Lees was like a saint's day to good Catholics after a long penance. He had in his boyhood been a prime favourite with Mrs. Lee—she was delighted to see him again, and thought the man even more charming than the boy. She made every effort to show off her hospitable home to Linwood in its old aspect of abundance and cheerfulness ; and, in spite of war and actual changes, she succeeded. She had the skilful housewife's gift "to make the worse appear the better,"—far more difficult in housewifery than in metaphysics. Herbert enjoyed, to her kind heart's content, the result of her efforts. The poor fellow's appetite had been so long mortified with the sorry fare of the American camp, that no Roman epicurean ever relished the dainties of an emperor's table (such as canaries' eyes and peacocks' brains) more keenly than he did the plain but excellent provisions at Lee Farm ; the incomparable bread and butter, ham, apple-sauce, and cream, the nuts the children cracked, and the sparkling cider they drew for him. We are quite aware that a hero on a sentimental visit should be indifferent to these gross matters, but our friend Herbert was no hero, no romantic abstraction, but a good, honest, natural fellow, compounded of body and spirit, each element bearing its due proportion in the composition.

Bessie yielded to the influence of old associations, and, as her mother thought, was more light-hearted, more *herself*, than she had been for many a weary month. "After all,'' she said, anxiously revolving the subject in her mind, "it may come out right yet. Bessie cannot help preferring Herbert Linwood, so good-humoured and open-hearted as he is, to Meredith, with his studied elegance, his hollow phrases, and expressive looks. Herbert's heart is in his hand ; and hand and heart he'll not be too proud to offer her ; for he sees things in their true lights, and not with the world's eye.''

Mrs. Lee was delicate and prudent ; but she could not help intimating her own sentiments to Bessie. From that moment a change came over her. Her spirits vanished like the rosy hues from the sunset clouds. Herbert wondered, but he had no time to lose in speculation. He threw himself at Bessie's feet, and there poured out his tale of love and devotion. At first he received nothing in return but silence and tears ; and, when he became more importunate, broken protestations of her gratitude and ill desert ; which he misunderstood, and answered by declaring "she owed him no gratitude ; that he was but too bold to aspire to her, poor wretch of broken fortunes that he was ; but, please Heaven, he would mend them under her auspices."

She dared not put him off with pretences. She only wept, and said "she had no heart to give ;" and then left him, feeling much like some poor mariner, who, as he is joyously sailing into a long-desired port, is suddenly enveloped in impenetrable mist.

Herbert was not of a temper to remain tranquil in this position. He knew nothing of the "blessing promised to those that wait," for he had never waited for anything ; and he at once told his perplexities to Mrs. Lee, who, herself most grieved and mortified, communicated slight hints which, by furnishing a key to certain observations of his own, put him sufficiently in possession of the truth. Without again seeing Bessie, he left Westbrook with the common conviction of even common lovers in fresh disappointments, that there was no more happiness for him in this world.

Mrs. Lee uttered no word of expostulation or reproach to Bessie ; but her sad looks, like the old mother's in the ballad, "gaed near to break her heart."

There are few greater trials to a tenderhearted, conscientious creature like Bessie Lee, than to defeat the hopes and disappoint the expectations of friends, by opposing those circumstances which, as it seems to them, will best promote our honour and happiness. "Eliot," said Bessie, in her secret meditations, "thinks I am weakly cherishing an unworthy passion—my mother believes that I have voluntarily thrown away my own advantage and happiness—thank Heaven, the wretchedness, as well as the fault, is all my own."

Many may condemn Bessie's unresisting weakness ; but who will venture to graduate the scale of human virtue ! to decide in a given case how much is bodily infirmity, and how much defect of resolution ! Certain are we, that when fragility of constitution, tenderness of conscience, and susceptibility of heart, meet in one person, the sooner the trials of life are over the better.

CHAPTER VIII.

A name which every wind to Heaven would bear,
Which men to speak, and angels joy to hear.

ANOTHER letter from Eliot broke like a sunbeam through the monotonous clouds that hung over the Lees.

"MY DEAREST MOTHER,—I arrived safely at head-quarters on the 22nd. Colonel Ashley received me with open arms. He applauded my resolution to join the army, and bestowed his curses liberally (as is his wont on whatever displeases him) on the young men who linger at home, while the gallant spirits of France and Poland are crossing the ocean to volunteer in our cause. He rubbed his hands exultingly when I told him that it was your self-originating decision that I should leave you. 'The only son of your mother—that is, the only one to speak of' (forgive him, Sam and Hal), 'and she a widow !' he exclaimed. 'Let them talk about their Spartan mothers, half men and demi-monsters ; but look at our women-folks, as tender and as timid of their broods as hens, and as bold and self-sacrificing as martyrs ! You come of a good stock, my boy, and so I shall tell the gen'ral. He's old Virginia, my lad ; and looks well to blood in man and horse.'

"The next morning he called, his kind heart raying out through his jolly face, to present me to General Washington. If ever I go into battle, which Heaven of its loving mercy grant, I pray my heart may not thump as it did when I approached the mean little habitation, now the residence of our noble leader. 'You tremble, Eliot,' said my colonel, as we reached the doorstep. 'I don't wonder—I always feel my joints give a little when I go before him. I venerate him next to the Deity ; but it is not easy to get used to him as you do to other men.'

"When we entered, the general was writing. If Sam wishes to know whether my courage returned when I was actually in his presence, tell him I then forgot myself—forgot I had an impression to make. The general requested us to be seated while he finished his despatches. The copies were before him, all in his own hand. 'Every *t* crossed, and every *i* dotted,' whispered the colonel, pointing to the papers. 'He's godlike in that ; he finishes off little things as completely as great.' I could not but smile at the comparison, though it was both striking and just. When the general had finished, and had read the letters of introduction from Governor Hancock and Mr. Adams, which I presented, 'You see, sir,' said my kind patron, 'that my young friend here is calculating to enter the army ; I'll answer for him, he'll prove good and true ; up to the mark, as his father Sam Lee was before him. He, that is, Sam Lee, and I *fit* side by side in the French war ; I was no flincher, you know, sir, and he was as brave as Julius Cæsar, Sam was ; so I think my friend Eliot here has a pretty considerable claim.'

"'But, my good sir,' said the general, 'you know we are contending against hereditary claims.'

"'That's true, sir ; and, thank the Lord, he can stand on his own ground. He shot one of the first guns at Lexington, and got pretty well *peppered* too, though he was a lad then, with a face as smooth as the palm of my hand.'

"'Something too much of this,' thought I ; and I attempted to stop my trumpeter's mouth by saying, 'I had no claims on the score of the affair at Lexington ;' that 'my being there was accidental, and I fought on instinct.'

"'Ah, my boy !' said the colonel, determined to tell his tale out, 'you may say that—there's no courage like that that comes by *natur*, gin'ral ;—

he stood within two feet of me, as straight as a tomb-stone, when, a spent ball bounding near him, he caught it in his hands, just as if he'd been playing wicket, and said, ' You may throw down your bat, my boys ; I've caught you out ! ' Was not that metal ! '

" General Washington's countenance relaxed as the colonel proceeded (I ventured a side glance), and at the conclusion he gave two or three emphatic and pleased nods ; but his grave aspect returned immediately, and he said, as I thought, in a most frigid manner, ' The request, Mr. Lee, of my friends of Massachusetts, that you may receive a commission in the service, deserves attention ; Colonel Ashley is a substantial voucher for your personal merit. Are you aware, sir, that a post of honour in our army involves arduous labour, hardships, and self-denial ! Do you know the actual condition of our officers— that their pay is in arrears, and their private resources exhausted ! There are among them men who have bravely served their country from the beginning of this contest ; gentlemen who have not a change of linen ; to whom I have even been compelled to deny, because I had not the power to divert them from their original destination, the coarse clothes provided for the soldiers. This is an affecting, but a true view of our actual condition. Should the Almighty prosper our cause, as, if we are true to ourselves, he assuredly will, these matters will improve ; but I have no lure to hold out to you—no encouragement but the sense of performing your duty to your country. Perhaps, Mr. Lee, you would prefer to reflect further, before you assume new obligations.'

" ' Not a moment, sir. I came here determined to serve my country at any post you should assign me. If a command is given me, I shall be grateful for it : if not, I shall enter the ranks as a private soldier.'

" General Washington exchanged glances with the colonel, that implied approbation of my resolution ; but not one syllable dropped of encouragement as to the commission ; and it being evident that he had no leisure to protract our audience, we took our leave.

" I confess I came away rather crest-fallen. I am not such a puppy, my dear mother, as to suppose my single arm of much consequence to my country ; but I felt an agreeable, perhaps an exaggerated consciousness, that I deserved—not applause, but some token of encouragement. However, the colonel said this was his way :— ' he never disappoints an expectation—seldom authorises one.'

" ' Is he cold-hearted ! ' I asked.

" ' The Lord forgive you ! Eliot,' he replied. ' Cold-hearted ! No ; his heat does not go off by flashes, but keeps the furnace hot out of which the pure gold comes. Lads never think there is any fire, unless they see the sparks and hear the roar.'

" ' But, sir,' said I, ' I believe there is a very common impression that General Washington is of a reserved, cold temperament——'

" ' The devil take common impressions ; they are made on sand, and are both false and fleeting. Wait, Eliot—you are true metal, and I will venture your impressions when you shall know

our noble commander better. Cold, egad ! ' he half muttered to himself. ' Where the deuse, then, has the heat come from that has cemented our army together, and kept their spirits up when their fingers and toes were freezing ! ' "

" Give me joy, my dear mother ; a kiss, Bessie ; a good hug, my dear little sisters ; and a huzza, boys ! General Washington has sent me a lieutenant's commission, and a particularly kind note with it. So, it appears, that while I was thinking him so lukewarm to my application, he lost no time in transmitting it to Congress, and enforcing it by his recommendation. Our camp is all bustle. Soldiers, just trained and fit for service, are departing, their term of enlistment having expired. The new quotas are coming in, raw, undisciplined troops. The general preserves a calm, unaltered mien ; but his officers fret and fume in private, and say that nothing effective will ever be achieved while Congress permits these short enlistments."

" ' Thanks to you, dear mother, my funds have enabled me to purchase a uniform. I have just tried it on. I wish you could all see me in it. ' Every woman is at heart a rake,' says Pope ; that every man is at heart a coxcomb, is just about as true. My new dress will lose its holiday gloss before we meet again ; but the freshness of my love for you will never be dimmed, my dear mother—for Bessie, and for all the little band, whose bright faces are even now before my swimming eyes.

" Yours devotedly,
" ELIOT LEE."

" P.S.—My poor jack-o'-lantern, Kisel, is of course of no use to me, neither does he give me much trouble. He is a sort of mountebank among the soldiers, merry himself, and making others merry. If he is a benefactor who makes two blades of grass grow where but one grew before, Kisel certainly is, while he produces smiles where rugged toil and want have stamped a scowl of discontent."

In this letter to his mother, Eliot enclosed one to Bessie, reiterating even more forcibly and tenderly what he had before said. It served no purpose but to aggravate her self-reproaches.

CHAPTER IX.

Come not near our fairy queen.

BEFORE mid-winter, Linwood joined Eliot Lee at West Point, and the young men renewed their acquaintance on the footing of friends. There was just that degree of similarity and difference between them that inspires mutual confidence, and begets interest. Herbert, with characteristic frankness, told the story of his love, disappointment, and all. Eliot felt a true sympathy for his friend, whose deserts he thought would so well have harmonised with Bessie's advantage and happiness ; but this feeling was subordinate to his keen anxiety for his sister. This anxiety was not appeased by intelligence from home. Letters were rare blessings in those days—scarcely to him blessings. His mother wrote about everything but Bessie, and his sister's letters were brief and vague, and most unsatisfactory. The winter, however, passed rapidly away. Though in winter quarters, he had incessant occupation; and the exciting novelty of military life, with the deep interest of the times, to an ardent and patriotic spirit, kept every feeling on the strain.

Eliot had that intimate acquaintance with nature that makes one look upon and love all its aspects, as upon the changing expressions of a friend's face; and as that most interests us in its soul-fraught seriousness, so he delighted even more in the wild gleams of beauty that are shot over the winter landscape, than in all its summer wealth. To eyes like his, faithful ministers to the soul, the scenery of West Point was a perpetual banquet.

Nature, in our spring-time, as we all know (especially in this blessed year of our Lord 1835), rises as slowly and reluctantly from her long winter's sleep as any other sluggard. On looking back to our hero's spring at West Point, we find she must have been at her work earlier than is her wont; for April was not far gone when Eliot, after looking in vain for Linwood to accompany him, sauntered into the woods, where the buds were swelling and the rills gushing. At first his pleasure was marred by his friend not being with him, and he now, for the first time, called to mind Linwood's frequent and unexplained absences for the last few days. Linwood was so essentially a social being, that Eliot's curiosity was naturally excited by this sudden manifestation of a love of solitude and secrecy.

He, however, pursued his way; and having reached the cascade which is now the resort of holiday visiters, he forgot his friend. The soil under his feet, released from the iron grasp of winter, was soft and spongy, and the tokens of spring were around him like the first mellow smile of dawn. The rills that spring together like laughing children just out of school (we borrow the obvious simile from a poetic child), and at their junction form "the cascade," were then filled to the brim from their just unsealed fountains. Eliot followed the streamlet where it pursues its headlong course, dancing, singing, and shouting, as it flings itself over the rocks, as if it spurned their cold and stern companionship, and was impatiently running away from the leafless woods to a holiday in a summer region. He forced his way through the obstructions that impeded his descent, and was standing on a jutting point which the stream again divided, looking up at the snow-white and feathery water, as he caught a glimpse of it here and there through the intersecting branches of hemlocks, and wondering why it was that he instinctively infused his own nature into the outward world: why the rocks seemed to him to look sternly on the frolicking stream that capered over them, and the fresh white blossoms of the early flowering shrubs seemed to yearn with a kindred spirit towards it, when his speculations were broken by human voices mingling with the sound of the waterfall. He looked in the direction whence they came, and fancied he saw a white dress. It might be the cascade, for that at a little distance did not look unlike a white robe floating over the

grey rocks, but it might be a fair lady's gown, and that was a sight rare enough to provoke the curiosity of a young knight-errant. So Eliot, quickening his footsteps, reached the point where the streamlet ceases its din, and steals loiteringly through the deep narrow glen, now called Washington's Valley. He had pressed on unwittingly, for he was now within a few yards of two persons on whom he would not voluntarily have intruded. One was a lady (a lady certainly, for a well-practised ear can graduate the degree of refinement by a single tone of the voice), the other party to the *tête-à-tête* was his truant friend Linwood. The lady was seated with her back towards Eliot, in a grape-vine that hung, a sylvan swing, from the trees; and Linwood, his face also turned from Eliot, was decking his companion's pretty hair with wood anemones, and (ominous it was when Herbert Linwood made sentimental sallies) saying very soft and pretty things of their starry eyes. Eliot was making a quiet retreat, when, to his utter consternation, a lady on his right, till then unseen by him, addressed him, saying,—"she believed she had the pleasure of speaking to Lieutenant Lee." Eliot bowed! whereupon she added, "that she was sure, from Captain Linwood's description, that it must be his friend. Captain Linwood is there with my sister, you perceive," she continued; "and as he is our friend, and you are his, you will do us the favour to go home and take tea with us."

By this time the *tête-à-tête* party, though sufficiently absorbed in each other, was aroused, and both turning their heads, perceived Eliot. The lady said nothing; Linwood looked disconcerted, and merely nodded without speaking to his friend. The lady rose, and with a spirited step walked towards a farmhouse on the margin of the Hudson, the only tenement of this secluded and most lovely little glen. Linwood followed her, and seemed earnestly addressing her in a low voice. By this time Eliot had sufficiently recovered his senses to remember that the farmhouse, which was visible from West Point, had been pointed out to him as the temporary residence of a Mr. Grenville Ruthven. Mr. Ruthven was a native of Virginia, who some years before had, in consequence of pecuniary misfortunes, removed to New York, where he had held an office under the king till the commencement of the war. His political partialities, however, were not so strong but that they might be deferred to prudence: so he took her counsel, and retired with his wife and two daughters to this safe nook on the Hudson, till the troubles should be overpast.

Eliot could not be insensible to the friendly and volunteered greeting of his pretty lady patroness, and a social pleasure was never more inviting than now when he was famishing for it; but it was so manifest that his presence was anything but desirable to Linwood and his companion, that he was making his acknowledgments and turning away, when the young lady, declaring she would not take "no" for an answer, called out, "Stop, Helen—pray, stop—come back, Captain Linwood, and introduce us regularly to your friend; he is so ceremonious that he will not go on with an acquaintance that is not begun in due form."

Thus compelled, Miss Ruthven stopped and submitted gracefully to an introduction, which Linwood was in fact at the moment urging, and she peremptorily refusing.

"Now, here we are, just at our own door," said Miss Charlotte Ruthven to Eliot, " and you must positively come in and take tea with us." Eliot still hesitated.

"Why, in the name of wonder, should you not?" said Linwood, who appeared just coming to himself.

"You must come with us," said Miss Ruthven, for the first time speaking, "and let me show your friend how very magnanimous I can be."

"Indeed, you must not refuse us," urged Miss Charlotte.

"I cannot," replied Eliot, gallantly, "though it is not very flattering to begin an acquaintance with testing the magnanimity of your sister."

Helen Ruthven bowed, smiled, and coloured; and at the first opportunity said to Linwood, "Your friend is certainly the most civilised of all the eastern savages I have yet seen, and, as *your* friend, I will try to tolerate him." She soon, however, seemed to forget his presence, and to forget everything else, in an absorbing and half-whispered conversation with Linwood, interrupted only by singing snatches of sentimental songs, accompanying herself on the piano, and giving them the expressive application that eloquent eyes can give. In the meanwhile Eliot was left to Miss Charlotte, a commonplace, frank, and good-humoured person, particularly well pleased at being relieved from the *rôle* she had lately played, a cipher in a trio.

Mr. and Mrs Ruthven made their appearance with the tea-service. Mr. Ruthven, though verging towards sixty, was still in the unimpaired vigour of manhood, and was marked by the general characteristics, physical and moral, of a Virginian: the lofty stature, strong and well-built frame, the open brow, and expression of nobleness and kindness of disposition, and a certain something, not vanity, nor pride, nor in the least approaching to superciliousness, but a certain happy sense of the superiority, not of the individual, but of the great mass of which he is a component part.

His wife, unhappily, was not of this noble stock. She was of French descent, and a native of one of our cities. At sixteen, with but a modicum of beauty, and coquetry enough for half her sex, she succeeded, Mr. Ruthven being then a widower, in making him commit the folly of marrying her, after a six weeks' acquaintance. She was still in the prime of life, and as impatient as a caged bird of her country seclusion, or, as she called it, imprisonment, where her daughters were losing every opportunity of achieving what she considered the chief end of a woman's life.

Aware of her eldest daughter's propensity to convert acquaintances into lovers, and looking down upon all rebels as most unprofitable suitors, she had sedulously guarded against any intercourse with the officers at the Point.

Of late, she had begun to despair of a favourable change in their position; and Miss Ruthven having accidentally renewed an old acquaintance with Herbert Linwood, her mother encouraged his visits from that admirable policy of maternal manœuvrers, which wisely keeps a *pis-aller* in reserve. Helen Ruthven was one of those persons, most uncomfortable in domestic life, who profess always to require an object (which means something out of a woman's natural, safe, and quiet orbit) on which to exhaust their engrossing and exacting desires. Mr. Ruthven felt there was a very sudden change in his domestic atmosphere; and though it was as incomprehensible to him as a change in the weather, he enjoyed it without asking or caring for an explanation. Always hospitably inclined, he was charmed with Linwood's good-fellowship; and while he discussed a favourite dish, obtained with infinite trouble, or drained a bottle of Madeira with him, he was as unobservant of his wife's tactics and his daughters' coquetries as the eagle is of the *modus operandi* of the mole. And all the while, and in his presence, Helen was lavishing her flatteries with infinite finesse and grace. Her words, glances, tones of voice even, might have turned a steadier head than Linwood's. Her father, good, confiding man, was not suspicious, but vexed when she called his companion away, just, as he said, "as they were beginning to enjoy themselves," to scramble over frozen ground or look at a wintry prospect, or to play over, for the fortieth time, a trumpery song. Helen, however, would throw her arms around her father's neck, kiss him into a good-humour, and carry her point; that is, secure the undivided attentions of Herbert Linwood. Matters were at this point, after a fortnight's intercourse, when Eliot entered upon the scene; and, though his friend Miss Charlotte kept up an even flow of talk, before the evening was over he had taken some very accurate observations.

When they took their leave, and twice after they had shut the outer door, Helen called Linwood back for some last word that seemed to mean nothing, and yet clearly meant that her heart went with him: and then

So fondly she bade him adieu,
It seem'd that she bade him return.

The young men had a long, dark, and at first rather an unsocial walk. Both were thinking of the same subject, and both were embarrassed by it. Linwood, after whipping his boots for ten minutes, said, "Hang it, Eliot! we may as well speak out; I suppose you think it deused queer that I said nothing to you of my visits to the Ruthvens?"

"Why, yes, Linwood—to speak out frankly, I do."

"Well, it is, I confess it. At first my silence was accidental—no, that is not plummet-and-line truth; for from the first I had a sort of a fear—no, not fear, but a sheepish feeling, that you might think the pleasure I took in visiting the Ruthvens quite inconsistent with the misery I had seemed to feel, and, by Heavens, did feel, to my heart's core, about that affair at Westbrook."

"No, Linwood—whatever else I may doubt, I never shall doubt your sincerity."

"But my constancy you do?" Eliot made no reply, and Linwood proceeded: "Upon my soul, I have not the slightest idea of falling in love with either of these girls, but I find it exceedingly pleasant to go there. To tell the truth, Eliot, I am wretched without the society of womankind ; Adam was a good sensible fellow not to find even Paradise tolerable without them. I knew the Ruthvens in New York : I believe they like me the better, apostate as they consider me, for belonging to a tory family ; and looking upon me, as they must, as a diseased branch from a sound root, they certainly are very kind to me, especially the old gentleman—a fine old fellow, is he not ? "

" Yes—I liked him particularly."

" And madame is piquant and agreeable, and very polite to me ; and the girls, of course, are pleased to have their hermitage enlivened by an old acquaintance."

Linwood's slender artifice in saying the "girls," when it was apparent that Miss Ruthven was the magnet, operated like the subtlety of a child, betraying what he would fain conceal. Without appearing to perceive the truth, Eliot said, " Miss Ruthven seems to restrict her hospitality to old acquaintance. It was manifest that she did not voluntarily extend it to me."

" No, she did not. Helen Ruthven's heart is in her hand, and she makes no secret of her antipathy to a rebel—per se a rebel ; however, her likes and dislikes are both harmless—she is only the more attractive for them."

Herbert had not been the first to mention Helen Ruthven ; he seemed now well enough pleased to dwell upon the subject. " How did you like her singing, Eliot ! " he asked.

" Why, pretty well ; she sings with expression."

" Does she not ! infinite !—and then what an accompaniment are those brilliant eyes of hers !"

" With their speechless messages, Linwood !" Linwood merely hemmed in reply, and Eliot added, " Do you like the expression of her mouth ? "

" No, not entirely—there is a little spice of the devil about her mouth ; but when you are well acquainted with her you don't perceive it."

" If you are undergoing a blinding process," thought Eliot. When the friends arrived at their quarters, and separated for the night, Linwood asked, and Eliot gave a promise, to repeat his visit the next evening to the glen.

CHAPTER X.

He is a good man.
Have you heard any imputation to the contrary?

FROM this period Linwood was every day at the glen, and Eliot as often as his very strict performance of his duties permitted. He was charmed with the warm-hearted hospitality of Mr. Ruthven, and not quite insensible to the evident partiality of Miss Charlotte. She did not pass the vestibule of his heart to the holy of holies, but in the vestibule (of even the best of hearts) vanity is apt to lurk. If Eliot therefore was not insensible to the favour of Miss Charlotte, an every-day character, Linwood could not be expected to resist the dazzling influence of her potent sister. A more wary youth might have been scorched in the focus of her charms. Helen Ruthven was some three or four years older than Linwood,—a great advantage when the subject to

be practised on combines simplicity and credulity with inexperience. Without being beautiful, by the help of grace and versatility, and artful adaptation of the aids and artifices of the toilet, Miss Ruthven produced the effect of beauty. Never was there a more skilful manager of the blandishments of her sex. She knew how to infuse into a glance " thoughts that breathe,"—how to play off those flatteries that create an atmosphere of perfume and beauty,—how to make her presence felt as the soul of life, and life in her absence a dreary day of nothingness. She had little true sensibility or generosity (they go together) ; but selecting a single object on which to lavish her feeling, like a shallow stream compressed into a narrow channel, it made great show and noise. Eliot stood on disenchanted ground ; and, while looking on the real shape, was compelled to see his credulous and impulsive friend becoming from day to day more and more inthralled by the false semblance. " Is man's heart," he asked himself, " a mere surface, over which one shadow chaseth another ? " No. But men's hearts have different depths. In some, like Eliot Lee's (who was destined to love once and for ever), love strikes a deep and ineradicable root ; interweaves itself with the very fibres of life, and becomes a portion of the undying soul.

In other circumstances Eliot would have obeyed his impulses, and endeavoured to dissolve the spell for his friend ; but he was deterred by the consciousness of disappointment that his sister was so soon superseded, and by his secret wish that Linwood should remain free till a more auspicious day should rectify all mischances. Happily, Providence sometimes interposes to do that for us which we neglect to do for ourselves.

As has been said, Linwood devoted every leisure hour to Helen Ruthven. Sometimes accompanied by Charlotte and Eliot, but oftener without them, they visited the almost unattainable heights, the springs and waterfalls, in the neighbourhood of West Point, now so well known to summer travellers that we have no apology for lingering to describe them. They scaled the coal-black summits of the " Devil's Peak ; " went as far heavenward as the highest height of the " Crow's Nest ; " visited " Bull-Hill, Butter-Hill, and Break-neck,"—places that must have been named long before our day of classic, heathenish, picturesque, and most ambitious christening of this new world.

Helen Ruthven did not affect this scrambling " thorough bush, thorough brier," through streamlet, snow, and mud, from a pure love of nature. Oh, no, simple reader ! but because at her home in the glen there was but one parlour—there, from morning till bedtime, sat her father—there, of course, must sit her mother ; and Miss Ruthven's charms, like those of other conjurers, depended for their success on being exercised within a magic circle, within which no observer might come. She seemed to live and breathe alone for Herbert Linwood. A hundred times he was on the point of offering the devotion of his life to her, when the image of his long-loved Bessie Lee rose before him, and, like the timely intervention of the divinities of the ancient creed, saved him from impending danger. This could not last much longer. On each successive occasion the image was less vivid, and must soon cease to be effective.

Spring was advancing, and active military operations were about to commence. A British sloop-of-war had come up the river, and lay at anchor in Haverstraw Bay. Simultaneously with the appearance of this vessel there was a manifest change in the spirits of the family at the glen—a fall in their mercury. Though they were still kind, their reception of our friends ceased to be cordial, and they were no longer urged, or even asked, to repeat their visits. Charlotte, who, like her father, was warm and true-hearted, ventured to intimate that this change of manner did not originate in any diminution of friendliness; but, save this, there was no approach to an explanation; and Eliot ceased to pay visits that, it was obvious, were no longer acceptable. The mystery, as he thought, was explained, when they incidentally learned that Captain Ruthven, the only son of their friend, was an officer on board the vessel anchored in Haverstraw Bay. This solution did not satisfy Linwood. "How, in Heaven's name," he asked, "should that affect their intercourse with us! It might, to be sure, agitate them; but, upon my word, I don't believe they even know it;" and, in the simplicity of his heart, he forthwith set off to give them information of the fact. Mr. Ruthven told him, frankly and at once, that he was already aware of it,—and Helen scrawled on the music-book which lay before them, "Do you remember Hamlet! 'ten thousand brothers!'" What she exactly meant was not plain; but he guessed her intimation to be, that ten thousand brothers and their love were not to be weighed against him. Notwithstanding this kind intimation, he saw her thenceforth unfrequently. If he called, she was not at home; if she made an appointment with him, she sent him some plausible excuse for not keeping it; and if they met, she was silent and abstracted, and no longer kept up a show of the passion that a few weeks before had inspired her words, looks, and movements. Herbert was not destined to be one of love's few martyrs; and he was fast reverting to a sound state, only retarded by the mystery in which the affair was still involved. Since the beginning of his intercourse with the family, his Sunday evenings had been invariably spent at the glen; and now he received a note from Miss Ruthven (not, as had been her wont, crossed and double-crossed), containing two lines, saying her father was ill, and as she was obliged to attend him, she regretted to beg Mr. Linwood to omit his usual Sunday evening visit! Linwood had a lurking suspicion—he was just beginning to suspect—that this was a mere pretext; and he resolved to go to the glen, ostensibly to inquire after Mr. Ruthven, but really to satisfy his doubts. It was early in the evening when he reached there. The cheerful light that usually shot forth its welcome from the parlour window was gone—all was darkness. "I was a rascal to distrust her!" thought Linwood, and he hastened on, fearing good Mr. Ruthven was extremely ill. As he approached the house he perceived that, for the first time, the window-shutters were closed, and that a bright light gleamed through their crevices. He put his hand on the latch of the door to open it, as was his custom, without rap-ping; but no longer, as if instinct with the hospitality of the house, did it yield to his touch. It was bolted! He hesitated for a moment whether to knock for admittance, and endeavour to satisfy his curiosity, or to return as wise as he came. His delicacy decided on the latter course; and he was turning away, when a sudden gust of wind blew open one of the rickety blinds, and instinctively he looked through the window, and for a moment was riveted by the scene disclosed within. Mr. Ruthven sat at a table on which were bottles of wine, olives, oranges, and other most rare luxuries. Beside him sat a young man—his younger self. Linwood did not need a second glance to assure him this was Captain Ruthven. On a stool at her brother's feet sat Charlotte, her arm lovingly resting on his knee. Mrs. Ruthven was at the other extremity of the table, examining, with enraptured eye, caps, feathers, and flowers, which, as appeared from the boxes and cords beside her, had just been opened.

But the parties that fixed Linwood's attention were Helen Ruthven and a very handsome young man, who was leaning over her chair while she was playing on the piano, and bestowing on him those wondrous glances that Linwood had verily believed never met an eye but his! What a sudden disenchantment was that! Linwood's blood rushed to his head. He stood as if he were transfixed, till a sudden movement within recalling him to himself, he sprang from the steps and retraced his way up the hill-side:—the spell that had well-nigh bound him to Helen Ruthven was broken for ever. No man likes to be duped, —no man likes to feel how much his own vanity has had to do with preparing the trap that ensnared him. Linwood, after revolving the past, after looking back upon the lures and deceptions that had been practised upon him, after comparing his passion for Helen Ruthven with his sentiments for Bessie Lee, came to the consoling conclusion that he had never loved Miss Ruthven. He was right—and that night, for the first time in many weeks, he fell asleep, thinking of Bessie Lee.

On the following morning, Linwood confided to Eliot the dénouement of his little romance. Eliot was rejoiced that his friend's illusion should be dispelled in any mode. After some discussion of the matter, they came to the natural conclusion that a clandestine intercourse had been for some time maintained by the family at the glen with the strangers on board the sloop-of-war, and that there were reasons for shaking Linwood and Eliot off more serious than Linwood's flirtation having been superseded by a fresher and more exciting one.

In the course of the morning Eliot, in returning from a ride, at a sudden turn in the road came upon General Washington and Mr. Ruthven, who had just met. Eliot was making his passing salutation when General Washington said, "Stop a moment, Mr. Lee, we will ride in together." While Eliot paused, he heard Mr. Ruthven say, "You will not disappoint me, general,—Wednesday evening, and a quiet hour—not with bat and whip in hand, but time enough to drink a fair bottle of 'Helicon,' as poor Randolph used to call it—there are but two left, and we shall ne'er look upon its like again. Wednesday evening—remember." General Washington assented, and the parties were separating, when Mr. Ruthven, in his cordial manner, stretched out his hand to Eliot, saying, " My dear fellow, I should ask you too ; but the general and I are old friends, and I want a little talk with him, by ourselves, of old times. Besides, no man, minus forty, must have a drop of my 'Helicon ;' but come down soon and see the girls,—they are Helicon enough for you young fellows, hey 1 "

As Mr. Ruthven rode away, " There goes," said General Washington, " as true-hearted a man as ever breathed. We were born on neighbouring plantations. Our fathers and grandfathers were friends. Our hearts were cemented in our youth, or at least in my youth, for he is much my elder, but his is a heart always fusible. Poor man ! he has had much ill-luck in life ; but the worst, and the worst, let me tell you, my young friend, that can befall any man, was an ill-starred marriage. His wife is the daughter of a good-for-nothing Frenchman ; bad blood, Mr. Lee. The children show the cross—I beg Miss Charlotte's pardon, she is a nice girl, fair Virginia stock ; but Miss Helen is—very like her mother. The son I do not know ; but his fighting against his country is *primâ facie* evidence against him."

The conversation then diverged to other topics. There was in Eliot that union of good sense, keen intelligence, manliness, and modesty, that excited Washington's esteem, and drew him out ; and Eliot had the happiness, for a half hour, of hearing him, whom of all men he most honoured, talk freely, and of assuring himself that this great man did not, as was sometimes said of him,

A wilful stillness entertain,
With purpose to be dress'd in an opinion
Of wisdom :

but that his taciturnity was the result of profound thought, anxiously employed on the most serious subjects.

Late in the afternoon of the same day, Linwood received a note from Helen Ruthven, enclosing one to General Washington, of which, after entreating him to deliver it immediately, she thus explained the purport. " It contains a simple request to your mighty commander-in-chief, to permit me to visit my brother on board his vessel. I know that Washington's heart is as hard as Pharaoh's, and as unrelenting as Brutus's ; still it is not, it cannot be in man to refuse such a request to the daughter of an old friend. Do, dear, kind, Linwood, urge it for me, and win the everlasting gratitude of your unworthy but always devoted friend, HELEN RUTHVEN."

" *Urge* it ! " exclaimed Linwood, as he finished the note, " urge General Washington ! I should as soon think of urging the sun to go backward or forward ; but I'll present it for you, my ' devoted friend, Helen,' and in merely doing that my heart will be in my mouth."

He obtained an audience. General Washington read the note, and, turning to Linwood, asked him if he knew its purport.

" Yes, sir," replied Linwood, " and I cannot," he ventured to add, " but hope you will find it fitting to gratify a desire so natural."

" Perfectly natural ; Miss Ruthven tells me she has not seen her brother for four years." Linwood felt his honest blood rush to his face at this

flat falsehood from his friend Helen. Washington perceived the suffusion, and misinterpreted it. " You think it a hard case, Mr. Linwood ; it is so, but there are many hard cases in this unnatural war. It grieves me to refuse Helen Ruthven— the child of my good friend." He passed his eye again over the note, and there was an expression of displeasure and contempt in his curling lip as he read such expressions as the following : " I cannot be disappointed, for I am addressing one who unites all virtues, whose mercy even surpasses his justice "—" I write on my knees to him who is the minister of Providence, dispensing good and evil, light and blessing, with a word." General Washington threw down the note, saying, " Miss Ruthven should remember that flattery corrupts the giver as well as the receiver. I have no choice in this matter. We have an inflexible rule prohibiting all intercourse with the enemy."

He then wrote a concise reply, which Linwood sent to the lady in a blank envelope.

" Ah ! " thought Helen Ruthven, as she opened it, " this would not have been blank three weeks ago—*mais n'importe*. Mr. Herbert Linwood, you may run free now ; I have nobler prey in my toils." She unsealed General Washington's note, and after glancing her eye over it, she tore it into fragments and dispersed it to the winds, exclaiming, " I'll risk my life to carry my point ; and if I do, I'll humble you, and have a glorious revenge ! "

She spent a sleepless night in contriving, revolving and dismissing plans on which, as she fancied, the destiny of the nation hung, and, what was far more important in her eyes, Helen Ruthven's destiny. She at last adopted the boldest that had occurred, and which, from being the boldest, best suited her dauntless temper.

The next morning, Tuesday, with her mother's aid and applause, she effected her preparations ; and having fortunately learned, during her residence on the river, to row and manage a boat, she embarked alone in a little skiff, and stealing out of a nook near the glen, she rowed into the current and dropped down the river. She did not expect to escape observation, for though the encampment did not command a view of the Hudson, there were sentinels posted at points that overlooked it, and batteries that commanded its passage. But rightly calculating on the general humanity that governed our people, she had no apprehensions they would fire on a defenceless woman, and very little fear that they would think it worth while to pursue her, to prevent that which she dared to do before their eyes and in the face of day.

Her calculations proved just. The sentinels levelled their guns at her, in token not to proceed ; and she in return dropped her head, raised her hands deprecatingly, and passed on unmolested.

At a short distance below the Point there is a remarkable spot, scooped out by nature in the rocky bank, always beautiful, and now a consecrated shrine—a " Mecca of the mind." On the memorable morning of Miss Ruthven's enterprise, the welcome beams of the spring sun, as he rose in the heavens, casting behind him a soft veil of light clouds, shone on the grey rocks, freshening herbage, and still-disrobed trees, of this lovely recess. From crevices in the perpendicular rocks that wall up the table-land above, hung a sylvan canopy ; cedars, studded with their blue berries, wild rasp-

berries, and wild rose-bushes ; and each moist and
sunny nook was gemmed with violets and wild gera-
niums. The harmonies of nature's orchestra were
the only and the fitting sounds in this seclusion :
the early wooing of the birds ; the water from the
fountains of the heights, that filtering through the
rocks, dropped from ledge to ledge with the regu-
larity of a water-clock ; the ripple of the waves as
they broke on the rocky points of the shore, or
softly kissed its pebbly margin ; and the voice of
the tiny stream, that, gliding down a dark, deep,
and almost hidden channel in the rocks, disappeared, and welling up again in the centre of the
turfy slope, stole over it, and trickled down the
lower ledge of granite to the river. Tradition has
named this little green shelf on the rocks " Kosciusko's Garden ; " but as no traces have been
discovered of any other than nature's plantings, it
was probably merely his favourite retreat, and as
such is a monument of his taste and love of nature.

The spring is now enclosed in a marble basin,
and inscribed with his name who then lay extended
beside it : Kosciusko, the patriot of his own country, the friend of ours, the philanthropist of all, the
enemy only of those aliens from the human family
who are the tyrants of their kind. An unopen
book lay beside him, while, gazing up through the
willows that drooped over the fountain, he perused
that surpassing book of nature, informed by the
Spirit and writen by the finger of God—a Book of
revelations of his wisdom, and power, and goodness.

Suddenly his musings were disturbed by approaching footsteps ; and looking up, he saw Linwood and Eliot winding down the steep pathway
between the piled rocks. He had scarcely exchanged salutations with them, when the little
boat in which Helen Ruthven was embarked shot
out from behind the dark ledge that bounded their
upward view of the river. They sprang forward
to the very edge of the sloping ground. Helen
Ruthven would most gladly have escaped their
observation, but that she perceived was impossible ;
and making the very best of her dilemma, she
tossed her head exultingly, and waved her handkerchief. The young men instinctively returned
her greeting. " A gallant creature, by Heaven !"
exclaimed the Pole ; " God speed you, my girl ! "
And when Linwood told him who she was, and her
enterprise, so far as he thought fit to disclose it,
he reiterated, " Again then, I say, God speed her !
The sweetest affections of nature should be free as
this gushing rill, that the rocks and the earth can't
keep back ; I am glad when they throw off the
shackles imposed by the cruel but inevitable laws of
war." They continued to gaze after the boat till it
turned and disappeared with the river in its winding
passage through the mountains.

On Wednesday morning it appeared that the
sloop-of-war had changed her position, and approached as nearly to West Point as was possible
without coming within the range of its guns. " I am
convinced," said Linwood to Eliot, taking up the
thread of conversation where they had dropped it
the day before, " I am convinced there is a plot
brewing."

" I am apprehensive of it too. Our obvious duty,
Linwood, is to go to General Washington and tell
him all we know of the Ruthvens."

" My service to you !—no, he is the wariest of
human beings, and has grounds enough for sus-

picion without our prompting. Can't he put this
and that together—the old man's pressing invitation, Helen's flight, and the movement of the
vessel ! "

" Ah, if his suspicions were excited, as ours are,
by previous circumstances, these would suffice ;
but he has entire confidence in his old friend ; he
is uninformed of the strong tory predilections of
the whole family ; and, though he does not like
Helen Ruthven, he has no conception of what we
have tolerable proof, that she has the talents of a
regular-bred French intriguer. Besides, as the
fact of your having seen those men at the glen
proves the practicability of their visiting it again,
the general should certainly be apprised of it."

" No, Eliot, I'll not consent to it—this is my
game, and I must control it. It is a violation of
the Arab bread-and-salt rule, to communicate that
which was obtained by our friendly intimacy at the
glen."

" I think you are wrong, Linwood ; it is a case
where an inferior obligation should yield to a superior one."

" I don't comprehend your metaphysical reasoning, Eliot ; I govern myself by the obligations I
feel."

" By the dictates of your conscience, my dear
fellow ; so do I ; therefore I shall go immediately
to the general, with or without you."

" Not with me—no, I'll not tell him what I
know, that's flat : and as to being questioned and
cross-questioned by him, heavens and earth ! when
he but bends his awful brow upon me, I feel as if
my heart were turning inside out. No, I'll not go
near him. Why can't we write an anonymous
letter ? "

" I do not like anonymous letters—my course
appears plain to me, so good morning to you."

" One moment, Eliot—remember, not a word of
what I saw through the window at the glen."

" Certainly not, if you insist." Eliot then went
to the general's marquee, and was told he would
see him in two hours. Eliot returned at the precise moment, and was admitted. " You are punc-
tual, Mr. Lee," said the commander, " and I
thank you for it. A young man should be as exact
in military life as the play requires the lover
to be ! ' he should not break a part of the thousandth part of a minute.' Your business, sir ! "

Eliot was beginning to disclose it, when they
were interrupted by a servant, who handed General Washington a note. A single involuntary
glance at the superscription assured Eliot it was
from Linwood. General Washington opened it,
and looked first for the signature, as one naturally
does at receiving a letter in an unknown hand.
" Anonymous ! " he said ; and refolding without
reading a word of it, he lighted it in a candle, still
burning on the desk where he had been sealing
letters, and suffered it to consume ; saying, " This
is the way I now serve all anonymous letters, Mr.
Lee. Men in public life are liable to receive
many such communications, and to have their
minds disturbed, and sometimes poisoned, by them.
They are the resort of the cowardly or the malig-
nant. An honest man will sustain by his name
what he thinks proper to communicate."

" There is no rule of universal application to
the versatile mind of man," thought Eliot, and
his heart burned to justify his friend ; when the

general reminded him they had no time to lose, he proceeded concisely to state his apprehensions and their grounds. Washington listened to him without interruption, but not without an appalling change of countenance. "I have heard you through, Mr. Lee," he said; "your apprehensions are perhaps natural; at any rate, I thank you for frankly communicating them to me; but, be assured, your suspicions have no foundation. Do you think such vile treachery could be plotted by a Virginian, my neighbour, my friend of thirty years, my father's friend, when all the grievous trials of this war have not produced a single traitor! No, no, Mr. Lee, I would venture my life—my country, on the cast of Ruthven's integrity. If I do not lightly give my confidence, I do not lightly withdraw it; and once withdrawn it is never restored."

Eliot left Washington's presence half convinced himself that his suspicions were unfounded. It never occurred to Washington or to Eliot that there might be a conspiracy without Mr. Ruthven being a party to it, and the supposition that he was so invalidated all the evidences of a plot.

In the afternoon Kisel asked leave to avail himself of a permit which Eliot had obtained for him, to go on the opposite of the river to a little brook, whence he had often brought a mess of trout for the officers' table; for our friend Kisel was skilled in the craft of angling, and might have served Cruikshank for an illustration of Johnson's definition of the word, "a fishing-rod, with a worm at one end and a fool at the other;" but happily, as it proved, our fool had some "subtlety in his simplicity." Eliot gave him the permission, with directions to row up to the glen when he returned, and await him there.

Eliot determined to go to the glen, and station himself on the margin of the river, where, in case (a chance that seemed to him at least possible) of the approach of an enemy's boat, he should descry it in time to give Washington warning. He went in search of Linwood, to ask him to accompany him; but Linwood was nowhere to be found. He deliberated whether to communicate his apprehensions to some other officer. The confidence the general had manifested had nearly dissipated his apprehensions, and he feared to do what might appear like officiousness, or like a distrust of Washington's prudence; that virtue, which, to remain, as it then was, the bulwark of his country's safety, must continue unsuspected.

Eliot in his anxiety had reached the glen while it was yet day-light; and, careful to escape observation, he stole along the little strip of pebbly beach where a mimic bay sets in, and seated himself on a pile of rocks, the extreme point of a hill that descends abruptly to the Hudson. Here the river, hemmed in by the curvatures of the mountains, has the appearance of a lake; for the passage is so narrow and winding through which it forces its way, that the eye scarcely detects it. Eliot for awhile forgot the tediousness of his watch in looking around him. The mountains at the entrance of the Hudson into the highlands, which stand like giant sentinels jealously guarding the narrow portal, appeared, whence he saw them, like a magnificent framework to a beautiful picture. An April shower had just passed over, and the mist was rolling away like the soft folds of a curtain from

the village of Newburgh, which looked like the abode of all "country contentments," as the setting sun shone cheerily on its gentle slopes and white houses, contrasting it with the stern features of the mountains. Far in the distance, the Catskills, belted by clouds, appeared as if their blue heads were suspended in the atmosphere and mingling with the sky, from which an eye familiar with their beautiful outline could alone distinguish them. But the foreground of this picture was most interesting to Eliot; and as his eye again fell on the little glen sleeping in the silvery arms of the rills between which it lies—"can this place," he thought, "so steeped in nature's loveliness, so enshrined in her temple, be the abode of treachery! It has been of heartlessness, coquetry, duplicity—ah, there is no power in nature, in the outward world, to convert the bad; blessings it has—blessings manifold, for the good."

The spirit of man, alone in nature's solitudes, is an instrument which she manages at will; and Eliot, in his deepening seriousness and anxiety, felt himself answering to her changing aspect. The young foliage of the well-wooded little knoll that rises over the glen had looked fresh and feathery, and as bright as an infant awaking to happy consciousness; but as the sun withdrew its beams, it appeared as dreary as if it had parted from a smiling friend. And when the last gleams of day had stolen up the side of the Crow's Nest, shot over the summit of Breakneck, flushed the clouds, and disappeared, and the wavy lines and natural terraces beyond Cold Spring, and the mass of rocks and pines of Constitution Island, were wrapped in sad-coloured uniform, Eliot shrunk from the influence of the general desolateness, and became impatient of his voluntary watch.

One after another the kindly-beaming homelights shot forth from hill and valley, and Eliot's eye catching that which flashed from Mr. Ruthven's window, he determined on a reconnoitre; and passing in front of the house, he saw Washington and his host seated at a table, served with wine and nuts, but none of those tropical luxuries that had been manifestly brought to the glen by the stranger-guests from the sloop-of-war. Eliot's heart gladdened at seeing the friends enjoying one of those smooth and delicious passages that sometimes vary the ruggedest path of life. That expression of repelling and immoveable gravity, that look of tension (with him the bow was always strained) that characterised Washington's face, had vanished like a cloud; and it now serenely reflected the social affections, bright and gentle spirits! that, for the time, mastered his perplexing cares. He was retracing the period of his boyhood; a period, however cloudy in its passage, always bright when surveyed over the shoulder. He recalled his first field-sports, in which Ruthven had been his companion and teacher; and they laughingly reviewed many an accident by flood and field. "No wonder," thought Eliot, as in passing he glanced at Ruthven's honest, jocund face; "no wonder Washington would not distrust him!"

Eliot returned to his post. The stars had come out, and looked down coldly and dimly through a hazy atmosphere. The night was becoming obscure. A mist was rising; and shortly after a heavy fog covered the surface of the river. Eliot wondered that Kisel had not made his appearance; for, desultory as the fellow was, he was as true to his master as the magnet to the pole.—Darkness is a wonderful magnifier of apprehended danger; and, as it deepened, Eliot felt as if enemies were approaching from every quarter. Listening intently, he heard a distant sound of oars. He was all ear. "Thank Heaven!" he exclaimed, "It is Kisel—a single pair of oars, and his plashy irregular dip!" In a few moments he was discernible; and nearing the shore, he jumped upon the rock where Eliot stood, crying out, exultingly, "I've dodged 'em, hey!"

"Softly, Kisel. Whom have you dodged?"

"Them red birds in their borrowed feathers. Cheat me! No! Can't I tell them that chops, and reaps, and mows, and thrashes, from them that only handles a sword or a gun, let 'em put on what ev'yday clothes they will!"

"Tell me, Kisel, plainly and quickly, what you mean."

A command from Eliot, uttered in a tone of even slight displeasure, had a marvellous effect in steadying Kisel's wits; and he answered with tolerable clearness and precision—"I was cutting 'cross lots before sunset with a mess of trout, long as my arm—shiners! when I stumbled on a bunch of fellows squatted 'mong high bushes. They held me by the leg, and said they'd come down with provisions for Square Ruthven's folks, and they had not got a pass, and so must wait for nightfall; and they'd have me stay and guide 'em across, for they knew they might ground at low water if they did not get the right track. I mistrusted 'em. I knew by their tongues they came from below; and so I cried, and told 'em I should get a whipping if I didn't get home afore sundown; and one of 'em held a pistol to my head, loaded, primed, and cocked, and told me he'd shoot my brains out if I didn't do as he bid me. 'Lo'd o' massy!' says I, 'don't shoot—'twon't do any good, for I ha'n't got no brains, hey!'"

"Never mind what you said or they said. What did you do?"

"I didn't do nothing. They held me fast till night; and then they pushed their boat out of a kind o' hiding-place, and come alongside mine, and put me into it, and told me to pilot 'em. You know that sandy strip a bit off t'other shore? I knew my boat would swim over it like a cob, and I guessed they'd swamp—and they did; diddle me if they didn't!"

"Are they there now?"

"There! not if they've the wit of sucking turkeys. The river there is not deep enough to drown a dead dog, and they might jump in and pull the boat out."

A slight westerly breeze was now rising, which lifted and wafted the fog so that half the width of the river was suddenly unveiled, and Eliot descried a boat making towards the glen. "By Heaven! there they are!" he exclaimed. "Follow me, Kisel;" and without entering the house, he ran to the stable close by. Fortunately, often having had occasion, during his visits at the glen, to bestow his own horse, he was familiar with the "whereabouts," and in one instant General Washington's charger was bridled and at the door, held by Kisel, while Eliot rushed into the house, and in ten words communicated the danger

and the means of escape. General Washington said not a word till, as he sprang on the horse, Ruthven, on whose astounded mind the truth dawned, exclaimed "I am innocent." He replied, "I believe you."

Washington immediately galloped up the steep embowered road to the Point. Eliot hesitated for a moment, doubting whether to attempt a retreat or remain where he was, when Mr. Ruthven grasped his arm, exclaiming, "Stay, for God's sake, Mr. Lee; stay, and witness to my innocence." The imploring agony with which he spoke would have persuaded a more inflexible person than Eliot Lee. In truth, there was little use in attempting to fly, for the footsteps of the party were already heard approaching the house. They entered, five armed men, and were laying their hands on Eliot, when Mr. Ruthven's frantic gestures, and his shouts of "He's safe—he's safe—he's escaped ye!" revealed to them the truth; and they perceived what in their impetuosity they had overlooked, that they held an unknown young man in their grasp instead of the priceless Washington! Deep were the oaths they swore as they dispersed to search the premises, all excepting one young man, whose arm Mr. Ruthven had grasped, and to whom he said—"Harry, you've ruined me—you've made me a traitor in the eyes of Washington—the basest traitor! He said, God bless him! that he believed me innocent. But he will not when he reflects that it was I who invited him—who pressed him to come here this evening—the conspiracy seems evident—undeniable! Oh! Harry, Harry, you and your mad sister have ruined me!"

The young man seemed deeply affected by his father's emotion. He attempted to justify himself on the plea that he dared not set his filial feeling against the importance of ending the war by a single stroke; but this plea neither convinced nor consoled his father. Young Ruthven's associates soon returned, having abandoned their search, and announced the necessity of their immediate return to the boat. "You must go with us, Sir," said Ruthven to his father; "for blameless as you are, you will be treated by the rebels as guilty of treason."

"By Heaven, Harry, I'll not go. I had rather die a thousand deaths—on the gallows if I must. I'll not budge a foot."

"He must go—there is no alternative. You must aid me," said young Ruthven to his companions. They advanced to seize his father. "Off—off!" he cried, struggling against them. "I'll not go a living man."

Eliot interposed; and addressing himself to young Ruthven, said, "Believe me, Sir, you are mistaking your duty. Your father's good name must be dearer to you than his life; and his good name is blasted for ever if in these circumstances he leaves here. But his life is in no danger—none whatever. He is in the hands of his friend, and that friend the most generous, as well as just, of all human beings. You misunderstand the temper of General Washington, if you think he would believe your father guilty of the vilest treachery without damning proof." Young Ruthven was more than half convinced by Eliot, and his companions had by this time become impatient of delay. Their spirit had gone with the hope that inspired their enterprise, and they were now only anxious to secure a retreat to their vessel. They had some little [debate among themselves whether they should make Eliot prisoner; but, on young Ruthven's suggestion that Lieutenant Lee's testimony might be important to his father, they consented to leave him, one of them expressing, in a whisper, the prevailing sentiment, "We should feel sheepish enough to gain but a paltry knight when we expected a checkmate by our move."

In a few moments more they were off; but not till young Ruthven had vainly tried to get a kind parting word from his father. "No, Harry," he said, "I'll not forgive you—I can't; you've put my honour in jeopardy—no, never!" and as his son turned sorrowfully away, he added, "Never, Hal, till this cursed war is at an end."

Early next morning Eliot Lee requested an audience of Washington, and was immediately admitted, and most cordially received. "Thank God, my dear young friend," he said, "you are safe, and here. I sent repeatedly to your lodgings last night, and, hearing nothing, I have been exceedingly anxious. Satisfy me on one point, and then tell me what happened after my forced retreat. I trust in Heaven this affair is not bruited."

Eliot assured him he had not spoken of it to a human being—not even to Linwood; and that he had enjoined strict secrecy on Kisel, on whose obedience he could rely.

"Thank you—thank you, Mr. Lee," said Washington, with a warmth startling from him, "I should have expected this from you—the generous devotion of youth, and the coolness and prudence of ripe age—a rare union."

Such words from him who never flattered, and rarely praised, might well, as they did, make the blood gush from the heart to the cheeks. "I am most grateful for this approbation, sir," said Eliot.

"Grateful! Would to Heaven I had some return to make for the immense favour you have done me, beside words; but the importance of keeping the affair secret precludes all other return. I think it will not transpire from the enemy,—they are not like to publish a baffled enterprise. I am most particularly pleased that you went alone to the glen. In this instance I almost agree with Cardinal de Retz, who says, 'he held men in greater esteem for what they forbore to do than for what they did.' I now see where I erred yesterday. It did not occur to me that there could be a plot without my friend being accessory to it. I did not err in trusting him. This war has cost me dear; but, thank Heaven, it has not shaken, but fortified, my confidence in human virtue!" Washington then proceeded to inquire into the occurrences at the glen after he left there, and ended with giving Eliot a note to deliver to Mr. Ruthven, which proved a healing balm to the good man's wounds.

Our revolutionary contest, by placing men in new relations, often exhibited in new force and beauty the ties that bind together the human family. Sometimes, it is true, they were lightly snapped asunder, but oftener they manifested an all-resisting force, and a union that, as in some chemical combinations, no test could dissolve.

CHAPTER XI.

Our will we can command. The effects of our actions we cannot foresee.—MONTAIGNE.

Herbert Linwood to his Sister.

July 30th, 1779.

"DEAREST BELLE,—I write under the inspiration of the agreeable consciousness that my letter may pass under the sublime eye of your commander-in-chief, or be scanned and sifted by his underlings. I wish to Heaven that, without endangering your bright orbs, I could infuse some retributive virtue into my ink to strike them blind. But the deuce take them. I defy their oversight. I am not discreet enough to be trusted with military or political secrets, and therefore, like Hotspur's Kate, I can betray none. As to my own private affairs, though I do not flatter myself I have attained a moral eminence which I may challenge the world to survey, yet I'll expose nothing to you, dear Belle, whose opinion I care more for than that of king, lords, and commons, which the whole world may not know without your loving brother being dishonoured thereby: so on, in my usual 'streak o' lightning style,' with facts and feelings.

"You have, before this, seen the official account of our successful attack on Stony Point, and have doubtless been favoured with the additional light of Rivington's comments, your veritable editor. These thralls of party editors! The light they emit, is like that of conjurors, intended to produce false impressions.

"Do not imagine I am going to send you a regular report of the battle. With all due deference to your superior mental faculties, my dear, you are but a woman, and these concernments of 'vile guns' must for ever remain mysteries to you. But, Belle, I'll give you the romance of the affair—'thy vocation, Hal.'

"My friend Eliot Lee has a vein of quixotism, that reminds me of the inflammable gas I have seen issuing from a cool healthy spring. Doctor Kissam, you know, used to say every man had his insanity. Eliot's appears in his affection for a half-witted follower, one Kisel; the oddest fellow in this world. His life is a series of consecutive accidents of good and bad *luck*.

"On the 10th he had been out on the other side of the river, *vagrantising* in his usual fashion, and returning late to his little boat, and, as we suspect, having fallen asleep, he drifted ashore at Stony Point. There he came upon the fort, and a string of trout (which he is seldom without) serving him as a passport, he was admitted within the walls. His simplicity, unique and inimitable, shielded him from suspicion, and a certain inspiration which seems always to come direct from Heaven at the moment of his necessity, saved him from betraying the fact that he belonged to our army, and he was suffered to depart in peace. The observations he made (he is often acute) were of course communicated to his master, and by him made available to our enterprise. Eliot and myself were among the volunteers. He, profiting by Kisel's hints, guided us safely through some 'sloughs of despond.' With all his skill, we had a killing scramble over pathless mountains, and through

D

treacherous swamps, under a burning sun, the mercury ranging somewhere between one and two hundred, so that my sal volatile blood seemed to have exhaled in vapour, and my poor body to be a burning coal, whose next state would be ashes.

"Our General Wayne (you will understand his temper from his *nom de guerre*, 'Mad Anthony') had ordered us to advance with unloaded muskets and fixed bayonets. He was above all things anxious to avoid an accidental discharge, which might alarm the garrison. At eight in the evening we were within a mile and-a-half of the fort, and there the detachment halted ; while Wayne, with Eliot and some other officers, went to reconnoitre. They had approached within gunshot of the works, when poor Kisel, who away from Eliot is like an unweaned child, and who had been all day wandering in search of him, suddenly emerged from the wood, and in a paroxysm of joy discharged his musket. Wayne sprang forward, and would have transfixed him with his bayonet, had not Eliot thrown himself before Kisel, and turned aside Wayne's arm ; some angry words followed, but it ended in the general leaving Kisel to be managed by Eliot's discretion. The general's displeasure, however, against Eliot, did not subside at once.

"When the moment for attack came, I felt myself shivering, not with fear, no, '*franchement*' (as our old teacher Dubois used to say, on the few occasions when he meant to tell the truth), *franchement*, not with fear, but with the recollection of my father's last words to me. The uncertain chances of a fierce contest were before me, and my father's *curse* rung in my ears like the voices that turned the poor wretches in the Arabian tale into stone. Once in the fight, it was forgotten ; all men are bulldogs then, and think of nothing past or to come.

"They opened a tremendous fire upon us ; it was the dead of night, Belle, and rather a solemn time, I assure you. Our commander was wounded by a musket-ball ; he fell, and instantly rising on one knee, he cried, 'Forward, my brave boys, forward.' The gallant shout gave us a new impulse ; and we rushed forward, while Eliot Lee, with that singular blending of cool courage and generosity which marks him, paused and assisted the general's aide in bearing him on, in compliance with the wish he had expressed (believing himself mortally wounded), that he might die in the fort. Thank God, he survived ; and, being as magnanimous as he is brave, he reported to the commander-in-chief Eliot's gallantry and good conduct throughout the whole affair, and particularly dwelt on the aid he had given him, after having received from him injurious epithets. In consequence of all this, Eliot is advanced to the rank of captain. Luck is a lord, Belle ; I would fain have distinguished myself, but I merely, like the rest, performed my part honourably, for which I received the thanks of General Washington, and got my name blazoned in the report to Congress.

"I hear that Helen Ruthven is dashing away in New York, not, as I expected, after her romantic departure hence, as the Honourable Mrs. O——. Well ! all kind vestals guard her ! Heaven knows, she needs their vigilance. Rumour says, too, that you are shortly to vow allegiance to my royalist friend. God bless you ! my dear sister. If it were true—alas ! nothing is more false—that matches are made in Heaven, I know *who* would be your liege lord. Another match there was, that in my boyhood—my boyhood ! my youth, my maturity, I believed Heaven had surely made. It is a musty proverb, that. Farewell, Belle : kiss my dear mother for me, and tell her I would not have her, like the old Scotch woman, pray for our side, 'right or wrong,' but let her pray for the right side, and then her poor son will be sure to prosper. Oh, would that I could, without violating my duty to my country, throw myself at my father's feet. His loyalty is not truer to King George, than mine to him.

"Dearest Belle, may Heaven reunite us all.

"Yours,
"H. LINWOOD.

"P.S.—Kind love, don't forget it, to Rose."

A day or two after Herbert's letter was despatched, Eliot received a summons from Washington ; and on his appearing before him, the general said, "I have important business to be transacted in New York, Captain Lee. I have despatches to transmit to Sir Henry Clinton. My agent must be intrusted with discretionary powers. An expedition to New York, even with the protection of a flag of truce, is hazardous. The intervening country is infested with outlaws, who respect no civilised usages. My emissary must be both intrepid and prudent. I have therefore selected you. Will you accept the mission ?"

"Most gratefully, sir—but—"

"But what ! if you have scruples, name them."

"None in the world, sir ; on my own account, I should be most happy, but I should be still happier if the office might be assigned to Linwood. It would afford him the opportunity he pines for, of seeing his family."

"That is a reason, if there were no other, why Captain Linwood should not go. Some embarrassment might arise. Your friend has not the coolness essential in exigencies."

Eliot well knew that Washington was not a man with whom to bandy arguments, and he at once declared himself ready to discharge, to the best of his ability, whatever duty should be imposed on him ; and it was settled that he should depart as soon as his instructions could be made out.

Eliot soon after met Linwood, and communicated his intended expedition. "You are always under a lucky star," said Linwood ; "I would have given all I am worth for this appointment."

"And you certainly should have it, if it were mine to bestow."

"I do not doubt it, not in the least ; but is it not hard ! Eliot, I am such a light-hearted wretch, for the most part, that you really have no conception how miserable my father's displeasure makes me. I don't understand how it is. The laws of Heaven are harmonious, and certainly my conscience acquits me, yet I suffer most cruelly for my breach of filial obedience. If I could but see my father, eye to eye, I am sure I could persuade him to recal that curse, that rings in my ears even now like a death-knell. Oh, one half hour in New York would be my salvation ! The sight of Belle and my mother would be Heaven to me! Don't laugh at me, Eliot," he continued, wiping his eyes, "I am a calf when I think of them all."

"Laugh at you, Linwood! I could cry with joy if I could give my place to you; as it is, I must hasten my preparations. I have obtained leave to take Kisel with me."

"Kisel! heaven forefend, Eliot. Do you know what ridicule such a *valet-de-place* as Kisel will call down on your head from those lordly British officers!"

"Yes, I have thought of that, and it would be sheer affectation to pretend to be indifferent to it; but I can bear it. Providence has cast Kisel upon my protection, and if I leave him he will be sure to run his witless head into some scrape that will give me ten times more trouble than his attendance."

"Well, as you please; you gentle people are always wilful." After a few moments thoughtful silence, he added, "How long before you start, Eliot?"

"The general said it might be two hours before my instructions and passports were made out."

"It will be dark then, and," added Linwood, after a keen survey of the heavens, "I think, very dark."

"Like enough; but that is not so very agreeable a prospect as one would infer from the tone of your voice."

"Pardon me, my dear fellow; it was New York I was thinking of, and not any inconvenience you might encounter from the obscurity of the night. Your passports are not made out?"

"Not yet."

"Do me a favour, then—let Kisel ride my grey. I cannot endure the thought of the Harlequin spectacle you'll furnish forth, riding down the Broadway with your squire mounted on Beauty; besides, the animal is not equal to the expedition."

"Thank you, Linwood. I accept your kindness as freely as you offer it. You have relieved me of my only serious embarrassment. Now get your letters ready; anything unsealed (my orders are restricted to that) I will take charge of, and deliver at your father's door."

"My father's door!" exclaimed Linwood, snapping his fingers with a sort of wild exultation that made Eliot stare, "oh, what a host of images those words call up! but as to the letters, there is no pleasure in unsealed ones; I sent a bulletin of my health to Belle yesterday; I have an engagement that will occupy me till after your departure: so farewell, and good luck to you, Eliot." The friends shook hands and parted.

The twilight was fading into night when Eliot was ready for his departure. To his great vexation Kisel was missing; and he was told he had ridden forward, and had left word that he would await his master at a certain point about three miles on their way. The poor fellow's habits were so desultory that they never excited surprise, though they would have been intolerable to one less kind-tempered than Eliot Lee. He found him at the point named. He had reined his horse up against the fence, and was awaiting his master, as Eliot saw, for he could just descry the outline of his person lying back to back to the horse, his legs encircling the animal's neck.

"Sit up, Kisel," said his master, in an irritated tone; "remember you are riding a gentleman's horse that's not accustomed to such tricks. And now I tell you, once for all, that unless you behave yourself quietly and reasonably, I will send you adrift."

Kisel whistled. He always either replied by a whistle or tears to Eliot's reproof, and the whistle now, as usual, was followed by a fit of sulkiness. The night was misty and very dark. Kisel, in spite of sundry kind overtures from his master, remained doggedly silent, or only answered in a muttered monosyllable. Thus they travelled all night, merely stopping at the farm-houses, to which they had been directed, to refresh their horses. On these occasions Kisel was unusually zealous in performing the office of groom, and seemed to have made a most useful transfer of the nimbleness of his tongue to his hands.

The dawn found them within the enemy's lines, at twenty miles' distance from the city of New York, and in sight of a British post designated in their instructions, where they were to stop, exhibit their flag of truce, show their passports, and obtain others to the city. "Now, Kisel," said Eliot, "you must have done with your fooleries; you will disgrace me if you do not behave like a man; pull up your cap—do not bury your face so in the collar of your coat—sit upright."

Kisel threw the reins upon his horse's neck, affected to arrange his cap and coat, and in doing so dropped his whip. This obliged him to dismount and go back a few yards, which he did as if he had clogs at his heels. In the meantime Eliot spurred on his horse, and rode up to the door where the enemy's guard was stationed. His passports were examined, and returned to him countersigned. He passed on; and the guard was giving a cursory glance at the attendant, when it seemed to strike him there was some discrepancy between the description and the actual person. "Stop, my man," said he, "let's have another glance. 'Crooked, ill-made person;' yes, crooked enough—'sandy hair;' yes, by Jove, sandy as a Scotchman's—'grey eyes, small and sunken;' grey to be sure, but neither small nor sunken."

"Well, now," said Kisel, with beseeching simplicity, and looking eagerly after Eliot, who was watering his horse at a brook a few rods in advance of him; "well, now, I say, don't *hender* me—smallness is according as people thinks. My eye an't so big as an ox's, nor 'tan't so small as a mole's; and folks will dispute all the way 'twixt the two: so what signifies keeping captain waiting!"

"Well, well, it must be right—go on. I don't know, though," muttered the inquisitor, as Kisel rode off at a sharp trot—"d—n these Yankees, they'd cheat the devil. The passport said, 'a turn-up nose'—this fellow's is as straight as an arrow. Here, halloo, sirs,—back." But Kisel, instead of heeding the recal, though seconded by his master, gallopped forward, making antic gestures, laughing and shouting; and Eliot, bitterly repenting his indiscretion in bringing him, retraced his steps. He found the inspector's faculties all awakened by the suspicion that he had been outwitted. "My friend," said Eliot, reproducing his passports, "this detention is unne-

D 2

cessary and discourteous. You see I am, beyond a question, the person here described ; and I give you my honour, that my companion is the attendant specified. He is a fellow of weak wits, as you may see by his absurd conduct, who can impose on no one, much less on a person of your keenness."

"That is to say, if he is he. But I suppose you know, sir, that a wolf can wear a sheep's clothing. There are so many rebels that have connexions in the city, outside friends to his majesty, that we are obliged to keep a sharp look-out."

"Certainly, my friend : all that you say is perfectly reasonable, and I respect you for doing your duty. But you must be satisfied now, and will have the goodness to permit me to proceed."

The man was conciliated ; and after making an entry in his note-book, he again returned the passports. Eliot put spurs to his horse ; and as the man gazed after him, he said, "A noble-looking youth. The Almighty has written his passport on that face ; but that won't serve him now-a-days without endorsements. That other fellow I doubt. Well, I'll just forward these notes I have taken down to Colonel Robertson, and he'll be on the look-out."

In the mean time Eliot followed Kisel at full speed ; but after approaching him within a few yards, he perceived he did not gain an inch on him : and, apprehensive that such forced riding might injure Linwood's horse, or, at any rate, that the smoking sides of both the steeds would excite suspicion, he reined his in, and wondered what new demon had taken possession of Kisel ; for, while he now rode at a moderate pace, he had the mortification of seeing that Kisel exactly, and with an accuracy he had never manifested in any other operation, measured his horse's speed by his master's, so as to preserve an undeviating distance from him. Thus they proceeded till they approached Kingsbridge, where a British picket was stationed. Here Kisel managed so as to come up with his horse abreast to Eliot's. The horse seemed to take alarm at the colours that were flying from the British flagstaff, and reared, whirled round, and curveted, so as to require all his rider's adroitness to keep on his back. Meanwhile the passports were being examined, and they were suffered to proceed without a particular investigation.

They had passed the bridge, and beyond observation, when Eliot, who was still in advance of his attendant, turned suddenly round, with the intention of trying the whole force of a moral battery ; but he was surprised by a *coup-de-main* that produced a sudden and not very agreeable shock to his ideas.

His follower's slouched and clownish attitude was gone, and in its place an erect and cavalier bearing. His head was raised from the muffler that had half buried it—his cap pushed back, and from beneath shone the bright laughing eye of Herbert Linwood.

"Now, Eliot, my dear fellow," he said, stretching out his hand to him, "do not look so, as if you liked the knave less than the fool."

"If I do look so, Linwood, it is because fools are easier protected than knaves. It is impossible to foresee what may be the consequence of this rash business."

"Oh, hang the consequence ! I wish you would get over that Yankee fashion, of weighing every possible danger ; you are such a cautious race."

"Granted, Linwood, we are ; and I think it will take all my caution to get us out of a scrape that your heroism has plunged us into."

The first shaft of Linwood's petulance had glanced off from the shield of his friend's good-temper, and he had not another. "I confess," he said, in an altered voice, "that the boldness is worse than questionable, that involves others in our own danger. But consider my temptations, and then try, my dear fellow, to pardon my selfishness. I have lived three years in exile—I, who never before passed a night out of my father's house. I am suffering the wretchedness of his displeasure ; and am absolutely famishing for the faces and voices of home. I could live a week upon the ticking of the old hall-clock."

"But what satisfaction can you expect, Linwood ! You have always told me you believed your father's displeasure was invincible——"

"Oh, I don't know that ; his bark is worse than his bite. I cannot calculate probabilities. One possibility outweighs a million of them. I shall at any rate see my sister—my peerless, glorious sister, and my mother. And, after all, what is the risk ! If you did not detect me, others will not, surely."

"You did not give me a chance."

"Nor will I them. The only catastrophe I fear is the possibility of General Washington finding me out. But it was deused crabbed of him not to give me the commission. He ought to know that a man can't live on self-sacrifice."

"General Washington requires no more than he performs."

"That is true enough ; but is it reasonable to require of children to bear the burdens of men !—of common men to do the deeds of heroes !"

"I believe there is no limit, but in our will, to our moral power."

"Pshaw !—and I believe the moral power of each individual can be measured as accurately as his stature. But we are running our heads into metaphysics, and shall get lost in a fog."

"A New England fog, Linwood !"

"They prevail there," he answered, with a quizzical smile. "But we are wandering from the point. I really have taken all possible precautions to keep my secret. I obtained leave for four days' absence, on the pretext that I was going up the river on my private business. The only danger arises from my having been compelled to make a confidant of Kisel."

"That occurred to me. How, in the name of wonder, did you manage him !"

"Oh, I conjured in your name. I made him believe that your safety depended on his implicitly obeying my directions ; so I obtained his holiday suit (which you must confess is a complete disguise), and sent him on a fool's errand up the river."

The friends entered the city by passing the pickets at the Bowery. They were admitted without scruple :—letting animals into a cage is a very different affair from letting them out. At Linwood's suggestion, they crossed into Queen-street. That great mart, now stored with the products of the commercial world, and supplying millions from its packed warehouses, was then chiefly occupied by the residences of the provincial gentry. Linwood had resumed his mufflers and his clownish air; but the true man from the false exterior growled forth many an anathema as he passed house after house belonging to the whig absentees—his former familiar haunts—now occupied, and as he thought desecrated, by British officers, or resident royalists, whose loyalty was thus cheaply paid.

"Look not to the right nor left, I pray you, Linwood," said Eliot; "you are now in danger of being recognised. We are to stop at Mrs. Billings's, in Broad-street."

"Just above my father's house," replied Linwood, in a sad tone. They rode on briskly; for they perceived that Eliot's American uniform and grotesque attendant attracted observation. They had entered Broad-street, and were near a large double house, with the carving about the doors and windows that distinguished the more ambitious edifices of the provincialists. Two horses, equipped for their riders, stood at the door, and a black servant in faded livery beside them. The door opened; and a gentleman of lofty stature, attended by a young lady, came forth. She patted the animal that awaited her, and sprang into the saddle. "It must be Isabella Linwood!" thought Eliot, turning his asking eye to his companion, who, he now perceived, had reined in his horse towards the flagging opposite to that where the parties who had attracted his observation were. "He is right and careful for once," thought Eliot. That Eliot would have thought it both right and inevitable to have indulged himself in a nearer survey of the beautiful young lady, we do not doubt; but as he again turned her horse suddenly reared his hind legs in the air. Her father screamed—there were several persons passing—no one dared approach the animal, who was whirling, floundering, and kicking furiously. Some, gazing at Miss Linwood, exclaimed, "she'll be dashed to pieces!"—and others, "Lord, how she sits!" She did sit bravely; her face colourless as marble, and her dark eyes flashing fire. Eliot and Linwood instinctively dismounted, and at the risk of their lives rushed to her rescue; and, at one breath's intermission of the kicking, stood on either side of the animal's head. She was an old acquaintance and favourite of Linwood, and with admirable presence of mind (inspiration he afterward called it) he addressed her in a loud tone, in his accustomed phrase, "Jennet—Jennet, softly—softly!" The animal was quieted; and, as Linwood afterward affirmed, spoke as plainly to him with her eye as ever human voice spoke. At any rate, she stood perfectly still while Eliot assisted the young lady to dismount. The people now gathered round; and at the first burst of inquiry and congratulation, Herbert disappeared. "Thank God, you are not hurt, Belle!" exclaimed her father, whose voice, though choked with emotion, was heard above all others. "What in Heaven's name possessed Jennet!—she never kicked before; and how in the world did you quiet her, sir?" turning to Eliot. "It was most courageously done!"

"Miraculously!" said Miss Linwood; her face, as she turned it to Eliot, beaming with gratitude. There are voices that, at their first sound, seem to strike a new chord that ever after vibrates; and this first word that Eliot heard pronounced by Isabella Linwood, often afterward rung in his ears like a remembered strain of sweet music. There were persons present, however, not occupied with such high emotions; and while Eliot was putting in a disclaimer, and saying, if there were any merit attending arresting the horse, it was his servant's, diligent search was making into the cause of the animal's transgression, which soon appeared in the form of a thorn, that, being entangled in the saddle-cloth, had pierced her side.

The first flow of Mr. Linwood's gratitude seemed to have been suddenly checked. "Papa has seen the blue coat," thought Isabella; "and the gushings of his heart are turned to icicles!" And infusing into her own manner the warmth lacking in his, she asked what name she should associate with her preservation.

"My name is Lee."

"A very short one. May we prefix Harry or Charles?" alluding to two distinguished commanders in the American army.

"Neither. Mine is a name unknown to fame, Eliot."

"Eliot Lee!—Herbert's friend!—Bessie's brother! Papa, you do not understand. Mr. Lee is the brother of your little pet, Bessie Lee, and," she added, "Herbert's best friend."

Her father coloured; and civilly hoped Miss Bessie Lee was well.

"Well! that is nothing," exclaimed Miss Linwood. "We hope all the world is well; but I must know where Bessie is—what she is doing—how she is looking, and a thousand million et ceteras. Papa, Mr. Lee must come home with us."

"Certainly, Isabella, if Mr. Lee chooses."

Thus bidden, Mr. Lee could only choose to refuse, which he did; alleging that he had no time at his own disposal.

Isabella looked pained, and Mr. Linwood felt uncomfortable; and making an effort at an amende honorable, he said, "Pray send your servant to me, sir; I shall be happy to express my obligations to him."

"Heaven smiles on Herbert!" thought Eliot; and he replied eagerly, "I will most certainly send him, sir, this evening, at eight o'clock." He then bowed to Mr. Linwood, took Isabella's hand, which she again graciously extended to him, and thanking her for her last kind words—"Best—best love to Bessie; be sure you don't forget it," he mounted his horse and was off.

"Send him!" said Mr. Linwood, reiterating Eliot's last words. "I'll warrant him!—trust a Yankee for not letting slip a shilling."

"He is quite right, papa. If he cannot obtain the courtesy due to the gentleman in return for the service he has rendered, he is right to secure the reward of the menial. You were savage, sir—absolutely savage. Mr. Lee will think we are barbarians—heathens—anything but Christians."

"And so am I, and so will I be to these fellows. This young man did only say what any other young man would have done upon instinct; so don't pester me any more about him. You know, Belle, I have sworn no rebel shall enter my doors."

"And you know, sir, that I have—not sworn—oh, no! but resolved, and my resolve is the feminine of my father's oath, that you shall hang me on a gallows high as Haman's, before I cease to plead that our doors may be opened to one rebel at least."

"Never, never !" replied her father, shutting his hall-door after him as he spoke, as if all the rebel world were on the other side of it.

CHAPTER XII.

Oui, je suis sûr que vous m'aimez, mais je ne le suis pas que vous m'aimiez toujours.—MOLIÈRE.

WHEN Eliot rejoined his friend at the appointed rendezvous, Mrs. Billings's, Herbert listened most eagerly to every particular of Eliot's meeting with his father and sister, and over and over again for so thoughtfully smoothing the way for his interview with them in the evening. "Oh, Eliot," he said, "may you never have such a hurricane in your bosom as I had when I stood by my father and Belle, and longed to throw myself at his feet, and take my sister into my arms. I believe I did kiss Jennet—what the deuce ailed the jade ! she is the gentlest creature that ever stepped. Never doubt my self-control after this, Eliot !" Eliot's apprehensions were not so easily removed. He perceived that Herbert was in a frame of mind unsuited to the cautious part he was to act. His feelings had been excited by his rencounter with his father and sister, and though he had passed through that trial with surprising self-possession, it had quite unfitted him for encountering the " botheration " (so he called it) that awaited him at Mrs. Billings's.

"We are in a beautiful predicament here," he said ; " our landlady, who is one of your ' 'cute Yankees,' will not let us in till she has sent our names and a description of our persons to the Commandant Robertson's :—this, she says, being according to his order. Now this cannot be—I will not implicate you—thus far I have proceeded on my sole responsibility, and if anything happens, I alone am liable for the consequences. Are your instructions to stop at this house positive ?"

" Yes ; and if they were not, we might not be better able to evade this police regulation elsewhere. I will see my countrywoman—' hawks won't pick out hawks' een,' you know they say ; perhaps one Yankee hawk may blind another."

A loud rap brought the hostess herself to the door, a sleek lady, who, Eliot thought, looked as if she might be *diplomatised*, though a Yankee, and entitled to the discretion of at least forty-five years.

"Mrs. Billings, I presume ?"

"The same, sir,—will you walk in ?"

"Thank you, madam. Kisel, remain here while I speak with the lady." Mrs. Billings looked at the master, then at the man, then hemmed, which being interpreted, meant, "I understand your mutual relations," and then conducted Eliot to her little parlour, furnished with all the display she could command, and the frugality to which she was enforced, a combination not uncommon in more recent times. A carpet covered the middle of the floor, and just reached to the stately chairs that stood like grenadiers around the room, guarding the uncovered boards, the test

of the house-wife's neatness. One corner was occupied by a high Chinese lackered clock ; and another by a buffet filled with articles, like the poor vicar's, " wisely kept for show," because good for nothing else ; and between them was the chest of drawers, that so mysteriously combined the uses which modern artisans have distributed over sideboards, wardrobes, &c. The snugness, order, and sufficiency of Mrs. Billings's household certainly did present a striking contrast to the nakedness and desolation of our soldier's quarters, and the pleased and admiring glances with which Eliot surveyed the apartment were quite unaffected.

" You are very pleasantly situated here, madam," he said.

" Why, yes ; as comfortably as I could expect."

" You are from Rhode Island, I believe, Mrs. Billings ? "

" I am happy to own I am, sir ;" the expression of hostility with which the lady had begun the conference abated. It is agreeable to have such cardinal points in one's history as where one comes from known—an indirect flattery, quite unequivocal.

" I have been 'told, madam," continued Eliot, " that you were a sufferer in the royal cause before you left your native state."

" Yes, sir, I may say that ; but I have never regretted it."

" The lady's loyalty is more conspicuous than her conjugal devotion," thought Eliot, who remembered to have heard that, with some other property, she had lost her husband.

" No, madam," he replied, " one cannot regret sacrifices in a cause conscientiously espoused."

" Your sentiments meet my views, sir, exactly."

" But your sacrifices have been uncommon, Mrs. Billings ; you have left a lovely part of our country to shut yourself up here."

" That's true, sir ; but you know one can do a great deal from a sense of duty. I am not a person that thinks of myself ; I feel as if I ought to be useful while I am spared." Our self-sacrificing philanthropist was driving a business, the gains of which she had never dreamed of on her sterile New England farm.

" I am glad to perceive, Mrs. Billings, that your sacrifices are in some measure rewarded. You have, I believe, the best patronage in the city ? "

" Yes, sir ; I accommodate as many as I think it my duty to : my lodgers are very genteel persons and good pay. Still, I must say, it is a pleasure to converse with one's own people. The British officers are not sociable except among themselves."

" I assure you our meeting is a mutual pleasure, Mrs. Billings. May I hope for the accommodation of a room under your roof for a day or two ? "

" I should be very happy to oblige you, sir. It appears to me to be a Christian duty to treat even our enemies kindly ; but our officers—I mean no offence, sir—look down upon the rebels, and I could not find it suitable to do what they would not approve."

" As to that, Mrs. Billings, you know we are liable to optical illusions in measuring heights—that nearest seems most lofty." Eliot paused, for he felt he had struck too high a note for his auditor ; and lowering his pitch, he added, " you are a New-England woman, Mrs. Billings, and know we are not troubled by inequalities that are imaginary."

" Very true, sir."

" If you find it convenient to oblige me, I shall not intrude on your lodgers, as I prefer taking my meals in my own room." This arrangement obviated all objection on the part of the lady, and the matter was settled after she had hinted that a private table demanded extra pay. Eliot perceived he was in that common case where a man must pay his *quid pro quo*, and acknowledge an irrequitable obligation into the bargain : he therefore submitted graciously, acceded to the lady's terms, and was profuse in thanks.

Looking over the mantel-piece, and seeming to see, for the first time, a framed advertisement suspended there, " I perceive, madam," he said, " that your lodgers are required to report themselves to the commandant ; but as my errand is from General Washington to Sir Henry Clinton, I imagine this ceremony will be superfluous ; somewhat like going to your servants for leave to stay in your house, after obtaining it from you, madam, the honoured commander-in-chief ! "

" That would be foolish."

" Then all is settled, Mrs. Billings. As my man is a stranger in the city, you will allow one of your servants to take a note for me to Sir Henry Clinton ! "

" Certainly, sir."

Thus Eliot had secured an important point by adroitly and humanely addressing himself to the social sympathies of the good woman, who, though ycleped " a 'cute calculating Yankee," was just that complex being found all the world over, made up of conceit, self-esteem, and good feeling ; with this difference, that, like most of her country people, she had been trained to the devotion of her faculties to the provident art of *getting along*.

In conformity to the answer received to his note, Eliot was at Sir Henry Clinton's door precisely at half-past one, and was shown into the library, there to await Sir Henry.

The house then occupied by the English commander-in-chief, and afterward consecrated by the occupancy of Washington, is still standing at the south-western extremity of Broadway, having been respectfully permitted by its proprietors to retain its primitive form, and fortunately spared the profane touch of the demon of change (*soi-disant* improvement) presiding over the city corporation.

In the centre of the library, which Eliot found unoccupied, was a table covered with the freshest English journals and other late publications : among them, Johnson's political pamphlets, and a poetic emission of light from the star just then risen above the literary horizon—Hannah More. Eliot amused himself for a half hour with tossing these over, and then retired to an alcove formed by a temporary damask drapery, inclosing some bookcases, a sofa, and a window. This window commanded a view of the Battery, the Sound, indenting the romantic shores of Long Island, the generous Hudson, pouring into the bay its tributary waters, and both enfolding in their arms the infant city, ordained by nature to be the queen of our country. " Ah ! " thought Eliot, as his eye passed exultingly over the beautiful scene, and rested on one of his majesty's ships that lay anchored in the bay, " How long are we to be shackled and sentinelled by a foreign power ! how long before we may look out upon this avenue to the ocean as the entrance to our independent homes, and open or shut it, as pleases us, to the commerce and friendship of the world ! "

His natural reverie was broken by steps in the adjoining drawing-room—the communicating door was open, and he heard a servant say, " Sir Henry bids me tell you, sir, he shall be detained in the council-room for half an hour, and begs you will excuse the delay of dinner."

" Easier excused than endured ! " said a voice, as soon as the servant had closed the door, which Eliot immediately recognised to be Mr. Linwood's. " I'll take a stroll up the street, Belle—a half hour is an eternity to sit waiting for dinner ! "

" If Dante had found my father in his Inferno," thought Isabella, " he certainly would have found him *waiting* for dinner ! "

The young lady, left to herself, did what we believe all young ladies do in the like case— walked up to the mirror, and there, while she was readjusting a sprig of jessamine, with a pearl arrow that attached it to her hair, Eliot, from his fortunate position, contemplated at leisure her image. The years that had glided away since we first introduced our heroine on her visit to Effie, had advanced her to the ripe beauty of maturity. The freshness, purity, and frankness of childhood remained ; but there was a superadded grace, an expression of sentiment, of thought, feelings, hopes, purposes, and responsibilities, that come not within the ken of childhood. Form and colouring may be described. Miss Linwood's hair was dark, and, contrary to the fashion of the times (she was no thrall of fashion), unpowdered, uncurled, and unfrizzed, and so closely arranged in braids as to define (that rare beauty) the Grecian outline of her head. Her complexion had the clearness and purity that indicates health and cheerfulness. " How soon," thought Eliot, as he caught a certain look of abstraction to which of late she was much addicted, " how soon she has ceased to gaze at her own image ; is it that she is musing, or have her eyes a sybilline gaze into futurity ! " Those eyes were indeed the eloquent medium of a soul that aspired to Heaven ; but that was not, alas ! above the " carking cares " of earth.

We must paint truly, though we paint the lady of our love ; and therefore we must confess that our heroine was not among the few favoured mortals whose noses have escaped the general imperfection of that feature. Hers was slightly —the least in the world—but incontrovertibly, of the shrewish order ; and her mouth could express pride and appalling disdain, but only did so when some unworthy subject made these merely human emotions triumph over the good-humour and sweet affections that played about this, their natural organ and interpreter.

Her person was rather above the ordinary height, and approaching nearer to *embonpoint* than is common in our *lean* climate ; but it had that grace and flexibility that make one forget critically to mark proportions and dimensions, and to conclude, from the effect produced, that they must be perfect. ✳ We said we could describe form and colour; but who shall describe that mysterious changing and all-powerful beauty of the soul, to which form and colour are but the obedient ministers?—who, by giving the form and dimensions of the temple, can give an idea of the exquisite spirits that look from its portals?

Eliot was not long in making up his mind to emerge from his hiding-place, and was rising, when he was checked by the opening of the library door, and the exclamation, in a voice that made his pulses throb—" Nymph, in thy orisons be all my sins remembered!"

"All, Jasper?" replied Miss Linwood, starting from her meditations, and blushing as deeply as if she had betrayed them—" all thy sins; I should be loath to charge my prayers with such a burden."

"Not one committed against you, Isabella," replied Meredith, in a tone that made it very awkward for Eliot to present himself.

"It would make no essential difference in my estimation of a fault whether it were committed against myself or another."

"Perhaps so!"

Miss Linwood took up one gazette and Meredith another. Suddenly recollecting herself—" Oh, do you know," she said, " that Eliot Lee is in town!"

"Now," thought Eliot, " is my time."

"God forbid!" exclaimed Meredith. Miss Linwood looked at him with an expression of question and astonishment, and he adroitly added, " Of course, if he is in town, he is a prisoner, and I am truly sorry for it."

"Spare your regrets—he comes in the honourable capacity of an emissary from his general to ours."

"It is extraordinary that he has not apprised me of his arrival;—you must be misinformed."

Isabella recounted the adventure of the morning, and concluded by saying, " He must have some reason for withholding himself. You were friends?"

"Yes, college friends—boy friendship, which passes off with other morning mists—a friendship not originating in congeniality, but growing out of circumstances—a chance."

"Chance friendship!" exclaimed Isabella, in a half-suppressed tone, that was echoed from the depths of Eliot's heart. He held his breath as she continued—" I do not understand this; the instincts of childhood and youth are true and safe. I love everything and everybody I loved when I was a child. I now dread the effect of adventitious circumstances—the flattering illusions of society—the frauds that are committed on the imagination by the seeming beautiful." Isabella was perhaps conscious that she was mentally giving a personal investment to these abstractions, for her voice faltered; but she soon continued with more steadiness and emphasis, and a searching of the eye that affected Meredith like an overpowering light—" Chance friendship! This chance friendship may remind you of a chance love, growing out of circumstances too."

"No, no, Isabella; 'on my honour, no. In these serious matters I am a devout believer in the divinity that shapes our ends. The concerns

of my heart never were, never could be, at the mercy of the blind blundering blockhead, Chance."

"Then, if it existed," continued Isabella, her eye still riveted to Meredith's face, where the pale olive had become livid—" if it had existed, you would not, or rather, if you speak truly, you could not, cast aside love for the sister as carelessly as you do friendship for the brother."

"If it existed!—my thanks to you for putting the question hypothetically; you cannot for a moment believe that I ever offered serious homage to that pretty little piece of rurality, Bessie Lee! Certainly, I found her an interesting exception to the prosaic world she lives in—a sunbeam breaking through those leaden New-England clouds—a wild rose-bud amid the corn and potatoes of her mother's garden-patch. She relieved the inexpressible dulness of my position and pursuits. It was like finding a pastoral in the leaves of a statute-book—Aminta in Blackstone."

Poor Eliot; his ears tingled, his brain was giddy.

"The case may have been reversed to Bessie," answered Isabella, " and you may have been the statute-book that gave laws to her submissive heart."

"Ça peut être!" replied Meredith; but he immediately checked the coxcomb smile that curled his lips, for it was very plain that Miss Linwood would bear no levity on the subject of her friend; and he added, apparently anxiously recalling the past,—" No—it is impossible—she could not make so egregious a mistake—she is quite unpresuming—she must have understood me, Isabella." There was now emotion, serious emotion in his voice. " Bessie Lee was not a simpleton; she must have known what you also know——" He faltered. Eliot would have given worlds for a single glance at Isabella's face at this moment; but even if the screen between them had fallen, he could not have seen it, for she had laid her hands on the table, and buried her face in her palms. " I appeal," continued Meredith, " from this stage of our being, troubled and darkened with distrust, to our childhood—that, you say, is true and unerring:—then, Isabella, believe its testimony, and believe that, from the fountain which you then unsealed in my heart, there has ever since flowed a stream, never diverted, and always increasing, till I can no longer control it. Not one word, not one look, Isabella! Again I appeal to the past:—were you unconscious of the wild hopes you raised when you said, ' I love everybody that I loved in my childhood!'"

"Oh!" cried Isabella, raising her head, " I did not mean that—not that!"

The drawing-room door opened, and Helen Ruthven appeared, calling out, " Isabella Linwood—a tête-à-tête—ten thousand pardons; but, Isabella, dear, as the charm is broken, do come here, and you too, Mr. Meredith—here is the drollest-looking fellow at Sir Henry's door. He was walking straight into the hall, when the sentinel pointed his bayonet at him. ' Now don't,' said he; ' that's a plaguy sharp thing, and you'll hurt me if you don't take care; I only want to speak a word to my kappen,' meaning captain, you know. Finding the sentinel would not let him pass, he screamed out to me as I was coming up the stairs—' Miss, just please give my duty to Gin'ral Clinton, and ask him if he won't be so accommodating as to let me speak to 'Kappen Lee.' Was it not comical!"

"What did you say to the poor fellow!" asked Isabella, who at once concluded he was the co-adjutor in her preservation.

"Say, my dear child! of course nothing."

They were now all gazing at the personation of Kisel, seated on the door-step, his head down, and he apparently absorbed in catching flies. "I think I know the poor fellow," said Meredith, who recognised some odd articles of Kisel's odd apparel—"he is a half-idiot, who from his infancy attached himself to Eliot Lee, and clung to him as you have seen a snarl of drifted sea-weed adhere to a rock. I am amazed that a man of Lee's common sense should have such an attendant."

"I honour him for it," said Isabella; "honest, heartfelt, constant affection, elevates the humblest and the meanest. From all I have heard of Eliot Lee," she continued, after a moment's pause, "it is not his fault if his friends in all conditions of life do not cling to him."

Isabella's remark was common-place enough; but the tremulous tone in which it was uttered struck Miss Ruthven. Judging, as most persons do, from her own consciousness, she thought there was but one key to a young lady's emotions; and, whispering to Isabella, she said, "Your blush is beautiful, but a tell-tale."

"False, of course, then," replied Isabella, nettled and embarrassed; and suddenly recollecting she had an unperformed duty towards the uncouth lad at the door, she left the drawing-room (declining Meredith's attendance) to perform it.

"This Captain Lee," said Miss Ruthven to Meredith, "must be a gentleman I sometimes saw at West Point. Our Charlotte was half in love with him."

"Indeed!"

"'Indeed,' yes; but be pleased now, Mr. Meredith, to recal your absent thoughts, and attend to me, who am cast upon your tender-mercies. I have a word to charm back the wanderers—Isabella Linwood!—Ah, I see you are here—now tell me honestly, do you not think that was a false sentiment of hers! Do you think one must of necessity be constant in friendship or love! You are in the constant vein now, but hear me out. Suppose I am interested, in love if you please, with a particular individual—I see another who is to him Hyperion to a satyr, and by a fixed law of nature one attraction must be overcome by the other. It is not a deliberate or a voluntary change—it certainly is not caprice: I am but the passive subject of an irresistible power."

"The object still changing, the sympathy true," said Meredith, with a satirical smile.

"That was meant," replied Miss Ruthven, "for a piquant satire: it is a mere truism," and fixing her lustrous eyes on Meredith, she continued: "The heart must have an object, but we are at the mercy of chance; and should we cling to that first thrown in our way, when taste is crude and judgment unripe, and cling to it after another appears ten thousand times more worthy! Should we, when daylight comes, shut out the blessed

sun, and continue to grope by a rush-light! We cannot—it will penetrate the crevices, and annihilate the stinted beam that we thought enough for us in the luminary's absence. Ah, Mr. Meredith, there is much puling parrotry about constancy, and first love, and all that; *I am sure of it*—am sure the object may change, and the *sympathy* remain, in the truest, tenderest hearts That sympathy—a queer name, is it not!—is always alive and susceptible—a portion of the soul—a part of life. A part!—life itself."

There was a strange confusion of ideas in Meredith's mind as he listened to this rhapsody of Helen Ruthven. By degrees one came clearly out of the mist: and "is the girl in love with me!" was his mental interrogatory.

CHAPTER XIII.

Is't possible that but seeing you should love her?

In the mean time Eliot had been released from his durance, where he had suffered, as mortals sometimes mysteriously do, what he seemed in nowise to have deserved; and passing unobserved into the entry, he had preceded Miss Linwood down the stairs, and was standing within the outer door in conversation with his attendant, so earnest that he did not perceive her approach till she said, "Am I intruding!"

She was answered by Herbert's suddenly turning his face to her, and uttering "Isabella!"

In the suddenness of surprise and joy she forgot everything but his presence; and would have thrown her arms around him but for Eliot's intervention.

"Herbert!—Miss Linwood! I entreat you to be cautious—your brother's safety is at stake—not a moment is to be lost—is concealment possible at your father's house!"

"Possible!—certain. I will instantly go home."

"Stop—pray hush, Herbert. Was the reason of your coming down stairs known to any one, Miss Linwood!"

"Only to Helen Ruthven and Mr. Meredith."

"Two foxes on the scent!—that's all," said Herbert.

"Oh, no, Herbert, they would be the last to betray; but they do not suspect you."

"Then all may be managed," said Eliot; "trust no one, Miss Linwood—you cannot serve your brother better than by appearing at Sir Henry's table, and letting it be known, incidentally, that you have seen my attendant."

"I understand you, and will do my best. Heaven help us! avoid by all means seeing mama, Herbert — she will not dare incur the responsibility of concealing your presence. Go in at the back gate—you can easily elude Jupe—trust all to Rose. God bless you, dear brother," she concluded; and, in spite of the danger of observation, she gave him one hasty embrace, and returned to the drawing-room to enact a part—a difficult task to Isabella Linwood.

The few guests expected soon after arrived; and Mr. Linwood reappeared from his walk with the air of a person who has tidings to communicate. "Ah, Isabella," said he, "I have news for you."

" The rebels have been crucifying more tories,
I suppose ?"

" Pshaw, Belle—you know I did not believe
that, any more than you did when Rivington first
published it. I have heard news of your Yankee
preservers."

" Only heard !—then I have the advantage of
you, for I have seen them."

" Seen them !—Lord bless me—where, child ?"

" In the hall below. I seized the opportunity
of relieving you from the interview appointed this
evening."

" You astonish me ! Well, after all, Robertson's suspicions may be groundless. He has just
received advice to look out sharply for the attendant of Captain Lee, who is suspected not to be
the person he passes for."

" And what if he is not, papa ? "

" What if he is not !—a true girl-question !
Why, he may be an officer, who, under the disguise of a servant, may be a very efficient emissary
for Mr. Washington. He may have come to con-
fer with some of our ' whited sepulchres'—pretended tories, but whigs to the back-bone—we
have plenty such."

" It would be very dangerous," said a sapient
young lady, " to let such a person go at large."

" But, papa," continued Isabella, without no-
ticing the last interlocutor, " it seems to me very
improbable that General Washington would be
accessory to any such proceeding."

" Ah, he'll take care to guard appearances.
He is as chary of his reputation as Cæsar was of
his wife's—a crafty one is Mr. Washington. The
passport seems to have contained a true description of the true servant of this Captain Lee.
Probably some young Curtius has assumed the
responsibility of the imposition. His detection
will reflect no dishonour on the great head of the
schismatics—only expose the poor youth to danger."

" Danger, papa !" Isabella's tone indicated
that the word fell on her ear associated with a
life she loved.

" Yes, Miss Linwood ; he may find a short and
complete cure for whiggism : for, I take it, that
in that department of t'other world which these
gentry go to, they will find rebellion pretty well
under."

" Oh my ! how you hate the whigs, Mr. Linwood ! " exclaimed the aforesaid young lady.
" Supposing it were poor dear Herbert who had
disguised himself just to take a peep at us all."

" Herbert !" echoed Mr. Linwood, his colour
deepening and flushing his high forehead, —
" Herbert !—he is joined to idols—I should let
him alone."

" My ! Isabella, is it not quite shocking to hear
your father speak in such a hard-hearted way of
poor Herbert ?" whispered the young lady, who
still cherished a boarding-school love for Herbert.
" But, dear me ! who is that coming in with Sir
Henry ?—He must be one of the young officers
who arrived in the ship yesterday. ' Captain Lee,
an American officer !' " reiterating Sir Henry's
presentation of his guest. " My ! I ought to have
known the uniform ; but I had no idea there was
such an elegant young man in the American army
—had you, Isabella ?"

Isabella was too much absorbed in her own
observations to return anything more than bows

and nods to her voluble companion. She saw
Meredith advance to Eliot with that engaging
cordiality which he knew so well how to throw
into his manner ; and she perceived that Eliot
met him with a freezing civility, that painfully
re-excited the apprehensions she had long felt,
that there was " something rotten in the state of
Denmark." Sir Henry, after addressing each of
his guests with that official and measured polite-
ness that marks the great man's exact estimate of
the value of each nod, smile, and word vouchsafed
to his satellites, advanced to her, and said in an
under tone, " My dear Miss Linwood, I have
sacrificed my tastes at your shrine—invited a
rebel to my table, in consideration of the service
he had the honour of rendering you, and my
valued friend your father, this morning."

" If all I have heard of the gentleman be true,"
replied Isabella, " Sir Henry will find his society
an indulgence rather than a sacrifice of taste."

" Perhaps so." Sir Henry shrugged his
shoulders. " He seems a clever person ! but you
know antipathies are stubborn ; and, entre nous,
I have what may be termed a natural aversion to
an American. I mean, of course, a rebel American."

England was so much the Jerusalem of the
loyal colonists, the holy city towards which they
always worshipped, that Sir Henry, in uttering
this sentiment, had no doubt of its calling forth a
responsive " amen" from Miss Linwood's bosom.
But her pride was touched. For the first time
an American feeling shot athwart her mind, and,
like a sunbeam falling on Memnon's statue, it
elicited music to one ear at least. " Have a care,
Sir Henry," she replied aloud : " such sentiments
from our rulers engender rebellion, and almost
make it virtue. I am beginning to think that if I
had been a man, I should not have forgotten that
I was an American." Her eye encountered Eliot
Lee's ; and his expressed a more animated delight
than he would have ventured to embody in words,
or than she would have heard spoken with complacency.

Sir Henry turned on his heel, and Eliot occupied his position. Without adverting to what he
had just overheard, or alluding to the discords of
the country, he spoke to Miss Linwood of her
brother, of course, as if he had left him in camp ;
from her brother they naturally passed to his
sister. Both were topics that called forth their
most eloquent feelings. The consciousness of a
secret subject of common concern heightened
their mutual interest, and in half an hour they
had passed from the terra incognita of strangers
to the agreeable footing of friends.

" I saw you bow to Miss Ruthven," said Isabella : " you knew her at West Point ?"

" Slightly," replied Eliot, with a very expressive curl of his lip.

" Did not I hear my name ?" asked Miss
Ruthven, advancing, hanging on Meredith's arm,
and seating herself in a vacant chair near Miss
Linwood.

" You might, for we presumed to utter it,"
replied Isabella.

" Oh, I suppose Captain Lee has been telling
you of my escape from that stronghold of the
enemy—indeed, I could endure it no longer. You
know, Captain Lee, there is no excitement there

but the scenery ; and even if I were one of those favoured mortals who find 'tongues in trees, books in the running brooks, and sermons in stones,' I have no fancy for them. I prefer the lords of the creation," fixing her eyes expressively on Meredith, "to creation itself."

" Pray tell me, Captain Lee," asked Isabella, " is your sister such a worshipper of nature as she used to be ! it seemed to be an innate love with her."

" Yes, it is ; and it should be so, if, as some poets imagine, there is a mysterious correspondence and affinity between the outward world and pure spirits."

" Dear Bessie ! I am so charmed to hear from her again. She has sent me but one letter in six months, and that a very, *very* sad one." Isabella's eye involuntarily turned towards Meredith, but there was no indication that the sounds that entered his ears touched a chord of feeling, or even of memory. It was worth remarking, that while subjects had been alluded to that must have had the most thrilling interest for both Miss Ruthven and Meredith, they neither betrayed by a glance of the eye, a variation of colour, or a faltering of voice, the slightest consciousness. Truly, " the children of this world are wiser in their generation than the children of light."

At the very moment Isabella was speaking so tenderly of her friend, Meredith interrupted her with, " I beg your pardon, Miss Linwood, but I have a controversy with Miss Ruthven which you must decide. I insist there is disloyalty in discarding the Queen Charlotte bonnet ; a fright, I grant, very like the rustic little affair your sister Bessie used to wear, Lee ; and absolute treason in substituting *la vendange*, a Bacchante concern, introduced by the Queen of France, the patroness of the rebel cause—pardon me, Captain Lee— your decision, Miss Linwood ; we wait your decision—"

Isabella carelessly replied, " I wear *la vendange ;*" but not thus carelessly did she dismiss the subject from her mind. " Meredith could not so lightly have alluded to Bessie, in speaking to her brother," thought she, while she weighed each word with a tremulous balance, " if he had ever trifled with the affections of that gentle creature. I have been unjust to him ! he is no heart-breaker after all." There is no happier moment in the history of the heart than when it is relieved of a distrust ; and most deeply to be pitied is a young, enthusiastic, and noble-minded creature, who, with a standard of ideal perfection, has her affections fixed, and her confidence wavering.

Eliot perceived that Miss Linwood's mind was abstracted, and feeling his position 'to be an awkward one, he withdrew to a distant part of the room. Meredith too made his observations. He was acute enough to perceive that he had allayed Isabella's suspicions. He was satisfied with the present, and not fearful of the future.

" Pray tell me, Meredith, do you know that Captain Lee !" asked a Major St. Clair.

" Very well ; we were at Harvard together !"

" Ah ! scholar turned soldier. These poor fellows have no chance against the regular-bred military. Homer and Virgil are not the masters to teach our art."

" Our army would halt for officers if they were," said Miss Linwood.

" St. Clair," said Meredith, " is of the opinion of the old Romans. Plutarch, you know, says they esteemed Greek and scholar terms of reproach."

" You mistake me, Meredith ; I meant no reproach to the learned Theban ; upon my word, he strikes me as quite a soldier-like looking fellow —a keen, quick eye—powerful muscles—good air —very good air, has he not, Miss Linwood !"

" Just now he appears to me to have very much the air of a neglected guest. Jasper, pray present Major St. Clair to your sometime friend."

" Excuse me, Miss Linwood," replied the major, " we have *roturiers* enough in our own household. I am not ambitious of making the acquaintance of those from the rebel camp."

" May I ask," resumed Isabella, " who our *roturiers* are !"

" Oh, the merchants—men of business, and that sort of people."

" Our city gentry !"

Major St. Clair bowed assent.

Isabella bowed and smiled too, but not graciously : her pride was offended. A new light had broken upon her, and she began to see old subjects in a fresh aspect. Strange as it may appear to those who have grown up with the rectified notions of the present day, she for the first time perceived the folly of measuring American society by a European standard—of casting it in an old and worn mould—of permitting its vigorous youth to be cramped and impaired by transmitted manacles and shackles. Her fine mind was like the perfectly organised body, that wanted but to be touched by fire from Heaven to use all its faculties freely and independently.

It was obvious that Meredith avoided Eliot, but this she now believed was owing to the atmosphere of the court drawing-room. Eliot was not so uncomfortable as she imagined. A common man in his position might not have risen above the vanities and littlenesses of self. He might have been fearful of offending against etiquette, the divinity of small polished gentlemen. He might, an irritable man would, have been annoyed by the awkward silence in which he was left, interrupted only by such formal courtesies as Sir Henry deemed befitting the bearing of the host to an inferior guest. But Eliot Lee cared for none of these things—other and higher matters engrossed him. He was meditating the chances of getting Herbert safe back to West Point, and the means of averting Washington's displeasure. He was eagerly watching Isabella Linwood's face, where it seemed to him her soul was mirrored, and inferring from its eloquent mutations her relations with Linwood ; and he was contrasting Sir Henry's luxurious establishment, and the flippant buzz of city gossip he heard around him, with the severe voluntary privations and intense occupations of his own general and his companions in arms. His meditations were suddenly put to flight.

Isabella had been watching for an opportunity to speak privately to Eliot of her brother. Miss Ruthven and Meredith never quitted her side. Miss Ruthven seemed like an humble worshipper incensing two divinities, while, like the false priest, she was contriving to steal the gift from the altar ;

or rather, like an expert finesser, she seemed to leave the game to others while she held, or fancied she held, the controlling card in her own hand. "I must make a bold push," thought Isabella, "to escape from these people;" and beckoning to Eliot, who immediately obeyed her summons, she said, "Permit me, Sir Henry, to show Captain Lee the fine picture of Lord Chatham in your breakfasting-room!"

"Lord Chatham has been removed to give place to the Marquis of Shelburne," replied Sir Henry, with a sarcastic smile.

"Shall I show you the marquis, then? The face of an enemy is not quite so agreeable as that of a friend, but I am sure Captain Lee will never shrink from either."

"This Captain Lee," whispered Helen Ruthven to Meredith, "has a surprising faculty in converting enemies into friends—have a care lest he make friends enemies."

Unfortunately, Isabella's tactics were baffled by a counter-movement. She was met at the door by the servant announcing dinner, and Eliot was obliged to resign her hand to Sir Henry, to fall behind the privileged guests entitled to precedence, and follow alone to the dining-room.

There were no indications on Sir Henry's table of the scarcity and dearness of provisions so bitterly complained of by the royalists who remained in the city. At whatever rate procured, Sir Henry's dinner was sumptuous. Eliot compared it with the coarse and scanty fare of the American officers, and he felt an honest pride in being one among those who contracted for a glorious future, by the sacrifice of all animal and present indulgence.

Dish after dish was removed and replaced, and the viands were discussed, and the generous wines poured out, as if to eat and to drink were the chief business and joy of life. "A very pretty course of fish for the season," said Major St. Clair, who sat near Eliot, passing his eye over the varieties on the table: "Pray, Captain Lee, have you a good fish-market at West Point?"

"We are rather too far from the seabord, sir, for such a luxury."

"Ah, yes—I forgot, pardon me; but you must have fine trout in those mountain-streams—a pretty resource at a station is trout-fishing."

"Yes, to idlers who need resources; but time, as the lady says in the play, 'time travels in divers paces with divers persons'—it never 'stays' with us."

"You've other fish to fry—he! he! very good—allow me to send you a bit of brandt, Captain Lee; do the brandt get up as far as the Highlands?"

"I have never seen them there."

"Indeed!—but you have abundance of other game—wild geese, turkeys, teal, woodcock, snipe, broad-bills!"

"We have none of these delicacies, sir."

"God bless me!—how do you live?"

Eliot was pestered with this popinjay, and he answered, with a burst of pardonable pride, "I'll tell you how we live, sir"—the earnest tone of his voice attracted attention—"we live on salt beef, brown bread, and beans, when we can get them; and when we cannot, some of us fast, and some share their horses' messes."

"Bless me—how annoying!"

"You may possibly have heard, sir," resumed Eliot, "of the water that was miraculously sweetened, and of certain bread that came down from Heaven; and we, who live on this nutriment that excites your pity, and feel from day to day our resolution growing bolder and our hopes brighter, we fancy a real presence in the brown bread, and an inspiration in the water that wells up through the green turf of our native land."

There is a chord in the breast of every man that vibrates to a burst of true feeling—this vibration was felt in the silence that followed. It was first broken by Isabella Linwood's delicious voice. She turned her eye, moistened with the emotion he had excited, towards Eliot; and filling a glass from a goblet of water, she pushed the goblet towards him, saying. "Ladies may pledge in the pure element—*our* native land! Captain Lee."

Eliot filled a bumper, and never did man drink a more intoxicating draught. Sir Henry looked tremendously solemn, Helen Ruthven exchanged glances with Meredith, and Mr. Linwood muttered between his teeth, "Nonsense! d—d nonsense, Belle!"

It must be confessed, that Miss Linwood violated the strict rules that governed her contemporaries. She was not a lady of saws and precedents. But if she sometimes too impulsively threw open the door of her heart, there was nothing there exposed that could stain her cheek with a blush. We would by no means recommend an imitation of her spontaneous actions. Those only can afford them to whom they are spontaneous.

After the momentary excitement had passed, Eliot felt that he had perhaps been a little too heroic for the occasion. Awkward as the descent is from an assumed elevation, he effected it with grace, by falling into conversation with the major on sporting and fishing; in which he showed a science that commanded more respect from that gentleman, than if he had manifested all the virtues of all the patriots that ever lived, fasted, starved, and died for their respective countries.

It was hard for Eliot to play citizen of the world, while he saw Meredith courted, admired, and apparently happy, mapping out, at his own will, a brilliant career, and thought of his sister wasting the incense of her affections; no more to Meredith than a last summer's flower. "He deserves not," he thought indignantly, as his eye fell on Isabella, "the heart of this glorious creature; no man deserves—I almost wonder that any man should dare aspire to it."

When a man begins to be humble in relation to a woman, he is not very far from love; and absurd as Eliot would have deemed it to fall in love at first sight, and utterly absurd for him, at any time, to fall in love with Miss Linwood, it was most fortunate for him that he was suddenly taken from her presence, by a request from Sir Henry (who had just had a note put into his hands) that he would accompany him to his council chamber. When there, he informed Eliot, that suspicions having been excited in relation to his attendant, a quest for him had been made at Mrs. Billings's—but in vain. "Captain Lee must be aware," he said, "that the disappearance of the man was a confirmation of the suspicions!"

Eliot replied, that "he was not responsible for

any suspicions that might be felt by the timid, or feigned by the ill-disposed."

"That may be, sir," replied Sir Henry; "but we must make you responsible for the reappearance of the man—your flag cannot exempt you from this!"

"As you please, sir," replied Eliot, quite undaunted; "you must decide how far the privilege of my flag extends. You, sir, can appreciate the importance of not violating, in the smallest degree, the few humanities of war."

Sir Henry pondered for a moment before he asked, "Is there anything in the character of your attendant which may betray him into an indiscretion?"

"I am an interested witness, Sir Henry; but if you do not choose to infer the character from the action, which certainly has been sufficiently indiscreet, give me leave to refer you to Mr. Meredith; he knew the poor lad in Massachusetts."

"But how can you identify him with this man?"

"He saw this man to-day."

Meredith was summoned and questioned. "He had seen Captain Lee's servant on Sir Henry's door-step, and recognised him at the first glance—the dullest eye could mistake no other man for Kisel."

"Do me the favour, Mr. Meredith," said Eliot, "to tell Sir Henry Clinton whether you think my man would be liable to a panic; for it appears that having overheard he was under suspicion, he has fled."

"True to himself, Kisel! He would most assuredly fly at the slightest alarm. He is one of those helpless animals whose only defence is the instinct of cowardice. I have seen him run from the barking of a family dog, and the mewing of a house cat; and yet, for he is a curious compound, such is his extraordinary attachment to Captain Lee, that I believe he would stand at the cannon's mouth for him. Poor fellow! his mind takes no durable impression; to attempt to make one is like attempting to form an image in sand; and yet, like this same sand, which, from the smelting furnace appears in brilliant and defined forms, his thoughts, kindled in the fire of his affections, assume an expression and beauty that would astonish you; always in fragments, as if the mind had been shattered by some fatal jar."

Meredith spoke *con amore*. He was delighted with the opportunity of doing Eliot a grace; and Eliot, in listening to the sketch of his simple friend, had almost forgot the subterfuge that called it forth. He was not, however, the less pleased at its success, when Sir Henry told him that his despatches and passports should be furnished in the course of the evening, and that no impediment would be thrown in the way of his departure.

The three gentlemen then parted, Meredith expressing such animated regret at their brief meeting, that Eliot was on the point of reciprocating it, when the thought of his sister sealed his lips and clouded his brow. Meredith's conscience rightly interpreted the sudden change of countenance; but his retained its cordial smile, and his hand abated nothing of its parting pressure.

Again we must quote that most apposite sentence—"Truly, the children of this world are wiser in their generation than the children of light."

CHAPTER XIV.

Oh, my home,
Mine own dear home.

WHILE Eliot was enjoying the doubtful advantage of Sir Henry's hospitality, Herbert Linwood, a fugitive in his native city, was seeking concealment in his father's house. His ardent temperament, which had plunged him into this perplexity, did not qualify him to extricate himself from it. So far from not giving to any "unproportioned thought its act," thought and action were simultaneous with him. His whole career had shown that discretion was no part of his valour. He never foresaw danger till he was in to the very lips; and, unfortunately, he manifested none of the facility at getting out that he did at getting in. In short, he was one of those reckless, precipitate, vivacious, kind, and whole-hearted young fellows, who are very dear and very troublesome to their friends.

After leaving Sir Henry Clinton's, he turned into a lane leading from Broadway to Broad-street, and affording a side-entrance to his father's premises. As he was about to turn into his father's gateway, he saw a man enter the lane from Broad-street, and, for once cautious, he continued his walk. He fancied the stranger eyed him suspiciously. As he turned into Broad-street the man also turned into Broadway, and Herbert eagerly retraced his steps; but as he entered his father's gate, he had the mortification to see the man repass the upper corner of the street, and to believe that he was observed by him. He was once more on his father's premises. His heart throbbed. The kitchen-door was half open, and through the aperture he saw Rose, who he was sure would joyfully admit him into the garrison if he could open a communication with her; but there were obstacles in the way. Jupiter, whom Isabella had warned him not to trust, was, according to his custom of filling up all the little interludes of life, eating at a side-table. Beside him sat Mars on his hind-legs, patiently waiting the chance mouthfuls that Jupe threw to him. Mars was an old house-dog, an *enfant gâté*, petted by all the family, and pampered by Jupe. An acquaintance of Jupiter's had dropped in for an afternoon's lounge; and Rose, who had a natural antipathy to loungers of every degree, was driving round with a broom in her hand, giving with this staff of office the most expressive intimations that his presence was unwelcome.

We must be permitted to interrupt our narrative, and recede some nine or ten years, to record the most remarkable circumstance in Rose's life. She was a slave, and most faithful and efficient. Slaves at that period were almost the only servants in the province of New York; and Rose, in common with many others, filled the office of nurse. Gifts and favours of every description testified her owner's sense of her value. On one memorable New-year's day, when Isabella was a child of eight years, she presented Rose a changeable silk dress. It was a fine affair, and Rose was pleased and grateful.

"Now," said Isabella, "you are as grand and as happy as any lady in the land—are you not, Rose?"

"Happy!" echoed Rose, her countenance changing ; "I may seem so ; but since I came to a thinking age, I never had one happy hour or minute, Miss Belle."

"Oh, Rose, Rose! why not, for pity's sake!"

"I am a *slave*."

"Pshaw, Rosy, dear! is that all?—I thought you was in earnest." She perceived Rose was indeed in earnest ; and she added in an expostulating tone, "Are not papa and mama ever so kind to you! and do not Herbert and I love you next best to them!"

"Yes, and that lightens the yoke ; but still it is a yoke, and it *galls*. I can be bought and sold like the cattle. I would die to-morrow to be free to-day. Oh, free breath is good—free breath is good!" She uttered this with closed teeth, and tears rolling down her cheeks.

Tears on Rose's cheeks! Isabella could not resist them, and pouring down a shower from her own bright eyes, she exclaimed, "You shall be free, Rose," and flew to appeal to her father. Her father kissed her, called her "the best little girl in the world," and laughed at her suit.

"Rose is a fool," he said ; "she had reason to complain when she lived with her old mistress, who used to cuff her ; but now she *was* free in everything but the name—far better off than nine-tenths of the people in the world." This sophistry silenced, but did not satisfy Isabella. The spirit of truth and independence in her own mind responded to the cravings of Rose's, and the thrilling tone in which those words were spoken, "it is a yoke, and it galls," continued to ring in her ears.

Soon after, a prize was promised in Isabella's school, for the best French scholar. She was sadly behind-hand in the studies that require patient application ; and her father, who was proud of her talents, was often vexed that she did not demonstrate them to others. "Now, Belle," he said, "if you will but win this prize, I'll give you anything you'll ask of me."

"Anything, papa!"

"Yes—anything."

"You promise for fair, sir!"

"You gipsy! yes."

"Then write it down, please ; for I have heard you say, papa, that no bargain is good in law that is not written down."

Mr. Linwood wrote, signed, and sealed a fair contract. Isabella set to work. The race was a hard one. Her competitors were older than herself, and farther advanced in the language ; but a mind like hers, with motive strong enough to call forth all its energy, was unconquerable. Every day and evening found her with increasing vigour at her tasks. Her mother remonstrated, Herbert teased and ridiculed, and Rose fretted. "What signified it," she asked, "for Miss Belle to waste her rosy cheeks and pretty flesh over books, when, without book-learning, she was ten times brighter than other girls!" Still Isabella, hitherto a most desultory creature in her habits, and quitting her tasks at the slightest temptation, persevered like a Newton ; and, like all great spirits, she shaped destiny. The prize was hers.

"Now, Belle," said her father, elated with the compliments that poured in upon him, "I will fulfil my part of the contract honourably, as you have done yours. What shall it be, my child!"

"Rose's freedom, papa."

"By Christopher Columbus (his favourite oath when he was pleased), you shall have it ; and in half an hour you shall give her, with your own hand, Belle, the deed of manumission."

"Could we but find the right sort of stimulus," he afterward said to his wife, "we might make Belle a great scholar." But the "right sort of stimulus" was not easily found ; and Isabella soon recovered her "rosy cheeks and pretty flesh." Her mind fortunately resembled those rich soils, where every chance sunbeam and passing shower brings forth some beautiful production. Her schoolmates studied, plodded, and wondered they did not know half as much, and were never half as agreeable, as Isabella Linwood. Human skill and labour can do much, but Heaven's gifts are inimitable.

Rose's outward condition was in no wise changed, but her mind was freed from galling shackles, by the restoration of her natural rights, and she now enjoyed the voluntary service she rendered.

We return from our digression. Herbert perceived, from a glance at the dramatis personæ that occupied the scene, that it was no time for him to enter ; and slouching his cap over his face, he seated himself on the door-step, and whittled a stick, listening, with what patience he could muster, to the colloquy within.

"'Pon my honour, Mr. Linwood" (the slaves were in the habit of addressing one another by the names or titles of their masters), "'pon my honour, Mr. Linwood, you were in a 'dicament this morning," said Jupiter's friend.

"Just 'scaped with my life, gin'ral."

"That's always safe," muttered Rose ; "that nobody would cry for if it were lost."

"That's not the case with me Mr. Linwood," resumed the general, "for Miss Phillis, in particular, turned as white as any lily when he stood by that kicking horse."

"It was a 'markable 'liv'rance, and I'll tell you how it happened, only don't tell anybody but Miss Phillis, with my 'spects. Just as Jennet had stopped one bout of kicking, and was ready to begin again, I heard an apparition of a voice crying out 'softly, softly Jennet, softly.' and 'pon my honour she stood stock still, trembling like a leaf—do you surmise who it was!"

"Miss Isabella, to be sure, you fool," said Rose.

"No such ting, Rose, I was as calm as——"

"A scared turkey, Jupe."

"I say I was as calm as them tongs, and there was nobody near the horse but that rebel officer when I heard the apparition. As true as you sit there, gin'ral, it was Mr. Herbert's voice that quieted Jennet. I'll lay the next news we hear will be his death—poor 'guided young man!"

"'Tis a pity," replied the believing general, "to cut him off 'fore he's a shock of wheat ; but then the rebels must die first or last, as they desarve, for trying to drive off the reg'lars. Pretty times we should have in New York if they were gone : no balls, no races, no t'eatres, no music, no cast-off regimentals, for your lawyers and traders an't genteel that way, Mr. Linwood."

"Very true, gin'ral. Here's 'fusion to the rebels!" and he passed his cup of cider to his compatriot.

"Now out on you, you lazy, slavish loons," cried Rose; "can't you see these men are raised up to fight for freedom for more than themselves? If the chain is broken at one end, the links will fall apart sooner or later. When you see the sun on the mountain-top, you may be sure it will shine into the deepest valleys, before long."

"I s'pose what you mean, Rose, is, that all men are going to be free. I heard Mr. Herbert say, when he *argied* with master, that 'all men were born free and equal;' he might as well say, all men were born, white and tall; don't you say so, gin'ral?"

"Be sure, Mr. Linwood, be sure. And I wonder what good their freedom would do 'em. Freedom an't horses and char'ots, tho' horses and char'ots is freedom. Don't you own that, Miss Rose?"

"He's a dog that loves his collar," retorted Rose.

"Don't be 'fronted, Miss Rose. Tell me now, don't you r'ally think it's Cain-like and ongenteel for a son to fight 'gainst his begotten father, and so on?"

"I would have every man fight on the Lord's side," replied Rose, "and that's every man for his own rights."

"La, Miss Rose, then what are them to do what has not got any?" Rose apparently disdained a reply to this argument, and the general interposed.

"It may be well Mr. Herbert is gone, if he an't dead, and gone; for, by what folks say, if the war goes on, there won't be too much left for Miss Isabella."

"'Folks say!'" growled Rose, "don't come here, Mart, with any lies but your own."

"Well, well, Miss Rose, I did not say noting. I know Miss Isabella is sure to have a grander fortin nor ever her father had, and that 'fore long too—Jem Meredith tells me all about it."

"That being the case, Rose," said Jupe, "hand us on a bit of butter. You are as close as if we were in a 'sieged city."

"Butter for you, you old cormorant! and butter a dollar a pound! No, no; up Jupe—out, out, Mars—let me clear away."

Rose was absolute in her authority. Jupiter rose, and Mars crawled most unwillingly out at the door. When there, the drowsy, surfeited animal was suddenly electrified; he snuffed, wagged his tail, barked, and ran in and out again. "What does all this mean?" demanded Rose; and pushing the door wide open, she espied a figure quietly seated on the steps, repressing Mars, and whittling with apparent unconcern. Now Rose, in common with many energetic domestics, had the same sort of antipathy to beggars that she had to moths and vermin of every description, considering them all equally marauders on the domicile.

"What are you doing here, you lazy varmint? pretty time of day for a great two-fisted fellow to be lying over the door, littering the steps this fashion. Fawning on a beggar, Mars! shame on you! clear out, sir!"—and she gave a stroke with her broom, so equally shared by the man and dog, that it was not easy to say for which it was designed. The dog yelped, the man sprang adroitly on one side of the step, raised his cap, and looked Rose in the face.

It was a Gorgon glance to Rose. For an instant she was transfixed; and then recovering her self-possession, she said, so as to appear to her auditors within to be replying to a petition,—"Hungry, are you?—well, well, go to the wash-house, and I'll bring you some victuals—the hungry must be fed."

"That's what master calls sound doctrine, Rose," said Jupiter; "I hope you won't forget it before my supper-time."

"You, you hound, you never fast long enough to be hungry; but I'll remember you at supper-time—I've some fresh pies in the pantry—if you'll take the big kettle to be mended. Now is a good time—Mart will lend you a hand."

Both assented, and thus in a few moments were disposed of; and Rose repaired to the wash-house to embark her whole heart in Herbert's concerns, provided her mind could be satisfied on some cardinal points. After she had given vent to the first burst of joy, something seemed to stick in Rose's throat—she hemmed, coughed, placed and displaced the moveables about her, and then speaking out her upright soul, she said, "you an't a deserter?"

"A deserter, Rose! I'd not look you in the face if I were."

"Nor a spy, Mr. Herbert?"

"Indeed I am not, Rose."

"Then," she cried, striking the back of one hand into the palm of the other, "then we'll go through fire and water for you; but Miss Belle and I could not raise our hands for spy or deserter, though he were bone of her bone."

These preliminaries settled, nothing was easier than for Rose to sympathise fully with the imprudent intensity of Herbert's longings to see his own family. Nothing beyond present concealment was to be thought of till a council could be held with Isabella. Her injunction was obeyed, and Rose immediately conducted Herbert to his own apartment. On his way thither he caught through a glass door a glimpse of his mother, who was alone, employing some stolen moments in knitting for her son:—stolen we say, for well-beloved as he was, she dared not even allude to him in his father's presence. Mrs. Linwood was thoroughly imbued with the conjugal orthodoxy, that

Man was made for God,
Woman for God in him.

She firmly believed that the husband ruled by divine right. She loved her son; but love was not with her, as with Isabella, like the cataract in its natural state, free and resistless; but like the cataract subdued by the art of man, controlled by his inventions, and subserving his convenience. Such characters, if not interesting, are safe, provided they fall into good hands. Such as she was, her son loved her tenderly, and found it hard to resist flying to her arms; and he would actually have done so when he saw her take up the measure-stocking lying in her lap and kiss it, and Rose said, "It is yours," but Rose held him back.

Everything in his apartment had been preserved, with scrupulous care, just as he had left it, and all indicated that he was daily remembered. There was nothing of the vault-like atmosphere of a deserted room, no dust had accumulated on the furniture. His books, his writing materials, his little toilet affairs, were as if he had left them an hour before. Herbert had never felt more tenderly than at this moment, surrounded by these mute witnesses of domestic love, the sacrifice he had made to his country. He was destined to feel it more painfully.

Rose reappeared with the best refreshments of her larder. "Times are changed, Mr. Herbert," she said, "since you used to butter your bread both sides, and when you dropped it on the carpet, say, 'The butter side is up, Rosy.' If the war lasts much longer we shall have no buttered side to our bread."

"How so, Rose—I thought you lived on the fat of the land in the city! Heaven knows our portion is lean enough."

"Oh, Mr. Herbert, it takes a handful of money now to buy one day's fare; and money is far from being plentiful with your father, though I'd pull out my tongue before I'd say so to any but your father's son. There's little coming in from the rents, when the empty houses of the rebels (as our people call them) are to be had for nothing, or next to nothing. They say the commandant does take the rent for some, and give it to the poor; which is like trying to cheat the devil by giving a good name to a bad deed."

"But, Rose, my father has property out of the city."

"Yes, Mr. Herbert; but the farms are on what's called the neutral ground; and the tenants write that what one side does not take t'other does not leave; and so between friends and foes it's all Miss Isabella and I can do to keep the wheels agoing. She has persuaded your father to dispose of all the servants but Jupe and me—plague and no profit were they always, as slaves always are. There's no telling the twists and turns that she and your mother make, that your father may see no difference on the table, where he'd feel it most. If he does, he's sure to curse the rebels; and that's a dagger to them."

"Rose, does my father never speak of me!"

"Never, Mr. Herbert, never."

"Nor my mother!"

Rose shook her head. "Not in your father's hearing."

"And my sister—is she afraid to speak my name!"

"She!—the Lord forgive you, Mr. Herbert. When did she ever fear to do what was right! There's not a day she does not talk of you, though your mother looks scared, and your father looks black; but I mistrust he's pleased. I heard her read to him out of a newspaper one day how General Washington had sent your name into Congress as one of them that had done their duty handsome at Stony Point or some of them places; and she clapped her hands, and put her arms round his neck, and said, with that voice of hers that's sweeter than a flute, 'Are you not proud of him!'"

"My noble sister!—what did he say, Rose!"

"Never a word with his lips; but he went out

of the room as if he'd been shot, his face speaking plainer than words."

"Oh, he'll forgive me!—I'm sure he will!" exclaimed Herbert, his ardent feelings kindling at the first light.

"Don't be too *sartin*, Mr. Herbert—will and heart are at war; and will has been master so long that I mistrust heart is weakest—if, indeed," she added, averting her eye, "you should join the Reformees—"

"Ay, then the fatted calf would be killed for me! No, Rose, I had rather die with my father's curse upon me."

"And better—better!—far better Mr. Herbert : your father's curse, if you don't *desarve* it, won't cut in ; but the curse of conscience is what can't be borne. I must not stay here longer. If you get tired sitting alone, you can sleep away the time. The bed has fresh linen—I change it every month, so it sha'n't get an old smell, and put them in mind how long you've been gone."

"After all," thought Herbert, as the faithful creature quitted the room, "I have never suffered the worst of absence—the misery of being forgotten!" But every solacing reflection was soon lost in the anxieties that beset him. A light-hearted, thoughtless youth is like the bark that dances over the waves when the skies are cloudless, breezes light, and tides favourable, but wants strength and ballast for difficult straits and tempestuous weather. "I have swamped myself completely," thought Herbert. "Eliot must inevitably leave me in the city. It was selfish in me to expose him to censure; that never occurred to me. Instead of getting my father's forgiveness—a fond, foolish dream—I stand a good chance, if Rose is right, of being handed over to the tender-mercies of Sir Henry Clinton. And, if I escape hanging here, I am lost with General Washington : imprudence and rashness are sins of the first degree with him. Would to Heaven I could get out of this net as easily as I ran into it ! I always put the cart before the horse—action before thought."

With such meditations the time passed heavily: and Herbert took refuge in Rose's advice, and threw himself on the bed within the closely-drawn curtains.

We hope our sentimental readers will not abandon him, when we confess that he soon fell into a profound sleep, from which he did not awaken for several hours. They must be agitating griefs that overcome the strong tendencies of a vigorous constitution to eating and sleeping. And besides, it must be remembered in Herbert's favour, that the preceding night had been one long fatiguing vigil. Kind nature ! pardon us for apologising for thy gracious ministry.

CHAPTER XV.

L'habitude de vivre ensemble fait naître les plus doux sentimens qui soient connus des hommes.—ROUSSEAU.

HERBERT'S sleep was troubled with fragments and startling combinations of his waking thoughts. At one moment he was at Westbrook, making love to Bessie, who seemed to be deaf to him, and intently reading a letter in Jasper Meredith's hand ; while Helen Ruthven stood behind her, beckoning to Herbert with her most seductive smile, which he fancied he was not to be deluded by. Suddenly the scene changed—he had a rope round his neck, and was mounting a scaffold, surrounded by a crowd, where he saw Washington, Eliot, his father, mother, and Isabella—all unconcerned spectators. Then, as is often the case, a real sound shaped the unreal vision. He witnessed his own funeral obsequies, and heard his father reading the burial service over him. By degrees sleep loosened the chain that bound his fancy, and the actual sounds became distinct. He awoke : a candle was burning on the table, and he heard his father in an adjoining apartment, to which it had always been his habit to retire for his evening devotions. He heard him repeat the formula prescribed by the church, and then his voice, tremulous with the feeling that gushed from his heart, broke forth in an extempore appeal to Him who holds all hearts in the hollow of his hand. He prayed him to visit with his grace his wandering son ; and to incline him to turn away from feeding on husks with swine, and bring him home to his father's house—to his duty —to his God. "If it please thee," he said, "humble thy servant in any other form—send poverty, sickness, desertion, but restore my only and well-beloved boy ; wipe out the stain of rebellion from my name. If this may not be, if still thy servant must go sorrowing for the departed glory of his house, keep him steadfast in duty, so that he swerve not, even for his son, his only son."

The prayer finished, his door was opened, and he saw his father enter without daring himself to move. Mr. Linwood looked at the candle, glanced his eye around the room, and then sat down at the table, saying, as if in explanation, " Belle has been here." He covered his face with both his hands, and murmured in a broken voice, "Oh, Herbert, was it to store up these bitter hours that I watched over your childhood—that I came every night here, when you were sleeping, to kiss you and pray over your pillow !—what fools we are ! we knit the love of our children with our very heart-strings—we tend on them—we pamper them—we blend our lives with theirs, and then we are deserted—forgotten !"

"Never, never for one moment !" cried Herbert, who with one spring was at his father's feet. Mr. Linwood started from him, and then, obeying the impulse of nature, he received his son's embrace, and they wept in one another's arms.

The door softly opened. Isabella appeared, and, her face irradiating with most joyful surprise, she called, "Mama, mama ; here, in Herbert's room !" In another instant, Herbert had folded his mother and sister to his bosom ; and Mr. Linwood was beginning to recover his self-possession, and to feel as if he had been betrayed into the surrender of a post. He walked up and down the room, then suddenly stopping and laying his hand on Herbert's shoulder, and surveying him from head to foot, "I know not, but I fear," he said, "what this disguise may mean—tell me, in one word, do you return penitent ?"

"I return grieving that I ever offended you, my dear father, and venturing life and honour to see you—to hear you say that you forgive me."

"Herbert, my son, you know," replied Mr. Linwood, his voice faltering with the tenderness against which he struggled, "that my door and my heart have always been open to you, provided—"

"Oh, no provideds, papa ! Herbert begs your forgiveness—this is enough."

"I wish, sir, you would think it was enough," sobbed Mrs. Linwood. :

"You must think so, papa ; it is the sin and misery of these unhappy times that divide you. Give to the winds your political differences, and leave the war to the camp and the field. Herbert has always loved and honoured you."

Mr. Linwood felt as if they were dragging him over a precipice, and he resisted with all his might. "A pretty way he has taken to show it !" he said ; "let him declare he has abandoned the rebels and traitors, and their cause, and I will believe it."

Herbert was silent.

"My dear father," said Isabella.

"Nay, Isabella, do not 'dear father' me. I will not be coaxed out of my right reason. If you can tell me that your brother abandons and abjures the miscreants, speak—if not, be silent."

"If it were true that he did abandon them, he would be no son of yours, no brother of mine. If he were thus restored to us, who could restore him to himself ? where could he hide him from himself ? Your own soul would spurn a renegado ! —think better of him—think better of his friends —they are not all miscreants. There are many noble, highminded—"

"What, what, Isabella ?"

"As deluded as he is."

"A wisely-finished sentence, child. But you need not undertake to teach me what they are. I know them—a set of paltry schismatics—pettifogging attorneys—schoolmasters—mechanics— shop-keepers—bankrupts—outlaws—smugglers— half-starved, half-bred, ragged sons of Belial ; banded together, and led on by that quack Catiline, that despot-in-chief, Washington. 'No son of mine if he abjures them !' I swear to you, Herbert, that on these terms alone will I ever again receive you as my son." Again he paused, and after some reflection added, "You have an alternative, if you do not choose to avail yourself of Sir Henry's standing proclamation, and come in and receive your pardon as a deserter—you may join the corps of Reformees. This opportunity now lost, is lost for ever. Is my forgiveness worth the price I have fixed ? Speak, Herbert."

"Have I not proved how inexpressibly dear it is to me ?"

"No faltering, young man ! speak to the point."

"Oh, my dear, dear son," said his mother, "if you but knew how much we have all suffered for you, and how happy you can now make us, if you only will, you would not hesitate, even if the rebel cause were a good one : you are but as one man to that, and to us you are all the world."

This argumentum ad hominem (tho only argument of weak minds) clouded Herbert's perception. It was a moment of the most painful vacillation ; the forgiveness of his father, the ministering, indulgent love of his mother, the presence of his sister, the soft endearments of home,

E

and all its dear familiar objects, solicited him. He had once forsaken them : but then he was incited by the immeasurable expectation of unrebuked youth, thoughts of high emprise, romantic deeds, and strange incidents ; but his experience, with few and slight exceptions, had been a tissue of dangers without the opportunity of brilliant exploits ; of fatigue without reward ; and of rough and scanty fare, which, however well it may tell in the past life of a hero, has no romantic charm in its actual details. He continued silent. His father perceived, or at least hoped, that he wavered.

"Speak," he said, in a voice of earnest entreaty, " speak, Herbert—my dear son, for God's sake, speak."

"It is right above all things to desire his forgiveness," thought Herbert, " and it is plain there is but one way of getting it. I am in a diabolical hobble—if I succeed in getting back to camp, what am I to expect ! Imprudence is crime with our general ; and, after all, what good have I done the cause !—and yet——"

"Herbert, exclaimed Isabella, and her voice thrilled through his soul, " is it possible you waver !"

He started as if he were electrified : his eye met hers, and the evil spirits of doubt and irresolution were overcome.

"Heaven forgive me !" he said, " I waver no longer."

"Then, by all that is holy," exclaimed Mr. Linwood, flushed with disappointment and rage, " you shall reap as you sow ; it shall never be said that I sheltered a rebel, though that rebel be my son." He rang the bell violently ; " Justice shall have its course—why does not Jupe come !— you too to prove false, Isabella ! I might have known it when I saw you drinking in the vapouring of that fellow Lee to-day ;" again he rang the bell : " you may all desert me, but I'll be true so long as my pulse beats."

No one replied to him. Mrs. Linwood, sustained by Herbert's encircling arm, wept aloud. Isabella knew the tide of her father's passion would have its ebb as well as flow ; she believed the servants were in bed, and that before he could obtain a messenger to communicate with the proper authority, which she perceived to be his present intention, his Brutus resolution would fail. She was however startled by hearing voices in the lower entry, and immediately Rose burst open the door, crying, " Fly, Mr. Herbert—they are after you !"

The words operated on Mr. Linwood like a gust of wind on a superincumbent cloud of smoke. His angry emotions passed off, and nature flamed up bright and irresistible. Every thought, every feeling but for Herbert's escape and safety, vanished. "This way, my son," he cried ; " through your mother's room—down the back stairs, and out at the side gate. God help you !" He closed the door after Herbert, locked it, and put the key into his pocket. Isabella advanced into the entry to meet her brother's pursuers, and procure a delay of a few moments on what pretext she could. She was met by two men and an officer, sent by Colonel Robertson, the commandant. "Your pardon, Miss Linwood," said the officer, pushing by her into the room where her father awaited him.

"How very rude !" exclaimed Mrs. Linwood, for once in her life speaking first and independently in her husband's presence ; " how very rude, sir, to come up stairs into our bedrooms without permission."

The officer smiled at this pretended deference to forms at the moment the poor mother was pale as death, and shivering with terror. " I beg your pardon, madam, and yours, Mr. Linwood—this is the last house in the city in which I should willingly have performed this duty ; but you, sir, are aware, that in these times our very best and most honoured friends are sometimes involved with our foes."

" No apologies, sir, there's no use in them—you are in search of Mr. Herbert Linwood—proceed— my house is subject to your pleasure."

The officer was reiterating his apologies, when a cry from the side entrance to the yard announced that the fugitive was taken. Mr. Linwood sunk into his chair ; but, instantly rallying, he asked whither his son was to be conducted.

" I am sorry to say, sir, that I am directed to lodge him in the Provost's—"

" In Cunningham's hands !—the Lord have mercy on him, then !"

The officer assured him the young man should have whatever alleviation it was in his power to afford him, until Sir Henry's further pleasure should be known. He then withdrew, and left Mr. Linwood exhausted by a rapid succession of jarring emotions.

Isabella retired with her mother, and succeeded in lulling her into a tranquillity which she herself was far enough from attaining.

The person whom, as it may be remembered, Linwood met in passing down the lane to his father's house, was an emissary of Robertson's, who had been sent on a scout for Captain Lee's attendant, and who immediately reported to the commandant his suspicions. He, anxious, if possible, not to offend the elder Linwood, had stationed men in the lane and in Broad-street, to watch for the young man's egress. They waited till ten in the evening, and then found it expedient to proceed to the direct measures which ended in Herbert's capture.

* * *

CHAPTER XVI.

Great is thy power, great thy fame,
Far kenn'd and noted is thy name!
An' tho' yon lowin' heugh's thy hame,
    Thou travels far.
                    BURNS.

ELIOT LEE returned to his lodgings from Sir Henry's in no very comfortable frame of mind. It was his duty, and this duty, like others, had the inconvenient property of inflexibility, to return to West Point with the despatches, without attempting to extricate his friend from the shoals and quicksands amid which he had so rashly rushed. He consoled himself, however, under this necessity, by the reflection that he could in no way so efficiently serve Herbert as by being the first to communicate his imprudence and its consequences to General Washington. His anxiety to serve him was doubled by the consciousness that he should thereby serve Isabella. An acquaintance of a day with a young lady ought not, perhaps, to have given a stronger impulse to the fervours of friendship ; yet the truest friend of three-and-twenty will find some apology for Eliot in his own experience, or would have found it, if, like Eliot, he had just seen the incarnation of his most poetic imaginings.

While he awaited in his room the despatches, he tried to adjust the complicated impressions of the day. He reviewed the scene in the library, and his conclusions from it were the result of his observations, naturally tinged by the character of the observer. Is it not impossible for any man to understand perfectly the intricate machinery of a woman's heart, its hidden sources of hope and fear, trust and distrust ; all its invisible springs and complex action ? " If," he thought, " Miss Linwood knew Meredith as I know him ; if she knew what she now fears, that he had fed his vanity, his idol, self, on the exhalations of homage, love, trust, and hope, from a pure heart that, like a flower, withered in giving out its sweets, she would not love him ; not that it is a matter of volition to love or not to love,—but she could not. If Isabella Linwood, gifted as she is in mind and person, were less sought—if, like my poor little Bessie, she were in some obscure, shady place of life, her preeminence unacknowledged and unknown, like her she would be deserted for an enthroned sovereign. This she cannot know ; and she is destined to be one of the ten thousand mismated men and women who have thrown away their happiness, and found it out too late. Find it out she must ; for this detestable selfishness dulls a man's perception of the rights of others, of their deserts, their wants, and their infirmities, while it makes him keenly susceptible to whatever touches self. He resembles those insects who, instead of the social senses of hearing and seeing, which connect one sentient existence with another, are furnished with feelers that make their own bodies the focus of all sensation."

Eliot was roused from his sententious revery by a whistle beneath his window. He looked out, and saw by the moonlight a man squatt·d on the ground, and so shaded by the wooden entrance to the door, as to be but dimly seen. Eliot conjecturing who it might be, immediately descended the stairs and opened the outer door. The man leaped from the ground, seized both Eliot's hands, and cried out in a half-articulate voice—" Could not Kisel find you ? hey ! when the dog can't find his master, nor the bean its pole, nor the flower the side the sun shines, then say Kisel can't find you, Misser Eliot—hey ! "

" My poor fellow ! how in the name of wonder did you get here alone ? "

" Ah, Misser Eliot, always told you you did not know what a salvation it was to pass for a fool, and all the while be just as wise as other folks. I have my own light,"—he pointed upwards,—" there's one that guides the owl as well as the eagle, and the fool better than the wise man."

" But how came the enemy to let you pass ? "

" Let me ! what for should not they ? What harm could such as I do them ? I told them so, and they believed me—good, hey ! "

" You cannot have walked all the way ? "

" Walked !—when did wit walk ? No, Misser Eliot, not a step of it. Hooked a fishing canoe, and poled 'long shore some,—jumped into a waggon with a blind nigger fiddler and his wife, and rode some,—then up behind a cow-boy, and paid him in whistling some,—boarded market-carts some,—and musquashed some."

" And here you are, and now I must take care of you."

" Yes, Misser Eliot, depend on you now, pretty much like other folks—Kisel, hey ! depends on Providence when he can get nothing else to depend on."

" Thank Heaven," thought Eliot, " I have not to draw on my extempore sagacity. Now that I have the real Dromio, I shall get on without let or hinderance." He re-entered the house, encountered his landlady, and, emboldened by the presence of Kisel, laughed at the unnecessary suspicion that had been excited, ordered his horses, and having received his despatches and his countersigned passports from Sir Henry, he determined to profit by the moonlight, and immediately set forth on his return.

As they passed Mr. Linwood's house, Eliot paused for a moment, but there was no intimation from its silent walls ; and hoping and believing that his friend was safe within them, and breathing a prayer for the peerless creature who seemed to him, like a celestial spirit, to sanctify the dwelling that contained her, he spurred his horse as if he would have broken the chain that bound him to the spot—the chain already linking in with his existence, and destined never to be broken till that should be dissolved.

He proceeded some twenty or five-and-twenty miles without incident, when, as he passed a narrow road that intersected the highway, five horsemen turned from it into the main road. Kisel, with the instinct of cowardice, reined his horse close to his master. The men remained in the rear, talking together earnestly in low tones. Suddenly, two of them spurred their horses and came abreast of the forward party, the one beside Kisel, the other beside Eliot. There was, at best, impertinence in the movement, and it annoyed Eliot. It might mean something worse than impertinence. He placed his hand on the loaded pistol in his holster, and calmly awaited further demonstrations from his new companions. A cursory glance assured him they were questionable characters. They wore cloth caps, resembling those used by our own winter travellers, drawn close over the eyes, and having a sort of curtain that hid the neck, ears, and chin. The mouth and nose were the only visible features ; and though they were dimly seen by the star-light (the moon had set), they seemed to Eliot, with a little aid from imagination, to indicate brutal coarseness and vulgarity. They had on spencers of a dreadnought material, girded around them with a leathern strap.—" Good evening," said the man at Eliot's side.

Captain Lee made no reply ; but his squire, eager to accept a friendly overture, and always ready on the least hint to speak, replied, " Good evening to you, neighbour ; which way are you riding ? "

" After our horses' noses," replied the fellow, gruffly.

" Oh, that's the way we are travelling—so we may as well be friendly ; for in these times there's many a bird on the wing at night besides owls and bats—hey ?"

" Where are you from, fellow ?" asked the first speaker.

" From below."

" Where are you going ?"

" Above."

The man, not disposed to be silenced by Kisel's indefinite replies, repeated his first question to Eliot.

" The true answer is safest," thought Eliot, who was determined, if possible, to avoid a contest where the odds were five to one ; and he briefly communicated his destination and errand.

" Despatches !" replied the man, echoing Eliot. " Is that all you have about you ? I wish you well, then, to your journey's end—and that wish is worth something, I can tell you. Come, Pat, spur your horse—we've no time to be lagging here."

" I'm thinking, captain, we had better change horses with these gentlemen, and give them our spurs to boot ;" and suiting the action to the word, he seized Kisel's bridle, and ordered him to dismount. At the same instant his comrade-captain made a lunge at Eliot, as if for a corresponding seizure ; but Eliot perceived the movement in time to evade it. He roused the mettle of his horse with a word—the fine animal sprang forward—Eliot turned him short round, and presented his pistol to Kisel's antagonist, who let fall the bridle, and turned to defend himself.

" Now spur your horse and fear nothing, Kisel," cried his master.

Not to fear was impossible to Kisel ; but the first injunction he obeyed, even to the rowels of his spurs ; and he and his master soon distanced their pusuers, who, now partly incited by revenge, pursued the hopeless chase for two or three miles.

Soon after losing sight of these men, Eliot reached Gurdon Coit's. Coit was a farmer, who, on the borders of the river and on the neutral ground, kept a public-house as supplemental to his farm, which, in these troubled times, was roughly handled by friends and foes. Friends and foes we say : for though Coit observed, as beseemed a man of his present calling, a strict outward neutrality, in heart he was on his country's side ; as he often testified, with considerable risk to himself, by affording facilities to secret emissaries to the city, and by receiving into his house valuable supplies, that were run up from the city (where Washington had many secret trusty friends) for the use of the army at West Point.

Eliot stopped at Coit's, and announced his intention, received by a hurra from Kisel, of remaining there till day-light. Coit was roused from a nap in his chair by the entrance of his new guests. In reply to Eliot's request for refreshment and lodging, he said, " You see, captain," (he recognised Eliot, who had been at his house on his way down,) " my house is brimful. Cæsar, and Venus, and all the little niggers, sleep in the kitchen. My wife's sisters are here visiting, and they've got the best bed-room, and my wife and the gals the other ; for you know we must give the best to the women, poor creturs—so a plank here in the bar-room is the best sleeping privilege I can give you, and the barn to your man."

" Oh, Misser Eliot, I've got a trembling in my limbs to-night," interposed Kisel ; " don't send me away alone."

Eliot explained the cause of poor Kisel's trembling limbs ; and it was agreed that he should share his master's *sleeping privilege*. In answer to Eliot's communication, Coit said, " As sure as a gun, you've met the Skinners : and you're a lucky man to get out of their hands alive. They've been harrying up and down the country like so many wolves for the last three weeks, doing mischief wherever 'twas to be done,—nobody has escaped them but Madam Archer."

" Who is Madam Archer ?"

" I mistrust, captain, you a'n't much acquainted with the quality in York state, or you'd know Madam Archer of Beech-hill ; the widow lady with the blind twins. I believe the Lord has set a defence about her habitation ; for there she stays, with those helpless little people, and neither harm nor the fear of it come nigh her, though she has nothing of mankind under her roof except one old slave ; and them that are brought up slaves, you know, have neither sense nor pluck for difficult times."

Kisel interrupted the landlord's harangue to hint to his master that his fright had brought on a great appetite ; and Eliot, feeling the same effect, though not from precisely the same cause, requested his host to provide him some supper, while he and his man went to look after their horses ; a duty that he gratefully performed, rejoicing in the rustic education that made it light to him to perform services for the want of which he often saw the noble animals of his more daintily-bred brother officers suffering.

" Who are these, my bedfellows ?" he asked of Coit, a few moments after, as he sat discussing some fine bacon and brown bread, and handing slice after slice to Kisel, who, squatting on the hearth, received it like a petted dog from his hand. The subjects of his inquiry were two long fellows wrapped in blankets, and their heads on their knapsacks, stretched on the floor, and soundly sleeping.

" They are soldiers from above," replied Coit, in a whisper, " who have come here to receive some tea and sugar, and such kind of fancy articles, for the ladies at the Point."

" And who is this noisy person on the settle ?"

" He does snore like all natur'," replied Coit, laughing, and then continued in a lowered voice :— " I don't know who he is, though I can make a pretty good guess ; and if I guess right, he a'n't a person I should like to interfere with, and it's plain he don't choose to make himself known. He has a rough tongue, that does not seem like your born quality—he does not handle his victuals like them—but he has that solid way with him that shows he was born to command the best of you in such times as these, when, as you may say, we value a garment according to its strength, and not for the trimmings. No offence, captain !"

" None in the world to me, my good friend ; I am not myself one of those you call the born-quality."

" A'n't ! I declare ! then you've beat me—I thought I could always tell 'em." Coit drew his chair near to Eliot, and added, in an earnest tone, " The time is coming, captain, and that's what the country is fighting for; for we can't say but we are desperately worried with the English yoke; but the time is coming when one man that's no better than his neighbour won't wear stars on his coat, and another that's no worse a collar round his neck; when one won't be born with a silver spoon in his mouth, and another with a pewter spoon, but all will start fair, and the race will be to the best fellow."

"Hey! Misser Eliot," cried Kisel, in his wonted tone, when a ray of intelligence penetrated the mists that enveloped his brain.

His shrill voice awakened the sleeper on the settle, who, lifting up his shaggy head, asked what "all this cackling meant!" Then, seeming to recover his self-possession, he keenly surveyed Eliot and his man, covered his face with his bandana handkerchief, and again composed himself to sleep.

Eliot, after securing a "sleeping privilege" for Kisel, received from our friend Coit the best unoccupied blanket and pillow the house afforded; and giving his fellow-lodgers, in seamen's phrase, the best berth the room admitted, he was soon lost in the deep refreshing sleep compounded of youth, health, and a good conscience.

Our host was left to his own musings, which, as he fixed his eye on Eliot's fine face, marked with nature's aristocracy, were somewhat in the following strain:—"'Not of the born quality!'—hum—well, he has that that is quality in the eye of God, I guess. How he looked after his dumb beast, and this poor cretur here, that seems not to have the wit of a brute: he's had the bringing up of a gentleman, anyhow. I see it in his bearing, his speech, his voice. Well, I guess my children will live to see the day when the like of him will be the only gentlemen in the land. The Almighty must furnish the material, but the forming, polishing, and currency, must be the man's own doings; not his father's or grandfather's, or the Lord knows who."

While Coit pursues his meditations, destined soon to be roughly broken, we offer our readers some extracts from a letter which fortunately has fallen into our hands, to authenticate our veritable history. It was written by Mrs. Archer, of Beechhill, to her niece, Isabella Linwood.

"No, no, my dear Belle, I cannot remove to the city—it must not be; and I am sorry the question is again mooted. 'A woman, and naturally born to fears,' I may be; but because I have that inconvenient inheritance, I see no reason why I should cherish and augment it. Your imagination, which is rather an active agent, has magnified the terrors of the times; and it seems just now to be unduly excited by the monstrous tales circulated in the city, of the atrocities the Yankees have committed on the tories. I see in Rivington's Gazette, which you wrapped around the sugar-plums that you sent the children (thank you), various precious anecdotes of Yankee tigers and tory lambs, forsooth! that are just about as true as the tales of giants and ogres with which your childhood was edified. The Yankees are a civilised race, and never, God bless them! commit gratuitous cruelties! If they still 'see it to be duty' (to quote their own Puritan phrase), they will cling to this contest till they have driven the remnant

of your Israel, Belle, every tory and Englishman, from the land; but they will commit no episodical murders; it is only the ignorant man that is unnecessarily cruel. They are an instructed, kindhearted, Christian people; and of this there will be abundant proof while the present war is remembered. Remember, Belle, these people have unadulterated English blood in their veins, which to you should be a prevailing argument in their favour; and, believe me, they have a fair portion of the spirit of their freedom-loving and all-daring ancestors. Our English mother, God bless her, too, should have known better than to trammel, scold, and try to whip her sons into obedience, when they had come to man's estate, and were fit to manage their own household. Thank Heaven, I have outlived the prejudices against the people of New England, which my father transmitted to his children. 'There they come,' he used to say, when he saw these busy people driving into the manor; 'every snow brings them, and, d—n them, every thaw, too.'

"What a pander to ignorance and malignity is this same prejudice, Belle! How it disturbs the sweet accords of nature, sacrilegiously severs the bonds by which God has united man to man, and breaks the human family into parties and sects! How it clouds the intellect and infects the heart with its earth-born vapours; so that the Englishman counts it virtue to scorn the American, and the *true* American cherishes a hatred of the Englishman! Our generous friends in the south look with contempt on the provident frugal sons of the Puritans; and they, blinded in their turn, can see nothing but the swollen pride of slave-owners and hard-heartedness of slave-drivers in their brethren of the south. Even you, dear Belle, have not escaped this *atmospheric* influence. After a general denunciation of the rebels, as you term the country's troops, you say, in the letter now before me, 'of course you have nothing to fear from the British regulars;' and I reply, like the poor brute in the fable, 'Heaven save me from my friends!' The British soldiers are aliens to the soil; they have neither 'built houses nor tilled lands' here; and they cannot have the same kindly and home feeling that a native extends to the denizens of his own land. Besides, they are, for the most part, trained to the inhuman trade of war; and though I have all due respect for English blood, and know many of their officers to be most amiable and accomplished men, I never see a detachment of their troops, with their colours flying (and such often pass within sight of us), without a sudden coldness creeping over me. Then there are the jagers and other mercenaries that our friends have brought over to fight out this family quarrel—is this right, Belle! you will suspect me of having turned whig—well, keep your suspicion to yourselves. The truth is, that, living isolated as I do, I have a fairer point of view than you, surrounded as you are by British officers and tories devoted to the royal cause, and to you, my beautiful niece, their elected sovereign.

"My only substantial fear, after all, is of the Cowboys and Skinners, more especially the last, who have done some desperate deeds in my neighbourhood. I have taken care to have it well known that I have sent all my plate and valuables to the city, and I hope and believe they will not pay me a visit. Should they, however, a widow and two blind children have little to dread from creatures who are made in the image of God, defaced as that image may be. Defenceless creatures have a fortress in every human heart. No, I repeat it, I cannot go to the city. You say I am afraid of the shackles of city life! I confess, that with my taste for freedom, and my long indulgence in it, they would be galling to me. I could, however, bear them without wincing to be near you; but my children, Belle—my *blind* children! my paramount duty is to them, and is prescribed and absolute. In the city they are continually reminded of their privation, and the kinder their friends the more manifold are the evidences of it; there they feel that they are merely objects of compassion, supernumeraries in the human family, who can only receive, not give. Here they have motives to exertion, dependants on their care. Their fruits and flowers, doves, rabbits, chickens, ducks, dogs, and kittens, live and thrive by them. Nature is to them a perpetual study and delight. I have just been walking with them over the hill beyond my house. You remember the hill is fringed with beech-trees, and crowned by their superior forest brethren, the old tory oak, the legitimate sovereign by the grace of God; the courtier elm, (albeit American!) that bows its graceful limbs to every breeze; the republican maple, that resists all hostility; and the evergreen pine, a loyalist—is it, Belle! well, be it so; it always wears the same coat, but they say its heart is not the soundest!—Pardon me, we fall so naturally into political allusions in these times.

"My children have learned so accurately to discriminate sounds, that, as we walked over the hill, they made me observe the variations of sound when the breezes whispered among the light beech leaves, when they stole through the dense masses of the maple foliage, fluttered over the pendent stems of the elm, rustled along the polished oak leaves, and passed in soft musical sighs, like the lowest breath of the Æolian harp, over the bristled pines. Do you remember the lively little stream that dashes around the rear of this hill, and winding quietly through the meadow at its base, steals into the Hudson? They, in their rambles, unattended and fearless, have worn a footpath along the margin of this stream, and wherever there is a mossy rock or fallen trunk of a tree, they may be seen tying up wild flowers, or the arm of each around the other, singing hymns and songs. I have seen men with hard features and rough hands arrested by the sound of their voices, and, as they listened, the tears trickling down their weather-beaten faces. Can I fear for them, Belle! They both delight in gardening; they love none but flowers of sweet odour; no unperfumed flower, however beautiful, is tolerated; but the lawn, the borders of the walks, all their shady haunts, are enamelled with mignonette, violets, lilies of the valley, carnations, clove-pinks, and every sweet-breathed flower. The magnificent view of the Hudson from the piazza they cannot see; but they have wreathed the pillars with honeysuckles and sweetbriers, and there they sit and enjoy the south-west breezes, the chief luxury of our climate. Could I pen them up in a city, where they will never walk into the fresh air but to be a spectacle, and where they

must be utterly deprived of the ministration of nature through which God communes with their spirits? I am sure you will acquiesce in my decision, my dear Isabella. You need not try to convince your father of my rationality; the reasonableness of any woman is a contradiction in terms to him. Whatever may happen, your mother will not reproach me; she will only say again what she has so often said before, ' that she expected it, poor sister Mary was always so odd.' This letter is all about myself. I have anxieties too about you, but for the present I keep to myself. The bright empyrean of hope is for youth to soar in, and your element shall not be invaded by croakings from the bogs of experience.

" Truly yours,
" MARY ARCHER."

The same conveyance that transported this letter, so full of resolution and trust, to Isabella, carried her information of the events related in the next chapter.

———◆———

CHAPTER XVII.

We are men, my liege.
Ay, in the catalogue ye go for men.

SURPRISE has sometimes been expressed by our English friends who have travelled among us, that the Americans should cherish such lively recollections of the war that achieved their independence, when their countrymen had almost forgotten that such a contest ever existed. They seem to have forgotten, too, that while their part was enacted by soldiers by profession and foreign mercenaries, our battle was fought by our fathers, sons, and brothers; that while the scene of action was three thousand miles from them, it was in our *home-lots* and at our fire-sides; and above all, that while they fought for the preservation of colonial possession, at best a doubtful good, we were contending for national independence—for the right and power to make the last and best experiment of popular government.

Such circumstances as it falls to our lot now to relate are not easily forgotten; and such, or similar, occurred in some of the happiest homes of our land.

Mrs. Archer was quietly sleeping with her children, when she was awakened by unusual sounds in the room below her; and immediately her maid, who slept in the adjoining apartment, rushed in, crying out, " that the house was full of men—she heard them on the stairs, in the parlour, hall, everywhere!"

Mrs. Archer sprang from the bed, threw on her dressing-gown, bade the girl be quiet, and beware of frightening the children; and then, as they, startled by the noise, raised their heads from their pillows, she told them in a calm and decidedly cheerful voice, that there were men in the house, who she believed had come to rob it: but that they would neither do harm to them, nor to her. She then ordered her maid to light the candles on the dressing-table, and again reassuring her trembling children, who had meanwhile crept to her side, she awaited the fearful visiters, whose footsteps she heard on the staircase.

A fierce-looking wretch burst into the apartment. The spectacle of the mother and her children arrested him, and he involuntarily doffed his cap. It was a moment for a painter, if he could calmly have surveyed the scene. The maid had shrunk behind her mistress's chair, and kneeling there, had grasped her gown with both hands, as if there were safety in the touch. Poor little Lizzy's face was hidden in her mother's bosom, and her fair silken curls hung over her mother's dark dressing-gown. Ned, at the sound of the opening door, turned his sightless eyeballs towards the villain. There was something manly and defying in his air and erect attitude, something protecting in the expression of his arm as he laid it over his sister; while the clinging of his other arm around his mother's neck, indicated the defencelessness of childhood, and his utter helplessness. Mrs. Archer had thrown aside her nightcap ; her hair was twisted up in a sort of Madonna style ; but not of the tame Madonna cast was her fine, spirited countenance, which blended the majesty of the ideal Minerva with the warmth and tenderness of the woman and mother.

The marauder, on entering, paid her, as we have said, an instinctive homage ; but immediately recovering his accustomed insolence, he replied to her calm demand, of " What is your purpose ?" " To get what we can, and keep what we get—my name is Hewson, which, if you've heard it, will be a warrant to you that I sha'n't do my work by halves."

The name of the Skinner was too notorious not to have been heard by Mrs. Archer. Her blood ran cold ; but she replied, without faltering, " Proceed to your work ; the house is open to you, not a lock in your way. Abby, give him my purse off the dressing-table—there is all the money I have by me—now leave my room, I pray you."

" Softly, mistress—catch old birds with chaff. First surrender your watch, plate, and jewels, which I take to be in this very room that you are so choice of."

" My watch, plate, and jewels, are in New York."

" The d—l they are !" Then emptying out and counting the gold and silver the purse contained, " This will never do," he said—" this will not pay the reckoning—live and let live—every one to his trade." He then proceeded, without further ceremony, to rip open beds and mattresses ; emptied the contents of every box, trunk, and drawer ; explored every corner and recess as adroitly as a trained dog would unearth his game, and seized on such light articles as attracted his eye, grumbling and swearing all the time at being cheated and out-manœuvred by a woman ; for in this light he seemed to view the measures Mrs. Archer had taken to secure her valuables.

In this humour he rejoined his comrades in the dining-room ; who he found, with the exception of a few dozen silver spoons and forks, had had an equally bootless search, and were now regaling themselves with cold meats, &c., from the pantry.

" Hey, boys—always after the provender before you've done your work."

" There's no work to be done, captain—we can't carry off chairs and tables—so what's the use of bothering ? we've done our best, and nobody can do better."

" Your best—maybe, Pat—but your and my best are two. We shall have whigs, tories, and reg'lars at our heels for this flash in the pan." He strode up and down the room, kicking out of his way whatever obstacle was in it, and muttering to himself a plan he was revolving : " Madam must turn out the shiners," he concluded aloud.

" Ay, captain—but how's the bird that won't sing to be made to sing ?—she is a cunning old one, I'm thinking."

" Old !—Time has never made a track on her yet—cunning she may be, but I don't believe she lied to me—she seems high as the stars above that—but if she has not got the money, boys, she can get it—I'll make her, too—I'll wager your soul on that, Pat."

" Wager your own, honey, that's forfeit to the devil long ago."

" A little more time was wasted in similar retorts, well shotted, in their own phrase, with oaths, and washed down with plentiful draughts of wine, when the captain returned to Mrs. Archer's apartment. " I say, mistress," he began, his flushed face and thickened voice indicating she had fresh cause for alarm, " I say, we can't be choused—so if you want to save what's choicer than money," he shook his fist with a tiger-like expression at the children, " you must have two hundred guineas put under ground for me, on the north side of the big oak, at the bridge, and that before Saturday night ; nobody to know it but you —no living soul but you and that gal there—no false play : remember ! Come, strike while the iron's hot, or we'll say three hundred."

Mrs. Archer reflected for a moment. She would have given a bond for any sum by which she could relieve herself of the presence of the outlaws. They had already produced such an effect on little Lizzy, a timid, susceptible creature, that she expected every moment to see her falling into convulsions ; and with this dread each moment seemed an hour. She replied, that the money should, without fail, be placed in the appointed spot.

" That is not quite all, madam ; I must have security. I know how the like of you look on promises made to the like of me. I got a rope good as round my neck by trusting to them once, and no thanks to them that I slipped it. I'll clinch the nail this time—I'll have security."

" What security ?" demanded Mrs. Archer, the colour for the first time forsaking her cheeks and lips ; for by the ruffian's glance, and a significant up and down motion of his head, she guessed his purpose.

" A pawn—I must have a pawn—one of them young ones. You need not screech and hold on so, you little fools. If you behave, I'll not hurt a hair of your head. The minute I handle the money, you shall have 'em back ; but as sure as my name's Sam Hewson, I'll make 'em a dead carcass if you play me false."

" You shall not touch my children—anything else—ask all—take all—anything but my children."

" Take all !—ay, that we shall—all we can take ; and as to asking, we mean to make sure of what we ask—'a bird in the hand,' mistress."

"Oh, take my word, my oath—spare my children!"

"Words are breath, and oaths breath peppered. Your children are your life ; and, one of them in our hands, our secret is as safe with you as with us—we've no time to chaffer—make one of them ready."

"Oh, mother !—mother !" shrieked Lizzy, clinging round her mother's waist.

"Hush, Lizzy—I'll go," said Edward.

"Neither shall go, my children—they shall take my life first."

The outlaw had advanced with the intention of seizing one of them ; but, awed by the resolution of the mother, or perhaps touched by the generosity of the boy, he paused and retreated, muttering to himself " It's a rough job—Pat shall do it." He once more left the apartment and returned to his comrades.

A sudden thought occurred to Mrs. Archer ; a faint hope dawned upon her. "Bring me the horn from the hall-table," she said to her servant. The girl attempted to obey, but her limbs sunk under. Mrs. Archer disengaged herself from the children, ran down the stairs, returned with the horn, threw open her window, and blew three pealing blasts. The outlaws were engaged in packing their spoil.

"Ha !" exclaimed Hewson, "it rings well—again—again. Never mind ; you'll wake nothing, mistress, but the dogs, cocks, and owls. Hear how they're at it ;—'bow—wow—wow—the beggars are come to town,'—ha, ha—well done. But boys, I say, we'd best be off soon. Pat, you know," (he had already communicated his plan to Pat,) " bring down one of them young ones."

Pat went—he lingered. "Come, boys, hurry," cried Hewson, who now began to apprehend the possibility of a response to Mrs. Archer's summons : " what the d—l ails that fellow !"—he went to the staircase and called. Pat appeared, but without the child, and looking as a wild beast might, subdued by a charm. "They're *blind*, captain—both *blind* !" he said. "I can't touch them—by all that's holy I can't—there's not strength in my arm to hold the sightless things—the one nor the t'other of 'em. So do it yourself, captain—I can't, and there's an end on't."

Hewson hesitated. The image of the mother and her blind children daunted even his fierce spirit. An expedient occurred to him :—"A sure way," he thought, "of drowning feelings." In ransacking the pantry he had seen a flask of brandy, and then prudently concealed it from his men. He now brought it forth, and passed it round and round. It soon began its natural work : consumed in its infernal fires all intellectual power, natural affection, domestic and pitiful emotion ; put out the light of Heaven, and roused the brute passions of the men.

Hewson saw the potion working ; their "human countenances change to brutish form." "It's a d—d shame,—a'n't it, boys," said he, "for this tory madam to balk us !—we shall have a hurra after us for this frolic, and nothing to show—we might as well have robbed a farmhouse, and who would have cared !"

"We'll tache her better, captain," said Pat ;

"we'll make an example of her, as the judges say in Ireland when they hang the lads. I'll give her a blow over the head, if you say so, handy like—or wring the chickens' necks—it's asy done."

"Pshaw, Pat—it's only your asses of judges that think examples of any use. If we hook one of the chickens, you know, Pat, she'll be glad to buy it back with the yellow shiners, boy, that's lodged safe in York—fifty a piece—share and share alike—my turn is it !—here's to you, boys—a short life and a merry one : I've charged 'em up to the mark," thought he ; and in raising the flask to his lips, it slipped through his hands and was broken to fragments. "Ah, my men ! there's a sign for us—we may have a worse slip than that ' 'tween the cup and the lip : ' so let's be off—come, Pat."

"Shall I fetch 'em both, captain !"

"No, no—one is as good as a thousand. But stay, Pat. Drunk as they are," thought Hewson, "I'll not trust them in the sound of the mother's screeches. First, Pat, let's have all ready for a start—tie up your bags, boys, come."

The men's brains were so clouded, that it seemed to Hewson they were an eternity in loading their beasts with their booty. Delay after delay occurred ; but finally all was ready, and he gave the signal to Pat.

Pat now obeyed to the letter. He mounted the stairs, sprang like a tiger on his prey, and returned with Lizzy, already an unconscious burden, in his arms. One piercing shriek Hewson heard proceeding from Mrs. Archer's apartment, but not another sound. It occurred to him that Pat might have committed the murder he volunteered ; and exclaiming, "The blundering Irish rascal has kicked the pail over !" he once more ascended the stairs to assure himself of the cause of the ominous silence. Edward was in the adjoining apartment when Lizzy was wrested from her mother's arms. He was recalled by Mrs. Archer's scream ; and when Hewson reached the apartment, he found Mrs. Archer lying senseless across the threshold of the door, and Edward groping around, and calling, " Mother !—Lizzy !—where are you ! —do speak, mother ! "

A moment after, Mrs. Archer felt her boy's arms around her neck. She returned to a consciousness of her condition, and heard the trampling of the outlaws' horses as they receded from her dwelling.

CHAPTER XVIII.

——————— Good vent'rous youth,
I love thy courage yet, and bold emprise.

"CAPTAIN !—Captain Lee ! don't you hear that horn !" said Gurdon Coit, shaking our soundly-sleeping friend, Eliot.

"Yes, thank you, I hear it ; it's daylight, is it !"

"No, no ; but there's something to pay up at Madam Archer's. Those devils you met on the road, I doubt, are there—the lights have been glancing about her rooms this hour, and now they've blown the horn—there's mischief, depend on't."

"Why in the name of Heaven did not you wake

me sooner?" exclaimed Eliot. Rouse up these fellows—wake that snoring wretch on the settle, and we'll to her aid instantly."

The offensive snoring ceased as Coit whispered, "No, don't wake him—edge-tools, you know." He then proceeded to wake the men from West Point, who were sleeping on the floor. Eliot, as they lifted their heads, recognised them—the one a common soldier, the other a certain Ensign Tooler— a man who had the most disagreeable modification of Yankee character; knowingness overlaid with conceit, and all the self-preserving virtues concentrated in selfishness, as bad liquor is distilled from wholesome grain. "Tooler, is that you?" exclaimed Eliot—"and you, Mason? up instantly!" and he explained the occasion for their prompt service.

"And who is this Madam Archer?" asked Tooler, composedly resting his elbow on the floor.

"She is a woman in need of our protection. This is enough for us to know," replied Eliot, discreetly evading more explicit information.

"She lives in the big house on the hill, don't she?"

"Yes, yes."

"Then I guess we may as well leave her to her luck, for she belongs to the tory side."

"Good Heavens, Tooler!—do you hesitate?—Mason, go with me, if you have the soul of a man."

"Lie still, Mason, we're under orders,—Captain Lee must answer for himself. It's none of our business if he's a mind to go off fighting windmills; but duty is duty, and we'll keep to the straight and narrow path."

"Cowardly, canting wretch!" exclaimed Eliot.

"I'm no coward, Captain Eliot Lee; and if Coit will say that Madam Archer is on our side, and you'll undertake to answer to General Washington for all consequences, I'll not hinder Mason's joining you.":

The terms were impracticable. There was no time to be lost: "You will go with me, Coit?" said Eliot.

"Why, Captain Lee, it's a venturesome business."

"Yes or no, Coit! not an instant's delay."

"I'll go, Captain Lee,—I'm not a brute."

Mason did not quite relish the consciousness of acting like a brute, and he half rose, balancing in his mind the shame of remaining, against the risk of disobeying his ensign's orders. "Lie still, Mason," said Tooler; "mind me, and you're safe—I'll take care of number one."

The person on the settle now sprang up and poured a torrent of vituperative oaths and invectives on Tooler. Tooler looked up with the abject expression of a barking cur when he hears his master's voice. "Why, gen'ral," said he, "if I had known———"

"Don't gen'ral me!—don't defile my name with your lips! A pretty fellow you, to prate of duty and orders in the very face of the orders of the Almighty commander-in-chief, to remember the widows and fatherless in their affliction. I always mistrust your fellows that cant about duty. They'll surrender the post at the first go-off, and then expect conscience to let them march out with the honours of war."

"I'm ready to go, sir,—ready and willing, if you say so."

"No, by George!—I'd rather fight single-handed with fifty Skinners, than have one such cowardly devil as you at my side." All this was said while "the gen'ral" was putting on his coat and hat, and arming himself; "are we ready, Captain Lee?" he concluded.

"Perfectly," replied Eliot, wondering who this sturdy authoritative auxiliary might be, but not venturing to ask, as he thought the "gen'ral" had implied his wish to remain incognito, and really not caring at this moment whose arm it was, provided it was raised in Mrs. Archer's defence. After one keen survey of the "gen'ral's" person, he concluded, "I never have seen him." He had not. Once seen, that frank, fearless countenance was never to be forgotten; neither could one well forget the broad, brawny, working-day frame that sustained it, or the peculiar limp (caused by one leg being shorter than the other), the only imperfection and marring of the figure of our rustic Hercules.

In an instant they were mounted, and in five minutes more, the distance not much exceeding half-a-mile, they were entering Mrs. Archer's hall. An ominous silence reigned there. The house was filled with smoke, through which the lighted candles, left by Hewson's crew, faintly glimmered, and exposed the relics of their feast, with other marks of their foray. A bright light shone through the crevices of the pantry door. Coit opened it, and immediately the flames of a fire which had been communicated (whether intentionally, was never ascertained) to a chest of linen, burst forth. "Good Heaven! where are the family?" exclaimed Eliot and his companion in a breath.

"Follow me," cried Coit, leading the way to Mrs. Archer's apartment, and shouting "Fire!" His screams were answered by the female servants, who now rushed from their mistress's apartment. "Where's your lady?" demanded "the general." They were too much bewildered to reply, and both he and Eliot followed Coit's lead, and all three paused at the threshold of Mrs. Archer's door, paralysed by the spectacle of the mother, sitting perfectly motionless with her boy in her arms, and looking like a statue of despair. The general was the first to recover his voice. "Lord of Heaven, madam!" he exclaimed, "your house is on fire!"

She made no reply whatever. She seemed not even to hear him. "Where is the little girl?" asked Coit.

Mrs. Archer's face became slightly convulsed. Her boy sprang from her arms at the sound of a familiar voice. "Oh! Mr. Coit," he cried, "they've taken off Lizzy!"

The crackling of the advancing flames, and the pouring in of volumes of smoke, prevented any farther explanation at the moment. The instinct of self-preservation, awakened in some degree, renerved Mrs. Archer; and, half sustained by Eliot's arm, she and her boy were conducted to an office detached from the house, and so far removed from it as to be in no danger from the conflagration. In the mean time the general had ascertained from the servants all that could be learned of the direction the Skinners had taken, and that they were not more than fifteen minutes in advance of them.

He and Coit had remounted their horses, and he was hallooing to Eliot to join them. "Come, young man," he cried, "let's do what's to be done at once, and cry afterwards, if cry we must."

"Recover her!" said Mrs. Archer, repeating the last words of Eliot's attempt to revive her hopes; "her lifeless body you may—God grant it!"

She paused, and shuddered. She still felt the marble touch of Lizzy's cheek—still saw her head and limbs drop as the ruffian seized her.

Eliot understood her. "My dear madam," he said, "she has fainted from terror, nothing more; she will be well again when she feels your arm around her. Take courage, I beseech you."

It is not in the heart of woman to resist such inspiring sympathy as was expressed in Eliot's face and voice. If Mrs. Archer did not hope, there was something better than despair in the feeling of intense expectation that concentrated all sensation. She seemed unconscious of the flames that were devouring her house. She did not hear the boyish exclamations with which Edward, as he heard the falling rafters and tumbling chimneys, interspersed his sobs for poor Lizzy; nor the clamorous cryings of the servants, which would break out afresh as they remembered some favourite article of property consuming in the flames.

A few yards from Mrs. Archer's house, a road diverged from that which our pursuers had taken They halted for a moment, when Coit, who was familiar with the localities of the vicinity, advised to take the upper road. "They both," he said, "came out in one at a distance of about three miles. They would thus avoid giving the forward party any warning of their approach, and their horses being the freshest and fleetest, they might possibly arrive at the junction of the roads first, and surprise the Skinners from an ambush."

"Lucky for us that there is another road," replied the general, as, conforming to Coit's suggestion, they turned into it. "The rascals we're after are foxes, and would be sure to escape if they heard the hounds behind them."

"I should think, from my observation of their horses," replied Eliot, "they have small chance of escaping us in a long pursuit."

"There I think you mistake. They get their jades for no *vartu* under heaven but running away; and I've heard of their distancing horses that looked equal to mine; speed a'n't Charlie's forte; though," he added, in a half-audible voice, and patting his beast lovingly, "you've done a feat at it once, Charlie. They know all the holes and hiding-places in the country," he continued, "and I have heard of their disappearing as suddenly as if the ground had opened and swallowed them up. I wish it would—the *varmin!*"

"Had we not best try the mettle of our horses!" asked Eliot, who felt as if his companions were taking the matter too coolly.

"If you please."

The general put up his Bucephalus to his utmost speed; but in spite of the feat his master boasted, he seemed to have been selected for other virtues than fleetness, for both Eliot and Coit soon passed him, and so far outrode him as

not to be able to discern the outline of the rider's figure when they reached the junction of the roads where they hoped to intercept the Skinners. They had perceived the faintest streak of dawn, while they could see the eastern horizon and the morning star trembling and glittering above it. Now they entered a little wood of thick-set pines and hemlocks, and the darkness of midnight seemed to thicken around them.

"Hark!" cried Eliot, suddenly halting; "don't you hear the trampling of horses?"

"Yes," replied Coit, "there is a bridge just ahead; let us secure a position as near it as possible." They moved on, and after advancing a few yards, again halted, still remaining under cover of the wood. "We are within twenty feet of the other road," resumed Coit; "it runs along just parallel to where we stand, and a few feet below us; there is a small stream of water on the other side of the pines, which we pass over by the bridge as we fall into the other road; tho rub will be to get on to the bridge before they see us. I wish the general would come up!"

"We must not wait for him, Coit."

"Not wait for him!" replied Coit, whose valour was at least tempered by discretion; "we are but two to five, and they such devils!"

"We have heaven on our side—we must not wait a breath—we *must* intercept them. Follow me when I give the spurs to my horse."

"Oh, if he would but come up!" thought Coit; "this young man is as brave as a lion, but the general *is* a lion!"

The Skinners had now approached so near to our friends that they fancied they heard the hard breathing of their horses. They halted at the brook, and Eliot distinctly heard Hewson say to Pat, "Don't she come to yet?"

"I can't just say—once or twice she opened her sightless eyes like, and she gasped, but she's corpse-cold; and captain, I say, I don't like the feel of her; I am afeard I shall drop her, there's such a wonderful weight in her little body."

"You cowardly fool!"

"By the soul of my mother it's true—try once the lift of her!"

"Pshaw! I've twice her weight in this bundle before me. Hold up her head while I dash some water in her face; they say the breath will go entirely if you let it stop too long. Hewson then dismounted, took from his pocket a small silver cup he had abstracted from Mrs. Archer's pantry, and was stooping to fill it, when he was arrested by the appearance of his pursuers.

"Now is our time!" cried Eliot, urging his horse down the descent that led to the bridge. There the animal instinctively stopped. The bridge was old, the rotten planks had given way; and as destruction, not reparation, was the natural work of those troubled times, the bridge had been suffered to remain impassable. Eliot looked up and down the stream; it was fordable, but the banks, though not high, were precipitous and ragged. Eliot measured the gap in the bridge accurately with his eye: "My horse can leap it," was his conclusion, and he gave him voice, whip, and spur. The animal, as if he felt the inspiration of his master's purpose, made a generous effort and passed the vacant space. Eliot did not look back to see if he were followed.

He did not heed Coit's exclamation, "You're lost!" nor did he hear the general, who, on arriving at the bridge, cried, "God help you, my boy!—I can't—my beast can't do it with my weight on him—follow me, Coit," and he turned to retrace his steps to a point where, as he had marked in stopping to water his horse, the stream was passable.

Eliot was conscious of but one thought, one hope, one purpose—to rescue the prey from the villains. He had an indistinct impression that their numbers were not complete. He aimed his pistol at Patrick's head—the bullet sped—not a sound escaped the poor wretch. He raised himself upright in his stirrups, and fell over the side of the horse, dragging the child with him.

At this moment two horsemen passed between Eliot and Pat, and one of them, dropping his bridle and stretching out his arms, screamed "Misser Eliot—oh, Misser Eliot!"

It was poor Kisel, but vain was his appeal. One of the men smartly lashed Kisel's horse:—Linwood's spirited grey darted forward as if he had been starting on a race-course; and Kisel was fain to cling to him by holding fast to his mane, so strong is instinct; though if he had deliberately chosen between death and separation from his master, he certainly would have chosen the former.

Meanwhile Hewson, springing forward like a cat, and disengaging the child from Pat's death-grasp, cried, "Fire on him, boys!—beat him down!" and remounted his horse, intending to pass Eliot, aware that his policy was to get off before the attacking party should, as he anticipated, be reinforced. Eliot prevented this movement by placing himself before him, drawing his sword, and putting Hewson to the defence.

Hewson felt himself shackled by the child, he was casting her off, when, changing his purpose, he placed her as a shield before his person, and again ordered his men to fire. They had been ridding themselves of the spoils that encumbered them, and now obeyed. Both missed their mark.

"D——n your luck, boys!" cried Hewson, who was turning his horse to the right and left to avoid a side stroke from Eliot, "out with your knives—cut him down!"

To defend himself and prevent Hewson from passing him, was now all that Eliot attempted; but this he did with coolness and consummate adroitness, till his horse received a wound in his throat that was aimed at his master, and fell dead under him.

"That's it, boys!" screamed Hewson, "finish him and follow me." But before the words had well passed his lips, a bullet fired from behind penetrated his spine. "I am a dead man!" he groaned.

His men saw him reeling; they saw Eliot's auxiliaries close upon them; and without waiting to take advantage of his defenceless condition, they fled, and left their comrade-captain to his fate.

The general was instantly beside Eliot. Coit received the child from the ruffian's relaxed hold. "Oh, help me!" he supplicated; "for the love of God, help me!"

"Poor little one," said Coit, laying Lizzy's cheek gently to his, "she's gone."

"Oh, I have not killed her! I did not mean she should be harmed—I swear I did not," continued Hewson. "Oh, help me! I'll give you gold, watches, silver, and jewels—I'll give them all to you."

"You are wounded, my dear boy, you are covered with blood," said the general to Eliot, as he succeeded in disengaging him from the superincumbent burden of his horse.

"It's nothing, sir; is the child living?"

"Nothing! bless your soul, the blood is dripping down here like rain." While he was drawing off Eliot's coat-sleeve, and stanching his wound, Hewson continued his abject cries.

"Oh, gentlemen," he said, "take pity on me; my life is going—I'll give you heaps of gold—it's buried in—in—in——" His utterance failed him.

"Can nothing be done for the poor creature?" said Eliot, turning to Hewson, after having bent over Lizzy, lifted her lifeless hand, and again mournfully dropped it.

"We will see," replied the general, "though it seems to me, my friend, you are in no case to look after another; and this car'on is not worth looking after; but come, we'll strip him and examine his wound—life is life—and he's asked for mercy, what we must all ask for sooner or later. Ah," he continued, after looking at the wound, "he's called to the general muster—poorly equipped to answer the roll. But come, friends—there's no use in staying here—there's no substitute in this warfare—every man must answer for himself."

"Oh," groaned the dying wretch, "don't leave me alone."

"'Tis a solitary business to die alone," said Coit, looking compassionately at Hewson as he writhed on the turf.

"It is so, Coit; but he that has broken all bonds in life can expect nothing better than to die like a dog, and go to the devil at last. I must be back at my post, you at yours, and our young friend on his way to the camp, if he is able. General Washington a'n't fond of his envoys striking out of the highway when they are out on duty. There's no use—there's no use," he continued to Eliot, who had kneeled beside the dying man, and was whispering such counsel as a compassionate being would naturally administer to a man in his extremity.

"Repent!" cried Hewson, grasping Eliot's arm as he was about to rise; "repent!—what's that! Mercy, mercy—Oh, it's all dark; I can't see you. Don't hold that dead child so close to me!—take it away! Mercy, is there!—speak louder—I can't hear you—oh, I can't feel you! Mercy! mercy!"

"He's done—the poor cowardly rascal," said the general, who, inured to the spectacle of death, felt no emotion excited by the contortions of animal suffering, and who, deeming cowardice the proper concomitant of crime, heard without any painful compassion those cries of the wretched culprit, as he passed the threshold to eternal justice, which contracted Eliot's brow, and sent a shuddering through his frame.

"There's something to feel for," said the general, pointing to Eliot's prostrate horse; "if ever I cried, I should cry to see a *spereted*, gentle beast like that cut off by such villanous hands."

"Poor Rover!" thought Eliot, as he loosed his girth, and removed the bits from his mouth, "how Sam and Hal will cry, poor fellows, when they hear of your fate! Ah, I could have wished you a longer life and a more glorious end: but you have done well your appointed tasks, and they are finished. Would to God it were thus with that wretch, my fellow-creature!"

"You're finding this rather a tough job, I'm thinking," said the general, stooping to assist Eliot; "our horses, especially in these times, are friends; and it's what Coit would call a solitary business to have to mount into that rogue's seat. But see how patiently the beast stands by his master, and how he looks at him! Do you believe," he added, in a lowered voice, "that the souls of these noble *critters*, that have thought, affection, memory—all that we have, save speech will perish; and that low villain's live for ever! —I don't."

Eliot only smiled in reply; but he secretly wondered who this strange being should be, full of generous feeling and bold speculation, who had the air of accustomed authority, and the voice and accent indicating rustic education. It was evident he meant to maintain his incognito; for when they arrived at the road which, diverging from that they were in, led more directly to Coit's (the same road that had proved fatal to poor Kisel), he said, "that he must take the shortest cut; and that if Eliot felt equal to carrying the poor child the distance that remained, he should be particularly glad, as Coit's attendance was important to him."

Eliot would far rather have been disabled than to have witnessed the mother's last faint hope extinguished; but he was not, and he received the child from Coit, who had carried her as tenderly as if she had been still a conscious, feeling, and suffering being.

Coit charged Eliot with many respectful messages to Mrs. Archer; such as, that his house was at her disposal—he would prepare it for the funeral, or see that she and her family were safely conveyed to a British frigate which lay below, in case she preferred, as he supposed she would, laying her child in the family vault of Trinity Church. Eliot remembered the messages, but he delivered them as his discretion dictated.

As he approached Mrs. Archer's grounds, he inferred from the diminished light that the flames had nearly done their work; and when he issued from the thick wood that skirted her estate, he saw in the smouldering ruins all that was left of her hospitable and happy mansion. "Ah," thought he, "a fit home for this lifeless little body!"

He turned towards the office where he had left the mother. She was awaiting him at the door. It seemed to her that she had lived a thousand years in the hour of his absence. She asked no questions—a single glance at the still, colourless figure of her child had sufficed. She uttered no sound, but, stretching forth her arms, received her, and sunk down on the door-step, pressing her close to her bosom.

Edward had sprung 'to the door at the first sound of the horse's hoofs. He understood his mother's silence. He heard the servants whispering, in suppressed voices, "She is dead!"

He placed his hand on Lizzy's cheek: at first he recoiled at the touch; and then again drawing closer, he sat down by his mother, and dropped his head on Lizzy's bosom, crying out, "I wish I were dead too!" His bursts of grief were frightful. The servants endeavoured to soothe him—he did not hear them. Her mother laid her face to his, and the touch of her cheek, after a few moments, tranquillised him. He became quiet; then suddenly lifting his head, he shrieked—"Her heart beats, mother! her heart beats! Lay your hand there. Do you not feel it! It does, it does, mother; I feel it, and hear it too!"

Eliot had dismounted from his horse, and stood with folded arms, watching with the deep sympathy of his affectionate nature the progress of this family tragedy, while he awaited a moment when he might offer such services as Mrs. Archer needed. He thought it possible that the sharpened senses of the blind boy had detected a pulsation not perceptible to senses less acute. He inquired of the servants for salts, brandy, vinegar—any of the ordinary stimulants; nothing had been saved—nothing was left but the elements of fire and water. These suggested to his quick mind the only and very best expedient. In five minutes a warm bath was prepared, and the child immersed in it. Mrs. Archer was re-nerved when she saw others acting from a hope she scarcely dared admit. "Station yourself here, my dear madam," said Eliot; "there, put your arm in the place of mine—let your little boy go on the other side and take her hand—let her first conscious sensation be of the touch most familiar and dear to her—let the first sounds she hears be your voices—nothing must be strange to her. I do believe this is merely the overpowering effect of terror; I am sure she has suffered no violence. Put your hand again on her bosom, my dear little fellow. Do you feel the beats now!"

"Oh yes, sir! stronger and quicker than before."

"I believe you are right; but be cautious, I entreat you—make no sudden outcry nor exclamation."

Mrs. Archer's face was as colourless as the child's over whom she was bending; and her fixed eye glowed with such intensity, that Eliot thought it might have kindled life in the dead. Suddenly he perceived the blood gush into her cheeks—he advanced one step nearer, and he saw that a faint suffusion, like the first almost imperceptible tinge of coming day, had overspread the child's face. It deepened around her lips—there was a slight distension of the nostrils—a tremulousness about the muscles of the mouth—a heaving of the bosom, and then a deep-drawn sigh. A moment passed, and a faint smile was perceptible on the quivering lip.

"Lizzy!" said her mother.

"Dear Lizzy!" cried her brother.

"Mother!—Ned!" she faintly articulated.

"Thank God, she is safe!" exclaimed Eliot.

The energies of nature, once aroused, soon did their beneficent work; and the little girl, in the perfect consciousness of restored safety and happiness, clung to her mother and to Edward.

The tide of gratitude and happiness naturally flowed towards Eliot. Mrs. Archer turned to express something of all she felt, but he was already gone, after having directed one of the servants to say to her mistress that Coit would immediately be at her bidding.

It was not strange that the impression Eliot left on Mrs. Archer's mind was that of the most beautiful personation of celestial energy and mercy.

CHAPTER XVIII.

Ignomy in ransom, and free pardon,
Are of two houses.

It is reasonable to suppose that the disclosures which occurred in Sir Henry Clinton's library, would be immediately followed by their natural consequences: that love declared by one party, and betrayed by the other, would, according to the common usages of society, soon issue in mutual affiancing. But these were not the piping times of peace, and the harmony of events was sadly broken by the discords of the period.

The conflict of Mr. Linwood's political with his natural affections, at his eventful meeting with his son, was immediately followed by a frightful attack of gout in the stomach—a case to verify the theories of our eminent friend of the faculty, who locates the sensibility in the mucous tissue of that organ. Isabella, afflicted on all sides, and expecting her father's death at every moment, never left his bed-side. In vain Meredith besieged the house, and sent her message after message; not he, even, could draw her from her post. "My life depends on you, Belle," said her father: "the doctor says I must keep tranquil—he might as well say so to a ship in a squall—but my child, you are my polar star—my loadstone—my sheet-anchor—my everything; don't quit me, Belle!" She did not for an instant.

"Bless me! Mr. Meredith," said Helen Ruthven, on entering Mrs. Linwood's drawing-room, and finding Meredith walking up and down, with an expression of impatience and disappointment, "what is the matter—is Mr. Linwood worse?"

"Not that I know."

"How happens it that you are alone, then?"

"The family are with Mr. Linwood."

"The family! the old lady surely can take care of him; is Isabella invisible?—invisible to *you?*"

"I have not seen her since her father's illness."

"My Heavens! is it possible! well, some people are better than others."

"I do not comprehend you, Miss Ruthven."

"My meaning is simple enough: a woman must be an icicle or an angel to hang over an old gouty father, without allowing herself a precious five minutes with her lover."

"Miss Linwood is very dutiful!" said Meredith, half sneeringly, for his vanity was touched.

"Dutiful!—she may be—she is undoubtedly—a very, very sweet creature is Isabella Linwood; but I should not have imagined her a person, if her heart were really engaged, to deny its longings and sit down patiently to play the dutiful daughter. I judge others by myself. In her situation—precisely in hers," she paused and looked at Meredith with an expression fraught with meaning, "I should know neither scruple nor duty."

There was much in this artful speech of Helen Ruthven to feed Meredith's bitter fancies when he afterwards pondered on it. "If her heart were engaged!" he said, "it is, I am sure of it—and yet, if it were, she is not, as Helen Ruthven said, a creature to be chained down by duty. *If* it were!—it is—it shall be—her heart is the only one I have invariably desired—the only one I have found unattainable. I believe, I am almost sure, she loves me; but there is something lacking—I do not come up to her standard of ideal perfection!—others do not find me deficient. There's poor Bessie, a sylvan maiden she—but there's Helen Ruthven—the love, the just appreciation of such a woman, so full of genius, and sentiment, and knowledge of the world, would be—flattering."

These were after-thoughts of Meredith, for, at the time, his interview with Miss Ruthven was interrupted by Rose putting a note into his hand, addressed to Sir Henry Clinton, and requesting him, in Miss Linwood's name, to deliver it as soon as possible.

"Pray let me see that!" said Miss Ruthven; and after examining it closely on both sides, she returned it, saying, "Strange! I thought to have found somewhere, in pencil, some little expressive, world-full-of-meaning word; as I said, some people are very different from others!"

Meredith bit his lips, and hastened away with the note. It contained a plain statement to Sir Henry Clinton, of the motives of Herbert's return, and every fact attending it. The note was thus finished:—

"I have told you the unvarnished and unextenuated truth, my dear Sir Henry. I think that justice will dictate my brother's release, or at least, require that he be treated as a prisoner of war; but if justice (justice perverted by artificial codes and traditionary abuses) cannot interpose in his behalf, I commend him to your mercy: think of him as if he were your own son; and then mete out to him, for the rashness of his filial affection, such measure as a father would allot to such offence.

"If my appeal is presuming, forgive me. My father is suffering indescribably, and we are all wretched. Send us, I beseech you, some kind word of relief."

Late in the afternoon, after many tedious hours, the following reply was brought to Isabella, written by Sir Henry's secretary:—

"Sir Henry Clinton directs me to present his best regards to Miss Linwood, and inform her that he regrets the impossibility of complying with her wishes,—that he has no absolute power by which he can remit, at pleasure, the offences of disloyal subjects. Sir Henry bids me add, that he is seriously concerned at his friend Mr. Linwood's illness, and that he shall continue to send his servant daily to inquire about him."

"Yes, no doubt," said Isabella, in the bitterness of her disappointment, throwing down the note, "these empty courtesies will be strictly paid, while not a finger is raised to save us from utter misery!"

"My dearest child!" said her mother, who had picked up the note and reverently perused it, "how you are hurried away by your feelings ! Sir Henry, or rather his secretary, which is the same thing, says as much as to say, that Sir Henry would aid us if he could ; and I am sure I think it is extremely attentive of him to send every day to inquire after your poor father. I do wonder a little that Sir Henry did not sign his name ; it would have seemed more polite, and Sir Henry is so strictly polite ! I am afraid, my dear, you were not particular enough about your note. Was it written on gilt paper and sealed with wax ! " Isabella, do you hear me, child ! "

" Indeed, mama, I did not observe the paper, and I forgot whether I sealed it all. ' Remit at pleasure the offences of disloyal subjects ! ' Herbert has transferred his loyalty to his country, and is no longer amenable to his sovereign in another hemisphere."

" Feminine reasoning ! " interposed Meredith, who entered at this moment. He stopped and gazed at Isabella, and thought he had never seen her so perfectly lovely. Watching and anxiety had subdued her brilliancy, and had given a depth of tenderness, a softness to her expression, bordering on feminine weakness. When a man has a dread, however slight it may be, that a woman is superior to him, her attractions are enhanced by whatever indicates the gentleness and dependence of her sex.

Meredith took her hand : his eyes expressed the emotion she produced, and his lips all the sympathy and none of the vexation he had felt for the last few days ; and then reverting to Sir Henry, he said, " I trust the current of your feelings will change when I tell you that I have obtained an order for Herbert's release."

" God bless you, Jasper !—Oh, mama, do you hear ! "

" Pray go, my dear madam," added Meredith, "and prepare Mr. Linwood for good news. You interrupted me, Isabella," he resumed, when Mrs. Linwood had left the room ; " your wishes always fly over the means to the end—a moment's reflection will show you that your brother's release cannot be unconditional."

" Well—the conditions are such as can in honour be complied with !—Sir Henry would propose no other."

" Honour is a conventional term, Isabella."

" The honour that I mean," replied Miss Linwood, " is not conventional, but synonymous with rectitude."

Meredith shook his head. He had an instinctive dislike of definitions, as they in Scripture, who loved darkness, had to the light. He was fond of enveloping his meaning in shadowy analogies, which, like the moon, often led astray, with a beautiful but imperfect and illusive light.

" Even rectitude must depend somewhat on position, Isabella," he replied. " He who is under the pressure of circumstances, and crowded on every side, cannot, like him who is perfectly free, stand upright and dispose his motions at pleasure."

" Do not mystify, Jasper, but tell me at once what the conditions are."

Isabella's face and voice expressed even more dissatisfaction than her words, and Meredith's reply was in the tone of an injured man.

" Pardon me, Miss Linwood, if my anxiety to prepare your mind by a winding approach has betrayed me into awkwardness. Certainly, Herbert's honour, the honour of your brother, cannot be dearer to any one than to me."

" You have always been his friend, I know," replied Isabella, evading Meredith's implication ; " watchful nights, and more anxious days, have made me peevish—forgive me."

Meredith kissed the hand she extended to him. " You cannot imagine, Isabella, what it costs me to infuse another bitter drop into the cup already overflowing with accumulated anxieties. But your aunt's disasters are followed with new trials. Do not be alarmed—the threatening storm may pass over."

" Oh, tell me what it threatens ! "

" Sir Henry has, within the last hour, received a despatch from Washington, disclaiming all part and lot in Herbert's return to the city, and expressing his deep regret that the sanctity of a flag of truce should be brought into question by one of his own officers."

" This was to be expected."

" Of course. But we all know that Washington has his resident spies in this city, and emissaries continually passing to and fro, in various disguises and under various pretences. However, assuming that he is exempt from any participation in this disastrous affair, common humanity would have dictated some plea for a brave and faithful officer,—some extenuation for a rash and generous youth. But Washington is always governed by this cold, selfish policy——"

" Is there not one word ! "

" Not one !—There is, indeed, a private letter from Eliot Lee, stating that the motives of Herbert's return were wholly personal, and containing the particulars you had previously stated ; and a very laboured appeal to Sir Henry, with a sort of endorsement from Washington, that these statements are entitled to whatever weight they might derive from the unquestionable integrity of Captain Lee."

" Thank Heaven ! Eliot Lee has proved a true friend."

" Certainly, as far as writing a letter goes ; but, as you must perceive, Isabella, Sir Henry cannot act officially from the statements of a sister and friend. He will do all he can. He has empowered me to offer Herbert not only his release, but favour and promotion, provided he will renounce the bad cause to which he has too long adhered, and expiate the sin of rebellion by active service in the royal army."

" Never, never ; never shall Herbert do this ! "

" You are hasty, Isabella—hear me. If I convince Herbert that he has erred, why should he not retrieve his error ! "

" Ay, Jasper, if you can convince him—but the mind cannot be convinced at pleasure—we cannot believe as we would—I know it is impossible."

Her voice faltered ; she paused for a moment, a moment of the most painful embarrassment, and then proceeded with more firmness :—" I will be frank with you, Jasper. Herbert is not—you know him as well as I do—he is not of a temper to suffer long and patiently. He is like a bird, for ever singing and on the wing in sunshine, but silent and shrinking when the sky is overcast. He may—it breaks my heart to think it possible

—but he may—his spirit broken by imprisonment and desertion, and stung by what will appear to him his commander's indifference to his fate,—he may yield to the temptation you offer, and abandon a cause that he still believes, in the recesses of his heart, to be just and holy.''

Meredith fixed his piercing eyes on Isabella. It seemed that something new had been infused into her mind. He forbore, however, from expressing a suspicion, and merely said, " You place me in a flattering light, Isabella,—as the tempter of your brother.''

" Oh no—you mistake me—you are only the medium through which temptation comes to him : but remember his infirmity—the infirmity of human nature, and do not increase the force of the temptation—do not make the worse appear the better reason, Jasper. I know you will not—at least I believe, I think, I hope——''

" For Heaven's sake, my dear friend," interrupted Meredith, " do not reduce your confidence in my integrity to anything weaker than a hope. Now as I perceive that you would choose accurately to limit and define my agency, I entreat you to do so—my hope, my wish, my purpose, Isabella, is to be in all things moulded and governed by your will. Let us understand each other. I go to Herbert the advocate of a cause in which I, at least, have unwavering confidence——''

" Thank Heaven for that !" said Isabella, replying courageously to the equivocal curl of Meredith's lip.

He proceeded :—" I am permitted, am I not, to communicate Sir Henry's generous offer ?''

" His offer—but do not call it generous. Nothing remitted—nothing forgiven. His oblivion of the past, and his future favour, are to be dearly paid for.''

" Sir Henry's offer, then, without note or comment.''

Isabella nodded assent.

" I may report à la lettre, Washington's renunciation, disclaimer, or whatever you may be pleased to call it ?''

" Literally, Jasper.''

" I may suggest to him—or do your primitive notions prohibit this ?—that Washington's communication and Eliot's letter enable us to give an interpretation to his return to the city that will relieve him from the appearance of having been forced by circumstances into our ranks. Indeed, without any essential perversion, this return to the path of duty may appear to have been his deliberate intention in coming to the city. This, of course, would very favourably affect his standing with his fellow-officers—you hesitate. Isabella, forgive me for quoting the vulgar proverb—be not ' more nice than wise.' Why should not Herbert avail himself of a fortunate position—a favourable light ?''

" Because it is a false light—a deceptive gloss. Do not, Jasper, over-estimate the uncertain, imperfect and ignorant opinions of others—pray do not be offended ; but is it not folly to look for our own image in others' minds, where, as in water, it may be magnified, or, as in the turbid stream, clouded and distorted, when in our own bosoms we have an unerring mirror ?''

" Your theory is right, undoubtedly, Isabella—

your sentiments lofty—no one can admire them more than I do ; but what is the use of standing on an eminence a hundred degrees above your fellow-mortals with whom you are destined to act ? It is certain they will not come up to you, and as certain that, unless you are unwilling to live in the solitude of a hermit, useless and forgotten, it is wisest to come down to them.'' Meredith paused. " We do not see eye to eye," thought Isabella ; but she did not speak, and Meredith proceeded :—" God knows, Isabella, that it is my first wish to conform my opinions, my mind and heart, to you ; but we must adapt ourselves to things as they are. Herbert is in a most awkward and fearful predicament. Sir Henry, like other public men, must be governed by policy. If your father's fortune or influence were important to the royal cause, Sir Henry might make an exception to the usual proceedings in similar cases in favour of his son ; but, as he remarked to me to-day, your father is injudicious in his zeal, and such a friend often harms us more than an enemy. He says, too, that he finds it essential not to relax in severity towards the rebel sons of royalists. Nothing is more common than for families to divide in this way ; their fathers remain loyal, the sons join the rebels ; and Sir Henry deems it most politic to cut them off from all hope of immunity on account of the fidelity of their fathers. If Herbert does not accept Sir Henry's terms, it will be particularly unfortunate for him that he came into the city under the protection of a flag of truce ; for, as Sir Henry remarked to me, it behoves us to seize every occasion to abate the country's confidence in Washington's integrity, and certainly this is a tempting one.''

" Does Sir Henry believe that Washington was privy to Herbert's coming to the city ?''

" Oh, Lord—no !''

" And yet, he will be guilty of the falsehood and meanness of infusing this opinion into other men's minds, and call it policy ! Jasper, how is it that the religious obligations of truth, which govern man in his intercourse with his fellow—which rule us in our homes and at our firesides, have never presided in the councils of warriors nor in the halls of statesmen ?''

" For no other reason that I know, Isabella, than that they would be exceedingly inconvenient there. ' Might makes right '—those that have the power will use it.''

" Ah, Jasper,'' said Isabella, without responding to Meredith's simile ; " the time is coming when that base dogma will be reversed, and right will make might. The Divinity is stirring within men, and the policy and power of these false gods, who fancy they have a chartered and transmitted right to all the good things of this fair world, shall fall before it, as Dagon fell prostrate before the ark of the Lord.''

" I do not comprehend you, Isabella.''

" I simply mean, that the time is at hand when the truth that all men are made in the image of God, and therefore all have equal rights and equal duties, will not only be acknowledged in our prayers and churchyards, but will be the basis of government, and of public as well as of private intercourse.''

" ' When the sky falls '—these are odd speculations for a young lady.''

" Speculations they are not. The hardest metals are melted in the furnace, to be recast in new forms; and old opinions and prejudices, harder, Jasper, than any metal, may be subdued and remoulded in these fiery times."

"And does our aunt Archer furnish the mould in which they are recast?—if she talks to you as she has to me of the redoubtable knight-errantry of the indomitable deliverer of her captive child, I do not wonder at this sudden inspiration of republicanism. It is rather a feminine mode, though, of arriving at political abstractions through their incarnation in a favourite hero."

A deep glow, partly hurt pride, partly consciousness, suffused Isabella's cheek. Her aunt's was the only mind whose direct influence she felt.

"You are displeased," he continued; "but you must forgive me, for I am in that state when 'trifles, light as air,' disturb me. My destiny, or rather, I should say, those hopes that shape destiny, seem to be under the control of some strange fatality, that I can neither evade nor understand. If I dared retrace to you the history of these hopes, from our childhood to this day, you would see how many times, when they have been most assured, you have dashed them by some evident and inexplicable alienation from me. At our last interview——"

"When was it—when was it?"—asked Isabella, in her nervousness and confusion, forgetting they had not met since the day of the dinner at Sir Henry Clinton's.

"When—have you forgotten our last meeting?"

"Oh, no—no; but ages have passed since—ages of anxiety and painful reflection."

"And have these ages, compressed as they have been into five days, changed your heart, Isabella? —or was it folly and presumption to hope—I will confess the whole extent of my presumption—to *believe*, that that heart, the object of all my hopes—that for which I only care to live, was—mine?" It was well that Isabella covered her face, for it expressed what she forbade her lips to speak.

"Anything but this mysterious silence," continued Meredith, aware how near a suppressed agitation was to the confession he expected. "Let me, I beseech you, know my fate at once. It is more important to us both that it should now be decided than you can imagine.'

"Oh, not now—not now, Jasper!"

Meredith was too acute not to perceive how near to a favourable decision was this "not now."

"And why not now, Isabella? Surely I have not seriously offended you. Think, for a moment, that after passing the last five days between the most anxious waiting at your door, and continued efforts for Herbert, when I at last got access to you, you receive my plans for your brother coldly and doubtingly; and I find that while I was burning with impatience to see you, you had been occupied with abstruse meditations upon the rights of man! I was galled, I confess, Isabella; and if I seemed merely to treat them with levity, I deserve credit for mastery over stronger feelings." Isabella was half-convinced that she had been unjust and almost silly. "You have it in your power," continued Meredith, "to infuse what opinions you will into my mind—to inspire my purpose—to govern my affections—to fix my destiny for time and eternity. Oh, Isabella! do not put me off with this silence. Let this blessed

moment decide our fate. Speak but one word, and I am bound to you for ever!"

That word of doom hovered on Isabella's lips; her hand, which he had taken, was no longer cold and passive, but returned the grasp of his; doubt and resolution were vanishing together; and the balance that had been wavering for years was rapidly descending in Meredith's favour, when the door opened and Mrs. Linwood appeared. At first starting back with delighted surprise, and then receiving a fresh impulse from her husband's impatient voice calling from his room, she said, "You must come to your father, instantly, Isabella." Isabella gave one glance to Meredith, and obeyed the summons. Meredith felt as if some fiend had dashed from his hand the sparkling cup just raised to his lips. His face, that expressed the conflict of hope just assured, and of sudden disappointment, was a curious contrast to Mrs. Linwood's smiling all over. She believed she at last saw the happy issue of her long-indulged expectations. She waited in vain for Meredith to speak; and finally came to the conclusion, that there were occasions in life when the best bred people forgot propriety. "I am quite mortified that I intruded," she said; "but you know Mr. Linwood—he is so impatient, and the gout you know is so teasing, and he never can bear Isabella out of his sight, and he is just on the sofa for the first time since this attack, and I unluckily hurt his foot. You know the gout has left his stomach and gone into his foot. It is much less dangerous there, but I don't think he is any more patient with it; and I happened just to touch the tip end of his toe in putting under the cushion, and he screamed out so for Isabella. He thinks she can do everything so much better than anybody else. Indeed, she is a first-rate nurse—so devoted, too—she has not left her father's bedside till now for five days and nights; she seemed to forget herself a little now (spoken in parenthesis, and significantly). Whatever man may think before marriage, Mr. Meredith, he finds afterward, especially if he is subject to the gout, good nursing is everything. I often say, All a good woman need know is how to take good care of her family and of the sick. However, that and something more Isabella knows."

"Madam?" said Meredith, waked from his revery by Isabella's name, the only word of this long speech, meant to be so effective and appropriate, that he had heard. He slightly bowed and left the house.

"How odd!—how very odd!" thought Mrs. Linwood. "When Mr. Linwood declared himself, he directly told my father and mother, and the wedding-day and all was settled before he went out of the house. I wish I knew just how matters stand. Belle will not say a word to me unless it's a fixed thing: so I shall find out one way or the other. I am sure I used to tell my mother everything; but Belle don't take after me: however, she is a dear girl, and I am sure I ought to be satisfied with her.—If she should refuse Jasper Meredith!!"

This last supposition of a tremendous possibility was quite too much for a solitary meditation; and the good lady started from her position at the window, where she had stood gazing after Meredith, and returned to her customary avocations.

CHAPTER XIX.

Un gentilhomme merveilleusement sujet à la goutte, estant pressé par les médecins de laisser de tout l'usage des viandes salées, avoit accoustumé de respondre plaisamment, que sur les efforts et tourmens du mal il vouloit avoir à qui s'en prendre ; et que s'escriant et mauldissant tantôt le cervelat, tantôt le jambon, il s'en sentoit d'aultant allegé.—MONTAIGNE.

ISABELLA returned to her father's apartment in a frame of mind rather adverse to her performing accurately the tasks of the "best nurse in the world."

"What the devil ails you, Belle !" exclaimed her father : "you are putting the cushion under the wrong foot !—there—there—that will do—that's right—now kiss me, Belle, dear. I did not mean to speak cross to you ; but your mother has been fidgeting here a little eternity. I wonder what the deuse is the reason she can never make anything lie easy. She does try her best, poor soul ! but she has no faculty—none in the world. What is this good news, Belle, she tells me Jasper has brought ?"

"It amounts to nothing, sir."

"Humph !—I thought as much." A pause ensued. "Hark !" resumed Mr. Linwood—"is not that Helen Ruthven's voice on the stairs ?—call her in, Belle." Miss Ruthven entered. "Glad to see you, my dear—like to see living folks alive. Belle is sitting up here like a tomb-stone, neither seeing, hearing, nor moving. ' How am I, child ?' —alive, thank God, and better—the enemy has cleared out of the citadel, and is firing away at the outworks—expect to eat a capital dinner to-day—Major St. Clair has sent me a brace of woodcock—a man of taste is Major St. Clair ! Woodcock, currant-jelly, and a glass of madeira, will make a Christian of me again. I should be as happy as the king if it were not—heigh ho, poor Herbert ! Oh, Jupiter Ammon, what a twinge !— Belle, do loosen that flannel—your mother has drawn it up like a vice—there—there—that will do. Do for conscience' sake tell me some news, Helen, my dear."

"I came on purpose, sir, to tell Isabella a famous piece of news ; but I met Jasper Meredith——"

"What of that, child ?"

"He has told the news, sir, of course."

"He may have told it to Belle ; but I am none the better for it : so pray tell on, my dear."

"Meredith's mother has arrived."

"His mother !" echoed Isabella.

"His mother !" repeated Mr. Linwood, in a voice that drowned hers—" When ?—how !— where !"

"Ah," thought Miss Ruthven, with infinite satisfaction, "they are not in smooth water yet, or this fact would have been announced."—" The ship," she replied to Mr. Linwood, " arrived last night, and is at anchor below waiting for a wind."

"What ship, child ?"

" The Thetis, or Neptune, or Minerva ?"

"It can't be, my child ; there's no such ship expected."

" It may be called by some other name, sir, I

never remember ships' names ; but Mrs. Meredith has most certainly arrived, and her niece, Lady Anne Seton, with her."

" Extraordinary — most extraordinary ! Did Jasper ever speak to you of expecting them, Belle ?"

" Never, sir."

"Do, for Heaven's sake, Belle, speak more than one word at a time—go on, Helen—what else did you hear ?"

Miss Ruthven was nothing loth to speak, and she proceeded :—"I met St. Clair at Mrs. Archer's. By-the-way, I admire your aunt excessively, Belle." Miss Ellen was a wholesale flatterer, and practised all the accesses to the heart through admiration of one's favourite friends and relations. "How sweetly she is settled ; but I could not but laugh at her scruples about using the Ludlows' furniture. I told her it was the good and universal rule of the city to make the most of what the rebel runaways had left behind them. You do not assent, Belle. I am sure your father agrees with me—do you not, Mr. Linwood ?"

"Mrs. Archer has a way of her own. Go on with your news, my child,—was Mrs. Meredith expected ?"

"I really do not know, sir ; Isabella has the best right to know."

Isabella blushed painfully. This was the answer Helen Ruthven wished, and she proceeded : —"St. Clair was with Jasper when the news arrived, and he says Meredith appeared delighted ; but then St. Clair does not penetrate below the surface, and Meredith is a bit of a diplomatist— don't you think so, Isabella ?"

"It is neither very flattering to Jasper nor to his mother," replied Isabella, evading Ellen Ruthven's annoying question, " to doubt his joy at the arrival after a ten years' separation."

" Perhaps not ; but then we must see things as they are—mothers are sometimes inconvenient appendages, and sometimes—troublesome spies. At any rate, I do not believe it is pure maternal love that has brought the lady out. St. Clair says she is not that kind of person ; she loves her ease, he says, and loves the world of London, and would not come here without a powerful motive. Your aunt said that the pleasure of seeing her son would be motive enough to most mothers ; but your aunt is all mother. By-the-way, what a sweet fellow Ned Archer is. I did not see Lizzy—her mother says she is not yet recovered from her fright—she is so nervous—poor thing ! I do not wonder."

"Go on, Ellen. What motive did you find out for Madam Meredith ?—wise heads yours ! to think a woman acts from motive."

"Ah, sir, but we did find one ; a right, rational, and probable one too. Perhaps you do not know that Lady Anne Seton is Mrs. Meredith's ward, and that she is, moreover, a rich heiress."

"Well, what of that ?"

"Oh, a vast deal ' of that '—a fortune is a most important item in a young lady's catalogue of charms ; and poor Mrs. Meredith flatters herself she has a son yet to be charmed."

Miss Ruthven fixed her eyes, that had the quality of piercing, on Isabella ; but Isabella's were riveted to the embroidery on which her hands were employed, and she did not raise them, nor move a muscle of her face.

Mr. Linwood breathed out an expressive "humph," and asked if fortune was the young lady's only charm.

"Oh, no! St. Clair gave me a catalogue of them as long as my arm. In the first place, she is just sweet eighteen—very pretty, though a little too much inclined to *embonpoint*—rather pale too—very sweet eyes, hazel, soft, and laughing—not a classic nose; but pretty noses are rare—hair of the loveliest brown; but that matters not now, when no one, save Isabella, wears 'hair of the colour God chooses'—a sweet pretty mouth she has, St. Clair says; and her hands, arms, and feet are such beauties, that she has been asked to sit to a sculptor."

"The deuse, girls! She'll cut you all out."

"She may prove a dangerous rival, Isabella."

Isabella looked disturbed, and was so; not so much at Miss Ruthven's allusion as at a sudden recollection. Meredith had urged her immediate decision as momentous to them both. "Is he," thought she, "afraid that his resolution, his affections, are not strong enough to resist a siege from his mother?" Rallying her spirits, she asked "if St. Clair had only furnished a schedule of Lady Anne's personal charms?"

"Oh, my dear friend, yes. She enters the lists armed *cap-à-pié*—she has been partly educated in France—dances like a sylph, and speaks French like a Parisian angel."

"Don't be gulled by that, girls; if she sputters away in French, it is a pretty sure sign she has nothing worth saying in English."

"But St. Clair says, Mr. Linwood, that she is agreeable and good-humoured—a sort of person that everybody likes."

"Then I sha'n't like her, that's flat; for I don't like that kind of fit that fits everybody."

"But you like her name?—Lady Anne Seton. There is such a charm in a name—a title too—a rose by any other name might be as sweet; but a name with the prefix of 'lady' is far more captivating for it. Lady Isabella! There is a coronet in the very sound.

"Do you know St. Clair says, that if Isabella were to appear in England, she might soon write herself lady?" She added, in a whisper, "he says, Belle—don't be offended—that if an earl, or even a baronet were to address you, it would fix a certain person at once; he has such deference for rank, that if you were merely to have it within your grasp, you would be perfectly irresistible to him."

"St. Clair talks idly," replied Isabella, proudly, and the tears, in spite of her efforts to repress them, starting into her eyes; "He knows very little of Jasper Meredith." Alas! such a suggestion, even from such a source, had power to wound her. "Helen," she added, "papa is getting tired, and must take his drops, and try for his nap."

"Bless me, my dear, forgive me for staying; I always get so interested in *your interests*. Good morning, dear Mr. Linwood; make haste and get well. Farewell, dear Isabella, I am going to reconnoitre, and will report progress;" and kissing both father and daughter, she departed.

"Helen Ruthven is very fond of you, Belle," said her father.

Isabella smiled; but it was a bitter smile. She did not care to rectify her father's opinion; but she thought Helen Ruthven much like a bee, who stings while laden with sweets.

"Very odd, Mrs. Meredith coming out just now," continued Mr. Linwood; "the ocean covered with rebel privateers—bringing over this girl too—a right woman's move. Give me my drops, Belle—they will sharpen my appetite—thank you, dear—Pah! what's this—that devilish rhubarb—you've spoiled my dinner, Belle."

"A thousand pardons, papa—take this water—now rest a little, and then your drops."

"Never mind, my dear—set down the glass, and come and kneel down by me, Belle. There's something the matter with you, my child; I am sure of it. You cannot deceive me, Belle—you are as transparent as that glass. Twice since you came from the parlour you have blundered, first with the cushion, and now the drops. It's an uncommon thing for you, my dear, to look one way and row t'other. Jasper was with you, Belle—has he offered himself?—Don't hesitate—I am in no condition to be trifled with—has Jasper done it?"

"Yes, sir."

"Have you accepted or rejected him?"

"Neither."

"Do you love him, Belle?"

"Dear papa!" said she, springing to her feet, and walking to the extremity of the room; "do not question me any farther."

"Come back to me, Belle—kneel down by me again, and listen to me. I can tell you a love-story: yes—little like a lover as I now seem. When I was eight-and-twenty, still in the hey-day of life, I loved, with my whole soul, your aunt Archer—don't flinch, child—listen. She was very young, just from school; twelve years younger than I, eight than your mother; but then she promised all she has since been. She rejected me. In a fit of pique I married your mother—mark the consequences. She has been the poor, subservient, domestic drudge———"

"Oh, papa! pray———"

"I am telling a plain story, Belle, and you must hear it; but never mind what she has been. You can't dispute that I have been unreasonable, peevish, passionate, and so we have worn away life together; and now, when the curtain is about to fall, I look back on my useless existence—my wasted talents—my lost opportunities, and mourn over it all—in vain!" His voice was choked with emotion.

"Oh, do not say so, sir; you are the dearest, kindest of fathers."

"To you, Belle; and what thanks to me for that? I have been proud of you—I have loved you—there it is; if I had loved your mother, I should have been the kindest of husbands. Love makes virtue easy. 'Love,' the Scripture says, 'is the fulfilling of the law.' I say those must be saints who fulfil the law without it. Conscience does not sleep even in such a self-lover as I am; and think you, Belle, I am not often tormented with the thought, that I was created for something better than to make my dinner the chief good of every day—to pamper myself with the bounties of Providence, and fret and fume at every straw in my way? No, my dear child, you never have

felt my petty tyranny; but you hold the master-
key to my heart. Poor Herbert! I sacrificed
him to a gust of passion. It was I that drove
him into the ranks of the rebels."

"Pray compose yourself, sir; do not say any
more."

"I must finish what I began upon—I have
gone aside from it—Jasper Meredith! Ah, Belle,
that name conjures the blood back to your cheeks
—Jasper Meredith has fortune, which, thanks to
this unnatural war, we want enough. He has
rank, which I honour, and talents, which all men
honour; but if he has not your whole heart, child,
let him and his fortune, rank and talents, go to
the devil."

"Thanks, dearest father, for your counsel;
and trust me, I will be assured of something better
and higher than fortune, rank, or talents, before
I bind myself in that indissoluble bond."

"I believe it, Belle; I know it." Mr. Linwood felt, though he did not perfectly comprehend, the emotions that at this moment irradiated
Isabella's beautiful face. "And, my child," he
continued, "ever since you have come to woman's
estate, I have resolved that whoever you loved,
let his name, condition, fortune, be what it would,
your hand should go with your heart, Belle; and
I fear not to stand by my resolve, for I know that
your giving your heart means your respect, honour,
esteem, and all that one of God's creatures can
feel for another."

"You are right, sir."

"I am sure of it—now kiss me, dear—that's a
seal to the bond. Read to me the last London
Gazette—no matter where. I'll doze away the
time till dinner."

CHAPTER XX.

Wherefore is light given to him that is in misery, and
life unto the bitter in soul?

WE ought not to tax too severely the ingenuity
of our readers, and therefore must briefly explain
our poor friend Kisel's sudden appearance with
the marauders. He had waked from his sound
sleep on Gurdon Coit's floor at the moment that
Eliot gallopped off with his associates towards
Mrs. Archer's, and in spite of all remonstrance
he had mounted his horse and followed him. He
had the dog's affection, but not his instinct: and
failing to find the right track, he fell in with the
Skinners instead of rejoining his master. It
occurred to Hewson that the poor fellow might be
a useful agent in reconveying the child to Mrs.
Archer; and ordering his men to ride on each
side of Kisel, he enforced his continuance in the
company into which he had unwittingly fallen.
One flash of hope came upon him at the sight of
his master, but he was soon beyond the possibility
of Eliot's pursuit or rescue; and with a heavy
heart he commended him to that Power that had
seemed hitherto to care for him as for the ravens
and all helpless things.

When Eliot reached Gurdon Coit's, he found
that the general and men from West Point had
been gone for a half-hour. Coit stood before the
door, holding by the halter a fine bay horse,
and as soon as he had expressed his heartfelt joy

at Eliot's report from Mrs. Archer's, he said "I
am thinking, Captain, you are pretty near breaking the tenth commandment—no wonder; this is
a noble animal; how he paws the dust, as though
he smelt the battle afar off! But here's a note
the Gen'ral left for you."

As some among the youth of the present day
may be shocked at the spelling of the canonised
old general, before Eliot reads the note we must
premise, that as neither reading, writing, nor
spelling (Jack Cade to the contrary notwithstanding) "come by nature," the general's accomplishment in these arts was very limited; and we beg
them to remember, that even in these days of
universal learning, a patriot-soldier might be
forgiven very imperfect orthography—but to the
note.

"DERE, GALUNT YOUNG FRIEND—I could have
huged you before we parted, I have been so
pleased with you from the beginin to the end of
this biznes. I felt for you in the loss of your
hors, and I can't bear the thots of your riden that
sorry jade, that's only been used to prouling
about o' nights, on all sorts of diviltry; so I've
ordered Gurden to put into your hands a *likely
cretur*, that our folks at home has sent up to be
sold to the ofisers in camp. Take it, my boy,
and don't feel beholden to me; for when the war
is at end, and it's conveneyent, we'll settle for it.

"Yours, tell death, and ever after, if the Lord
permits.

"ISRAEL PUTNAM."

We will leave Eliot's surprise, joy, and gratitude to be imagined. The last emotion was
greatly augmented by his benefactor's exempting
him from the pain of a pecuniary obligation. He
was soon mounted on his new steed, and retracing
his way, with many a delightful recollection to
counteract his anxieties. These, however, prevailed when he was ushered into Washington's
presence, and felt the whole weight of the task
Herbert's rashness had imposed on him. He
first delivered his despatches, and had the happiness of receiving his commander's thanks for the
manner in which he had performed his mission.
Washington wasted no time in formal compliments, and Eliot felt his approval to be more
than the praise of other men. Might not that
approval be withdrawn! Eliot must encounter
the risk, and he proceeded to ask the general's
patience while he recounted the misdemeanors
and misfortunes of his friend.

It is well known that Washington's moderation
and equanimity were the effects of the highest
principle, not the gift of nature. He was consti-
tutionally subject to gusts of passion, but he had
acquired a power, almost divine (and doubtless
from a divine source), by which he could direct
the whirlwind and subdue the storm;—a power
that has seemed to the believing to verify that
prophetic verse in Proverbs, which accords with
his natal day, and which so truly graduates and
expounds his virtues—"He that ruleth his own
spirit is greater than he that taketh a city."

Eliot saw, as he proceeded in his narrative, that
Washington's brow contracted, and that "the
angry spot" glowed there; but he continued to
speak with the calmness and manly freedom that

suited a man conscious of his own integrity, and zealous for his friend; nor did he change colour till Washington, checking the hasty strides he was making up and down the apartment, said, " What *proof* is there, Captain Lee, that you were not privy to this mad and disgraceful expedition of your friend ?"

" None, sir," replied Eliot, unappalled, but not unmoved. Washington seemed struck with the dignity of his manner; his countenance somewhat relaxed as Eliot proceeded :—" There may be probabilities as conclusive to a generous mind as proofs to a common one. You will perceive, sir, that the same action that was indiscretion in my friend would have been crime in me, honoured as I was, by your trust. And further, that I could have had no temptation to a violation of that trust but a desire to oblige my friend, while he was urged on and blinded to consequences by the intensity of filial and fraternal love, which, allow me to say, sir, has been kept in long and painful abeyance by his devotion to his country."

" Your zeal for your friend is generous, Captain Lee. Fidelity in friendship is a bond for integrity in other matters; be assured, I will not hastily withdraw the confidence I have with so much reason placed in you. I must take time to reflect on this matter. To what did you allude as having occurred last night ?"

Eliot briefly related the affair at Mrs. Archer's. He saw a smile on Washington's lips, when he spoke of his hearty coadjutor " the gen'ral." He concluded by saying, he trusted he had not offended by following what seemed to him the imperative dictates of humanity.

" No, my friend—no," replied Washington, not unmoved; " war too often cuts us off from the humanities—in God's name, let's perfect them when we may. I am engaged now; come to me again this evening."

Eliot left his commander somewhat relieved, but still, not without deep anxiety for Linwood. He had reason for solicitude. No man that ever lived more jealously guarded against the appearance of evil than Washington. One who kept with his exactness the account with conscience, might, in ordinary circumstances, have afforded to be careless of appearances, and regardless of public opinion; but he was aware that his reputation belonged to his country; that it was identified with the cause he had espoused; the cause of liberty and popular government; and how has that glorious cause profited by it ! Heralded by his spotless name, it has gone forth to restore the order of God's providence; to abase the high, and raise up those that were bowed down; to break the golden sceptre, and to overthrow thrones, to open Bastiles, to unbind chains, to reclaim the deserts that man had made, and to sow at broadcast the seeds of knowledge, virtue, and happiness.

The issue of Eliot's second interview with Washington is already known, so far as it appeared by the despatches sent to New York. He had the consolation of being assured that not a shadow of distrust remained on Washington's mind. Never man more needed solace in some shape than did Eliot at this conjuncture of his affairs. On first going to his quarters, he found there a packet from his mother. He pressed it to his lips, and eagerly broke the seal. The following is a copy of his mother's letter.

" MY DEAR SON,—I perceive by your letters of the first, which, thanks to a kind Providence, have duly come to hand, that it is now nearly three months since you have heard from us. Much good and much evil may befall in three months ! Much good have I truly to be grateful for: and chiefly that your life and health have been thus precious in the sight of the Lord, and that you have received honour at the hand of man (of which our good Dr. Wilson made suitable mention in his prayer last Sabbath); and, as I humbly trust, approval from Him who erreth not.

" We have had a season of considerable worldly anxiety. The potatoe-crop looked poorly, and our whole harvest was cut off by the blight in the rye, which, as you see in the newspapers, has been fatal through Massachusetts. This calamity has been greatly aggravated by the embargo they have laid on their flour in the Southern States. The days seemed to be coming upon us when ' plenty should be forgotten in our land, and sore famine overspread the borders thereof.'—Our people have been greatly alarmed, and there have been fasts in all our churches; at which the carnally-minded have murmured, saying—it would be time enough to fast when the famine came. It is indeed a time of desolation in our land—' there is no more in our streets the voice of mirth and the voice of gladness—the voice of the bridegroom and the voice of the bride'—the step of the father and the brother are no more heard on our thresholds, and we stretch our ears for tidings of battles that may lay them in the dust. Think you, my son, that our children's children, when they bear their sheaves rejoicing, will remember those who sowed in tears, and with much patience and many prayers ?

" For my own part, my dear Eliot, I have had but little part in this worldly anxiety, for divers reasons which you will presently see. One care eats up another." (Bessie's name was here written and effaced.) " Let me tell you, before I forget it, that the Lord has smiled on our Indian corn. I had an acre put in the south meadow, which you know is a warm soil, and Major Avery tells me it will prove a heavy yield. He is a kind neighbour (as indeed we all try to be in these times), and called yesterday to ask me to get into his wagon, and take a ride, saying it would cheer me up to see the golden ears peeping out of their seared and rustling leaves; but I did not feel inclined to go."—(Here again Bessie's name was written, and again effaced—the tender mother shrunk from giving the blow that must be given.) " Do not have any care, dear Eliot, about our basket and our store; they are sufficiently filled. The children are nicely prepared for winter, even to their shoes. Just as I was casting about to see how I should get them made, there being no shoemaker left short of Boston, Jo Warren came home, his term of service having expired, and he, as he says, ' liking much better the clack of his hammer and lapstone than bloody soldiering.'

" My dear son, I have written thus far without touching on the subject which fills heart and mind, day and night. I felt it to be suitable to mention the topics above ; but I knew if I left them to the last you would read without reading, and thereby lose the little comfort they might give you. Fain would I finish here ! God grant you may receive with submission what follows.— You know, that never since you went away have I been able to hold out any encouragement to you about your poor sister. The dear child struggled, and struggled, but only exhausted her strength without making any head way ; I shall always think it was from the first more weakness of body than anything else, for she had such a clear sense of what was right ; and this it was that weighed her down—a for ever tormenting sense that she was wasting in idle feelings the life and faculties that God had given to her. She tried to assist me in family duties, but she moved about like a machine ; and often her sewing would drop from her hands, and she would sit silent and motionless for hours. ·

"In the first part of Herbert Linwood's visit she was more like her former self—old feelings seemed to revive, and I had hopes—but oh ! they were suddenly dashed ; for immediately on his going away she seemed to have such self-reproach —such fear that she had foregone her duty, and had for ever forfeited your confidence. All night she was feverish and restless, and during the day she would sit and weep for hours together. She never spoke but to accuse herself of some wrong committed, or some duty unperformed. When the clock struck she would count the strokes, and you could see the beatings of her heart answer to each of them, and then she would weep till the hour came round again. Dr. Wilson and some of our godly women hoped she was under conviction ; but I did not favour their talking to her as often as they wished, for I knew that her health was much broken, her mind hurt, and that in this harp of a thousand strings (as Dr. Watts says) there were many they did not understand.

"Through the summer her flesh has wasted away till she seemed but the shadow of her former self. Her eyes appeared larger, and as the shadows deepened about them, of a deeper blue than ever—sometimes as I looked at her she startled me ; it seemed to me as if all of mortality was gone, and I was standing in the presence of a visible spirit. There was such a speaking, mournful beauty about her, that even strangers— rough people too—would shed tears when they looked at her.

"She never spoke of——. If the children mentioned his name, or but alluded to him, she seemed deaf and palsied. She never approached the honeysuckle window where they used to sit. She never touched the books he read to her—her favourite books ! and, one after another, she put away the articles of dress he had noticed and admired. Still with all these efforts she grew worse, till her reason seemed to me like the last ray of the sun before its setting.

"Two weeks ago she brought me a small box, enveloped and sealed, and asked me to keep it for her. 'Be sure,' she said, ' and put it where I cannot find it —be sure, mother.' From this moment there was a change ; it seemed as if a pressure was taken off. From hour to hour her spirits rose. She talked with more than her natural quickness

and cheerfulness, joined in the children's sports, and was full of impracticable plans of doing good, and wild expectations of happiness to all the world. I saw a fearful brightness in her eye. I knew her happiness was all a dream ; but still it was a relief to see the dear child out of misery. I hoped, and feared, and lived on, trembling from hour to hour. Last night she asked me for her box, and when she had taken it she threw her arms around me, and looked in my face smiling. O ! what a wild, strange smile it was ! She then kissed the children and went to her room. She has scarcely been in bed five minutes together for the last fortnight ; and as she did not come to breakfast in the morning, I hoped she was still sleeping ; and truly thankful for this symptom that her excitement was abating, I kept the house still. Ten o'clock came, and not yet a sound from her room. An apprehension darted through my mind—I ran up stairs — her room was empty, her bed untouched.

"On the table, unsealed, was the packet I inclose to you. I read it, and was relieved of my worst fear. Our kind neighbours went yesterday in search of her, but in vain. Last evening we heard the tramp of a horse to the door, and it proved to be Steady. He has been kept in the home-pasture all the fall ; and it seems the poor child, who you know is so timid that she never before rode without you or ——at her side, had put on the saddle and bridle, and started in the night. How far she rode we can only conjecture from Steady appearing quite beat out : Major Avery judges he may have travelled eighty miles, out and home. You will conclude with me that it is Bessie's intention to go to New York ; and when I think of her worn and distracted condition, and the state of the country through which she must pass, filled with hostile armies and infested with outlaws, do I sin in wishing she were dead beneath her father's roof ! If anything can be done, you will devise and execute—my head is sick with thinking, and my heart faint with sorrowing. Farewell, my beloved son. Let us not, in our trouble, forget that we are all, and especially the poor, sick, wandering lamb of our flock, in the hands of a good Being who doth not willingly afflict us.

"Your loving, grieving mother,
"S. LEE."

The first part of Bessie's letter appeared to have been written at intervals, and some weeks antecedent to the conclusion : it was evidently traced with a weak and faltering hand, and had been drenched with her tears. She began—

"DEAR BROTHER ELIOT.—(The word "dear" was effaced and re-written)—I am but a hypocrite to call you ' dear ' Eliot, for all permitted affections are devoured by one forbidden one. The loves that God implanted have withered and died away under the poisonous shadow of that which has been sown in my heart—think you by the evil spirit, Eliot ! I sometimes fear so. I used to love our overkind mother, and for our little brothers and sisters my heart did seem to be one fountain of love, ever sweet, fresh, and overflowing ; and you, O Eliot, how fondly, proudly I loved you ! And now, if I were to see you all dead before me, it would move me no more than to see the idle leaves falling from the trees."

"I have read your letters over and over again, till they have fallen to pieces with the continual dropping of my hot tears ; but every syllable is imprinted on my heart. You did not believe your 'sister would waste her sensibility, the precious food of life, in moping melancholy.' Oh, Eliot, how much better must I have appeared to you than I was ! I have been all my life a hypocrite. You believed 'my mind had a self-rectifying power,' and I imposed this belief on you ! I am ready now to bow my head in the dust for it. 'Love,' said your letter, 'can never be incurable when it is a disease ; that is to say, when its object is unworthy.' Ah, my dear brother, there was your fatal mistake. It was I that was unworthy—it was your simple sister that, in her secret, unconfessed thoughts, believed he loved her, knowing all the while that his lot was cast with the high, the gifted, the accomplished—with such as Isabella Linwood, and not with one so humble in condition, so little graced by art, as I am. I do not blame him. Heaven knows I do not. 'Self-rectifying power !' Eliot, talk to the reed, that has been uprooted and borne away by the tides of the ocean, of its 'self-rectifying power !'"

A long interval had elapsed after writing the above, and the subsequent almost illegible scraps indicated a mind in ruins.

"Oh, Eliot, pray—pray come home ! They are all persecuting me. The children laugh at me, and whistle after me ; and when I am asleep, they blow his name in my ears. Mother looks at me, and will not speak."

"They have printed up all the books. Even the Bible has nothing but his name from beginning to end. I can never be alone ; evil spirits are about me by day and by night. My brother, I am tormented."

"Eliot, my doom is spoken ! Would that it were to cut down the cumberer of the ground ! But no ! I am to stand for ever on the desolate shore, stricken and useless, and see the river of life glide by. The day, as well as the night, is solitary, and there is no joyful voice therein."

"Oh, memory !—memory !—memory ! what an abyss of misery art thou ! The sun rises and sets —the moon rolls over the sky—the stars glide on in their appointed paths—the seasons change, but no change cometh to me—the past, the past is all —there is no present, no future !

"I remember hearing Dr. Wilson preach about sin deserving infinite punishment, because it was against an Infinite being. I did not comprehend him then—now I do. In vain I raise my faded eyes and fevered hands to God."

The remainder was written in a more assured and rapid hand.

"Eliot, you have seen those days, have you not ! when clouds gathered over the firmament ; when, one after another, each accustomed and dear object was lost in their leaden folds, when they grew darker and came nearer, till you felt yourself wrapped about in their chilling drapery, and you feared the blessed sun was blotted out of Heaven. Suddenly God's messenger hath come forth—the clouds have risen at his bidding, and unveiled his beautiful works. The smiling waters and the green fields, one after another, have appeared—the silvery curtain has rolled up the mountain's side, and then melted away and left the blue vault spotless. Such darkness has oppressed me ; such brightness is now above and around me. Dear Eliot, how glad you will be ! My spirits dance as they did in my childhood. The days are all clear, and the nights so beautiful, that I would not sleep if I could. Shame to those who steep themselves in the dull and brutish oblivion of sleep, when the intelligences of Heaven are abroad on the moonbeams, calling to the wakeful spirit to leave the drowsy world, and join their glorious company— to career from star to star, and commune in the silence of night with their Creator. Oh, Eliot ! I have heard the music 'of the young-eyed cherubim ;' and I have learned secrets—wonderful secrets of the offices and relations of spirits, if I were sure you would believe them—but no, you cannot. The mind must be prepared by months of suffering—it must pass a dark and winding way to reach (*while yet on earth*) the bright eminence where I stand. But take courage, brother ; when you pass the bounds of time you will hear, and see, and know what I now do.

"You will wonder how I have escaped the manacles that so long bound me. I cannot explain all now ; but thus much I am permitted to say, that they were riveted by certain charms : and I cannot be assured of my freedom till I myself return them to him from whom they came—to him who has so long been the lord of my affections and master of my mind. Then, and not till then, shall I be the 'self-rectified' being you blindly but truly predicted. I must go to New York ; but mind, dear brother, and indulge no idle fears for me. Do you remember once, when we read Comus together, wishing your sister might, like the sweet lady there, be attended by good spirits !— dear Eliot, I am. I cannot always see them through this thick veil of mortality, but I can both hear and feel them.

"Our good mother pesters me so. Should you think, brother, that a being accompanied as I am could eat and drink, and lie down and sleep as other mortals do ! Oh, no ! And, besides, are they not all the time praying that the Lord would send corn into their empty garners ; and yet, poor dull souls, they cannot see their prayer is answered, when I am fed and satisfied with bread from Heaven—sweet, spiritual food !

"I shall set forward to-night, when they are all steeped in this sleep they would fain stupify me with. I have not hinted to our mother my purpose, because, dear Eliot, since you are gone she is quite different from what she was. I would say it to none but you in the world ; but the truth is, she has grown very conceited, and would not believe one word of my superior knowledge. I do not blame her. The time is coming when the scales will fall from her eyes. Farewell, dear brother, —'angels guard thee,' as Jasper used to say ;—I can write his name now with a steady hand—what a change! They do guard me—the blessed angels! Once more, fear nothing, Eliot. In going, I am attended by that 'strong siding champion, conscience;' if I stay, he will desert me."

Eliot's manliness was vanquished, and he wept like a child over his sister's letter. He reproached himself for having left home. He bitterly reproached himself for not having foreseen the danger of her long, exclusive, and confiding intercourse with Meredith. He was almost maddened when he thought of the perils to which she must have been exposed, and of his utter inability to save her from one of them. The only solacing thought that occurred to him was the extreme improbability that her fragile and exhausted frame could support the fatigues she must encounter, and that even now, while he wept over her letter (a fortnight had elapsed since it was written), her gentle spirit might have entered upon its eternal rest.

CHAPTER XXII.

This fierce spirit of liberty is stronger in the English colonies, probably, than in any other people of the earth.
BURKE.

MEREDITH's last interview with Isabella, broken off so inopportunely by her mother, had left him perplexed and disappointed. His love for her, if analysed, might have exhibited much of the dross that belongs to a selfish and worldly spirit,—pride and vanity, and something perhaps yet lower than these; still it was a redeeming sentiment, and if it had not force enough to conquer all that was evil in him, it at least inspired some noble aspirations.

He had been apprised of his mother's arrival by a sort of official note which she sent him from the Narrows, the amount of which was, "that she had come out because she could see no prospect of an end to the atrocious war—that she had brought her dear niece, Lady Anne, because it was as impossible to separate her from her as to prolong her own cruel absence from her son." Meredith interpreted this note as readily as if he were reading a conventional diplomatic cipher, and thus re-read it. "The term of my dear niece, Lady Anne's mourning, is nearly expired—she will have scores of suitors, and her fortune will pass out of the family; while you, my dear son, are throwing yourself away upon the broken-down Linwoods—the only hope is in my crossing the horrible Atlantic, and braving storms and privateers."

Strange as it may seem, though thus forewarned, he felt that he was not fore-armed, at least in panoply divine; he distrusted his power of resistance, and was anxious to secure himself with grappling-irons before he should be wafted by his mother's influence whither she would. Once assured by her own lips, of what he had but the faintest doubt, that Isabella Linwood loved him, his fate would be fixed. He could tell his mother it was so, and she would be saved the trouble of setting her toils, and he from the necessity of avoiding her snare, and—from the danger of falling into it. If Jasper Meredith's virtue was infirm, he was sagacious, and had at least the merit of being conscious of the tottering base on which it rested.

When he left Isabella, he deferred his filial duties, and proceeded forthwith to the city prison, then called the Provost, where the prisoners of war who were in the city, with the exception of such officers as were on their parole, were herded together, and treated in all respects like criminals.

Meredith, provided with an order from Robertson, the commandant, and countersigned by Cunningham (of infamous memory), the keeper of the city prison, made his way through dens crowded with American soldiers, to a small inner cell, which Linwood was allowed the privilege of occupying alone. Meredith had paid Linwood daily visits, had reported to him his father's condition, and had each day laboured to give such a bias to his mind, as to lead him to the course which he was now authorised to set before him.

"Good morning, and good news for you, Linwood!" he said, as he shut the door after him.

"Ha! has General Washington interposed for me?"

Meredith shrugged his shoulders: "I alluded to your father."

"God forgive me! he is better then?"

"Quite relieved—the gout has gone to the feet, and if—if he were easy about you, there would be no danger of a relapse. But, my dear Linwood, you are looking ill yourself."

"Not ill—no, but deused hungry. Cunningham's short and sour commons leave an aching void, I assure you." Linwood placed his hands upon the seat of his most painful sensations at the moment.

"I hoped the partridges and madeira I smuggled in yesterday, would have made you independent of Cunningham's tender mercies, for twenty-four hours at least."

"Don't mention them just now, if you love me. I worked myself up to making them over to some poor wretches out there, who are dying by inches of bad and insufficient food—but hunger is selfish, and sharp-set as I now am, I am afraid I shall repent me of my good deeds—so don't speak of them. Are there no despatches, no letters, nothing from West Point?"

Meredith told him of the official communication received from Washington, and the letter from Eliot; of the one he spoke contemptuously, of the other coldly. He then paused for Herbert to give utterance to the disappointment expressed in his truth-telling face, but he was silent, and Meredith proceeded:—'One would think that a brave young officer who, like you, had sacrificed everything to a fancied duty, deserved a kind word at least from his commander; but these old-fashioned courtesies have a little too much of the aristocratic feudal taint for your republican leader. They savour of the protection the lord extends to his follower, in return for services that are more cheaply paid in continental rags, or in the promises of King Congress! It is a hard service where there is neither honour, favour, nor profit." Meredith again paused. Linwood was still silent, and he went on to make the proposition authorised by Sir Henry, and which he enforced by arguments of policy so artfully and plausibly urged, that an older and sterner casuist than our friend Herbert might have been puzzled, if not tempted. But "it was a joyous sight to see" how he brushed away the web that was spun about him. He opened the door that communicated with the adjoining apartment, and the generous blood mounting to his cheeks, "Do you see that young man!" he asked, in a low but energetic voice, and pointing to a youth who, pale and haggard, was stretched on the floor in one corner, wrapped in his camp-cloak, eating a crust of mouldy bread; "he is from Carolina, and as bold and generous a soldier as ever shouldered a musket. He and his two brothers joined the American army and came to the north —by the way, Jasper, please mark how the scattered and distant members of our vast country are drawn and bound together by one sentiment—we fight for Carolina, and Carolina fights for us. This poor fellow is the survivor of his two brothers—they fell in battle. His widowed mother lives on a small plantation. Her slaves have been decoyed away by the offer of freedom from your British officers—generous, forsooth! and she is left with one son. Yesterday this young man contrived to get a letter forwarded, entreating his mother to give up this son to her country. Look at that man with the frame of a Hercules, his joints loosened, and staggering as he crawls about from the effects of starvation, and the cursed fetid atmosphere of this hole! He is a Connecticut farmer, who began his career at Bunker's Hill. Think you he spends his time in bewailing unrequited services, and whining about continental money ? No, but in stimulating the spirits of these poor fellows by visions of the future glory of their free and independent country. 'Never mind, boys,' he says ; 'let 'em burn our houses (his was burned at Fairfield), our children shall live in better, and shall tie the flag with thirteen stripes, and maybe more, to the mast-head of their own ships.' Jasper, there is not one of these most abused men whose heart does not beat true to his country : to die doing battle for her would be nothing, that is the common lot of a soldier—but they are pining, starving, dying by inches here, without one thought disloyal to her. And I," he continued, after reclosing the door, " am to be humbled and gulled with offers that the most squalid wretch among them would spurn. Perhaps I deserve it ; there was one moment—but one, thank God! when, tempted by more than all the gold and all the honour in the king's gift, I swerved. I was saved by a look from Isabella. Do you think I could ever meet that eye again after I had joined Sir Henry's *honourable* corps of *Reformees.* I am humble, and with reason, Heaven knows ; but I do marvel, Jasper, that you could suggest dishonour to Isabella's brother."

"Pardon me, Mr. Linwood, we have different views of the honour of the course I proposed, which appears to me simply a return to your inalienable duty."

"We certainly have very different views, Jasper. You call those poor fellows out there rebels ; I, patriots. You think they deserve to be ground to the dust, I that they are infernally abused. You think Washington is cold, selfish, calculating, ambitious ; and I believe that he is generous, disinterested, just (thereby I suffer) ; and humane I know him to be, for there is

not a man within these walls, myself excepted, who has not received some intimation that he is remembered and cared for by his general. Now, with these *views,* I could as easily put on the poisoned tunic of Nessus as the uniform of the *Reformees.*"

The young men were both awkwardly silent for a few moments. Meredith was discomfited and mortified. Linwood's vexation had effervesced in his long speech ; to use a household simile, the scum had boiled over and left the liquor clear. "Hang it, Jasper," he resumed, in his natural good-humoured tone, "don't let's quarrel, though the more you will serve me the more I won't be served. We will agree to make over these contested topics to dame Posterity, who, instead of peering forward, as we must, into the dark future, has only to cast her eyes behind her to award an infallible decision. Fifty years hence, my dear fellow, would that we could be here to see it, New York will still be, if you are right, a petty colonial station for British officers ; if I am, the rich metropolis of an independent empire. But, *allons*—is there no news, no gossip, no agreeable scandal afloat !"

Meredith suddenly recollected and communicated the arrival of his mother and Lady Anne Seton, and the propriety of hastening to receive them. Linwood heartily congratulated him, little thinking how deeply his own fate was involved in this arrival.

Meredith went to play his filial part, and Herbert was left to solitary, but not sad, reflection. He felt a most comfortable, and perhaps unexpected assurance, that his virtues were purified and strengthened in the fires of adversity.

CHAPTER XXIII.

She, the fair sun of all her sex,
Has bless'd my glorious day ;
And shall a glimmering planet fix
My worship to its ray !—Burns.

Meredith, after leaving the Provost, was hastening down Broad Street, when he perceived a carriage approaching him. At this moment a band of black musicians, who were in training, bearing the British flag, turned from Beaver into Broad Street ; and as they turned, struck up a march in the faces of the horses. The suddenness of the apparition and the clamour terrified them ; they reared and plunged. A lady screamed from the coach to the musicians to stop ; but the souls of the Africans were lapped in the elysium of their own music, and they neither heard nor heeded till Meredith, springing forward, dashed the instrument of their leader to the ground. The music then ceased, and the coachman, by great adroitness or strength, or both, checked the progress of his steeds, while two ladies sprang from the coach, and were followed by shrieking waiting-maids and broken bandboxes, with their contents of feathers, flowers, ribands, fans, &c., showering over the pavement.

The elder of the two ladies looked as if she could have lifted up her hands and wept ; the younger did lift up hers and laugh. "Make haste, Nancy," said the elder ; " oh, the coloured hair-powders—shut up the box, they are all blowing away—we can get none here."

" *Dépêchez-vous, Thérèse*," cried the young lady ; " oh, *mes fleurs—mes plumes* ! "

" *Ah, oui, mon Dieu ! qu'est-ce que c'est qu'une demoiselle sans plumes, sans fleurs !* ' replied the little trig Française, fluttering hither and yonder to reclaim her treasures from the dispersing winds.

" My dear mother !" exclaimed a voice, that for a moment silenced the chattering, and called forth a parenthetical and *sotto-voce* exclamation from Thérèse—"*Ah, le fils de madame—un bel homme !* "

While the usual expressions of a joyful meeting were interchanging, Mrs. Linwood, who from her window had watched the affair to its *dénouement*, appeared at her door, calling " Jasper, bring the ladies here, I entreat you. My dear Mrs. Meredith, I am so sorry you have had such a fright, and yet so very glad to see you."

" For the love of Heaven, who is she !" asked Mrs. Meredith, so averting her face as to limit her query to her son.

" Mrs. Linwood."

A shadow passed over Mrs. Meredith's face ; but she instantly replied, " My dear Mrs. Linwood, how very happy I am to see you again—an awkward *début*, this," shrugging her shoulders ; " but so fortunate it should have happened at your door ;—that the first house my foot enters in America should be that of a friend."

" A friend ! Mrs. Linwood ! strange, I never heard my aunt mention the name," thought Lady Anne.

" Lady Anne Seton," continued Mrs. Meredith, presenting her niece ; " and how is the dear husband ! and Herbert, my harum-scarum little friend, as I used to call him ! Miss Belle—ah, ten years make such changes—' the boy and girl to man and woman grown ;' and yourself—upon my word, Mrs. Linwood, the ten years have slipped by without touching you."

" Aunt forgets she did not recognise her," thought Lady Anne ; and she conveyed her observation of the discrepancy by such an arch glance at her aunt, that she checked the floodtide of her civilities, and gave Mrs. Linwood, who was nearly overpowered by them, time to rally. She, good woman, received them all literally ; and, in return, furnished the most circumstantial details of her husband's late illness, told when he took physic and when he did not ; when his laudanum made him sleep and when it would not—to all of which Mrs. Meredith " lent the pitying ear" of a thorough-bred lady, while she was mentally wondering the woman could be such a fool as to think she cared whether her husband were dead or alive. After having threaded the mazes of the materia medica, Mrs. Linwood concluded with, " Bless me ! I have not sent for Isabella !" The good lady trusted she had given Isabella time to make her toilette. Mrs. Linwood's artifices were very pardonable, and never exceeded some trifling manœuvre to keep the best foot forward without apparent limping. She rang the bell ;—no one answered. " Jasper, will you have the goodness," she said, " to tap at her father's door, and let Belle know who is here—you see Jasper is quite one of us, Mrs. Meredith."

A more acute observer than Mrs. Linwood would have understood the lowering of Mrs. Meredith's brow, as her eye followed her son. " Jasper has been fortunate, indeed, in making such friends," she said ; " a great security is it, my dear Mrs. Linwood, for a young man to have domestic influences, and *such* influences."

On opening Mr. Linwood's door, Meredith found Isabella apparently absorbed in reading a political pamphlet to her father. " Ah, Jasper, I am glad to see you !" cried out Mr. Linwood : " I give you joy. I have been trying, ever since I heard your mother was below, to drive this girl down ; but she sticks to me like the breath of my nostrils. Now Jasper has come for you, you *must* go, Belle."

" Not *must*, sir, unless Miss Linwood prefers to do so."

" Did you come for me—I mean, did my mother send for me !"

" Do not go down if it is disagreeable to you," said Meredith, replying to rather more than met her ear.

" Pshaw ! go Belle ; your dress is well enough ; the ladies—no disrespect, Jasper, it's the nature of the animal—will like you all the better for being worse dressed than themselves."

Isabella was not sorry to have her reluctance ascribed to her dishabille ; but that, though she had some womanish feeling about it, constituted a very small portion of her shrinking from a presentation to Jasper's mother and fair cousin. She had, however, enough self-control to do well whatever must be done ; and without farther hesitation she gave her arm to Meredith. As soon as her father's door was closed after them, he paused. He was intensely anxious to intimate to his mother, at their first meeting, the relation that he believed would subsist between them : but while he hesitated how to word this wish, Isabella prevented him.

" You have seen Herbert !"

" Yes."

" And the result !" she added, with a quivering lip.

" Precisely as you wished."

" Dear, dear Herbert !" she exclaimed, and sprang forward with a lightened heart and buoyant step. The first flush of elevated and gratified feeling beamed from her soul-lit eye and dyed her cheek.

The light within shone on all without her. Her personal anxieties were forgotten ; and to her natural elegance of manner there was a graciousness and brightness that made her at once shine forth as the sun of the little circle. Mrs. Meredith had proposed to herself to be condescending to Miss Linwood ; and was quite sure that Lady Anne, whom she had induced, with an eye to a first impression on Jasper, to array herself before leaving the ship in a French walking-dress, would be *frappante*. But both ladies were destined to feel in Isabella's presence they were lesser lights. Her simple morning dress, and the classic arrangement of her dark rich hair, unspoiled and untouched by the profane fashion of the times, contrasted most favourably with the forced, prim, and fantastical mode of the day.

Mrs. Meredith was as near being astounded as a woman of the world ever can be, and was actually embarrassed and uncomfortable ; but Lady Anne, though surprised, was charmed. For a moment she might have felt overshadowed ; but nothing could, for more than one moment, cloud her sunny self-complacency. " *Qu'elle a l'air noble !*" she whispered to her cousin—" She has been abroad ?—in France ?"

" No," he replied ; " but undisputed superiority anywhere is apt to produce '*l'air noble.*'" Meredith was not a man of independent opinions ; and he had never felt a more assured admiration of Isabella than now, that he witnessed her impression on his reluctant and lady-of-the-world mother, and his *à-la-mode* cousin.

" You find Isabella grown ?" said Mrs. Linwood, expecting to elicit a flood of compliments.

" Oh, certainly," replied Mrs. Meredith, " very much grown : ten years, you know, makes a vast difference. Miss Linwood was not, I believe, much over twelve when I went home."

" Ten—twelve—twenty-two—bless me ! no, dear Mrs. Meredith, she is not yet quite twenty," said the simple mother, as eagerly as if she were putting in the plea " not guilty."

" Scarcely three years older than my niece," replied Mrs. Meredith, with an evident satisfaction in the three years minus.

" And what are three years ?" exclaimed Lady Anne ; " they shall make no gulf between us, Miss Linwood ; we will be friends at once—intimate—will we not ?"

" You are very kind."

" Oh, not in the least. It will be quite as much my gain as yours. Aunt has brought me out to make my *début* here ; and half the pleasure, I think, must consist in having a friend—a confidante, to talk over one's conquests with."

" Lady Anne, my love, you are so elated by getting out of that odious ship, that you hardly know what you are talking about."

" I beg your pardon, aunt, I do. I was talking on the most enchanting subjects : lovers, conquests, and confidantes."

" And what do you know about lovers and confidantes, my dear child ? They are the unknown inhabitants of a *terra incognita* to you."

" My veteran mother," thought Meredith, " would fain shelter my pretty cousin with the *ægis* of simplicity." But simplicity was not in the *rôle* of the young lady. " *Mille pardons, chère tante,*" she replied—" have you not for the last twelve months been teaching me the geography of this unknown world ?—and, besides, what think you we read of, talk of, dream of, at a boarding school—history ?—Greeks and Romans ?—no, no, dear lady : young lords and nice officers in scarlet coats and epaulettes, and, now and then, *par parenthèse—un beau cousin.*" A bright glance at Jasper with these last words propitiated his mother, and Lady Anne was permitted to proceed. " I take it for granted, Miss Linwood, that New York is quite a paradise just now ?'"

" If ' nice young officers' are the birds of your paradise, Lady Anne, it is."

" The *beau cousin* might perhaps be admitted into yours," retorted the young lady, archly looking at Isabella for the blush she expected to provoke ; but the blush called for came not to Isabella Linwood's cheek.

Mrs. Meredith explored another face. Jasper's brilliant eyes impulsively turned towards Isabella, and there came a revelation from them that she would not admit, and yet could not misunderstand. " My dear son," said she, " I must trouble you to order a carriage for us. I am quite forgetting myself in the happiness of meeting an old friend."

Mrs. Linwood interposed. The time had not yet passed away when such primitive hospitalities were frankly offered and unceremoniously accepted, and she insisted on her friends staying to pass the day. Mrs. Meredith declined as resolutely as courtesy would permit ; but Lady Anne, independent in all her proceedings, expressed so strong an inclination to remain, and brushed away her aunt's objections of meeting with such evident and relentless assurance of their flimsiness, that Mrs. Meredith was reduced, as a last resource, to yield with grace.

The day, on many accounts, was oppressive to Isabella. Her sisterly thoughts were much with Herbert ; she was anxious for his future ; and in imagination painfully contrasted his solitary prison with the seeming cheerfulness of his father's house. There was something in Meredith's manner that offended her. It was constrained and elaborate, and it was evident to her that he shunned disclosing their actual relations to his mother, and sheltered them from her penetration by appearing quite engrossed in playful devotion to his pretty cousin. She was annoyed with Mrs. Meredith's hollow and emphasised superlatives. She bore a strong personal resemblance to her son. Isabella was now and then painfully startled by a corresponding mental resemblance, which affected her somewhat like those family likenesses where an ugly face, by a sort of travestie, brings into question the beauty of a more fortunate one. The qualities that were glaring and obtrusive in the mother, were in the son sheltered by a nicer tact, and a more acute perception of their effect on others. " But," Isabella asked herself, " were they less real or less hopeless ?"

Isabella, in her turn, was the subject of passing speculation to Mrs. Meredith. At first, when she appeared all radiant with animation, the sagacious lady concluded that she had taxed all her powers to take the heart of Jasper's mother by a *coup-de-théâtre ;* but afterwards she could find no satisfactory solution to Isabella's abstractedness and apparent carelessness whether she pleased her or not. Nothing is so incomprehensible to a mere worldly spirit, spell-bound within a narrow circle of selfish interests, as the workings of an independent, lofty mind.

Isabella's sole enjoyment that day was from a source whence it would be least expected—from her probable rival—from the light-hearted, good-humoured Lady Anne ; and before they parted they had made fair progress towards an intimacy.

The intimacies that occur between persons of powerful and inferior character, probably result from the same necessity of the mind that drives a statesman to relaxation over a senseless game of cards, or (if, as with Edmund Burke, his heart overflows with the milk of human kindness) leads him to play at leap-frog with children. The same principle may furnish a solution for some puzzling disparities in matrimonial alliances.

" And what sort of a person is this Lady

Anne!" asked Mr. Linwood of his daughter, who had been giving him such particulars of the day as she thought might entertain him.

"Very pretty, and graceful, and agreeable too. I am sure you will like her, papa. It is amusing to see how she goes straight forward to her point, like a bird by an air line, while her aunt winds about as if she were manœuvring a ship into port in presence of an enemy; oh, above all things, I like truth, straightforwardness! Lady Anne is not brilliant, nor has she, I imagine, any great depth of feeling; but she is independent, true, and kind-hearted, and in such good-humour with herself, that she makes small demands upon others;—I like her."

"And do not fear her, Belle!"

Isabella answered to her father's probing glance proudly. "Fear her!—no, sir—no," she reiterated, but in a less assured tone.

"Bravo, my girl! but depend on't she will be a star in our firmament, this Lady Anne. What a match she would have been for Herbert—obstinate, foolish, dear boy."

"Thank you for that, papa! he is dear and noble, and like his father in clinging to what he believes to be right."

"That is like me," replied Mr. Linwood, wiping the mist from his eyes; "but not like me, Belle, not at all like me, in mistaking wrong for right."

Strangely is the human mind compounded. Mr. Linwood had been informed of Herbert's rejection of Sir Henry Clinton's proffer. This bonâ fide intimation of the resemblance Herbert had manifested to his father in this rejection, placed the action in a fresh and favourable aspect. Vanity has its uses.

CHAPTER XXIV.

Come può ritarre il piedo
Inesperto pellegrino
Dagli inciampi che non vede,
Dai perigli che non sa?—METASTASIO.

IT was long before the dawn of one of the few soft days of October, 1779, that Bessie Lee left her safe home to begin a perilous journey. The light of reason was not quite extinct, and with some forecast she took a few coins, keepsakes, that had long lain idly in a drawer, and transferred them to her pocket; then placing in her bosom the little ivory box containing, as she wildly fancied, the charms that bound her to Jasper Meredith, she equipped herself for her journey. A regard to dress is an innate idea in a woman, that no philosopher can deny to the sex. In all her mutations, that remains.

The resemblance of the dress of an insane person to the ill-sorted and imperfect equipment in a dream, verifies Rush's remark, that derangement is a long dream—a dream a short derangement. Bessie, after looking over her moderate wardrobe, selected the only gala dress it contained—a white silk petticoat and blue bodice; but after dressing herself in them, either from the instinct of neatness, or from the glimmering of the unfitness of such travelling apparel, she took off the silk petticoat, and after tying it in a handkerchief with some more essential articles, she laced the bodice over a dimity skirt, and put over that a long linen night-gown. Delighted with her own provident sagacity in arraying herself for day and night, she threw over the whole a brown silk cardinal, and a chip gipsy hat tied down with a blue gauze handkerchief. "He always told me I had inspiration in dress," she said, as she gave a pleased, parting glance at the glass. In passing her mother's door, she paused: "I have heard it was a bad sign," thought she, "to leave home without your parent's blessing; but I go forth with Heaven's, and hers must follow." She then proceeded to equip her horse, and set out on the New York road, which she pursued unerringly. She fancied that the same providential exemption from the necessity of sustenance vouchsafed to her was extended to her horse Steady, and the animal, happening to be full-fed, sturdy, and of hard-working habits, seemed to acquiesce in his supposed destiny, save now and then, when he resolutely halted at a stream of water to slake his thirst. The part of New England through which Bessie's route lay, was sterile and thinly settled. She was unmolested, and for the most part unobserved. She would sometimes pass a house where the children would pause from their play, stare, and ask one of the other—who that pretty lady could be! and wonder that, with such a nice cloak, she should ride without gloves! Once a kind-hearted farmer stopped her, and after asking her numberless questions, to which he received no satisfactory replies, he earnestly begged her to stop at his house for some refreshment. She declined his hospitality with an assurance that she did not need it, and a smile that so little harmonised with her blanched cheek, and wild melancholy eye, that the good man said her looks haunted him. In truth, so unearthly was her appearance, that two gossips, whom she passed on the road, stopped, drew nearer to each other, and, without speaking, gazed after her till she was out of sight; and then, with feminine particularity, compared their observations.

"She's master beautiful!" exclaimed one of them.

"Call you that beautiful!" replied her companion; "why, she has neither flesh nor blood—I felt a chill when I looked at her."

"And I felt my blood rush to my heart, as if I had seen something out of nature. I might have taken her for an angel, but for her silk cardinal, and her horse, that looked more like our old roan than like the horses in Revelations."

Nancy was less imaginative. "I did not see nothing mysterious," she said, "but her pale little hands that looked as if they could hardly hold a thread of silk."

"My! did not you see those long curls that streamed down below the hood of her cloak, looking as bright and soft as Judith's baby when we laid it out—poor thing! and the colour of her cheeks, that were as white as my poor man's fresh tombstone—and her eyes, that shone like stars of a frosty night! don't tell me, Nancy; we must expect to see visions, and dream dreams when there's war in the land, and famine at the door!" The unconscious subject of this colloquy went on, her innocent heart dilating with a hope as assured and buoyant as that of a penitent on her way to a shrine where absolution and peace await her.

It was late in the afternoon, when, emerging from a wood, she observed that at a short distance before her the road forked. She was hesitating which direction to take, when seeing two men seated on a log by the fence, she reined her horse towards them. They were soldiers returning from service, who had laid down their knapsacks and halted to refresh themselves with some coarse food, which was spread on the ground. Bessie was close upon them, and had stopped her horse, when their broad insolent stare awakened her timidity, and she was turning away when one of them seized her bridle, exclaiming, " Not so fast, my pretty mistress! first thoughts are best; what did you come here for?"

" Oh!" she answered, confused and stammering, " I—I—I do not know—I came for—for—nothing."

" Then don't be scared—for nothing can come of nothing—(a rare sight, a petticoat, hey, Mart!) —come, dismount, lady fair."

Bessie seemed paralysed. Mart's face expressed an emotion of compassion—" I say, Raphe," he interposed, " be civil; let her go on."

" I mean to be civil, you sir; don't you see her horse is half starved " (the poor beast was eagerly cropping the grass), " and she looks as if she had not tasted victuals for a month—come come, little one, what are you 'fraid of!" and slipping her foot from the stirrup, he lifted her from the saddle and seated her on the log. He then took up the blue check handkerchief on which their repast (coarse brown bread, slices of raw pork, and apples) was spread; " come, take some and eat away," he continued, " that's a nice girl!" Bessie, the delicate, shrinking Bessie, seized the food thus offered and thus served, and ate ravenously. In her disordered state she seemed to exist in two separate natures; the mind took no cognizance of the necessities or sensations of the body, and the body, at the first opportunity, asserted and gratified its cravings. While she ate, the men talked apart. " This is droll, by jiminy!" said Mart; " who or what do you guess she is, Raphe?"

" Some stray cast-off of some of the old-country folks—German gin'rals or English lords."

" She don't look like it," said Mart, after having cast at Bessie a surveying glance, in which pity was mingled with curiosity.

" Don't look like it! you can't tell what she does look like. She's worried, and pale, and scared out of her wits; but I tell you what does look like it—do you see that fandango finery (Bessie's blue bodice) peeping out of the neck of her gown! By the living jingo, she eats like a Trojan, don't she! This way she'll soon get the blood back to her pretty cheeks. But I say, Mart, we must make some sort of a calculation what to do—"

" What to do! That's plain enough—let her go her way, and we'll go ours."

" You're a fool, Mart, and t'ant the first time I've thought so."

" And you're a rogue, Raphe, nor is it the first time I've thought so."

Raphe's angry blood mounted to his cheeks: but well aware this was not the moment for a broil, he gulped down his passion, and resumed, in a more conciliating tone: " There's no use in falling out, Mart; we've had lean fortin long enough, and when a streak of fat comes, I don't see no reason in turning our plates bottom side upwards—do you?"

" No."

" It's plaguy tedious walking barefoot." He looked significantly at the horse. " There's a hundred long miles to foot it before I see home."

" And a hundred and fifty to boot, before I see the top of our steeple."

" Then I conclude 'twould be an accommodation to you, as well as to me, to ride and tie that stout beast?"

" And she?" said Mark, interrogatively, and pointing to Bessie.

" Why, she—she's as light as a feather. She can ride behind while she behaves and holds her tongue, and we find it convenient. The like of her can't expect to pick and choose."

" You're a d—d rascal, Raphe!" This exclamation, spoken with energy and in a louder voice than the previous conversation, roused Bessie's attention, and she listened to and comprehended what followed. " I'm going home, to our folks," continued Mart, " and do you think I could look mammy in the face after such a trick as that?"

" Well, well, man—don't be mad; if one shoe don't fit, another may. Supposing we just slip into this wood with this traveller, just so far that she can't rouse people on the high road here with crying 'stop thief!' and then we'll be off on the beast; that, on my conscience, I believe is no more hers than ours." Before the sentence was finished, Bessie had sprung into her saddle. Raphe, whose fierce passions had been kept in abeyance by the necessity of his companion's co-operation, now sprang forward and seized her bridle. " Oh, mercy! mercy!" cried the terrified girl.

A blow from Mart's fist on his side obliged Raphe to turn and defend himself; and Bessie, thus released, urged her horse onward, leaving her champion to do battle in her righteous cause, which he did so manfully and thoroughly that Raphe was disabled for the present, and left to curse his own folly and to pursue his pedestrian journey alone.

Bessie's horse fortunately selected the right road; and refreshed by his half-hour's rest, he obeyed his mistress' signals to hasten onward. These signals she reiterated, from an impression of some indefinite danger pursuing her. By degrees, however, her thoughts reverted to their former channels, and she dwelt no more on her recent alarm than a dreamer does on an escaped precipice. A languor stole over her that prevented her from observing Steady's motions. From a fast trot he had slackened to a walk, and after thus creeping on for a mile or two, he stood stock-still.

Bessie sat for a while as if waiting his pleasure, and then looking at the setting sun, she said, " Well, Steady, you have done your day's duty, and I'll not be unmerciful to you. I too have a tired feeling," and she passed her hand over her throbbing temples; " but, Steady, we will not stay here by the roadside, for I think there be bad people on this road; and besides, it is better to be alone where only God is."

The country through which Bessie was now passing was rocky, hilly, and wooded, excepting narrow intervals and some few cleared and cultivated slopes. She had just passed a brook, that glided quietly through a very green little meadow on her left, but which, on her right, though screened from sight, sounded its approach as in the glad spirit of its young life it came leaping and dancing down a rocky gorge. Bessie, as it would seem from the instinct of humanity, let down some bars to allow her hungry steed admittance to the meadow, saying, as she did so, " You shall have the green pastures and still waters, Steady, where those home-looking willows are turning up their silvery leaves as if to kiss the parting sunbeams, and the sun-flower and the golden rod are still flaunting in their pride, poor things ! But I will go on the other side, where the trees stand bravely up, to screen and guard me—and the waterfall will sing me to sleep.''

She crossed the road and plunged into the wood, and without even a footpath to guide her, she scrambled along the irregular margin of the brook. Sometimes she swung herself round the trunk of a tree by grasping the tough vines encircling it ; sometimes, when a bold perpendicular rock projected over the water, she surmounted it, as if the danger of wetting her feet must be avoided at all pains and risks ; then a moss-covered rock imbedded in the stream attracting her eye, she would spring on to it, drop her feet into the water, doff her little chip hat, and bathe her burning temples in the cool stream ; and when she again raised her head, shook back her curls and turned her face heavenward, her eye glowing with preternatural brightness, she might have been mistaken for a wanderer from the celestial sphere gazing homeward. After ascending the stream for about a hundred yards, she came to a spot which seemed to her excited imagination to have been most graced

By the sovereign planter, when He formed
All things for man's delightful use;

and, in truth, it was a *resting-place* for the troubled spirit, far more difficult to find than a bed of down for the wearied body.

The thicket here expanded and spread its encircling arms around a basin worn into the earth by the force of the stream, which leaped into it over a rock some thirty feet in height. Here and there a rill straggled away from the slender column of water, and as it caught the sun's slant ray, dropped down the rock in sparkling gems. The trees were wreathed with grape-vines, whose clusters peeped through the brown leaves into the mirror below. The leaves of the topmost branches of the trees were touched with the hues of autumn, and hung over the verdant tresses below them like a wreath of gorgeous flowers. The sky was clear, and the last rays of the setting sun stole in obliquely, sweet and sad, as the parting smile of a friend, glancing along the stems of the trees and flashing athwart the waterfall.

" Here will I lay me down and rest," said Bessie, rolling up with her foot a pillow of crisp crimson leaves that had fallen from a young delicate tree, fit emblem of herself, stricken by the first touch of adversity. " But first I will say my prayers, for I think this is one of God's temples." She knelt and murmured forth the broken aspirations of her pure heart, and then laying herself down, she said, " I wish mother and Eliot could see me now— they would be so satisfied ! "

Once she raised her head, gazed at the soft mist that was curling up from the water, and seemed intently listening. " I have somewhere read," she said, " that

Millions of spiritual creatures walk the earth,
Unseen, both when we wake and when we sleep.

I believe it ! " Again her head fell back on its sylvan pillow, and utterly incapable of farther motion or thought, she sank to deep repose. Night came on, the watchful stars shone down upon her, the planets performed their nightly course, the moon rose and set, and still the unconscious sufferer slept on.

CHAPTER XXV.

Alas ! what poor ability's in me
To do him good !
Assay the power you have.—MEASURE FOR MEASURE.

" AH, Belle, is that you ! " said Mrs. Archer, as Miss Linwood just as twilight stole into her aunt's room to have a *tête-à-tête* with the only person in the world with whom she had a strictly confidential intimacy. " What is Sir Henry's answer ! "

" Just such as we might have expected. He does, to be sure, in good set terms, beg me to have no apprehensions about my brother. But he says it is impossible for him just now to grant me an opportunity to speak to him in private on the subject : ' it would be quite useless,' and ' he's particularly occupied,' and all such trumpery excuses."

" Then take my advice, Belle, and make the opportunity he will not grant :—go to his ball this evening. Never mind the gossip of kind friends, who will wonder you can have the heart to appear there when your brother is in such unfortunate circumstances. You and I agree in the principle of never sacrificing the greater to the less—go ; Sir Henry will not refuse you his ear when you are before him ; and if you cannot obtain all you desire, you may get some mitigation of poor Herbert's condition.''

" I have made up my mind—I will go."

" You will meet Lady Anne Seton ! The ball is given in honour of her arrival, I hear."

" Yes."

" You are very pensive and *monosyllabic*, Belle: has any thing occurred ! Have you seen Jasper since that last critical conjuncture in your affairs ! "

" No—oh, yes, he has called two or three times with Lady Anne."

" Then something has *not* occurred, which amounts to pretty much the same thing ; or, perhaps, my dear child, you are beginning to feel a little tremulous about this pretty and rich cousin ! "

" No aunt, I assure you that my first serious doubt on that subject would fix my wavering judgment.''

" And your feelings ! "

" They go in the same scale with my judgment. You know that I do not expect perfection. If ever I marry, which I think very doubtful—you may smile, aunt Mary, but I think it more than doubt-ful—I shall expect faults in abundance. Heaven knows I am no match for perfection ; I only ask that they may not be such faults as affect the vitality of the character."

"And you would cease to love, Isabella, where you suspected such ?"

"If I merely suspected," replied Isabella, fal-tering, "I cannot say ; but if I were sure, most certainly."

"A suspicion of ten years' standing is, I should think—" assurance doubly sure, she would have added ; but wondering at the subtleties of that sentiment that could mystify the perceptions of the clear-sighted Isabella Linwood, she merely said, "it matters not what I think—you will both feel and act right ; and if you ought to get rid of the shackles, you will not wait till they rust off."

Mrs. Archer had never interposed her advice in Isabella's affair with Meredith, though she watched its progress with far more interest than if it had been a disease that might issue in death. She thought it was a case where she must and would work out her own salvation ; and where, at any rate, she must be left to the free decision of her own heart. Still she found it impossible in their confidential womanly intercourse not to betray her own biases ; and whenever they were betrayed, Isabella felt them the more, as they produced the only discord in the perfect harmony of their minds. The souls of the aunt and niece seemed to be in-formed by the same spirit. They had the same independence of mind, the same acute perception of truth through all the adventitious circumstances and artificial forms of society, the same restive-ness under the everlasting trifling of frivolous minds, the same kindling at what was beautiful in thought, and the same enthusiasm for the beauti-ful in action.

After Mrs. Archer's last words to her, Isabella sat thoughtful and silent, till her aunt reminded her that it was quite time she should go home and dress for Sir Henry's ball.

"I will go," she replied, "though there is nothing in life I detest quite so much as playing suitor to a great man."

"Then, my dear child, you had best come on our side, for so long as we are colonists, and wear the yoke, suing and obsequiousness is the necessity of our condition."

"You would take advantage of my pride to make me a republican. The very first rebel, if I remember, was he who ' could not bow and sue for grace with suppliant knee.' "

"An arch-rebel he was, but no republican ; our champions are republicans, and no rebels, since they claim only their original and indefea-sible rights. But here come Ned and Lizzy to assert theirs."

The children were attracted by Isabella's voice. Her hearty devotion to them made them regard her much in the light of the good genius of an eastern tale, who never appears without conferring some signal happiness. "Tell me, Ned," said she, "are you whig or tory ?"

"I used to be a tory, cousin Belle, because you were, and I thought mama was."

"And now ?"

"I'm for Washington ; but don't you tell," he replied, kissing her.

"And you, Lizzy, do you know what whig and tory means ?"

"To be sure : I know whig means the very best man in the world, and that is Captain Lee ; and I shall always love the whigs best——"

"And I begin to love their cause best too, my dear children ; and with this parting con-fession, which pray keep to yourselves, good-bye to you all."

Mrs. Archer hailed the change of Isabella's sentiments (a woman's political conclusions are rather sentiments than opinions) as a good omen. It was a link broken in the chain that bound her to Meredith ; and it indicated, as she thought, the weakness of the whole chain. She thus concluded a long reverie : "Belle thinks and feels inde-pendently. No woman in the unimpaired perfection and intensity of love does this. Milton understood our nature when he put those words of dependence and tenderness into Eve's mouth :—

" God is thy law, thou mine : to know no more,
Is woman's happiest knowledge, and her praise."

The gala days of Sir Henry Clinton's reign in New York are still celebrated in traditionary fire-side-stories, as a brilliant period in the colonial *beau-monde.* However unsuited to the times, the exiled whigs, who were driven forth from their homes, might have deemed this pomp, pageantry, feasting, and revelry ; however much it might have exasperated the Americans, who, half-starved and half-clothed, were contending for their rights, it served to kill the ennui of foreign officers, to bring *en scène* the pretty candidates for husbands, and, in short, to do what is done for us by the balls and company (society ?) of our own gay seasons. Never, according to the grandmamas, was there such abundance of the elements of a belle's happiness—such music !—such dresses !—so many, and such admirers !

"My dear Jasper," said Mrs. Meredith, while Lady Anne, in Sir Henry's antechamber, was telling a bevy of admiring young ladies that her French milliner had fashioned her dress after one of Maria Antoinette's ; "my dear Jasper, is not your cousin looking perfectly lovely this evening ?"

"For the first time I think her beautiful."

"She is beautiful !—Colonel Davidson says she is by far the prettiest woman on this side the Atlantic." The lady paused ; and then, being in her arguments what is called an authority lawyer, proceeded. "Sir Edward remarked, as he handed me up-stairs, how superior her air is to that of the young women here : indeed how should they have an air, poor things, in this demi-savage world ?"

Meredith could not but smile as he compared his cousin to that model of elegance enthroned in his mind. He coolly replied, "Lady Anne is easy."

"Easy !—bless me, Jasper, Helen Ruthven is what I call easy ; and a very engaging girl she is —but Lady Anne ! Sir Henry himself remarked her grace, her faultless proportions. There is that troublesome St. Clair peering through the door ; he means to ask her for the first dance—pray anticipate him, Jasper : it is her *début ;* you will oblige me infinitely, my son."

"What are you and aunt caballing about ?" asked Lady Anne, approaching.

"Conspiring against the world, fair cousin : I am entreating my mother to interpose her authority, and command you to lead down the first dance with me."

"Her authority! I cannot dance with a collar round my neck. If you wish it, authority out of the question, I will dance with you with all my heart. Of course you know, cousin Jasper," she added, as at the striking up of the music Meredith led her into the dancing-room, "I prefer you to a tiresome stranger."

"You flatter me!"

"No, indeed," replied the young lady, without perceiving that Meredith was piqued by her unvarnished truth, "I never flatter : one gets so tired of flattery, that hears nothing else all day from her admirer down to her dressing-maid. I never should flatter where I particularly wished to please."

Meredith was always inferring a little more than met the ear, winding in a labyrinthine path where he was not likely to meet one who, like his literal cousin, went straight forward. "Ah, my pretty coz, are you there!" thought he. "You would have me understand that though you do not wear my mother's collar, you are well enough inclined to go where she would guide you."

Lady Anne took the station assigned her in the dance by the ritual of precedence ; but as soon as she moved, it was plain that, whatever rank was assigned her, nature and art had decreed she should there be first. Those who went before her through the mazes of the long dance, sighed, panted, and puffed at the imminent risk of breaking the bounds of their whalebone prisons, or sinking under their brocades. She, in a dress that for lightness and grace would have suited an Ariel or a Persian dancing-girl, moved like a bird through its own element. There was no sign of effort or fatigue. Her eyes, instead of being set by overpowering exertion, or wandering like an ambitious performer's, sparkled with animation, and her coral lips parted in a child-like smile. She seemed to have surrendered herself to the music, and to be a poetic manifestation of the pleasure of motion. The observers followed her to the foot of the dance : the dancers became mere observers.

Lady Anne received this tribute as a matter of course, and if she were not surprised, she was not elated by it. Not so Mrs. Meredith ; she enjoyed it as a triumph. She had anticipated the sensation to be produced on the assembly, and had made a pretty accurate estimate of that which, by a very natural reaction, would be felt by Meredith ; and when, stationed near them, she heard the eloquent flood of compliments he poured out,—heard him, this time unbidden, earnestly beg his cousin's hand for another dance, she turned away satisfied that the first step was taken.

Every one present who might aspire to such distinction, asked Lady Anne's hand, and each solicitation enriched the prize to Meredith, for (if it be allowed thus to speak of such high concernments), he graduated even ladies' favours by their market value.

Miss Ruthven had not been dancing herself; she was conscious of not dancing well ; but hovering about the dance, and expressing, whenever she caught Meredith's eye, by animated gestures

and significant glances, her admiration of his partner. At the first opportunity she said to Lady Anne, in a low voice, but not too low to be heard by Meredith,—"How very glad I am that my dear friend, Isabella Linwood, is not here."

"And how very sorry I am!—but pray, Miss Ruthven, why are you glad?"

"Oh, you know—you faultless creature, I am sure you know."

"Indeed, I cannot conjecture."

"Then, if I must tell, one does not like to see one's friends outshone. Isabella Linwood has so long been the brightest star in our firmament. Ah, Mr. Meredith, sic transit !—as you learned in the tongues say."

Meredith made no reply, for at this moment he caught Isabella's eye as she entered the room, leaning on Sir Henry's arm. She was dressed in a white silk gown, without any ornament or decoration whatever, save a rich Brussels lace veil, which she had put on partly to screen and partly to apologise for her very simple and rather inappropriate toilet.

"Ah, console-toi, mon amie !" exclaimed Lady Anne, touching Miss Ruthven's arm with her fan, "look at that peerless creature, and tell me now whose light will wax dim. I like my own looks as well, I am sure, as anybody else likes them, but I can see that I am quite une chose terrestre compared with Isabella Linwood—n'est-ce pas, mon cousin !"

"Les choses terrestres are best adapted to the sphere for which they are created," said Meredith, turning, with a bitter smile, from what he thought a very cold salutation from Miss Linwood, to begin the second dance with Lady Anne.

Isabella stood for a moment with the rest, admiring and wondering at Lady Anne's performance ; then, intent on the object which alone brought her to Sir Henry's, she begged five minutes' audience in the library. "There she goes," thought Mrs. Meredith, taking a long breath, as if relieved from a load, "I knew it would make her very uncomfortable."

"Ah," thought Meredith, as following Isabella with his eyes he blundered in the dance—"there is something of the terrestre in that movement—I will profit by it."

"Quite as terrestrial as the rest of us," thought Helen Ruthven ; and as she stationed herself next to Mrs. Meredith, and made some very acceptable remarks about Miss Linwood, she felt like a political manœuvrer, who, having started rival candidates, flatters himself he shall run into the goal between them.

"To what am I indebted for this grace, Miss Linwood!" asked Sir Henry, rather to relieve Isabella than to inform himself of what he already anticipated.

"I am here a beggar, Sir Henry."

"In your brother's behalf!—I understand,—a very painful subject, my dear young lady ;—I feel, on my honour I do, the deepest sympathy with your father. You are aware that I have done all in my power for the misguided young man, and that he has not accepted my overtures."

"And that his refusal is the warrant of his honour—is it not, Sir Henry!"

"Why, there are many modifications of this principle of honour. You would not hold a thief bound by his oath to his comrades, if he were offered pardon and enrolment among honest men as his reward for abandoning them ?"

An indignant reply rose to Isabella's lips, but she remembered in time that she came as a suitor, and saying that she would not waste Sir Henry's time with arguing on a subject on which they must utterly differ, she went straight to her point. "You must, sir," she said, "believe that my brother came to the city for the motive he avows, and for no other."

"What proof have I of this ?" asked Sir Henry, with a tormenting smile.

"The word of a man of truth."

"And the faith of an all-believing girl. This may be very sufficient evidence in a *cour d'amour* —it would hardly suffice in a court-martial. But proceed, my dear Miss Linwood, and tell me precisely your wishes. You may rely on my desire to serve you."

Sir Henry's tone was earnest and sincere, and Isabella was encouraged. "My brother," she said, "has, thank Heaven, shown himself equal to bearing well the adverse turns of a soldier's fortune. He endures manfully his imprisonment in the dark, filthy, crowded prison allotted to the Americans—the honest yeomen of the land. He suffers, without complaint, Sir Henry, the petty tyranny of the atrocious keeper of these poor men."

"Tut, tut, my dear,—it is the fortune of war."

Isabella had again to quell her pride, before she could command her voice to proceed with due humility. "All he asks, Sir Henry, all that I ask for him is, that you will put him on the footing of a prisoner of war, and thus relieve him from an imputation that compels General Washington to withhold all interference in his behalf, and to leave him here a degraded man, suffering for an act of rashness what is alone due to crime."

"It is impossible, my dear girl—you overrate my powers—I am responsible——"

"To God—so are we all, Sir Henry, and happiest are those who have most of such deeds as I ask of you to present at this tribunal. But are you not supreme in these provinces ? and may you not exercise mercy without fearing that man shall miscall it ?"

"My powers, thanks to my gracious sovereign, are ample ; but you have somewhat romantic notions of the mode of using them. I am willing to believe—or rather," he added with a gracious smile, "to believe that you believe your brother's story to be a true one ; but, Miss Linwood, this view of the ground must not alter, to speak *en militaire*, our demonstration. We are bound, as I have communicated to you, through our friend Mr. Jasper Meredith—we are bound, by the policy of war, to avail ourselves of the accident, if it be one, that enables us plausibly to impute to Washington an act held dishonourable in all civilised warfare."

"Then, in plain English," said Isabella, with a burst of indignation this time irrepressible, "the 'policy of war' compels you to profess to believe a falsehood, in order to stain a spotless name."

Sir Henry made no reply, but strided with folded arms up and down the apartment. A glance at his irritated countenance recalled Isabella to herself. "Forgive me, Sir Henry," she said,

"if feeling only that my poor brother is a victim to this horrible 'policy of war,' I have spoken more boldly than was fitting a humble miserable suitor."

Whether it is that the tone of submission is that which Heaven has ordained for women, and that which is the natural vehicle of a lofty sense of superiority, is a falsetto in which she rarely succeeds, we cannot say ; but true it is, that the moment Isabella's voice faltered, Sir Henry's brow relaxed, and condescending to her weakness, he said, "It can hardly be expected, Miss Linwood, that a young lady should comprehend a subject quite out of her line—we will, therefore, if you please, waive its farther discussion, and return to the drawing-room."

"Excuse me, Sir Henry, I cannot go back to the drawing-room," replied Isabella, in spite of her efforts bursting into tears,—"I came here solely for the purpose of obtaining something for poor Herbert, and I have utterly failed." It is not in man—a gentleman and a soldier, to be unmoved by the tears,—the real distress of a young and beautiful woman. Sir Henry too, to his friends—to those of his own household (we have it on poor André's testimony), was generous and kind-hearted.

"My dear girl," he said, "pray do not make yourself so unhappy. You know not how much your brother is already indebted to you—if he were not fenced about by such friends, your father on one side, and yourself and your devoted knight on the other—do not blush, my dear young lady—he would have fared much worse than he has, I assure you. He has only to suffer durance with patience—our bark is worse than our bite ; and, believe me, the war cannot last much longer."

"And he must remain in prison while the war lasts ?"

"I fear so."

"Then, for mercy's sake, Sir Henry, grant us one favour. My father is old. His health and fortune, as you know, are shattered. This cruel war severed him from his only son, and drew down on poor Herbert the displeasure which has ended in all this wretchedness. Something may be saved from the wreck, their disjointed affections may be re-united if—if they are permitted to meet."

"If your father wished to visit your brother, he would have asked permission—it certainly would not have been refused."

Isabella well knew that her father, after having once (to use his favourite phrase) set his foot down, would not make so violent a recession as such a step demanded ; but not choosing to allude to his infirmities, and anxious to secure for Herbert a greater alleviation than a single interview, she availed herself of an obvious reason. "My father," she said, "is still confined to his apartment. He cannot go to Herbert—if Herbert might come to him ?"

"This would be indeed an extraordinary departure from all form and precedence."

"Yes ; but it would be the very essence of kindness, which is better than all form and precedence. Oh, Sir Henry, have you not sometimes sleepless hours in the silent watches of the night ; and will not then the thought that you have solaced an old man, your friend, and restored peace and love to his habitation, be better than the memory of victories—dear Sir Henry, will it not!"

"I should be too happy to oblige you—it would be a very great pleasure; but indeed, indeed, my dear Miss Isabella, this is an extraordinary proposition."

"So much the better fitting you to accede to it; you who have the power to depart from the vulgar beaten track. You may have little reason to remember, with pleasure, this vexatious war, Sir Henry; but the good you have done by the way will be like the manna of the wilderness."

Isabella had touched the right chord. "Well, my dear Miss Belle, tell me precisely what you want, and what security you can give that my trust will not be abused."

"I want an order from you to Cunningham, directing him to permit my brother to leave the prison in the evening between any hours you shall see fit to assign; and for your security, Sir Henry, I can offer the surest, the word not only of a man of honour, as you have said there are many and uncertain modifications of that principle, but the word of a man bound to you by every tie of gratitude and good faith."

"You have persuaded me, my dear, against my better reason, it may be, but you have persuaded me; and to-morrow, after our cabinet-council, I will send you the order."

"Oh, no—to-night, Sir Henry," urged Isabella, with her characteristic decision, determining to leave nothing to the possible influence of a cabinet-council or a treacherous to-morrow; "to-night, if you would make me completely happy. Here on the table is pen, ink, and paper; and here is a chair—sit down, and write three lines, and I will go home with them, and fall down on my knees, and pray God to bless you for ever and ever."

If Sir Henry had been told one hour before that he should be persuaded to such an act, he might have exclaimed with Hazael—"Am I a dog," that I should be thus *managed?* But, like many other great men, he yielded to a superior mind, albeit in the form of woman. He wrote the order, taking care to qualify it by requiring Cunningham to guard young Linwood's egress and ingress from observation, and stipulating that he should be attended by Cunningham himself, the most formidable of the bull-dog race of gaolers.

"Now," said Sir Henry, after Isabella, with a transport of gratitude, had received the order, and was about to take her leave, "you must not run away—you, of all others, are bound to grace a fête given to Jasper Meredith's cousin—you owe me this."

"And most gratefully will I pay you all I can of the debt I owe you, Sir Henry," she replied, giving him her hand, and returning to the drawing-room. The consciousness of the advantage she had gained, the buoyant spirit of youth, that having taken one step from the starting-point believes the race won, lit up her eye and cheek with their natural brightness. If a mask had fallen from her face, the change would not have been more startling to some of her observers, nor more puzzling to others.

"I do marvel, cousin Jasper," said Lady Anne, when they were driving home, "that you have never fallen in love with Isabella Linwood!"

"And how do you know that I have not!" he asked, willing to try the ground of her conclusions.

"How! bless me, do you think I am stone-blind!—you have not danced with her—you have scarcely spoken to her this evening, when she appeared so perfectly irresistible."

"I fancy, my dear," interposed Mrs. Meredith, "that your cousin Jasper, like other men of his stamp, prefers a person less *prononcée*—more quiescent—more ductile than Miss Linwood."

"You mean, aunt, not shining with a light of her own—more of a reflector."

"Pardon me, my dear Lady Anne, you interrupted me. I was going on to say, that men who are conscious of eminent talents, prefer those who, not ambitious to shine, will amuse and soothe their hours of relaxation."

"Lesser lights—I understand you perfectly," said Lady Anne, cutting in to escape her aunt's tedious circumlocution: "do tell me, Jasper," she continued, "if you observed how changed Miss Linwood appeared when she returned to the drawing-room! I was dancing with that tiresome colonel, and you were talking to me."

"I was talking with you—how could I observe another!"

"Miss Linwood mistakes," said Mrs. Meredith, "in assuming such violent contrasts—in making such sudden transits from grave to gay. He is a poor artist who resorts to glaring lights and deep shadows to set off his pictures—she wants *toning down.*"

The mother was not more at fault in her expressed opinion, whether sincere or not, than her son was in his mental inference from the sudden change in Isabella's deportment. None are more fallible in their judgment than people of the world, and simply because they make no allowance for truth as a basis of action. Notwithstanding Meredith's disclaimer, he had observed, and narrowly, the change so obvious, and thus had reasoned upon it:—"Isabella was piqued at my devotion to my cousin; she was, for no woman is above these little vanities, vexed at Lady Anne's superlative dancing; but she soon rallied, and determined to appear high as the stars above me, and all these matters. Her pride is invincible; it is quite time to show her that her power is not. Women *are* destined to be the 'lesser lights.' I have most generously committed myself, while she has remained as silent, if not as cold, as a statue; therefore I am at liberty to retreat, if I should—at any future time—choose to do so. When I am with her, I feel her full supremacy; but away from her, on reflection, I can perceive that an alliance with my cousin might, in the end, be quite —that is, very tolerable, and vastly more eligible (and in these times that must be thought of) than this long, long *dreamed*-of marriage with Isabella Linwood."

CHAPTER XXVI.
The wonder, or a woman keeps a secret!

ISABELLA moulded and arranged everything to profit by Sir Henry's boon. She persuaded her father (one is easily led the way the heart inclines), in consideration of Herbert's past sufferings and uncertain future, to acquiesce in a present obli-

vion of his offences. She exacted a promise from
Herbert that he would hear her father laud King
George, his ministers, and all their acts, without
interposing a disqualifying word, or even a glance;
and, what was a greater feat for him, that he
would sit quietly and hear the names of Washington, Franklin, Jay, Hamilton, La Fayette—all
that he most honoured, coupled with the most
offensive epithets. This vituperation she knew
was a sort of safety-valve, by which her father let
off the passion that might otherwise burst on poor
Herbert's head. She felt that no sacrifice, short
of that of principle, was too great to obtain affectionate intercourse between the father and son;
that, between those thus related, there never could
be a " good war, nor a bad peace."

As Sir Henry had exacted a strict secrecy as
to his indulgence, Isabella congratulated herself
that she had long before this persuaded her father
to dismiss Jupiter (an irreclaimable gossip), on
the ground that he was a useless piece of lumber;
but really because Rose had declared that it exceeded the ability of her commissary department
to supply his rations. Rose herself was worthy
of all confidence. Mrs. Archer, of course, was
one of the family cabinet.

The awkwardness of the first meeting got over,
all difficulties were past. Little differences, if *let
alone*, soon melt away in the warmth of hearty
affection. Herbert was obliged sometimes to bite
his lips, and at others, when his frank and hasty
spirit prompted a retort, a glance from Isabella
kept him silent.

It was not till Herbert's second or third visit
that Mr. Linwood manifested the uneasiness incident to persons of his age and habits when put
out of their accustomed track. Rivington's Royal
Gazette, issued twice a week, and the only newspaper in the city, was to Mr. Linwood, as newspapers are to most men, one of the necessaries of
life. " My dear," he asked his wife, " where is
the paper?"

" I left it below, my dear; there is nothing in
it." Mrs. Linwood had ventured this omission
from consideration to Herbert, whose temper she
feared might boil over at the hearing of one of
those high-toned tory gazettes.

" Pshaw—nothing in it! just so all women say,
unless they find some trumpery murder or shipwreck. Belle, be good enough to bring the paper,
and read it to me; and do ask Rose to bring us
in a stick of wood—it is as cold as Greenland
here—five pounds I paid Morton yesterday for a
cord of hickory. D—n the rebels, I wish I had
their bones for firewood."

" They do their best, sir, to make it hot for the
tories," said Herbert, very good-humouredly.

" Ah, Herbert my son, I forgot you were here;
I did indeed. But I can't be mealy-mouthed—I
must speak out, come what come will. But it is
hard not to be able to get the wood from our own
farms, is it not?"

" Very hard, sir, to be deprived of any of our
rights."

" Rights!" Isabella entered, and Mr. Linwood
added, in a softened tone, " have a care, my boy;
there are certain words that fall on my ear like
sparks on gunpowder."

" Here is something to prevent your emitting
any more sparks just now, Mr. Herbert," said

Isabella, giving him a Boston paper, while she
retained the orthodox journal to read aloud.

" What's that?—what's that?" asked her
father.

" A Boston paper, sir, sent to you with Colonel
Robertson's compliments."

Herbert read aloud a few lines written on the
margin of the paper, chuckling in spite of his filial
efforts to the contrary:—" Major-General Putnam presents his compliments to Major-General
Robertson, and sends him some American newspapers for his perusal. When General Robertson
shall have done with them, it is requested they
may be given to Rivington, in order that they
may print some truth."

" The impudent renegado! Come, Isabella, what
says Rivington to-day?"

Isabella read aloud an order from Sir Henry
Clinton, " That all negroes taken fighting in the
rebel cause should be sold as slaves: and that all
deserting should live at what occupation they
pleased within the British lines!"

" Very salutary that!" interposed Mr. Linwood.
" Black sons of Belial—they fighting for liberty,
d—n 'em!"

Herbert cleared his throat. " My father—my
upright father applauding a bounty offered to
cowardice and treachery!—Oh the moral perver-
sions engendered by war!" thought Isabella; but
she wisely kept her reflections to herself, and
striking another chord, ran over one of Rivington's
advertisements of fancy articles for sale by himself, the sole editor and publisher in the city. Oh,
Smetz, Stewart, Gardiner, Tryon, Baily, ye ministers to the luxury of our city! well may ye ex-
claim, in your rich repositories of the arts and
industry of the old world—

Great streams from little fountains flow.

For the curious in such matters, we permit our
heroine to read aloud verbatim: " For sale at this
office, scarlet dress-frocks, with silk lining and
capes, the work of celebrated operators west of
London; the celebrated new-fashioned buckle,
which owes its origin and vogue to the Count
d'Artois, brother to the King of France; of the
locket or depository for preserving the gentle
Saccharissa's hair, a great variety; crow-quills
for the delicate Constantia; scarlet riding-dresses
for ladies, made to suit the uniform of their husbands or *lovers;* canes for the gallant gay Lo-
thario; gold and silver strings for plain walking-
canes, with silver and gold tassels for plain Master
Balance; vastly snug shaving equipages; bro-
caded shoes and slippers; ladies' shuttles for the
thrifty in the knotting amusements; songs suited to
the various humours and affections of the mind."

" Bravo, friend Rivington!" exclaimed Herbert, " you do not expend all your imagination in
the invention of news."

" Is there nothing but this nonsense in the
paper, Belle? What is that in capitals about
letters from England?"

Isabella resumed: " Letters from England say
they will never acknowledge the Independence of
the United States, while there is a soldier to be
raised, or a tester to be expended, in the three
kingdoms!"

" John Bull for ever! What say you to that,
Mr. Herbert?" asked his father, exultingly.

"*Nous verrons*, sir !—but, mercy upon us ! what is this !" Herbert read aloud from the Boston paper : "We regret to state that the daughter of Mrs. Lee, of Westbrook, left her mother's house two weeks since, with the supposed intention of going to New York. The young lady has been for some time in a state of partial mental alienation." A description of Bessie's person followed, and an earnest request that any information obtained might be transmitted to the unhappy mother.

Both Herbert and Isabella were filled with consternation and anxiety ; and, after revolving the past, both came to the same conclusion as to the probable origin of poor Bessie's mental malady. Mr. Linwood, who only recollected her as a quiet, pretty little girl, exhausted his sympathy in a few inquiries and exclamations, became somewhat impatient of the sadness that had overclouded his children. "We are as doleful as the tombs here," he said : "What can keep your aunt Archer tonight, Isabella ?—Ah ! here she comes — right glad to see you, Mary. Belle and Herbert are knocked up by an unlucky bit of news." The news was communicated to Mrs. Archer, who entered deeply into their feelings.

"Ah !" said she, "this explains a note I received this morning from Captain Lee."

"From Eliot !" exclaimed Herbert.

"Yes ; he sent by a courier, who came to Sir Henry, a most acceptable present—a set of chessmen for the children, which he has contrived, and, aided by an ingenious private, made for them."

"Chessmen contrived by a rebel !" said Mr. Linwood—"of course he has left out the king, queen, and bishop !"

"Pardon me—he may think kings, queens, and bishops, very fit playthings."

"But what says the note !" asked Herbert, impatiently.'

"It says, that if the chessboard should fail to be of use to Ned and Lizzy, it has at least served the purpose of partially diverting his thoughts from a grief that almost drives him mad. Of course he alludes to the sad affair."

"Undoubtedly," replied Herbert ; "and this business of the chessboard is just like himself—he is the most extraordinary fellow ! I never knew him in any trouble, small or great, that he did not turn to doing something for somebody or other by way of a solace—a balm to his hurt mind."

"I do not wonder you love him so devotedly," said Isabella.

"Oh, Belle," whispered Herbert in return, "had Heaven but put him in Jasper's place, or made Jasper like him !"

Mrs. Archer caught the words, and in spite of her own discretion and Isabella's painful blushes, she uttered a deep and insuppressible "Amen !"

"Come, come, what are you all about !" said Mr. Linwood : "suppose you imitate this wonderful hero of yours in the use of his mental panacea, and comfort me with a game of whist. Do you play as deep a game as you used to, Herbert ; trump your partner's trick and finesse with a knave and ten !"

Herbert confessed he had forgotten the little he knew. "Well, then, you may brood over your Yankee paper, and we will call in your mother,

who, in five-and-twenty years' drilling, has learned just enough *not* to trump her partner's tricks."

Mrs. Linwood was summoned, and the party formed. Mr. Linwood was in high good-humour ; and though Isabella made some inscrutable plays, all went smoothly till the family party was alarmed by, a tap at the door ; and before any one had time to reply to it, the door was opened, and Lady Anne Seton appeared. Startled by the appearance of a stranger, and somewhat disconcerted by perceiving the embarrassment caused by her intrusion, "Shall I go back !" she asked, her hand still on the door.

"Oh, no—no," cried Mr. Linwood, "come in, my dear little girl, by all means ; you promised me a game of piquet, and I, an old savage, forgot it, and so I have forfeited my right, and now make it over to this young man, my son Herbert." Lady Anne turned a surprised, sparkling, and inquiring glance to Herbert, as much as to say, "Is it possible !" and Herbert made his bow of presentation. "You know," continued the father, "that this young man is in limbo ; but you do not know, and be sure you let no one else know, that Sir Henry, God bless him ! permits the rascal to visit us privately."

"Am I really trusted with an important secret ! —delightful !—and does anything depend on my keeping it !"

"The continuance of my brother's visits and Sir Henry's favour," replied Isabella, emphatically, alarmed at the necessity of confiding their secret to one so gay and inexperienced as Lady Anne.

Inexperienced she was, but true and single-hearted. "Do not look so solemn, my dear Miss Linwood," she said ; "indeed I will not tell. I am too much puffed up with the first important secret I ever had in my keeping, to part with it carelessly. I am even with aunt and Jasper now, with their everlasting private talks ; and when it is stupid at home, I may come here, may I not !"

"Always," interposed Mr. Linwood, really delighted with the accession of the charming girl to their circle. Mrs. Linwood, who only waited for her husband to strike the key-note, was voluble in her hospitable expressions. Herbert looked the most unequivocal welcome ; and Lady Anne, never querulous, did not trouble herself about Isabella's merely civil assent, and, perhaps, did not notice it. From this time her visits were almost as regular as Herbert's. She was little addicted to romance ; but every young girl has a spice of it, and Herbert's romantic and precarious position increased the charm of his frank and spirited character. A dear lover of sunshine was Herbert ; and these short domestic interludes, brightened by Lady Anne, were hours in paradise to him. All day in his gloomy prison he looked forward to his release from purgatory ; and, once engaged at a side-table with his lively partner in the most fascinating of all *tête-à-tête* games, or round the *petit-souper*, which his good mother spent the day in contriving and concocting, he forgot the ills of life, till the summons from his keeper reminded him that he had still to buffet with his portion of them.

"If I do not mistake," said Mrs. Archer to Isabella, after the breaking up of one of their evening meetings, "Herbert and Lady Anne are beginning to see visions, and dream dreams."

"Heaven forbid !"

"And why, my dear Belle, should Heaven forbid so natural and pleasant a consequence of their familiar intercourse ?"

"How can you ask, aunt Mary ! I could not forgive Herbert if he were so soon to forget poor Bessie."

"We must take man as he is, Belle. Herbert is too light-hearted to cherish a hopeless passion ; he regards his love for Bessie Lee as a dream, and, rely on it, he is thoroughly awakened from it. You must have perceived that he has not been desperately afflicted about your unfortunate little friend ?"

"Yes, I have—but men do not show their feelings."

"Some men do not, but Herbert does ; and rely on it, Belle, he is not of a temper to continue to love a person (even if poor little Bessie were not, as she must now be, utterly lost to him) whose heart is another's."

"I suppose you are right, aunt Mary," replied Isabella, after a moment's hesitation, colouring deeply ; "the whole sex are alike incapable of the generosity of unrequited affection !" *Unacknowledged* was her mental reading of unrequited.

"Substitute folly or weakness for generosity, Belle, and you will take a more masculine, and, it may be, a more rational view of the case."

"Oh, aunt Mary, are you, like the rest of the world, giving up all feeling for what you call rationality ?"

"No, my dear child, but I have learned that what you call *feeling*, what constitutes the dream of a few weeks, months, or it may be years of youth, makes but a small portion of the reality or the worth of life. Providence has kindly so organised man, that he cannot waste his affections in one hopeless, fruitless concentration ; nor lose life in a tissue of vain regrets. The stream that is obstructed in one course will take another, and enrich and beautify regions for which it did not, at first, seem destined."

Isabella was not just now in a humour to assent to Mrs. Archer's conclusions, but her mind was the good ground in which the seed could not be lost. She was conscious that, though her aunt's strictures were ostensibly directed to Herbert, they had some bearing on herself. She was in a position the most tormenting to a mind prompt both to decide and act. Since Lady Anne's arrival she had rarely seen Meredith. This she admitted was in part her own fault. She had been restrained by her promise to Sir Henry Clinton from communicating to Jasper the favour granted to Herbert. "But when she gave the promise to Sir Henry, ought she not to have excepted Jasper ? Was it not due to him ! and would she not have made the exception, through all the blushing and faltering it must have cost her, had she not felt sure that Sir Henry himself would have made Meredith a party to the secret ?"

Sir Henry, after a little reflection, was ashamed of the spell that had been wrought on him, and communicated it to no one.

Meredith, partly spurred by pride, partly led on by the incessant manœuvres of his mother, partly incited by the worldly advantages of an alliance with Lady Anne, and flattered too by his cousin's frank and affectionate manner, was fast verging towards that point, to attain which his mother had compassed sea and land.

He had confidently expected that Isabella would at once and fully have reciprocated his declarations of attachment. Her reserve had abased his pride, piqued his vanity, and disappointed his affection. He believed he truly loved her, and he did, as truly as he could love. But Jasper Meredith's love, like water that rises through minerals, was impregnated with much foreign material. He at first had no formed purpose in his devotion to Lady Anne ; but after being twice or thrice repulsed from Mr. Linwood's door by "My master is better, sir, but not yet down stairs," and "Miss Isabella is very much engaged," he half resolved no longer to resist the "tide in his affairs that was leading on to fortune."

———◆———

CHAPTER XXVII.

Some die of weariness,
Some of disease and some insanity,
And some of withered or of broken hearts ;
For this last is a malady which slays
More than are numbered in the lists of fate,
Taking all shapes, and bearing many names.
						BYRON.

———

BESSIE LEE's sylvan lodge harmonised so well with her wild fancies, that when she awoke it seemed no more strange to her than her accustomed sleeping-place. Whatever she might be destined afterward to suffer from this exposure on the damp earth through a cold autumnal night, she was as unconscious of the ills that flesh is heir to as if she were a disembodied spirit. "Sluggard that I am !" she exclaimed, starting up and shaking off the heavy dew-drops, "the spirits of morning are at worship, and I sleeping ! the birds are singing their hymns, and I, that have been watched and guarded, am silent." She leaned her cheek on the mossy stem of a tree, and began to repeat the Lord's Prayer : "'Our Father'—ay, nature worships with me — beautiful waterfall, majestic trees, glad light, is he not *our* father !— 'hallowed be his name,'—ye hallow his name, for ye are the manifestations of his wisdom, the ministers of his love, the shadows of celestial beauty !—'thy kingdom come'—it is come here— obedience, peace, serenity, are his kingdom—war is not—care is not—love is not—love to fallible mortals, for there no peace is—so I will on my pilgrimage, and break the last link in the chain— then will I return here, finish my prayer, and lay me down and rest again."

Thus mingling with her celestial meditations one earthly purpose, she retraced her way to the road, and looked about in vain for her horse, who, having obeyed his rational impulses, was now far on his way homeward. "It was not kind of you, Steady," she said, as she came to the conclusion he had abandoned her ; but without one thought of relinquishing her purpose, or one doubt of her ability to effect it, she walked on for about half a mile, and probably began to have some obscure sense of tremulousness and weakness, for, seeing a horse equipped with saddle and bridle hitched to the fence, and a basket standing by him containing biscuits and apples, she laughed aloud, exclaiming, "Who would have thought it !" and then checking herself, raised her eyes devoutly and added, " yet, I might have known they would be provided by the wayside, just when I wanted them. I wonder there is not a woman's saddle, but I can manage ;" and taking the basket in one hand, she mounted, and rode briskly on. She proceeded without any hindrance or molestation whatever, now and then, probably, from an insupportable feeling of weariness, dismounting and lying for a moment under the shadow of a tree. It was about the middle of the afternoon, when she was entering the street of a little village, that she heard behind her the trampling of horses on the full gallop, and outcries of " Stop thief !" Her horse, incited more by the uproar at his heels than by any impulse she was able to give him, sprang forward. The people rushed from their houses—their screams bewildered her. She gazed fearfully around her, her wearied horse soon slackened his speed, and one of her pursuers reached her just at the moment that, having dropped the bridle from her powerless hand, she was falling from her saddle. " Time you was spent, young madam," cried her rough assistant, as, supporting half her weight, he prevented her sinking to the ground.

The people of the village, chiefly women and children, gathered around, all gazing on Bessie with scrutinising glances. Her wandering eye and blanched cheek must have half told her story, for not one of them spoke till she, drawing up from the arm that supported her, asked, with an air of offended dignity, " Why are ye so unmannerly to me ?"

" Ha, ha—not quite so topping, Miss—serve your writ, Mr. Sheriff," replied one of her pursuers. " Pretty high, to talk about manners, when you've been riding fifty miles on a stolen horse."

" Stolen !" echoed Bessie, " indeed, I did not steal him."

" How upon 'arth did you get him then ? answer that."

" I took him—" the standers-by interrupted her with a coarse laugh ; but Bessie, without heeding them, proceeded : " I took him, where he stood awaiting me."

" Now, if that is not a high joke ! Just hear me, good people—the sheriff can swear to all I say. This is Squire Saunders's horse—you have all heard of the squire !" They had all heard of Squire Saunders, whose fame rayed through a large circle. " Well, the squire rode up to his wood-lot this morning, to see about a trespass that's committing there—you know, sheriff ; and the squire just hitched his horse to the fence, and went up into the woods, and got out of his reckoning ; and two hours after, when he came upon the road——"

" Take care of that poor young woman," cried a benevolent-looking man who was passing in an ox-cart, " don't you see she can't stand ?"

" I am tired," said Bessie, sinking to the ground, and putting her hand to her head ; " this noise tires me."

The spectators exchanged glances of inquiry and pity ; the sheriff looked compassionate ; his companion, sturdy, and resolved not to be *taken*

in. The man of the ox-cart stopped his vehicle, and joined the group : " Are ye all blind and deaf," he added, " that ye do not see the poor girl's mind is unsettled ?"

" Oh, no, friend," said Bessie, shaking her head, and looking up with a faint smile, " you are very much mistaken—my mind is not the least unsettled—indeed, it every day becomes stronger and more capable than it was."

Her champion looked to the standers-by for their assent to this confirmation of his opinion, and then turning to the sheriff, said, " You will not, I am sure, trouble her farther ?"

" No, I'll be hanged if I do !"

" Nor you ?" appealing to the sheriff's attendant.

" I don't know—if I were sure—I don't like to be outwitted—remember, sheriff, it was for horse and *thief* the squire offered the reward."

" The devil take the reward, Dan !"

" You may say so—for you that's got an office can afford it, but I'm a volunteer. But since you all take on so about it, if you're a mind to contribute and pay something towards my expenses and trouble and so on, I'll trust to the squire for the rest."

" I have not one copper to pay," said Bessie's friend.

" Pay ! is that all he wants ?" asked Bessie, thrusting her hand into her pocket, and giving into his greedy grasp her few coins ; " perhaps it was meant," she added, in a confidential tone to her champion, " that I should pay for the use of the horse, but I know he was provided for me. Are you satisfied ?" she asked, in a tone to pierce the heart ; " indeed I have given you all."

" He shall be satisfied—he must be satisfied !" cried every voice at once ; and the man, perceiving the general sentiment was against him, was glad to mount his horse and follow the sheriff, who was already leading away Squire Saunders's recovered property. It was evident the sheriff's organ of benevolence had resisted the influence of his station.

" And now what is to be done with this poor helpless thing ?" asked Barlow, the kind-hearted man who had so far befriended Bessie. At this question, two or three of the spectators slunk away ; the rest exchanged fearful and uncertain glances ; one or two murmured that they " did not love to have crazy folks in their houses ;" and it was obvious that the benevolence of all was restrained by that irrational fear which so much increases the sufferings of those who are mentally diseased. No one offering an asylum for the poor wanderer, Barlow turned to her and asked, " What will you do now, my poor child ?"

" Oh, go on."

" Go on ! where, in the name of wonder ?"

" To New York."

" Impossible ! how are you to go ?"

" I must go—more than life depends on it—now, I cannot tell exactly. I do not think I could walk very far," she vainly attempted to rise ; " but do not be concerned about me, for certainly He who hath helped me so far will not now desert me."

The gentle girl's unconsciousness of her wants was more touching than the most passionate appeal.

"Will you go home with me ?" asked Barlow, after wiping his eyes, and clearing his voice.

"Oh, no, I thank you ; I cannot lose any time."

"Poor child ! but," he added, "I live six miles nearer to New York than this, and I can take you so far on your way."

"Then indeed I will go. Did I not tell you, O ye of little faith, that the way would be provided ?" Again, and again without success, she attempted to rise.

"Lend a hand, neighbours," said Barlow ; "the straw on my cart is clean, and we will lay her on it." Bessie was placed in the cart, and driven to Barlow's humble habitation, a dwelling-house adjoining a blacksmith's shop, within a few miles of Hartford, in Connecticut.

Barlow would have been justifiable, if ever man was, in going "on the other side," and leaving Bessie Lee to the chance mercies of others. But Barlow's heart bore a faint resemblance to his own anvil ; the stroke of his fellow-creature's necessities always brought forth sparks of kindness.

"Dear me !" exclaimed his wife, when he entered their little dwelling, supporting Bessie with one arm ; "whom have you got here ?"

"Open the door into the bedroom, Martha, and I'll tell you afterwards." The door was promptly opened, the bedspread turned down, and Bessie laid upon the clean inviting bed.

"Oh, thank you, thank you !" she said : "I shall tell mother and Eliot how very kind you are to me."

"Dear me !" said pitiful Mrs. Barlow.

"Oh, ma'am, I am very well," said Bessie, replying to her compassionate look ; "only a little tired—do not let me oversleep to-morrow morning."

"Give her some warm milk, Martha ; and let her sleep, if she can—it's her only chance."

The hospitality was done, and Bessie left to the ministry of nature, while Barlow related to his marvelling wife all he knew of her. "Well," said she, as he concluded, "I do feel for her folks ; and yet she don't look as if she belonged to this world. I have dreamed of seeing angels, and she looks like them ; but like nothing made out of clay. I'm glad you brought her home, Barlow ; it's a great easement to the heart to do a kindness, though we are in a poor case to entertain strangers, even if they be angels."

"We be in a poor situation ; but it would have been awful to have left such a young, delicate, innocent, beautiful fellow-creature to perish by the wayside !"

"Dear me ! yes, indeed."

"Or to have left her to people that were so slack about helping her."

"It would."

"And so, knowing your feelings, Martha, I've done what I have done."

"You've done right, Barlow."

"I don't know, you are so poorly, and the boys sick. Have they missed their chill to-day !"

"No, neither they nor I."

Barlow rose, looked at the pale faces of his little boys, who were lying in a truckle-bed, then at his sickly wife, and shook his head.

"Martha, I am afraid I have been presumptuous."

"Dear me, husband ! don't worry about that ; what would be the use of sickness if it did not give us feelings for others ! "

"True, Martha ; and somehow I could not help it ; and now I can't but think Providence will help us through with what his finger pointed out. I have repented of a great many things in my day ; but I never saw reason to repent of a good deed—look in the bedroom, Martha, and see if she is sleeping."

"Dear me, no ! but there's a quiet smile on her lips, and her beautiful eyes are raised ; and she seems just like a lamb looking at the shepherd."

"If she's still, she may fall asleep ; so let us ask a blessing on her and the rest of us, and then we'll to bed ourselves."

What grace and dignity do the devotion and compassion of such pure hearts impart to the dwelling of the poor man ! Oh ye, who fare sumptuously every day, imitate him in his only luxury—the luxury of deeds never to be repented of !

CHAPTER XXVIII.

The man I speak of cannot in the world be singly counterpoised.

A WEEK subsequent to Bessie Lee's arrival at Barlow's, a violent hallooing and knocking were heard at the blacksmith's shop ; and no answer being given, Barlow's house-door was soon beset with impatient knocks and cries of—"Halloo, blacksmith, you are wanted ! "

Barlow rose from the bed, where he had been laid by a severe attack of intermittent fever, and answered, that he was utterly unable to go to his workshop. "What does he say !" asked a young gentleman in a foreign accent, who, with two or three attendants, was impatiently awaiting Barlow's services.

"He says he cannot come, sir."

"Cannot ! *Ce n'est pas le mot d'aujourd'hui.*"

"Neither, I think, sir," replied the first speaker, "is *must* current in these parts."

"*Vous avez raison, mon ami ; mais, mon Dieu !* what are we to do !"

The gentleman, being very much in the habit of overcoming other men's impossibilities every day of his life, dismounted, gave his bridle to an attendant, and walked up to the open door of our friend Barlow, who, on seeing the uniform of an American general officer, was somewhat abashed, though its wearer was a fair young man, with a remarkably gentle and benignant countenance. "If it were barely possible, sir," said Barlow, "I should be happy to serve you ; but I am scarcely able to stand."

"Ah, my good friend, I see you are in a bad position, and your wife too. How long have you been ill, madame !"

"I have had the *fever 'nagur,* six weeks, off and on."

"Fever 'nagur ! *Qu'est-ce que c'est ?*" asked the gentleman, aside, of his companion.

"Fever and ague."

"Ah, *je comprends !* very bad malady, madame, very bad ; you should take every day a little port wine."

Mrs. Barlow smiled. "Dear me! yes, sir, if I had it."

"You go or send often to Hartford?" resumed the stranger, addressing Barlow.

"Almost every day, sir."

"Ah, very well! I have some port wine there in a friend's cellar. I will give you an order for a bottle or two; and I pray you to send for it; and you and your wife, and these little fellows, who by their blue lips have the ague too, shall drink to my health and your own."

"Thank you, sir," said Mrs. Barlow; "a little port wine is what I have been all along thinking would cure us—dear me!"

"Is it only one horse, sir, that wants shoeing?" asked Barlow, tying a handkerchief round his throat.

"Only one, my good friend; my own brave beast, who has done much good service, and has much more to do. *Pauvre bête!* it goes to my heart to have his hoof broken up."

Barlow felt as if his strength came with the sympathy and consideration manifested by the person who needed it. "I guess, sir," he said, "I could stand long enough to do so small a job."

"Ah, my friend, *mille*—a thousand thanks; but spare your strength to do what no one else can do. Here, orderly, kindle up the blacksmith's fire quickly." While this was in preparation, the stranger took writing materials from his pocket, and addressed the following note to a person whose munificence is still remembered, though he has long ago gone to the enjoyment of his treasures, where he was then wisely laying them up.

"MY DEAR WADSWORTH,—I have just chanced to call at a poor blacksmith's, who, with his worthy family, is at death's door with a protracted intermittent. It seems to me that port, like that I drank with you yesterday, might restore them. As the man looks like too *independent* an American to beg a favour, I have taken the liberty to give him this order for a bottle or two, telling him with a *poetic* truth, that I had wine in your cellar. It is your own fault if all your friends feel that they have a property in your possessions. Adieu."

Just as the stranger had signed and sealed this billet, the inner door opened, and Bessie Lee appeared, her cheeks dyed with fever, her eyes bright as gems, her lips of the brightest vermilion, and her beautiful hair hanging, in many a tangled curl, over her face and neck. "*Mon Dieu!*" exclaimed the stranger.

"Dear me! my child, go back," said Mrs. Barlow, gently repulsing her. Bessie, however, without heeding her, pressed forward, and addressing herself to the stranger in an energetic business sort of way, "You are going to New York?" she said.

"Not exactly, young lady; but I am going in that direction."

"Do go back into the bedroom,—do, husband, persuade her—"

"No, no, Martha, let her have her own way."

"Thank you," said Bessie. "Will you be kind enough, sir to step into my room?—this buzzing confuses me."

The stranger, with characteristic sagacity, had already half penetrated the truth. He motioned to Bessie to precede him, saying in a low voice to Mrs. Barlow, "Your husband is right. It is best your child should have her own way."

"Dear me, she is not our child, sir!"

"She does not look as if she were," thought the stranger; but there was no time for farther explanation. As soon as they were fairly within the inner room, Bessie shut the door. She seemed at first disconcerted; but instantly rallying, she said, "I am unknown to you, sir, but your face seems to have that heavenly sentence written on it: 'Ask and it shall be given to you.'"

"Then why do you hesitate?"

"*They* would think it so strange that I should be asking such a favour of a stranger—a young gentleman——"

"Who are *they*?"

"My mother and brother."

"Their names, my friend?"

"I cannot tell their names. My present object is to get to New York as soon as possible, where I have business of the greatest importance. I have been staying here for some days with very kind people. I would not wound their feelings on any account," she added, in a whisper; "but they are very weak-minded—no judgment at all; indeed, there are few people that have, so I do not choose to confide to them the reason of my actions. All will be explained and published when I return from New York."

"But, my dear young lady, are you aware that New York is in possession of the enemy?"

"Oh, sir, I have no enemies."

"Rough soldiers—foreign soldiers, my fair friend, will make no exception in your favour."

"You do not know," she replied, drawing up her little person with an air of assured but mysterious superiority,—"you do not know that I am one of those of whom it was said, that 'their angels do always stand before my Father;' and I could tell you of such difficult passes where invisible spirits have guided and tended me—so faithfully! but that at another time. There is not the slightest danger in my going to New York—indeed, I have no choice; I must go."

"Do you know any one in New York?"

"Yes, Miss Linwood, the friend to whom I am going."

"Miss Linwood! Miss Isabella Linwood? Ah, I have heard of her."

"She is not my only—" friend, she was going to say; a shade passed over her countenance, and she added, "acquaintance in New York. Now, sir, all that I am going to ask of you is for liberty to ride behind you, or one of your attendants, as far as you go on my way."

The stranger, compassionate as he felt, could scarcely forbear a smile. "We should be hardly a proper escort for you, my fair friend," he replied.

"Oh, fear not for that; I am so fenced about—so guarded by unseen and powerful spirits, that it matters not with whom, if I but get forward."

After a moment of anxious thought, "Tell me, young lady," he replied, "the name of that brother of whom you spoke, and on my honour I will do all in my power for you."

"No—never—this is a temptation of that evil one who so long led me astray, to turn me again from the straight path, to frustrate my purpose. I do not blame you, sir. He has before, in my dreams and at other times, whispered to me, that if I were but to speak my brother's name, I should be cared for ; but this would be trusting to a human arm. No : his name must not pass my lips." If she had then spoken it, how different would have been the fate of many individuals !

The benevolent stranger perceived that the impressions (whether illusions or not) from which Bessie acted were ineffaceable, and that she had that fixedness of purpose from which it seems impossible, by reason or art of any sort, to turn an insane person. He was at an utter loss what to do or say, and merely murmured, " Would to Heaven I could serve you !"

" You would and cannot ! Indeed, you look to me like those favourites of Heaven, who both will and can. Who are you ?"

" I am more generous than you, my friend, and I will tell you. My name is La Fayette."

" La Fayette ! Now is it not wonderful," exclaimed Bessie, clasping her hands and looking upward, her whole face bright and rapturous—" Is it not wonderful that he who is chosen and set apart of God for the cause of freedom, the friend of Washington, the best friend of my struggling country, should be guided to this little dwelling to find me out and aid me ? You cannot choose but serve me," she added, laying her hand on his, and faintly and wildly laughing.

" And I will serve you, my poor girl, so help me God !" he replied, kissing her faded, feverish hand. " Sit you here quietly, and I will see what can be done."

" I will wait patiently ; but remember, there is but one thing to be done."

La Fayette appeared in the outer room. His eyes were suffused with tears, and for a moment he found it difficult to command his voice. " You can make nothing of her," said Mrs. Barlow, looking inquiringly. " No ! I thought so—she is the meekest and the beautifullest mortal, the gentlest and the most obstinate, that ever I came across."

" Where is your husband, my good friend ?"

" Shoeing your horse, sir."

" Ah, that's very kind, very kind indeed. I will go and speak with him." Accordingly, he proceeded to the workshop, and there received from Barlow all the particulars he could communicate of poor Bessie Lee. " It is not only her master beautiful looks, sir," said Barlow, in conclusion ; " but she seems so pure in heart, and so well nurtured, and so pretty spoken. She draws many a tear from us—being weak and sick, sir, makes one easy to cry."

" The fountain of such tears is a good heart, my friend ; and no one need apologise for letting them gush out now and then. You say you have made every effort to find out who the poor girl is ?"

" Yes, sir, indeed I have ; but it is impossible. I have thought of advertising the stray lamb," he added, with a smile ; " but somehow I did not love to put her in the newspapers."

" That, perhaps, would have been wisest ; but now I think the best thing that can be done is to gratify her ruling desire, and get her to New York as soon as possible."

" Ay, indeed, sir ; but how get her there now ?"

" Why, my friend, you must furnish the way, and I the means. You know that those of us who are best off in these times have no superfluity. I cannot spare more than a guinea from the small sum I have with me."

" A guinea is a great sum, sir, in these hard times ; but—"

" But not enough to get the young lady to New York, I am aware of that ; and therefore, in addition, I shall give you my watch, which, being of gold and a repeater, will enable you to raise enough for her necessities, and a surplus to make your family comfortable till you come to the anvil again."

" This is too much," replied Barlow, bending low over the horse's hoof, either his gratitude or his sickness making it " easy for him to cry again."

" Not too much, nor quite enough, my friend. You will find some worthy man and woman to accompany her to the American lines ; and I will do what I can to secure her safe-conduct. She will certainly go safely to the British posts, and beyond, I trust. Surely none of God's creatures, who have a trace of his image, can be inhuman to her ; but we must take all precautions."

" Yes, indeed, sir. War, like a slaughter-house, breeds vermin ; and there be those abroad whose hearts are as hard as my anvil."

" We will do our best to protect her from such."

La Fayette then wrote an earnest recommendation of Bessie to the protection and kindness of all Americans. He requested the American officer to forward her under the protection of a flag ; and finally addressed a note to the British commander, and all his officers and agents, stating the condition of the young person whom he commended to their humanity, and praying them to expedite her progress to New York, where (as he thought proper to state, knowing Mr. Linwood to be a tory) the friend to whose house she was going, Robert Linwood, Esq., resided. The surprise of Barlow when he received these notes, and saw the powerful, all-honoured, and loved name of La Fayette attached to them, is indescribable. La Fayette gave the watch into his hands, and without waiting for his thanks, he pressed Barlow's hand, mounted his horse, joined his companions, and rode off at full speed. Barlow gazed after him till the cavalcade disappeared ; then, after a fervent thanksgiving to God, he said, looking at the watch, " I must pledge this ; but if Heaven prosper me, I will redeem it, and leave it, as better than all my fast property, to my children."

We have graced our page by recording here one of His unnumbered good deeds, who has filled up the measure of human benevolence by every manifestation, from the least to the greatest, of this divine quality.

CHAPTER XXIX.

But this was what I knew had come to pass,
When, answering with your vacant no, and yes,
You fed upon your thoughts and mark'd me not.

" My dear Lady Anne," said Mrs. Meredith to her niece, as they were one morning sitting together, " you seem to have taken a wonderful liking to that knotting (Lady Anne had become, as our friend Rivington has it, 'thrifty in the knotting amusement') ; where in the world did you learn it ? "

" Mrs. Linwood taught me."

" So I should think. It is as monotonous as she is."

" Oh, aunt, I find it charming ! It is the very perfection of existence to have an occupation like this for your fingers, while your heart and mind are left free to rove to the end of the world, or, what is better still, to be at the service of some agreeable companion you may chance to have beside you."

"*Chacun à son goût !* " said Mrs. Meredith, taking up a book, with a vexing consciousness that she was not the " agreeable companion" preferred to her niece's maiden meditations. Lady Anne had not spoken five words for the hour they had been sitting together. As the morning was rainy, the ladies were likely to remain uninterrupted ; and it was too tempting an opportunity for Mrs. Meredith to make an attack she had long been meditating, to be foregone ; so she put aside her book and her vexation, and said, in a voice sufficiently *untoned* for an old diplomatist, " You seem quite fond of the Linwoods, my love ? "

" I am, aunt."

" You find the choleric, peevish, egotistical old man charming ? "

" Indeed I do sincerely think him a delightful old gentleman."

" And that living manifestation of all the mediocrities, his patient consort ? "

" The most amiable woman in the world."

" And their lofty, capricious daughter, now silent and infolded in her own sublimities, like a worshipped idol on its pedestal, and now gracious as a new-made queen ? "

" And always captivating and gentle, aunt." Mrs. Meredith threw up her hands and eyes. " I mean *almost* always gentle, as a woman should be. For my part, I do not fancy perpetual sunshine. I am much of a certain English sea-captain's way of thinking, who, after being becalmed in the sunny waters of France, sailed away in one of his own north-easters and thick fogs, and thanked Heaven he was out of that d—d sunshine."

" Your illustration is a fortunate one, Lady Anne. I congratulate you on your peculiar taste. But for this gusty variety in the temper of your friend, your long evenings with that little family *coterie* would be rather of the becalmed order."

" The evenings never seem long to me," replied Lady Anne, her face dimpling with recollected pleasure.

" How in the world do you kill time ? "

" Oh, the old gentleman and Mrs. Archer, and Isabella and her mother, play whist."

" And you sit by and look on ? This is inscrutable, that you, my dear child, who are so admired, courted, worshipped, should be content to play so obscure a part. If there were a young man in the case—if that son of Mr. Linwood were at home—by the way, they seem to make themselves exceedingly comfortable while he is in durance. Yes, if the juice of 'that little western flower' were on your eyelids, I could understand why you should thus 'madly dote.' "

Lady Anne laughed and shook her head, as if to say, " Puzzle it out if you can."

Mrs. Meredith was displeased ; but, like many persons who have self-command and good taste, she chose to show her angry feelings in the light of gentle emotions. Her voice faltered, and her eyes filled with tears (her eyes, it may be remembered, were fine, the prototypes of her son's brilliant orbs). " I ought, my dear girl," she said, " to be satisfied if you are ; but I have so set my heart upon you, the only child of my dear lamented brother. I had hoped that Jasper and I should make our home attractive to you, that we might have, at least, a portion of your affection."

" My dear aunt ! " exclaimed Lady Anne, throwing down her knotting, " I—I—" do love you dearly, she was on the point of adding, but she was too honest to indulge her good-nature at the expense of truth, and she said, " I feel your kindness to me. I should be most ungrateful if I did not."

" Grateful, undoubtedly you are, and so you would have been to any faithful guardian ; but the heart asks something more. You manifest neither to me nor Jasper more than the affection of a common relative. Whatever place I may take in the scale of your friends, your cousin is certainly no common person."

" No, indeed, that he is not," said Lady Anne, charmed that she could soothe her aunt and speak sincerely. " Jasper is by far the most agreeable gentleman you have introduced to me here. He is a little abstracted now and then ; but when he knows what he is saying, he is perfectly delightful. I told Isabella Linwood last evening that it was a mystery to me—*une véritable merveille*—that she had never fallen in love with Jasper."

" What did she say ? " asked Mrs. Meredith eagerly, and off her guard.

" I do not remember. I believe she said nothing."

" A provoking, inscrutable person she is," thought Mrs. Meredith ; and then made a remark which she meant to be what the lawyers call *leading* :— " There was a report, before we came, of an attachment between Jasper and Miss Linwood."

" Bless me ! was there ? "

" Why are you surprised ? "

" For the best reason in the world, aunt—neither seems to fancy the other. As for Isabella, whenever I praise cousin Jasper, she is either quite silent, or turns the conversation, as if she did not like to appear to disagree with me."

" Ah, my young lady," thought the aunt, " you do not see quite through a millstone."

Jasper at this moment entered. " Come here, cousin," said Lady Anne ; and when he had approached, she added, in a playful voice, putting her hand (the prettiest hand in the world) on his arm, " Were you *ever* in love with—" her mischievous pause nearly suspended the pulsations of Meredith's heart, " with—don't be scared—the most loveable person in the world ? "

He had recovered himself. " If I never have been," he replied, seizing her hand and kissing it, " I shall soon be—irretrievably."

The past, the future, rushed upon him, and overpowered his self-command. He turned from Lady Anne, and left the apartment. " Oh, Jasper ! Jasper ! " cried Lady Anne, blushing, laughing, and springing after him, " stop one minute—you did not understand me." But before she reached the stairs, the outer door closed after Meredith. Mrs. Meredith clasped her hands. Jasper was won— Lady Anne must of course be !—and she seemed to herself to have reached the summit of her Pisgah, and thence to descry the promised land for which she had come *to* the wilderness. That "there is many a slip between the cup and the lip," is a proverb somewhat musty ; but it pithily indicates the sudden mutations to which poor humanity is liable.

CHAPTER XXX.

I would to Heaven I had your potency,
And you were Isabel! should it then be thus?
No! I would tell what 'twere to be a judge,
And what a prisoner.

We change the scene from Mrs. Meredith's drawing-room to the gloomiest cell in the city prison, where, stretched on a heap of straw, lay a poor wretch condemned to be hung at four o'clock in the afternoon of that day. The door opened, and Isabella entered, attended by Rose, and escorted by a turnkey, who, having set down a candle to aid the feeble light of the cell, went out himself, and locked the door upon them.

"Take up the light, Rose," said Isabella, who was shivering, not so much from the unsunned air of the apartment, as at the presence of a fellow-creature in such circumstances ; "hold it near him, Rose, so that I can see his face."

Rose approached close to him and said, as if announcing the visit of an angel, "Here's a lady come to see you." He made no reply ; and, after an eager survey, she turned to her young mistress and said, "His senses are clean gone ! " Isabella held Rose's arm while she gazed at him. His face was ashen, his hair was in matted masses, and his pale blue eye wandered inexpressively.

"Who are you ? " asked Isabella. The music of her voice for an instant fixed his uncertain gaze, but he made no reply ; and again his eye was bent on vacancy. "Who are you, friend ? " she repeated.

"I a'n't nobody," he replied, in a broken voice between a laugh and a sob.

"Have you no friend ? " He turned his face to the straw, and muttered something inaudibly. "What does he say, Rose ? "

"Turn up your face so the lady can hear," said Rose. He obeyed ; but Rose's voice seemed to have broken the spell of her mistress's, and he remained silent.

"Rouse yourself, my good friend," said Isabella ; "I wish to be of service to you. Can you give me any reason why you should not die the death to which you are sentenced ? "

"No—lief as not."

"It cannot be—you must have something— some friend for whom you would like to live and come out of this place."

"Had !—had ! " the poor creature sobbed like a child.

"Tell me," said Isabella, eagerly, "the name of this friend ? " But the obstinate mood had again seized him ; and though she varied the question, and put it in every possible form, he gave no sign of answer.

"Try him upon some other hook, Miss Belle," whispered Rose.

"How long had you been with the Skinners when you were taken ? "

Now he answered promptly—"Years !—years !"

"Years !—that cannot be."

"Cannot ? A'n't the minutes years to the child that's crying for its mammy, hey ! " He had risen on his elbow ; but he again sank back on the straw, and renewed his piteous crying.

"What does this mean ! What can be done for him ! " exclaimed Isabella. "My poor friend, death is very near to you—do you know it ! "

"Yes, yes, lady. Ha'n't they brought me a new suit ? " He pointed to the execution suit that was folded up and lying beside him. "There be three times in every one's life when they're sure of a new suit :—when they're born, when they're married, and when they die. I've got my last and prettiest, I'm thinking ; for I remember granny reading about the angels being in white robes."

His mind seemed now more collected, and Isabella ventured to ask him if he were willing to die !

"Glad on't—don't look at me, lady, with that bright watery eye—I *am* glad on't."

"Have you prayed for the pardon of your sins ? "

"Haven't any—never had—never wronged anybody, nor wished it, nor thought on't."

"Merciful Heaven ! " exclaimed Isabella, "what is to be done ? "

"For me, lady ?—nothing."

"Do you not wish to live ? "

"Yes—with him. 'Out him ?—no."

"Who ? " Isabella spoke too eagerly. He looked at her, shook his head, then broke into an exulting laugh, like a boy who has seen a trap and escaped it.

"Miss Belle," said Rose, "you are wasting your tears and your feelings—we must all die once, and the stroke can't come in better time to him than now, when he's so willing to go."

"Willing ! glad, hey ! nobody cares for me, and I cares for nobody but him ; I think he be dead ; but," he added, laying his hand on Isabella's arm, "be he dead, or be he living, you'll see him—your soul is kin to his, lady—and mind you tell him how the Skinners kept me till the reg'lars came—did not tell 'em I was not a Skinner—cheated 'em, hey !"

Isabella waited till he was through, and then said quietly, "Who did you tell me to give your message to ? "

"Misser Eliot." At the utterance of this name poor Kisel sank back on the straw, laughed and cried, and attempted to whistle, but he was too weak to control the muscles of his lips. By degrees his voice subsided into low moanings, and his eye wandered without light or direction from his mind. The name had produced its effect upon Isabella also. She had been incited to this visit to the prison by Herbert, who had communicated to her, the previous evening, some particulars he had received from a sub-keeper in the prison, in relation to this condemned man, which had excited a fear in Herbert's mind that there was some mistake in relation to the culprit. Herbert had not, however, the slightest suspicion that the poor victim was Kisel. One or two particulars of the convict's apparent innocence and simplicity had touched Isabella's heart, and all night she had been disturbed by the impression that he was unjustly condemned. Some young ladies would have rested satisfied with dropping a few pitiful tears over such a mischance, but Isabella Linwood was of another temper; and having no male friend on whom she could rely, she went herself to the prison, and easily obtained access to the prisoner's cell. The moment Kisel pronounced Eliot's name, she was convinced the condemned must be the half-witted attendant of Captain Lee, whom she had often heard Herbert describe; and she doubted not that, by going to Sir Henry Clinton and communicating her conviction, she might obtain an order for having him identified by confronting him with Herbert, or, at any rate, that she should procure a respite of his sentence. Her carriage was awaiting her; and having communicated her intentions to Rose, she directed her to walk home, saying she should go immediately to Sir Henry's. Rose remonstrated. "What if he be the poor man you think for, Miss Belle! life is nothing to him—he can do nothing with it—he would not thank you for it."

"But, Rose, the life of an innocent man is sacred."

"La, Miss Belle, they don't stand on such trifles as innocence in war-times—please don't go to Sir Henry's. He won't think the man belonging to Captain Lee alters the case much, and you don't love to be denied, and—I don't love to have you."

Rose was right. Her young mistress did not "love to be denied," but the discipline of events was fast subduing her self-will, and counteracting the indulgence and flattery of her friends. A common nature is not taught by experience, and may, therefore, be either the tool or victim of circumstances; but a creature like Isabella Linwood, composed of noble elements (if, as with her, these elements are sustained by religious principle), has within herself a self-rectifying and all-controlling power. "Rose little dreams," said she, as the carriage-door closed upon her, "how my fondest wishes and expectations have been *denied* and defeated! God grant that the affections thus cast back upon me may not degenerate to morbid sensibility or pining selfishness, but that they may be employed vigorously for the good of my fellow-beings! This poor harmless, broken creature, if I could but save him!—save him and render Eliot Lee a service—Herbert's friend—poor Bessie's brother—and the preserver of my dear little pet, Lizzy!"

In the midst of these meditations she was shown into Sir Henry's library, where she perceived Jasper Meredith seated at the table, reading, in the identical spot where, a few weeks before, she had received so passionate a declaration from him. A most embarrassing reminiscence of the scene struck them both. He started from the table, and she asked the servant to show her to the drawing-room.

"The drawing-room was occupied;" and thus, though the awkwardness of entering was increased tenfold by the effort to avoid it, enter she must. Seldom have two persons been placed in a more singular position in relation to each other. Their destiny, while it was governed by inflexible principles, seemed to have been at the mercy of the merest accidents. "If," as Meredith had thought a thousand times, while pursuing his retrospections, "if Isabella had not hesitated, and while she hesitated, Helen Ruthven had not broken in upon us, our fate would then have been fixed; or if, on the second occasion, when I urged her decision, she had not again hesitated till her impatient father called her, I should not now be wavering between my inclination and my *better judgment!*"

But Isabella did hesitate, and that hesitation, proceeding from the demands of her pure and lofty nature, was her salvation, and a fatal rebuke and spur to his vanity.

They exchanged the ordinary salutations. Isabella sat down. They were in the same chairs they had occupied at that memorable moment of their lives; the same table was before them—the same books on the table. Feelings have their habits, and so easily revert to their customary channels! A spell seemed to have been cast over them. Neither spoke nor moved, till Isabella, starting as one starts from a thrilling dream, rose and walked to the window. "Ah," thought she, "what memories, hopes, *dreams,* 'poor fancy's followers,' has this place conjured up!"

Jasper, moved by an irresistible impulse, followed her, and was arrested, in his half-formed purpose, by the vision of Helen Ruthven, who, as she was passing on the opposite side of the street, had seen Isabella come forward, and had vainly tried to catch her eye. She was smiling and bowing. When she saw Meredith, she beckoned. "You had best go to Miss Ruthven," said Isabella; "I have some business with Sir Henry."

"I will go, Miss Linwood," he replied; and adding bitterly, "the will of man is by his reason swayed," he disappeared. Isabella burst into tears. Was ever a woman disenthralled from such a sentiment as Isabella had felt, without efforts repeated and repeated, and many such pangs as she now suffered, secretly endured! The struggle is a hard one—the conquest worth it.

Sir Henry entered. "Your pardon, my dear Miss Isabella. I believed Meredith was here, and thought you might chance to profit by the blessing promised to those who wait—but you look troubled—your father is not worse, no!—your brother has not abused his liberty!—papa does not frown upon the faithful knight!"

"Oh, no, no—nothing of all this, Sir Henry—I have again come a petitioner to you, but not now in my own cause." Isabella then proceeded to state concisely and eloquently the case of the condemned; Sir Henry became graver as she proceeded; and as she ended, losing a good deal of his habitual courtesy, he said, "Really Miss Linwood, these are not matters for a young lady to interfere with. The day for voluntary and romantic righters of wrongs is past. This fellow has been adjudged to death after due investigation, before the proper tribunal, and I do not see that it makes any essential difference in his favour even if he should have had the honour of once being in the service of a man who is so fortunate as to be the friend of your brother, and to have rendered an accidental service to your aunt. The poor wretch, as you allow, was one of the band of Skinners when captured by a detachment of our soldiers. His comrades were hung last week, and I have already granted a respite to this man for some reason, (what, I do not precisely recollect,) alleged by the proper officer."

" He was ill—unable to stand, when the others suffered."

" Ah, yes—I remember."

Isabella urged her conviction that the prisoner had been accidentally involved with the Skinners. She described his simplicity and imbecility of mind, and, as it seemed to her, his utter incapacity to commit the energetic and atrocious crimes perpetrated by a band of desperadoes. But to all her pleadings Sir Henry still returned the answer so satisfactory to an official conscience :—" His death had been decreed by the laws in such cases made and provided."

Isabella said that so slight seemed to be the prisoner's tenure of life, that if he were reprieved for a week, Sir Henry might be relieved from the responsibility of taking a life perhaps not forfeited. But Sir Henry did not shrink from responsibility, and though she still reasoned, and urged, it was all in vain.

He alleged that the press of important affairs rendered it impossible for him to make a personal investigation of the business ; and that indeed it was out of the question, occupying the station he did, to attend minutely to such a concern. The truth was, that Sir Henry was somewhat fortified in his present decision by a secret consciousness, that on a former occasion, he had surrendered a point purely to the influence of a lovely young woman ; and he was now resolved to maintain the invincible.

Isabella was obliged to take her leave, having failed in her errand of mercy, and feeling a just indignation at the carelessness with which a man could make his station an apology for neglecting the rights of his fellow ; and struck with the truth, that the only reason for one man's occupying a station more elevated than another, is that it gives him the opportunity of better protecting and serving his fellow-beings.

———◆———

CHAPTER XXXI.

All torment, trouble, wonder, and amazement,
Inhabit here ! Some heavenly power guide us
Out of this fearful country.

THE hour appointed for Kisel's execution drew nigh. The premonitory bell was already sounding, when a countryman, who had come from the other side of the Hudson, sheltering his little boat in a nook under some cedars growing where Warren-street now terminates, was proceeding towards the city with a market-basket, containing butter, eggs, &c. As he was destined to enact an important part in the drama of that day, it may not be superfluous to describe the homely habiliments in which he appeared. He had on a coarse dark-grey overcoat, a sort of dreadnought, of domestic manufacture, double-breasted, and fastened with black mohair buttons, as large as dollars, up to his throat ; his cravat was a blue and white linen handkerchief—an enduring article, then manu-

factured by all thrifty housewives ; his stockings were blue and white yarn, ribbed ! his shoes cow-hide, and tied with leather thongs. A young man is rarely without a dash of coxcombry, and our humble swain's was betrayed in a fox-skin cap, with straps of the fur that decorated his cheek, much in the mode of the brush-whisker of our own day. The cap was drawn so close over his brow as nearly to hide his dark pomatumed hair ; and finally, his hands were covered by scarlet and white mittens, full fringed, and with his name, *Harmann Van Zandt*, knit in on their backs.

The storm of the morning had passed over. The sun was shining out clear and warm for the season ; and as every one is eager to enjoy the last smiles of our stinted autumn, the countryman must have wondered, as he passed the few habitations on his way to the populous part of the town, not to see the usual group—the good-man with his pipe, the matron knitting, and the buxom Dutch damsel leaning over the lower portal of the door. As he approached Broadway, however, the sounds of life and busy movement reached his ear, and he saw half-a-dozen young lads and lasses issue from a house on his left, dressed in their Sunday gear, their faces full of eager expectation, and each hurrying the other.

The good *vrow*, who stood on the door-step, was giving them a last charge to hear everything and see everything to tell her ; for she " always had to stay at home when anything *lively* was going on." As she turned from them, her house-wife eye fell on the countryman's market-basket. " Stop, neighbour," said she, " and tell us the price of your butter and eggs."

" Butter one dollar the pound, eggs three for a shilling."

" That's the prettiest price asked yet ; but——"

" Ay, mother ; but live and let live, you know."

" *Let live*, truly. You Bergen people are turning your grass into gold."

" We must make hay while the sun shines."

" While the sun shines ! Ah, it does shine as through a knot-hole on a few, but the rest of us are in solid darkness. Go your ways, friend ; you'll find lords and generals, admirals, commandants, and gaol-keepers, to buy your butter and eggs ; honest people must eat their bread without butter now-a-days. The hawks have come over the water to protect the doves, forsooth, and the doves' food, doves and all, are like to be devoured."

This was a sort of figurative railing much indulged in by those who were secretly well affected to the country's cause, but who were constrained by motives of prudence to remain within the British lines.

It seemed to have struck a sympathetic chord in the countryman ; for drawing near the good woman, whose exterior expressed very little resemblance to the gentle emblem by which she had chosen to personify herself, he said, kindly smiling, " Bring me a knife, mother, and I'll give you a slice of butter to garnish your tea-table when your comely lasses come home."

" This is kind and neighbourlike," said the woman, hastily bringing the knife and plate ; " I thought, the first minute you opened your lips, you were free-hearted. This a'n't the common way of the Bergen people—they sell the cat and her skin too—you have not their tongue, neither —mine is more broken than yours, and I'm only Dutch on the mother's side."

" Ah, mother, trading with gentlefolks, and such fair-spoken people as you, gets the mitten off one's tongue. But I must be going. Can you direct me to Lizzy Bengin's ! our Lida wants a pink ribbon against Christmas."

" Now don't say you come to market, and don't know where Lizzy Bengin lives ! Did you never take notice of the little one-story building at the very lower end of Queen-street, with the stoop even with the ground, and plenty of cochinia, and cookey horses, and men and women, in the window, and a parrot hanging outside that beats the world for talking !" The man gave the expected assent, and his informant proceeded—" That is Lizzy's ; and without going a step out of your way, you may turn your butter and eggs into silver before you get there. Call at the Provost—Cunningham starves the prisoners, and eats the fat of the land himself—or at Admiral Digby's, who has the young prince William under his roof, and therefore a warrant for the best in the land—or at Tryon's, or Robertson's, or any of the quality ; their bread is buttered both sides ; but the time is coming——."

" When the bread shall be fairly spread for all. I think so, mother ; but I must be going—so, good-day."

" Good-day, and good luck to you—a nice youth and a well-spoken is that," said she, looking after him ; " and if butter must be a dollar a pound, I'm glad the money finds its way into the pockets of the like of him."

Meanwhile the subject of her approbation pursued his way, and soon found himself in the midst of a throng, who were hurrying forward to the place of execution. The usual place for military executions was in an apple orchard, where East Broadway now runs ; but the condemned having to suffer as one of the infamous band of Skinners, was not thought worthy to swing on a gallows devoted to military men. Accordingly, a gallows was erected in a field just above St. Paul's church. Our friend of the butter and eggs found himself, on reaching Broadway, retarded and encompassed by the crowd. " Hold your basket up, fellow, and let me pass," said a gentleman, who seemed eager to get beyond the crowd. The countryman obeyed, but turned his back upon the speaker, as if from involuntary resentment at his authoritative tone.

" Whither are you hastening, Meredith !" asked another voice.

" Ah, St. Clair, how are you ! I am trying to get through this abominable crowd to join my mother and Lady Anne, who have gone to take a drive ; my servant is waiting with my horse beyond the barracks."

"Your mother, Lady Anne, and Miss *Linwood !*"

An opening now before the countryman would have allowed him to pass on, but he did not move. " Upon my honour, St. Clair, I did not know that Miss Linwood was with them. They talked of asking Helen Ruthven "

" And so they did. Lady Anne sent me to her, but Miss Ruthven said, not very civilly I think, she had no inclination for a drive, and begged me to stop while she wrote you this note."

Meredith opened the note, sealed with an anchor, and containing only these two lines, exquisitely written in pencil :—" Could I endure anything called pleasure on the same day with my *tête-à-tête* walk with you this morning ! Oh, no—there is no next best.—H. R."

" You seem pleased, Meredith," resumed St. Clair, as he saw Meredith's eye kindle and his cheek brighten. Meredith made no reply, but thrust the note into his pocket. He was pleased. He felt much like a musician, whose ears have been tormented by discords, when the keys are rightly struck. " Lady Anne had hard work," continued St. Clair, " to persuade Miss Linwood to go with her. It seems she has got up her nerves for this poor devil of a Skinner. Lady Anne persuaded her at last ; indeed, I believe she was glad to get beyond the tolling of the bell till the rumpus is over."

" Women are riddles," thought Meredith ; " they feel without reason, and will not feel when reason bids them." He had lost his desire to go alone to join the ladies ; and he offered St. Clair his horse, saying he would himself ride his servant's. St. Clair eagerly accepted his courtesy, and the two gentlemen elbowed their way through the crowd. The countryman turned to gaze after them ; and while his eye followed Meredith with its keenest glance, the wave of the multitude had set towards him, and so completely hedged his way in front, that, not being able to proceed, he thought best to retreat a few yards to where the crowd was less dense, and wait till the pressure was past, which must be soon, as the procession with the prisoner had already moved from the Provost. Meanwhile he secured the occupation of a slightly elevated platform, an entrance to a house, where, setting down his basket, he folded his arms, and while he detained had the benefit of the various remarks of the passers-by.

" What a disgrace it is," said a British subaltern to his companion, " that those rebels," pointing to some American officers, prisoners on parole, " are permitted to walk the streets in uniform. It is too annoying—I hate the sight of them."

" Yes," retorted his companion laughing, " and so you have ever since they distanced you skating on the Kolch last winter."

" A crying shame is it," said an honest burgher to a fellow-vestryman, " that a human creature is going to his doom, and but one bell tolling. But the Lord's temples are turned aside from all holy uses—our own sanctuary is a prison for soldiers, and the Middle Dutch a riding-school !"

" A soul's a soul," returned his companion ; " but the lordly English bells may not toll for the parting of this poor wretch's ; only the tinkling bell of the methodist chapel, that's kept open, forsooth, because John Wesley and his followers are loyal."

" We shall have our pains for our trouble," said a fellow, who seemed to have come to the spectacle *en amateur !* " the boys say he never will stand it to get to the gallows."

" Move on—move on," cried a voice that heralded the procession ; and the crowd was driven forward, in order to leave an open space around the prisoner and his assistants.

It is impossible for a benevolent man to look on a fellow-creature about to suffer a violent death (be his doom ever so well merited) without a feeling of intense interest. The days of the culprit's youth, of his innocence, of his parents' love and hope ; the tremendous present, and the possible future, all rush upon the mind ! It would appear that our country friend was a man of reflection and sentiment ; for, as he gazed at the prisoner, his cheek was blanched, his brow contracted, and the exclamation, " Oh, God ! Oh, God !" burst from lips that never lightly uttered that holy name.

Poor Kisel appeared as if nature would fain save him from the executioner's touch. His head had fallen on his bosom, his knees were bent and trembling, and his step as wavering and uncertain as that of a blind man. He was supported and helped forward by a stout man on his right. When he was within a few feet of the countryman, a ray of consciousness seemed to shoot athwart his mind. He raised his head, shook back his shaggy locks, cast a wild inquiring glance around him, when his eye encountering the stranger, he seemed electrified, his joints to be reset, his nerves restrung. He drew up his person, uttered a piercing shriek, sprang forward like a cat, and, sinking at his feet, sobbed out, " Misser Eliot, hey !"

The multitude were for an instant palsied ; not a sound—not a breath escaped them : and then a rush, and a shout, and cries of " Seize him !" and shrieks from those who were trodden under foot.

" Stand back—back—back, monsters !" cried Eliot, himself almost wild with amazement and grief—" give him air, space, breath, he is dying !" He raised Kisel's head, and rested it on his breast, and bent his face over him, murmuring, " Kisel, my poor fellow !"

Kisel's eye, gleaming with preternatural joy, was riveted to Eliot's face. A slight convulsion passed over his frame ; drops of sweat, like rain, gushed from every pore ; and, while his quivering, half-smiling lips murmured inaudibly, " Misser Eliot !—Misser Eliot !" they stiffened, his eyes rolled up, and his released, exulting spirit fled.

Eliot was but for one instant unmanned ; but for one instant did he lose the self-possession on which even at this moment of consternation he was conscious that much more than his own individual safety depended. He made no effort to escape from observation ; that would have excited suspicion ; but said, calmly, still supporting Kisel's head, " The poor man, I think, is gone ; is there not some physician here who can tell whether he be or not ?" A doctor was called for ; and, while one was bustling through the crowd, there were various conjectures, surmises, and assertions. Some said " he looked as good as dead when he came out of the prison ;" some asked " if he could have hoped to have got away ?" and others believed that the excitement of the scene had maddened his brain. Eliot said he had fallen at his feet like a spent ball ; and, while he was internally blessing God that his poor follower had escaped all farther suffering, the medical man announced, with the authority of his art, that " life was extinct." The body was conveyed to the prison for interment. The crowd dispersed ; and Eliot, feeling that Heaven had conferred its best boon on Kisel, and extended a shield over him, pursued his way to Lizzy Bengin's shop.

CHAPTER XXXII.

Les revers de la vérité a cent milles figures, et un champ indefiny.

Les Pythagoriens font le bien certain et finy, le mal incertain et infiny.—MONTAIGNE.

WHILE the circumstances related above were in action, the ladies, in their drive, had stopped at an opening to the Hudson, where the shore was shelving and indented with a footpath, on which the full mellow rays of the afternoon sun shone. And who would not pause to gaze at the noble Hudson, which, coming from its source in distant mountains, infolds in its arms the city it has created, wears on its bosom its little emerald island gems, reposes in the bay, and then finishes its course through the portal of the Narrows !

The river is now precisely what it then was, for " man's hand cannot make a mark upon the waters ;" but on its shores what changes has that marvellous instrument wrought ! Where nature sat, like a hermit, amid the magnificence of her solitary domain, are now bustling cities, fortified islands, wharves and warehouses, manufactories, stately mansions, ornamented pleasure-grounds, and citizens' cottages, and the parent city extending up and branching out in every direction, from the narrow space it then occupied, covering with its thronged streets the wooded heights and bosky dells, now, alas ! reduced from the aristocracy of nature to one uniform level. Then the city's tributary waters bore on their surface a few fishing-skiffs, and some two or three British men-of-war. Now see the signals of population, enterprise, and commercial prosperity : schooners from our own eastern and southern ports, neatly rigged vessels from a hundred river-harbours, mammoth steamers bringing in and carrying out their hundreds at every hour of the day, ferry-boats scudding to and fro, sail-boats dancing over the waves ; row-boats darting out and in, hither and yon ; packets taking their semi-weekly departure for England and France, ships with the star-spangled banner floating from the mast-head, and rich freighted argosies from all parts of each quarter of the globe. What a change !

Lady Anne heard the trampling of horses, and put her head out of the coach-window. A blush suffused her sunny face at the recollection of her parting with Meredith in the morning. Her embarrassment was as transient as the suffusion. " Ah, cousin Jasper," she said, " you have come at last ; I have been waiting impatiently, sitting here, like a dutiful niece (as I am), because aunt has heard bugbear stories about American rattlesnakes, and absolutely forbade my strolling along the shore with Isabella. You will not be afraid, aunt, if the gentlemen are with me ?"

" Not in the least, my love ; indeed, I will alight myself, if Major St. Clair will give an old lady his arm."

" She understands tactics," thought St. Clair ; " she will defile with me, and leave Jasper to a tête-à-tête on vantage-ground !" He, however, bowed, en militaire, and gave Mrs. Meredith his arm ; and she, as he had foreseen, led him off in an opposite direction from that which Lady Anne had taken.

Isabella had before alighted, and left her companion, on the pretext of looking for an autumnal flower, that she knew grew on the river's bank; but really, that she might, in the freedom of solitude, and in the calm of a sweet country walk, indulge her sad reflections. Isabella had learned to master herself in great trials; but she had not yet learned that far more difficult lesson, to be patient and serene under small annoyances. She was vexed and wearied with Mrs. Meredith's pompous talk and common-place and hollow sentiment, and somewhat disturbed by Lady Anne's kind-hearted, but too manifest efforts, to divert her thoughts from the tragedy enacting in the city, to which she had imputed all the sadness that might have been in part ascribed to another cause.

Lady Anne had no enthusiasm for scenery: she had never lived in the country, never been trained in Nature's school, nor a guest at her perpetual and sweetest banquet; but she had youthful spirits stirred to joyousness by a ride, or a walk, or any other exciting cause; and she laughed, rattled, and bounded on, wondered where Isabella could be, and at last, quite out of breath, sat down on a grassy bank by a very high rock, around which the pass was narrow and difficult. "I will not venture that," said she, pointing to the path. "You may go for Isabella, Jasper, and I will wait here for you."

"Thank you, sweet coz; but I prefer staying here too, if you will permit me."

"You may as well, I fancy. Isabella is rather *penseroso* this afternoon; and as she very faintly seconded my entreaties to aunt that I might go with her, I think she prefers *la solitaire*. To tell you the truth, Jasper, she is horribly blue to-day, though I would not own it to aunt."

"And why not?"

"Oh, you know she is no favourite with aunt; and when we really love a person, as I do really and fervently Isabella Linwood, we are not fond of speaking of their faults to those who do not like them."

"Then perhaps you think she is a favourite of mine?"

"Certainly I do—is she not?"

"She *was*."

With what different import do the same words fall on different ears! This "she *was*" hardly reached Lady Anne's sensorium. Her thoughts were weighing something more important than any of Meredith's words could be to her. Meredith's heart throbbed as he pronounced them. Uttered to Lady Anne, they seemed to him to cut the Gordian knot that bound him to Isabella. There was another unseen, unwilling, and involuntary auditor, who, as on the other side of the rock she leaned breathless against it, proudly responded from the depths of her soul, "She *was*—it is past—a finished dream to us both!"

"How very nice these little scarlet berries are!" said Lady Anne, picking some berries from their evergreen leaves.

"Very nice."

"This is a lovely river, Jasper. How I should like a nice cottage on this very spot!"

"And when your imagination builds the cottage, coz, is there no one permitted to share it with you?"

Lady Anne picked the leaves from the stem in her hand, strewed them around, and, laughing and blushing, said, "that absolute solitude in a cottage would be just as stupid as in a palace."

"On this hint shall I—*can* I speak?" thought Meredith.

"Formerly, when I built castles in the air," continued Lady Anne, engrossed in her own sweet fancies, and not dreaming of the interpretation Meredith's deluded vanity was giving to her words, "I always put wings to them, and would lodge them in London, Paris, or Italy, as suited the humour of the moment—now I make them fixtures in America."

Meredith felt somewhat like the sportsman, who, accustomed to the keen pursuit of game that incites and eludes him, cares not for the silly prey that runs into his toils. "Heigh-ho!" resumed Lady Anne, awaking from a reverie, after a short pause, "it is time we returned—the sun is setting—you are very stupid, Jasper—you have not spoken three words."

"My dear cousin, there are moments when it is far more agreeable to look, and to listen, than to speak."

"But then, sir, you should look 'unutterable things.'"

"We may feel them without looking or speaking them—do not go now—there are few delicious moments in life—why not prolong them?"

"You talk limpingly, Jasper, like one who has conned a task, and recites it but half learned; there should be a *vraisemblance* in compliments."

"On my honour!"

"Oh, never swear to them; these are like beggars' oaths, nobody believes them." Lady Anne was already on the wing. "Bless us," thought Meredith, "a little dash of coquetry might make her quite charming;" and springing after her, he gave her his arm. When they met his mother at the road-side, his face and air were so changed and so animated, that, in the flush of her hopes, she ventured to whisper to him—

"Not Hermia, but Helena I love;
Who would not change a raven for a dove!"

He smiled assentingly, and his mother was perfectly happy.

"Where is Isabella?" and "Where is Miss Linwood?" "I thought she was on your side;" and "I thought she was on yours," was asked and reiterated, and answered by the person in question appearing. She had left the shore, scrambled through the wood, and come into the road in advance of the party. They rallied her on her preference of solitude, and she them (for she had regained her self-command), on the willing forbearance with which they had permitted her to enjoy it. Mrs. Meredith, of course, first entered the carriage; and while the young ladies were getting in, putting on their cloaks, &c., she wrote on a card and gave to her son the following hint from Metastasio:—

E folle quel nocchiero
Che cerca un' altra stella,
E non si fida a quella
Che in porto lo guidò.

"My sage mother is this sure star, by whose directing 'light I am to pilot my bark,'" thought

Meredith, as he read the pencilled words—" well, be it so."

Mrs. Meredith's carriage stopped at Mrs. Linwood's door. Isabella alighted, and Lady Anne was following her, when her aunt interposed.— "My dear child," she said, " I particularly wish you to go home with me this evening."

" I would, aunt—but—but I have promised Mr. Linwood————"

" I appeal to your generosity, Miss Linwood; I have not your passion for solitude, and I am quite wretched without Lady Anne."

Lady Anne's back was to her aunt; and she turned up her eyes imploringly to Isabella, who consequently resolutely professed herself afraid to encounter her father if she should resign Lady Anne. Lady Anne finished the parley by springing from the carriage, and promising her aunt to be at home an hour earlier than usual. Mrs. Meredith, vexed, puzzled, and disconcerted, drove home.

The young ladies were met at the door by Rose, with a message from Mrs. Archer, requesting Isabella, without a moment's delay, to come to her house. "Make my excuses to papa," said Isabella to Lady Anne, "and enact the good daughter till I return."

" Yes, that I will," said Lady Anne; " and the good daughter would I be in reality all my life to him," she thought; " but Herbert Linwood will not, in his forlorn circumstances, declare his love for me if he feels it; and I, like all the rest of my sex, must keep the secret of my pure love as if it were a crime." Whether the open-hearted girl's eyes and cheeks would betray the secret which the austere proprieties of her sex forbade her to tell, and whether on this hint Linwood would be emboldened to speak, was soon put to the proof; for one hour after, arriving on his evening visit, Rose conducted him into the breakfast-room, informing him that he must wait till a person who was with his father on business should be gone. Rose, sagaciously divining her young master's inclinations, then went to Lady Anne and whispered—" Mr. Herbert is in the breakfast-parlour; and do, Miss, happen in there; poor boy, he has enough of his own company in prison."

Lady Anne did not wait for the request to be repeated. She went, nor did she and Herbert appear in Mr. Linwood's room till after a repeated, and finally, very impatient summons from him; and then they entered, and kneeling together at his feet, asked his blessing on their plighted loves.

He did not speak for half a minute, and then laughing, while the tears gushed from his eyes, "God bless you, my children!" he said; " God bless you!—kiss me, my dear little girl—this has been pretty quickly hatched, though; but I don't wonder; I loved you the first minute I saw you."

" And I, like a good son, dutifully followed my father's example."

" Vous n'avez fait que votre devoir filial; fort bien, monsieur!" said Lady Anne, archly.

" My dear child!" interposed Mr. Linwood, " now you are going really to be my child, don't torment me with interlarding your English with French. There's nothing I detest like cutting up a plain English road with these French ditches. It's a slipshod tongue, good enough for those that are born to parlez-vous and gabble all their lives; but English, my dear, is for men of sense and true-hearted girls like you, that speak what they mean."

Lady Anne promised to cure herself of a habit into which she had unconsciously fallen; and a pause followed, which gave Mr. Linwood time for a reflection that clouded his brow.

" This won't do, Herbert," he said; " I forgot myself entirely, and so have you. What business have you to be making love, and stealing away this dear little generous girl's heart—you, a proscribed man—holding your life by sufferance—disgraced?"

" Not disgraced, sir!"

" Oh, no! dear Mr. Linwood, not disgraced."

" Well, well, 'tis a devilish ugly word to bestow on one's own flesh and blood, but, my dear little girl, we must look truth in the face. Your aunt is a woman of the world; she will accuse us; and she may very well suspect us of conniving at this business—you have fortune—we are poor." The proud old man's blood mounted to his face—" No, no; it must not be. I take back my consent."

Herbert's face expressed the conflict of his love with his sense of rectitude—the last prevailed. " My father is right," he said; " and I, headlong as usual, have done just what I ought not to do."

" You're right now, anyhow, my boy; you show blood—go up to the mark, though a lion—" A glance at poor Lady Anne, leaning on the side of his easy-chair, with tearful eyes, mended his sentence—" I should say, though an angel were in the way."

" I have been far enough from the mark, sir; I should have remembered in time that I was in the enemy's talons; and what is far worse, under the censure of my own general."

" As to that, Herbert, as to that——"

" Be kind enough to hear me out, sir. I should have remembered that I was penniless; that Lady Anne is very young, careless of herself, and an heiress; but how could I think of any thing," he added, taking her hand, and pressing it to his heart, " when I heard her generous, bewildering confession, that she loved me—but that I loved her with my whole soul!"

" It's—it's—it's hard; but you must come to it, my children. You must just set to work and undo what has been done; you must forget one another."

" Forget, dear Mr. Linwood! Herbert may forget; for I think it seems very easy to him to recede——"

" Anne!"

" Forgive me, Herbert; but really you and your father place me in such an awkward position. Give you up, I will not; forget you, I cannot. I cannot extinguish my memory; and there is no thought in it, waking or sleeping, but what concerns you. I know it is very shocking and improper to say this before you, Mr. Linwood, but it is true."

" I love truth, my child—such truth—God knows I do, too well."

" Then, sir," she continued, smiling archly through her tears, " let me go on and speak a little more of it." Her voice faltered. "I wish Isabella were here—any woman would feel for me."

"God bless me, child, don't I feel for you!—look at Herbert, the calf — don't he feel for you?"

"Herbert says I am so very young. I am sure seventeen and past has years and *wisdom* enough for *not quite* two-and-twenty. He says I am careless for myself; if I were as calculating as my aunt Meredith, what could I do better for myself than to supply the cruel deficiencies of my lot! than to provide for myself the kindest and best of fathers and mothers, and a sister that has not her peer in the wide world! Herbert says I am an heiress—I am so; but what is fortune to me, if I may not select the object with whom to share it? If I am not two-and-twenty——" she cast an arch glance at Herbert, "I have lived long enough to see that fortune alone is perfectly impotent. It does not create friends, nor inspire goodness, nor secure happiness; but when it comes as an accessory to a happy home, to love, and health, and liberal hearts; ah, then it is indeed a boon from Heaven! Am I not right, Mr. Linwood?"

"Yes, by Jupiter, you are! Your views could not be juster if you were as old as Methuselah, and as wise as Solomon. But, my dear, we must come back to the point—what is very right for you, and noble, would be very wrong for us. The Linwoods have always had a fair name, and now, when everything else is gone, they must hold fast to that. Oh, Herbert, if you had only stuck to your king, all would be well; but I won't reproach you now—no, no, poor boy! I never felt so much like forgiving you for that d—d blunder."

"Then, for Heaven's sake, sir, say you forgive me—let that account be settled."

"I will—I do forgive you, my son; but it's the devil and all to forget!" Herbert grasped the hand his father extended to him. There was a silence of a few moments, broken by Mr. Linwood saying, "It's tough to come to it, my children; but this must be the last evening you meet."

"Lady Anne," said Rose, opening the door, "Mrs. Meredith's carriage is waiting for you."

"Let it wait, Rose."

"But the footman bade me to tell you, my lady, that your aunt is ill, and begs you will come home immediately."

"Then I must go," said the poor girl, bursting into tears, all her natural buoyancy and courageous cheerfulness forsaking her at the foreboding that this might be a final separation. Mr. Linwood hemmed, wiped his spectacles, put them on, threw them down on the table, stirred the fire, knocked down shovel, tongs, and fender, and cursed them all; while Lady Anne retired with Herbert to the farthest part of the room, to exchange words that can never be appreciated rightly but by the parties, and therefore must not be repeated. They verily believed that mortals had never been so happy—never so wretched as they.

Once there was a reaction in Lady Anne's mind. She started from Herbert, and, appealing to his father, said—"Think once more of it, Mr. Linwood; why should you heed what my aunt or any one else may impute to you? We have all felt and acted right, naturally, and honestly. I cannot, for my life I cannot, see why we should sacrifice ourselves to their false judgments."

Mr. Linwood shook his head. "It cannot be," said Herbert; "we must cast ourselves upon the future; if," he added, lowering his voice, "it should please Heaven to permit me to regain my freedom, if—but I am wrong—I must not cherish these hopes. Years may pass away before the war ends; and in the mean time, you may bless another with that love which——"

"Never end that sentence, Herbert Linwood. You may take back your own vows—you cannot give me back mine—I will not receive them. My love will not depend on your freedom, your name with friend or foe; it will not be touched by circumstance, or time, or absence. Farewell, Herbert."

One fond embrace she permitted—the first— *was it the last?*

CHAPTER XXXIII.

Thou hast by moonlight at her window sung,
With feigning voice, verses of feigning love;
And stolen the impression of her fantasy,
With bracelets of thy hair—rings, gawds, conceits,
Knacks, trifles, nosegays, sweetmeats, messengers
Of strong prevailment in unhardened youth.

It will be remembered that Isabella, at her aunt's summons, had gone to her house. She met Mrs. Archer at her street-door. Her face spoke of startling intelligence before she uttered it. "My dear Belle," she said, "I have the strangest news for you. I went to your father's while you were out; and just as my foot was on your door-step, a man drove up in a wagon, with a girl as pale as death—such a face! The moment he stopped, she sprang from the wagon. At once I knew her, and exclaimed, "Bessie Lee!"

"Bessie Lee! Gracious Heaven!"

"Yes; she asked eagerly if you were at home. I perceived the inconvenience—the impossibility of your taking care of her in the present state of your family. I felt anxious to do anything and everything for the sister of young Lee; I therefore told her you were not at home, but she could see you at my house; and I persuaded her to come home with me."

"Dear Bessie! can it be possible that she is here!"

"Yes, I have left her in that room. Her attendant told me that she arrived this morning at Kingsbridge, with a decent man and woman, who had passports from La Fayette, and a letter from him to the commander of that post, commending the unfortunate person to his humanity, and entreating him to convey her, under a proper escort, to Mr. Linwood's."

"Poor Bessie! Heaven has miraculously guided her into the best hands. How does she appear!"

"With scarcely enough of mortality to shield her troubled spirit; fluttering and gentle as a stricken dove—pale, unnaturally, deadly pale—a startling brightness in her deep blue eye—her cheeks sunken; but still her features preserved the exquisite symmetry we used to think so beautiful when, a pensive, quiet little girl, she stole after you like a shadow. And her voice, oh, Belle! you cannot hear it without tears. She is mild and submissive, but restless, and excessively impatient to see you and Jasper Meredith. Twice she has come to the door to go out in search of him. I have ordered the blinds to be closed, and the candles lighted, to make it appear darker without than it really is. I could only quiet her by the assurance that I would send for him immediately."

"Have you done so?"

"No; I have waited to consult you."

The house Mrs. Archer occupied was of the common construction of the best houses of that day, being double, the two front apartments separated by a wide hall, a drawing-room in the rear, and a narrow cross-passage opening into a carriage-way to the yard. A few moments before Isabella arrived, a person had knocked at the door, and asked to see Mrs. Archer; and being told that she was particularly engaged, he asked to be shown to a room where he might await her convenience, as he had business of importance with her. He was accordingly shown into an apartment opposite to that occupied at the moment by Mrs. Archer and Bessie.

There he found the blind children, Ned and Lizzy, so absorbed in a game of chess, that, although he went near them, and overlooked them, they seemed just conscious of his presence, but not in the least disturbed by it. They went on playing and managing their game with almost as much facility as if they had their eyesight, till, after a closely-fought battle, Lizzy declared a check-mate. Ned (only not superior to all the chess-players we have ever seen) was nettled by this unexpected defeat, and gave vent to his vexation by saying, "Anyhow, Miss Lizzy, you would not have beaten, if I had not thought it was my knight, instead of yours, on number four."

"Oh, Ned!"

"You would not; you know I always get puzzled about the knights—I always said it was the only fault in the chessmen—I always said I wished Captain Lee had made them more different."

"That fault is easily rectified," said the looker-on.

"Captain Lee!" exclaimed Ned, whose memory was true to a voice once heard, and who never, in any circumstances, could have forgotten the sound of Eliot's voice.

"Hush, my dear little fellow—for Heaven's sake, hush!" cried Eliot, aware of the imprudence he had committed; but it was too late.

Ned's feelings were as susceptible as his hearing. He impetuously sprang forward, and opening the door into the entry, where Mrs. Archer had just uttered the last sentence we reported of her conversation with Isabella, he cried out—"Oh, mama, Captain Lee is here!"

Eliot involuntarily doffed his fox-skin cap, and advanced to them. Both ladies most cordially gave him their hands at the same moment, while their brows were clouded with the thoughts of the sad tidings they had to communicate. Conscious of the precarious position he occupied, he naturally interpreted the concern so evident on their faces, as the expression of a benevolent interest in his safety. "Do not be alarmed, ladies," he said; "I have nothing to fear, if my little friends here

be quiet; and that I am certain they will be, when they know my life depends on my remaining unknown."

"Oh, what have I done!" exclaimed Ned, bursting into tears; but he was soon soothed by Eliot's assurances that no harm as yet was done.

Mrs. Archer withdrew the children, while Miss Linwood communicated to Eliot, as briefly as possible, the arrival and condition of his sister; and he, rather relieved than distressed by the information, told her that his deepest interest in coming to the city was the hope of obtaining some tidings of the poor wanderer. They then consulted how and when they had best present themselves before her; and it was decided that Miss Linwood should first go into the apartment, and prepare her to see Eliot.

Eliot retreated, and stood still and breathless to catch the first sound of Bessie's voice; but he heard nothing but the exclamation, "She is not here!" Eliot sprang forward. The door of the apartment which led into the side passage and the outer door were both open, and Eliot, forgetful of everything but his sister, was rushing into the street, when Bessie entered the street-door with Jasper Meredith! Impelled by her ruling purpose to see Meredith, she had, on her first discovery of the side passage, escaped into the street, where the first person she encountered was he whose image had so long been present to her, that seeing him with her bodily organ seemed to make no new impression, nor even to increase the vividness of the image stamped on her memory. She had thrown on her cloak, but had nothing on her head, and her hair fell in its natural fair curls over her face and neck. Singular as it was for the delicate, timid Bessie to appear in this guise in the public street, or to appear there at all, and much as he was startled by her faded, stricken form, the truth did not at once occur to Meredith. The wildness of her eye was subdued in the dim twilight; she spoke in her accustomed quiet manner; and after answering to his first inquiry that she was perfectly well *now*, she begged him to go into Mrs. Archer's with her, as she had something there to restore to him. He endeavoured to put her off with a common-place evasion—"He was engaged now, would come some other time," &c., but she was not to be eluded; and seeing some acquaintances approaching, whose observation he did not care to encounter, he ascended Mrs. Archer's steps, and found himself in the presence of those whom he would have wished most to avoid; but there was no retreat.

Bessie now acted with an irresistible energy. "This way," said she, leading Meredith into the room she had quitted; "come all of you in here," glancing her eye from Meredith to Isabella and Eliot, but without manifesting the slightest surprise or emotion of any sort at seeing them, but simply saying, with a smile of satisfaction, as she shut the door and threw off her cloak, "I expected this—I *knew* it would be so. In visions by day, and dreams by night, I always saw you together."

It was a minute before Eliot could command his voice for utterance. He folded his arms around Bessie, and murmured, "My sister!—my dear sister!"

She drew back, and placing her hands on his shoulders and smiling, said, " Tears, Eliot, tears ! Oh, shame, when this is the proudest, happiest moment of your sister's life ! "

" Is she mad ! " asked Meredith of Isabella.

Bessie's ear caught his last word. " Mad ! " she repeated. I think all the world is mad ; but I alone am not ! I have heard that whom the gods would destroy they first make mad. Men and angels have been employed to save me from destruction."

" It is idle to stay here to listen to these ravings," said Meredith, in a low voice, to Miss Linwood ; and he was about to make his escape, when Isabella interposed. " Stay for a moment, I entreat you," she said ; " she has been very eager to see you, and it is sometimes of use to gratify these humours."

In the mean time Eliot, his heart burning within him at his sister's being gazed at as a spectacle by that man of all the world from whose eye he would have sheltered her, was persuading her, as he would a wayward child, to leave the apartment. She resisted his importunities with a sort of gentle pity for his blindness, and a perfect assurance that she was guided by light from Heaven. " Dear Eliot," she said, " you know not what you ask of me. For this hour my life has been prolonged, my strength miraculously sustained. You have all been assembled here—you, Eliot, because a brother should sustain his sister, share her honour, and partake her happiness ; Jasper Meredith to receive back those charms and spells by which my too willing spirit was bound ; and you, Isabella Linwood, to see how, in my better mind, I yield him to you."

She took from her bosom a small ivory box, and opening it, she said, advancing to Meredith, and showing him a withered rose-bud, " Do you remember this ? You plucked it from a little bush that almost dipped its leaves in that cold spring on the hill-side. Do you remember ? It was a hot summer's afternoon, and you had been reading poetry to me ; you said there was a delicate praise in the sweet breath of flowers that suited me ; and some silly thing you said, Jasper, that you should not, of wishing yourself a flower that you might breathe the incense that you were not at liberty to speak ; and then you taught me the Persian language of flowers. I kept this little bud : it faded, but was still sweet ! Alas ! alas ! I cherished it for its Persian meaning." Her reminiscence seemed too vivid—her voice faltered, and her eye fell from its fixed gaze on Meredith ; but suddenly her countenance brightened, and she turned to Isabella, who stood by the mantel-piece resting her throbbing head on her hand, and added, " Take it, Isabella, it is a true symbol to you."

Eliot for the first time turned his eye from his sister, and even at that moment of anguish a thrill of joy shot through every vein when he saw Isabella take the bud, pull apart its shrivelled leaves, and throw them from her. Meredith stood leaning against the wall, his arms folded, and his lips curled into a smile that was intended to express scornful unconcern. He might have expressed it, he might possibly have felt it towards Bessie Lee ; but when he saw Isabella throw away the bud, when he met the indignant glance of her eye

flashing through the tears that suffused it, a livid paleness spread around his mouth, and that feature, the most expressive and truest organ of the soul, betrayed its inward conflict. He snatched his hat to leave the room ; Bessie laid her hand on his arm. " Oh, do not go ! I shall be cast back into my former wretchedness if you go now."

" Stay, sir," said Eliot. " My sister shall not be crossed."

" With all my heart. I have not the slightest objection to playing out my dumb show between vapouring and craziness."

" Villain ! " exclaimed Eliot. The young men exchanged glances of fire. Bessie placed herself between them, and stretching out her arms, laid a hand on the breast of each, as if to keep them apart. " Now this is unkind—unkind in both of you. I have come such a long and wearisome journey to make peace for all of us ; and if you will but let me finish my task, I shall lay me down and sleep—for ever, I think."

Eliot pressed her burning hand to his lips. " My poor, dear sister," he said, " I will not speak another word if I die in the effort to keep silence."

" Thanks, dear Eliot," she replied ; and putting both her arms around his neck, she added, in a whisper, " Do not be angry if he again call me crazy ; there be many that have called me so—they mistake inspiration for madness, you know." Never was Eliot's self-command so tested ; and retiring to the farthest part of the room, he stood with knit brows and compressed lips, looking and feeling like a man stretched on the rack, while Bessie pursued her fancied mission. " Do you remember this chain ? " she asked, as she opened a bit of paper, and let fall a gold chain over Meredith's arm. He started as if he were stung. " It cannot harm you," she said, faintly smiling, as she noticed his recoiling. " This was the charm." She smoothed the paper envelope. " As often as I looked at it, the feeling with which I first read it shot through my heart—strange, for there does not seem much in it." She murmured the words pencilled by Meredith on the envelope,

Can she who weaves electric chains to bind the heart,
Refuse the golden links that boast no mystic art ?

" Oh, well do I remember," she cast up her eyes as one does who is retracing the past, " the night you gave me this : Eliot was in Boston ; mother was—I don't remember where, and we had been all the evening sitting on the porch. The honeysuckles and white roses were in bloom, and the moon shone in through their leaves. It was then you first spoke of your mother in England, and you said much of the happy destiny of those who were not shackled by pride and avarice ; and when you went away, you pressed my hand to your heart, and put this little packet in it. Yet," turning to Isabella, " he never said he loved me. It was only my over-credulous fancy. Take it, Isabella ; it belongs to you, who really weave the chain that binds the heart."

Meredith seized the chain as she stretched out her hand, and crushed it under his foot. Bessie looked from him to Isabella, and seemed for a moment puzzled ; then said, acquiescingly, " Ah, it's all well ; symbols do not make nor change realities. This little brooch," she continued, steadily pursuing her purpose, and taking from the box an old-fashioned brooch in the shape of a forget-me-not, " I think was powerless. What need had I of a forget-me-not, when memory devoured every faculty of my being? No, there was no charm in the forget-me-not ; but oh, this little pencil," she took from the box the end of a lead pencil, '' with which we copied and scribbled poetry together. How many thoughts has this little instrument unlocked—what feelings has it touched—what affections have hovered over its point, and gone thrilling back through the heart! You must certainly take this, Isabella, for there is yet a wonderful power in this magical little pencil —it can make such revelations."

" Dear Bessie, I have no revelations to make."

" Is my task finished?" asked Meredith.

" Not yet—not quite yet—be patient—patience is a great help; I have found it so. Do you remember this?" She held up before Meredith a tress of her own fair hair, tied with a raven lock of his in a true-love knot. " Ah, Isabella, I know very well it was not maidenly of me to tie this ; I knew it then, and I begged it of him with many tears, did I not, Jasper? but I *kept* it—that was wrong too. Now, Mr. Meredith, you will help me to untie it?"

" Pardon me ; I have no skill in such matters."

" Ah, is it easier to tie than to untie a true-love knot? Alas, alas! I have found it so. But you must help me. My head is growing dizzy, and I am so faint here!" She laid her hand on her heart. " It must be parted—dear Isabella, you will help me—you can untie a true-love's knot?"

" I can sever it," said Isabella, with an emphasis that went to the heart of more than one that heard her. She took a pair of scissors from the table, and cut the knot. The black lock fell on the floor ; the pretty tress of Bessie's hair curled around her finger :—" I will keep this for ever, my sweet Bessie," she said ; " the memorial of innocence, and purity, and much-abused trust."

" Oh, I did not mean that—I did not mean that, Isabella. Surely I have not accused him ; I told you he never *said* he loved me. I am not angry with him—you must not be. You cannot be long, if you love him ; and surely you do love him."

" Indeed, indeed I do not."

" Isabella Linwood! you *have* loved him." She threw one arm around Isabella's neck, and looked with a piercing gaze on her face. Isabella would at this moment have given worlds to have answered with truth—" No, *never!*" She would have given her life to have repressed the treacherous blood, that, rushing to her neck, cheeks, and temples, answered unequivocally Bessie's ill-timed question.

Meredith's eye was riveted to her face, and the transition from the humiliation, the utter abasement of the moment before, to the undeniable and manifested certainty that he had been loved by the all-exacting, the unattainable Isabella Linwood, was more than he could bear, without expressing his exultation. " I thank you, Bessie Lee," he cried ; " this triumph is worth all I have endured from your raving and silly drivelling. Your silent confession, Miss Linwood, is *satisfactory*, full, and plain enough ; but it has come a thought too late. Good evening to you." " A fair good night to you, sir." " I advise you to

take care that your sister sleep more and *dream* less."

There is undoubtedly a pleasure, transient it may be, but real it is, in the gratification of the baser passions. Meredith was a self-idolater ; and at the very moment when his divinity was prostrate, it had been revived by the sweetest, the most unexpected incense. No wonder he was intoxicated. How long his delirium lasted, and what were its effects, are still to be seen. His parting taunt was lost on those he left behind.

Bessie believed that her mission was fulfilled and ended. The artificial strength which, while she received it as the direct gift of Heaven, her highly-wrought imagination had supplied, was exhausted. As Meredith closed the door, she turned to Eliot, and locking her arms around him, gazed at him with an expression of natural tenderness, that can only be imagined by those who have been so fortunate as to see Fanny Kemble's exquisite personation of Ophelia ; and who remember (who could forget it?) her action at the end of the flower-scene, when reason and nature seeming to overpower her wild fancies, she throws her arms around Laertes' neck, and with one flash of her all-speaking eyes makes every chord of the heart vibrate.

The light soon faded from Bessie's face, and she lay as helpless as an infant in her brother's arms. Isabella hastened to Mrs. Archer ; and Eliot, left alone and quite unmanned, poured out his heart over this victim of vanity and heartlessness.

Mrs. Archer was prompt and efficient in her kindness. Bessie was conveyed to bed, and Eliot assured her that everything should be done for her that human tenderness and vigilance could do. After obtaining a promise from Mrs. Archer that she would write a letter to his mother and forward it with some despatches which he knew were to be sent to Boston on the following day, and after having arranged matters for secret visits to his sister, he left her, fervently thanking God for the kind care that watched over her flickering lamp of life.

Shall we follow Eliot Lee to his hiding-place? shall we betray his secret meditations? shall we show the golden thread that ran through their dark web? shall we confess, that, amid the anxieties (some understood by our readers, and some yet unexplained) that lowered over him, a star seemed to have risen above his horizon? Yes—we dare confess it ; for a little reflection rebuked his presumption, and he exclaimed, " What is it to me if she be free?"

Isabella passed the night in watching with Mrs. Archer over her unconscious little friend ; and as she gazed on her meek brow, on the beautiful features that were stamped with truth and tenderness, her indignation rose against him who, for the poor gratification of his miserable vanity, could meanly steal away the treasure of her affections—that most precious boon, given to feed the lamp of life, and light the way to heaven.

Mrs. Archer, at this crisis, felt much like one who, having seen a rich domain relieved by the sudden interposition of Providence from a pernicious intruder, is impatient to see it in possession of a lawful proprietor. It was womanly and natural, that when she and Isabella were watching at Bessie's bed-side, she should descant on Eliot—should recal his tenderness and gentleness to Bessie, and the true heroism with which, for her sake, he repressed the indignation that was ready to burst on Meredith. Mrs. Archer thought Isabella listened languidly, and assented coldly. She told her so. "Dear aunt Mary," she replied, "my mind is absorbed in a delicious, devout sense of escape. From my childhood I have been in thraldom—groping in mist. Now I stand in a clear light—I see objects in their true colours—I am mistress of myself, and am, as far as relates to myself, perfectly happy. Some other time we will talk over what your friend said, and did, and did not do, and admire it to your heart's content. Now I am entirely selfish ; I have but one idea—but one sensation !" Mrs. Archer was satisfied.

CHAPTER XXXIV.

Chi può dir com' egli arde e in picciol fuoco.

MEREDITH left Mrs. Archer's in a state of feverish excitement. He paced up and down the street, trying by projects for the future to drive away the memory of the past. The thought of his degradation before Isabella Linwood was insupportable ; and the recollection that Eliot Lee had bestowed the stinging epithet of villain on him in her presence, roused his strongest passions and stimulated him to revenge. He turned his steps toward Sir Henry Clinton's. "I shall but do a common duty," he said, "in giving information that a rebel officer, high in Washington's favour, is in disguise in the city—I shall, indeed, be summarily avenged, if Tryon should requite on Lee's head the death of Palmer." The man to whom his thoughts adverted was he in relation to whom Putnam had addressed to Tryon the famous laconic note.

"SIR,—Nathan Palmer, a lieutenant in the service of your king, has been taken in my camp as a spy, condemned as a spy, and will be hung as a spy.

"P.S.—He has been hanged."

The thought of such a catastrophe changed Meredith's purpose. He had no taste for tragedy. He believed that Eliot's visit to the city had relation only to Bessie, and, shrinking from adding such an item to his account with her as the betrayal of her natural protector, he turned back, and retraced his way homeward, meditating a retaliation better suited than revenge, to his shallow character. Passions flow from deep sources. Meredith's relations with Isabella were far more interesting to him than the life or death of Eliot Lee, or his poor sister ; and in trying to devise some balm for his wounded vanity, he hit upon an expedient on which he immediately resolved. This alluring expedient was none else than an immediate engagement with Lady Anne Seton ; which, being antedated but by a few hours, would demonstrate to Isabella Linwood that he, and not she, had first thrown off the shackles ; and would leave for ever rankling in her proud bosom the tormenting recollection, that she had involuntarily confessed she loved him, as he had tauntingly said, "a thought too late."

His decision made, he hastened home, dwelling with the most soothing complacency on his recent meeting with his cousin on the banks of the Hudson, and smiling, as he thought how delighted she would be at his profiting by her hint, in thus soon offering to be joint tenant of her love-built American cottage.

"Where is my cousin ?" he asked, at he entered the drawing-room, and found his mother sitting alone.

"Where she eternally is," replied his mother, throwing down her book and eyeglass, and rising with the air of one who has borne a vexation till it is no longer supportable ; "it is the most inexplicable infatuation ; the girl seems absolutely bewitched by Isabella Linwood."

"But Miss Linwood is not at home this evening. I left her at her aunt Archer's."

"At Mrs. Archer's !—you were with her there, Jasper ?"

Meredith replied, smiling, and without attempting to evade his mother's probing eye, "Yes, I was there, but much against my will, for I had hoped to pass this evening with you and my cousin."

"Thank you, my son, thank you. I flattered myself that all was settled in your mind—definitively settled—when you so gallantly assured Anne that you soon should be 'irretrievably in love,' leaving her to supply the little hiatus which no girl, in like case, would fail to fill with her own name. And now I will be perfectly frank with you, Jasper—indeed, if there is any thing on which I pride myself, it is frankness. You understood the intimation in the Italian stanza, I gave you from the carriage this afternoon ?" Meredith bowed. "It conveyed a little history in a few words, my son ; I have simply aimed to be 'la stella,' by which you, a wise and skilful 'nocchiero,' should, taking advantage of fair winds and favourable tides, guide your vessel into port. But why speak in figures when we perfectly understand one another ! Our dear little Anne—a sweet attractive creature, is she not !—was left to my guardianship, or rather matronship, for your poor uncle was so very thoughtless as to vest me with no authority to control her fortune, or her choice of a husband."

"Bless my soul ; is it possible !"

"Too true, indeed. You now perceive in what embarrassing circumstances I was placed. This pretty girl on my hands, with her immense and unencumbered property ; nothing short of the utmost prudence and energy on my part, could save her from being the prey of fortune-hunters, (alas! for poor human nature !—the lady uttered this without a blush,) rest assured, Jasper, that nothing would have induced me in these perilous times to cross the Atlantic, but my duty to my orphan niece."

"And the remote prospect of benefiting me, my dear mother."

Mrs. Meredith was too intent on the interesting subject upon which she was entering, to notice the sarcasm her son had not the grace to suppress. "I had my anxieties," she continued, "I frankly confess to you, I had my anxieties before I arrived, about Miss Linwood, and—some few I have had since——"

Mrs. Meredith paused and fixed her eyes on

Jasper. "On my honour, you have not the slightest ground for them," he said.

She proceeded. "Miss Linwood is in some respects a superior young person—she has not the—the—the talent of Helen Ruthven—nor the —the—the grace of Lady Anne (no wonder the perplexed diplomatist hesitated for a comparative that should place Isabella Linwood below these young ladies) ; but as I said, she is a superior young person—a remarkable-looking person, certainly ; at least, she is generally thought so. I do not particularly like her style—tenderness and manageableness, like our dear Anne's, are particularly becoming in a female. Miss Linwood is too lofty—one does not feel quite comfortable with her. On the whole, I consider it quite fortunate you did not form an attachment in that quarter— prudence must be consulted—not that I would be swayed by prudential considerations—certainly not—no one thinks more than I do of the heart ; but when, as in your case, Jasper, the taste and affections accord with a wise consideration of— of——"

"*Fortune*, my dear mother ?"

"Yes, Jasper, frankly, fortune—I esteem it a remarkably happy circumstance. Your own fortune may or may not be large. The American portion of it depends upon contingencies, and, therefore, it would have been rash for you to have encumbered yourself with a ruined family ; for, as I am informed, the Linwoods have but just enough to subsist decently upon from day to day. It is true they keep up a respectable appearance. Anne, by-the-way, tells me they get up the most delicate *petits soupers* there. It is amazing what pride will do !—what sacrifices some people make to appearances !"

"There must be something besides mere table luxuries to make these suppers so attractive to my cousin."

"Undoubtedly ; for as to that, you know, we have everything that money can purchase in this demi-savage country ; to be sure, Anne might have a foolish, girlish liking for Miss Linwood, but then, I am quite confident—I hesitate, for if there is *any* thing on which I pride myself, it is being scrupulous towards my own sex in affairs of the heart ; but I betray nothing ; for though you are perfectly free from coxcombry, you are not blind, and you must have seen——"

"Not seen, but *hoped*, my dear mother," replied Meredith, with a smile that indicated assurance doubly sure.

"Hope is the fitting word for *you*—but your hope may be *my* certainty—I betray no secrets. Anne has not been confidential, but the dear child is so transparent——"

"She seems, however, to have been rather opaque in this Linwood attachment."

"Yes, I confess myself baffled there—you may have opened a vein of coquetry, Jasper. I know not what it means, but it can mean nothing to alarm us. It is very odd, though—there is nothing there to gratify her, and everything here. This very evening Governor Tryon called, with the young Prince, to propose to get up a concert for her. By-the-way, a pretty youth is Prince William !—he left this bouquet for Lady Anne. The Honourable Mr. Barton and Sir Reginald were here too, and the Digbys—and there she is

mewed up with that old fretful Mr. Linwood. She must think, Jasper, you are not sufficiently devoted to her."

"She shall not think so in future."

"Hark, there is the carriage !—I sent her word that I was not well. In truth, her absence has teased me into a headache, and my own room will be the best place for me." Thus concluding her tedious harangue, the lady made a hasty retreat ; and before Lady Anne had exchanged a salutation with Meredith, and thrown aside her hat and cloak, her aunt's maid appeared with a message from this "frank" lady, importing the sense of Lady Anne's kindness in coming home, and informing her that prudence obliged her to abstain from seeing her niece till morning.

"I am very sorry !" said Lady Anne, heaving a deep sigh, sinking down in the arm-chair her aunt had just left, resting her elbow on it, and looking pensively in the fire.

"You need not be so deeply concerned, my kind cousin ; my mother is not *very* ill," said Meredith, with difficulty forbearing a laugh at the disparity between the cause and the effect on his apparently sympathising cousin.

"Ill !" exclaimed Lady Anne, starting ; "I did not suppose that she was ill."

"Then, why, in the name of Heaven, that deep sigh ?"

"There are many causes of sighs, cousin Jasper."

"To you, Lady Anne, so young, so gifted, so lovely, so *beloved*."

"That should be happiness !" she replied, covering her face with hands to hide the tears, that, in spite of all the anti-crying tendencies of her nature, gushed from her eyes.

"Those dimpled hands," thought Meredith, "hiding so childishly her melting face, might move an anchoret ; but they move not me. I am too pampered—to know that I have been loved by Isabella Linwood, with all the bitter, cursed mortification that attends it, is worth a world of such triumphs as this. Poor Bessie ! I remember too—but, *allons*, I will take the good ' the gods provide,' since I cannot have that which they deny. Cousin——"

"Did you speak to me, Jasper ?"

"Now, by my life," thought Meredith, "my words are congealed—they will not flow to such willing ears."

"I am playing the fool," exclaimed Lady Anne, suddenly rising and dashing off her tears. "Good night, Jasper—I have betrayed myself—no, no, I did not mean that—pray forget my weakness—I am nervous this evening for the first time in my life, and I know nothing of managing nerves— Good night, Jasper !"

Meredith seized her hand and held her back. "Indeed, my sweet coz, you must not go now."

"Must not go ! Why not ?" she replied, excessively puzzled by the expressive smile that hovered on his lips.

"Why not ? Because you are too much of an angel to shut your heart so suddenly against me, after allowing me a glimpse at the paradise within."

"What do you mean ?" she asked, now beginning, from Meredith's manner, and from the well-tutored expression of his most sentimental eyes, to have some dim perception of his meaning, and to be disconcerted by it.

"Dear Anne, did you not, with your own peculiar, enchanting ingenuousness, say you had betrayed yourself! Never was there a sweeter—a more welcome treachery." He fell on his knee, and pressed her hand to his lips.

"For the love of Heaven, Jasper," she cried, snatching her hand away, "tell me what I have said or done."

"Nothing that you should not, dearest cousin; your betrayal, as you called it, was, I know, involuntary, and for that the dearer."

"Are you in earnest, Jasper!"

"In earnest! most assuredly; and do you, Lady Anne, like all your sex, delight in torturing your captives!—your captive I certainly am, for life."

The truth was now but too evident to Lady Anne; but she was so unprepared for it, her mind had been so wholly pre-occupied, that it seemed to her the marvellous result of some absurd misunderstanding. At first she blushed, and stammered, and then, following her natural bent, laughed merrily.

To Meredith, this appeared a childish artifice to shelter her mortification at having made, in military phrase, a first demonstration. His interest was stimulated by this slight obstacle; and rallying all his powers, he began a passionate declaration in the good set terms "in such cases made and provided;" but Lady Anne cut him off before he had finished his peroration. "This is a most absurd business, Jasper; I entreat you never to speak of it again. Aunt, or somebody, or something, has misled you—misled, you certainly are. I never in my life thought of you in any other light, than as a very agreeable cousin, nor ever shall. I am very sorry for you, Jasper; but really, I am not in fault, for I never, by word or look, could have expressed what I never felt. Good night, Jasper." She was running away, when she turned back to add, "Pray, say nothing of this to my aunt, and let us meet to-morrow as we have always met before." She then disappeared, and left Meredith baffled, mortified, irritated, and most thoroughly awakened from his dreams. Her face, voice, and manner, were truth itself; and rapidly reviewing their past intercourse, and carefully weighing the words that had misled him, he came to the conclusion that he had been partly misguided by his mother, and partly the dupe of his previous impressions. The measure of his humiliations was filled up.

But his vanity survived the severe and repeated blows of that evening. Vanity has a wonderful tenacity of life: it resembles those reptiles that feed greedily on every species of food, the most delicate and the grossest, and that can subsist on their own independent vitality.

CHAPTER XXXV.

Heart! what's that?
Oh, a thing servant-maids have, and break for John the footman.

If Meredith could have borne off his charming heiress-cousin, his love for Isabella might have gone to the moon, or to any other repository of lost and forgotten things. But, balked in that pursuit, it resumed its empire over him. He passed a feverish, sleepless night, revolving the past, and reconsidering Isabella's every word and look during their interview of the preceding evening; and finally, he came to a conclusion not unnatural (for few persons give others credit for less of a given infirmity than they themselves possess), that Isabella's vanity had been wounded by the conviction that she had been, for a time, superseded by Bessie Lee; and that the ground he had thus lost might, by a dexterous manœuvre, be regained. Engrossed with his next move, he appeared at breakfast-table as usual, attentive to his mother, and polite to Lady Anne, who, anxious to express her good-will, was more than ordinarily kind; and Mrs. Meredith concluded that if matters had not gone as far as she had hoped, they were going on swimmingly. The breakfast finished, Lady Anne ran away from her aunt's annoying devotions to the Linwoods, and Meredith retired to his own room to write, after weighing and sifting each word, the following note to Isabella. He did not send it, however, till he had taken the precaution to precede it by a written request to Lady Anne (with whom he had found out too late that honest dealing was far the safest) that she would, on no account—he asked it for *her own sake*—communicate to *any one* their parting scene of the preceding evening. His evil star ruled the ascendant, and Lady Anne received the note too late.

To Miss Linwood.

"Montaigne says, and says truly, that '*toutes les passions qui se laissent gouster et digérer ne sont que médiocres*;' but how would he—how shall I characterise a passion which has swallowed up every other passion, desire, and affection of my nature—has grown and thriven upon that which would have seemed fatal to its existence!

"Isabella, these are not hollow phrases; you know they are not; and be not angry at my boldness; I know your heart responds to them, and, though I was stretched on the rack to obtain this knowledge, I thank my tormentors. Yes, by Heaven! I would not exchange that one instant of intoxicating, bewildering joy, when, even in the presence of witnesses, and such witnesses! you confessed you *had* loved me, for ages of a common existence. Thank Heaven, too, the precious confession was not through the hackneyed medium of words. Such a sentiment is not born in your bosom to die. I judge from my own inferior nature. I have loved on steadily, through absence, coldness, disdain, caprice (pardon me, my proud, my adored Isabella), in spite of the canker and rust of delay after delay; in spite of all the assaults of those temptations to which the young and fortunate are exposed. Can I estimate your heart at a lower rate than my own!

"As to that silly scene last evening, though it stung me at the moment, and goaded me to an unmeaning impertinence, yet, on a review of it, do you not perceive that we were both the dupes of a little dramatic effect! and that there is no reality in the matter, except so far as concerns the lost wits of the crazed girl, and the very natural affliction of her well-meaning brother, whose unjust and hasty indignation towards me, being the result of false impressions, I most heartily forgive.

"As to poor Bessie Lee, I can only say, God help her! I am most sincerely sorry for her; but neither you nor I can be surprised that she should be the dupe of her lively imagination, and the victim of her nervous temperament. I ask but one word in reply. Say you will see me at any hour you choose; and, for God's sake, Isabella, secure our interview from interruption."

In half an hour, and just as Meredith was sallying forth to allay his restlessness by a walk in the open air, he met his messenger with a note from Miss Linwood. He turned back, entered the unoccupied drawing-room, and read the following.

———

"I have received your note, Jasper; I do not reply to it hastily; hours of watchfulness and reflection at the bed-side of my friend have given the maturity of years to my present feeling. *I have loved you*, I confess it now; not by a treacherous blush, but calmly, deliberately, in my own hand-writing, without faltering or emotion of any sort. Yes, I have loved you, if a sentiment springing from a most attachable nature, originating in the accidental intercourse of childhood, fostered by pride, nurtured by flattery, and exaggerated by an excited imagination, can be called love.

"I have loved you, if a sentiment struggling with doubt and distrust, seeking for rest and finding none, becoming fainter and fainter in the dawning light of truth, and vanishing, like an exhalation in the full day, can be called love.

"You say truly. Bessie Lee *is* the dupe of a too lively imagination, and the victim of a nervous temperament. To these you might have added, an exquisitely organised frame, and a conscience too susceptible for a creature liable to the mistakes of humanity. Oh, how despicable, how cruel, was the vanity that could risk the happiness of such a creature for its own gratification! I have wept bitterly over her; I should scarcely have pitied her, had she been the unresisting slave and victim of a misplaced and unrequited passion.

"After what I have written, you will perceive that you need neither seek nor avoid an interview with me; that the only emotion you can now excite, is a devout gratitude that our former interviews *were interrupted*, and circumstances were made strong enough to prevail over my weakness. "ISABELLA LINWOOD.

"P.S.—I have detained my messenger, and opened my note to add, that your cousin has just come in, and, with a confidence befitting her frank nature, has communicated to me the farce with which you followed up the tragedy of last evening."

———

Meredith felt, what was in truth quite evident, that Isabella Linwood was herself again. He threw the note from him in a paroxysm of vexation, disappointment, and utter and hopeless mortification; and covering his face with his hands, he endured one of those moments that occur even in this life, when the sins, follies, and failures of by-gone years are felt with the vividness and acuteness of the actual and present, and memory and conscience are endued with supernatural energy and retributive power.

What a capacity of penal suffering has the All-wise infused into the moral nature of man, even the weakest!

> The mind is its own place, and in itself,
> Can make a heaven of hell, a hell of heaven.

Meredith was roused by the soft fall of a footstep. He started, and saw Helen Ruthven, who had just entered, and was in the act of picking up the note he had thrown down. She looked at the superscription, then at Meredith. Her lustrous eyes suffused with tears, and the tears formed into actual drops, and rolled down her cheeks. "Oh, happy, most happy Isabella Linwood!" she exclaimed. Meredith took the note from her and threw it into the fire. Miss Ruthven stared at him, and lifted up her hands with an unfeigned emotion of astonishment. After a moment's pause, she added, "I still say *most* happy Isabella Linwood. And yet, if she cannot estimate the worth of the priceless kingdom she sways, is she most happy? You do not answer me; and you, of all the world, cannot." Meredith did not reply by word; but Miss Ruthven's quick eye perceived the cloud clearing from his brow, and she ventured to try the effect of a stronger light. "I cannot comprehend this girl," she continued; "she is a riddle—an insolvable riddle to me. A passionless mortal seems to me to approach nearer to a monster than to a divinity deserving your idolatry, Meredith. She cannot be the cold, apathetic, statue-like person she appears——"

"And why not, Miss Ruthven?"

"Simply because a passionless being cannot inspire passion—and yet—and yet, if she were a marble statue, your love should have been the Promethean touch to infuse a soul. Pardon me —*pity* me, if I speak too plainly; there are moments when the heart will burst the barriers of prudence—there are moments of desperation, of self-abandonment. I cannot be bound by those petty axioms and frigid rules that shackle my sex —I cannot weigh my words—I must pour out my heart, even though this prodigality of its treasures 'naught enriches you, and makes me poor indeed!'"

Helen Ruthven's broken sentences were linked together by expressive glances, and effective pauses. She gave to her words all the force of intonation and emphasis, which produce the effect of polish on metal, making it dazzling, without adding an iota to its intrinsic value. Meredith lent a most attentive ear, mentally comparing the while Miss Ruthven's lavished sensibilities to Isabella's jealous reserve. He should have discriminated between the generosity that gives what is nothing worth, and the fidelity that watches over an immortal treasure; but vanity wraps itself in impenetrable darkness. He only felt that he was in a labyrinth of which Helen Ruthven held the clew; and that he was in the process of preparation to follow whithersoever she willed to lead him.

We let the curtain fall here; we have no taste for showing off the infirm of our own sex. We were willing to supply some intimations that might be available to our ingenuous and all-believing young male friends; but we would not reveal to our fair and true-hearted readers the flatteries, pretences, false assumptions, and elaborate blandishments, by which a hackneyed woman of the world dupes and beguiles ; and at last (obeying the inflexible law of reaping as she sows) pays the penalty of her folly in a life of matrimonial union without affection—a wretched destiny, well fitting those who profane the sanctuary of the affections with hypocritical worship.

While the web is spinning around Meredith, we leave him with the wish that all the Helen Ruthvens in the world may have as fair game as Jasper Meredith.

CHAPTER XXXVI.

Adventurous I have been, it is true,
And this fool-hardy heart would brave—nay, court,
In other days, an enterprise of passion ;
Yea, like a witch, would whistle for a whirlwind.
But I have been admonished.

OUR humble story treats of the concerns of individuals, and not of historical events. We shall not, therefore, embarrass our readers with the particulars of the secret mission on which Eliot Lee had been sent to the city by the commander-in-chief. He needed an agent, who might, as the exigency should demand, be prudent or bold, wary or decided, cautious or gallant, and self-sacrificing. He had tested Eliot Lee, and knew him to be capable of all these rarely-united virtues. Eliot had confided to Washington his anxieties respecting his unfortunate sister, and his burning desire to go to the city, where he might possibly ascertain her fate. Washington gave him permission to avail himself of every facility for the performance of his fraternal duty, consistent with the public service on which he sent him. His sympathies were alive to the charities of domestic life. While the military chieftain planted and guarded the tree that was to overshadow his country, he cherished the birds that made their nests in its branches.

Eliot was instructed to seek a hiding-place in the city at a certain Elizabeth Bengin's, a woman of strong head and strong heart, whose name is preserved in history as one who, often at great personal risk, rendered substantial service in the country's cause. Dame Bengin and her parrot Sylvy, who seemed to preside over the destinies of the shop, and did in fact lure many a young urchin into it, were known to all the city. The dame herself was a thickset, rosy little body, fair, fat, and forty ; her shop was a sort of thread and needle store : but as the principle of division of labour had yet made small progress in our young country, Mistress Bengin's wares were as multifarious as the wants of the citizens. Mrs. Bengin's first principle was to keep a civil tongue in her own and in Sylvy's head, she holding civility (as she often said and repeated) to be the most disposable and most profitable article in her shop. It was indeed seriously profitable to her, for it surrounded her with an atmosphere of kindness, and enabled her, though watched and suspected by the English, to follow her calling for a long while unmolested.

She gave Eliot an apartment in a loft over her shop, to which, there being no apparent access, Eliot obtained egress and ingress by removing a loose board that, to the uninstructed eye, formed a part of the ceiling of the shop.

From this hiding-place Eliot sallied forth to execute his secret purposes, varying his disguises, which were supplied by Mrs. Bengin, as caution dictated. As all sorts of persons frequented the shop, no attention was excited by all sorts of persons coming out of it. Eliot's forced masquerading often compelled him to personate various characters during the day, and at evening, with simply a cloak over his own uniform, and a wallet over his arm, like those still used by country doctors, and precisely, as Dame Bengin assured him, like that carried by the " doctor that attended the quality," he made his way, sheltered by the obscurity of the night, to Mrs. Archer's, where he was admitted by one of the children, whose acute senses caught the first sound of his approaching footsteps. Eliot, in spite of remonstrances from his prime minister, Mrs. Bengin, had persisted in appearing in his own dress at Mrs. Archer's. In vain the good dame speculated and soliloquised ; she could not solve the mystery of this only disobedience to her counsel. " To be sure," she said, " it makes a sight of difference in his looks, whether he wears my tatterdemalion disguises, wigs, scratches, and what not, or his own nice uniform, with his own rich brown hair, waving off his sunshiny forehead —a bright, pleasant, tight-built looking youth he is, as ever I put my two eyes upon; and if he were going to see young ladies, I should not wonder that he did not want to put his light under a bushel; but, my conscience ! to keep up such a brushing and scrubbing—my loft is not so *very* linty either —just to go before the widow Archer—to be sure, she is a widow ; but then, there never was a man yet that dared to have any courting thoughts of her, any more than if she were buried in her husband's grave; and this is not the youth to be presuming."

Dame Bengin knew enough of human nature to have solved the mystery of Eliot's toilet, if she had been apprised of one material fact in the case. At Mrs. Archer's, watching at Bessie's bedside, Eliot always found Miss Linwood ; and though the truest, the most anxious, and tender of brothers, he was not unconscious of her presence, nor unconscious that her presence mingled with his sufferings for his sister a most dangerous felicity. His fate was inevitable ; he at least thought it so ; and that fate was an intense and unrequited devotion to one as unattainable to him as if she were the inhabitant of another planet. He did not resist his destiny by abating one minute of those hours that were worth years of a drawing-room intercourse. In ordinary circumstances, Isabella's soul would have been veiled from so new an acquaintance ; but now constantly under the influence of strong feeling and fresh impulses, and a most joyous sense of freedom, her lofty, generous, and tender spirit glowed in her beautiful face, and inspired and graced every word and movement.

Her devotion to Bessie was intense ; not simply from compassion nor affection, but remembering, that in her self-will she had insisted, in spite of her father's disinclination, and her aunt's most reasonable remonstrances, on Bessie's visit to the city, she looked upon herself as the primary cause of her friend's misfortunes, and felt her own peace of mind to be staked on Bessie's recovery. What a change had the discipline of life wrought in Isabella's character! the qualities were still the same; the same energy of purpose, the same earnestness in action, the same strength of feeling, but now all flowing in the right channel, all having a moral aim, and all governed by that religious sense of *duty*, which is to the spirit in this perilous voyage of life what the compass is to the mariner.

Of Bessie's recovery there seemed, from day to day, little prospect. One hopeful circumstance there was. The intelligent physician consulted by Mrs. Archer had frankly confessed that his art could do nothing for her, and had advised leaving her entirely to the energies of nature. Would that this virtue of *letting alone* were oftener imitated by the faculty! that nature were oftener permitted to manifest her power unclogged, and unembarrassed by the poisons of the drug-shop!

Bessie was as weak and helpless as a new-born infant, and apparently as unknowing of the world about her. With few and brief exceptions, she slept day and night. Her face was calm, peaceful, and not inexpressive; but it was as unvarying as a picture. Her senses appeared no longer to be the ministers of the mind; she heard without hearing, and saw without seeing, and never attempted to speak. At times, her friends despaired utterly, believing that her mind was extinct; and then again they hoped it was a mere suspension of her faculties, a rest preluding restoration.

While fear and hope were thus alternating, a week passed away. Eliot's mission was near being accomplished. The evening of the following day was appointed for the consummation of his plans. The boats, with muffled oars and trusty oarsmen, were in readiness, and the plan, for the secret seizure of a most important personage, so well matured, that it was all but impossible it should be baffled. The most brilliant result seemed certain: and well balanced as Eliot's mind was, it was excited to the highest pitch when a communication reached him from head-quarters, informing him that Washington deemed it expedient to abandon the enterprise of which he was the agent; and he was directed, if possible, to cross the Hudson during the night, and repair to the camp near Morristown. And thus ended the hope of brilliant achievement and sudden advancement; and he went to pay his last visit to his sister—for the last time to see Isabella Linwood!

She met him with good news lighting her eyes. "Bessie is reviving!" she said; "she has pressed my hand, and spoken my name!"

"Thank God!" replied Eliot, approaching the bed-side. For the first time Bessie fixed her eye on him, as if conscious at whom she was looking; then, as he bent over her, she stretched out her arms, drew his face to hers, and kissed him, feebly murmuring, "Dear Eliot!"

The effort exhausted her, and she reverted to her usual condition. "This must be expected," said Miss Linwood, replying to the shade of disappointment that passed over Eliot's brow; "but having seen such a sign of recovery, you will leave her with a light heart?"

Eliot smiled assentingly; a melancholy smile enough. "You still," she continued, "expect to get off to-morrow evening?"

"No; my business in the city is finished, and I go this very night."

"To night! would to Heaven that Herbert were going with you!"

"Not one regret for my going!" thought Eliot, and he sighed involuntarily. "You seem," resumed Isabella, "very suddenly indifferent to Herbert's fate—you do not care to know, before you go, how our plans are ripening?"

"Indifferent to Herbert's fate!—to aught that concerns you, Miss Linwood!"

"A common-place compliment from you, Captain Lee—well, as it is the first, I'll forgive you—not so would Herbert, for making him secondary in a matter where he is entitled to the honour, as he has the misery of being principal. Poor fellow! his adversities have not taught him patience; and Rose tells me he is very near the illness he has feigned, and that if he does not get off by to-morrow night, he will fret himself into a fever."

"Have you made Lady Anne acquainted with your project?"

"Yes, indeed! and her quick wit, loving heart, and most ingenious fingers, have been busy in contriving and executing our preparations. She is wild enough to wish to be the companion of Herbert's flight. This is not to be thought of; but I have promised her that she shall see him once more. Lizzy Bengin will go with us to the boat, where, if Heaven prosper us, he will be by eight to-morrow evening. And then, Captain Lee, should you persuade General Washington to receive and forgive him, we shall be perfectly happy again."

"Perfectly happy!" echoed Eliot, in a voice most discordant with the words he uttered.

"Oh, pardon me! I did not mean that. It is cruel to talk to you of happiness while Bessie is in this uncertain condition—and most unjust it is to myself, for I never shall be happy unless she is restored, and mistress of herself again."

"Ah, Miss Linwood, that cannot be. In her best days she had not the physical and mental power required to make her 'mistress of herself;' no, it can never be. If it were not for my mother, who I know would wish Bessie restored to her, even though she continue the vacant casket she now is, I should, with most intense desire, pray God to take her to himself; there alone can a creature so sensitive and fragile be safe and at peace!"

"You are wrong—I am certain you are wrong. There is a flexibility in our womanly nature that is strength in our weakness. Bessie will perceive the delusion under which she has acted and suffered, and which had dominion over her, because, like any other dream, it seemed a reality while it lasted. Yes, her affections will return to their natural channels to bless us all." Eliot shook his head despondingly. "You are faithless and unbelieving," continued Isabella; and then added, smiling and blushing, "but *I* reason from experience, and therefore you should believe me."

This was the first time that Meredith had been alluded to. The allusion was intrepid and generous; and if a confession of past weakness, it was an assurance of present, conscious, and all-sufficient strength. That Eliot at least thought so, was evident from the sudden irradiation of his countenance; a brightness misinterpreted by Isabella, who immediately added, "I have convinced you, and you will admit I was not very rash in saying that we should all again be perfectly happy."

Eliot made no reply ; he walked to the extremity of the room, paused, returned, gazed intently yet abstractedly at his sister, then at Isabella, and then mechanically took up his hat, laid it down, and again resumed it.

Isabella was perplexed by his contradictory movements. "You are not going so soon !" she said. He did not reply. "Shall I call my aunt !" she added, rising.

Eliot seized her hand, and withheld her. "No, no, not yet—Miss Linwood, I am playing the hypocrite. It is not alone my anxiety for my sister that torments me—that made your prediction of happiness sound to me like a knell." He paused, and then yielding to an irresistible impulse, he impetuously threw himself at Isabella's feet. "Isabella Linwood, I love you—love you without the presumption of the faintest, slightest hope—before we part for ever, suffer me to tell you so."

"Captain Lee, you astonish me !—you do not mean——"

"I know I astonish you, but I will not offend you. Is it folly—rashness—obtrusiveness to pour out an affection before you, that expects nothing in return—asks nothing but the satisfaction of being known, and not offensive to you !"

"Oh, no, no ; but you may regret——"

"Never, never. From this moment I devote my heart—I dedicate my existence to you ; insomuch as God permits me to love aught beneath himself, I will love you. I must now part from you for ever ; but wherever I go, your image will attend me—that cannot be denied me ; it shall defend me from temptation, incite me to high resolves, pure thoughts, and good deeds."

"Such homage might well make me proud," replied Isabella, "and I am most grateful for it ; but your imagination is overwrought ; this is a transient excitement—it will pass away."

"Never !" replied Eliot, rising, and recovering in some degree the steadiness of his voice ; "hear me patiently ; it is the only time I shall ever ask your indulgence. I am not now, nor was I ever, under the dominion of my imagination or my passions. I have been trained in the school of exertion, of self-denial, and self-subjection ; and I would not, I could not love one who did not sway my reason, who was not entitled to the homage of my best faculties. I have been moved by beauty—I have been attracted by the lovely—I have had my fancies and my likings—what man of two-and-twenty has not !—I never *loved* before ; never before felt a sentiment that, if it were requited, would have made earth a paradise to me ; but that unrequited, unsustained but by its own independent vitality, I would not part with for any paradise on this earth."

The flush of surprise that first overspread Isabella's face had deepened to a crimson glow. If a woman is not offended by such language as Eliot's, she cannot be unmoved. Isabella's was a listening eye. It seemed to Eliot, at this moment, that its rays touched his heart, and burned there. She passed her hand over her brow, as one naturally does when the brain is becoming a little blurred in its perceptions. "This is so very strange, so unexpected," she said, in the softest tone of that voice, whose every tone was music to her lover's ear—" in one short week—it cannot be !"

Isabella but half uttered her thoughts : she had been misled, as most inexperienced observers are in similar cases, by the tranquillity of Eliot's manner ; she respected and liked him exceedingly ; but she thought him unexcitable, and incapable of passion. She had yet to learn that the strongest passions are reducible to the gentlest obedience, and may be so subjected as to manifest their power, not in irregular and rebellious movements, but only in the tasks they achieve. She did not now reflect or analyse, but she felt, for the first time, there was that in Eliot Lee that could answer to the capacities of her own soul.

"This is, undoubtedly, unexpected to you," resumed Eliot, "but should not be strange. When I first saw you, I was struck with your beauty ; and I thought, if I were a pagan, I should embody my divinity in just such a form, and fall down and worship it ;—that might have been what the world calls *falling in love*, but it was far enough from the all-controlling sentiment I now profess to you. Our acquaintance has been short (*I* date farther back than a *week*) ; but in this short period I have seen your mind casting off the shackles of early prejudices, resisting the authority of opinion, self-rectified, and forming its independent judgments on those great interests in which the honour and prosperity of your country are involved. I have gloried in seeing you willing to sacrifice the pride, the exclusiveness, and all the little idol vanities of accidental distinctions, to the popular and generous side.

"Nay, hear me out, Isabella : I will not leave you till you have the reasons of my love ; till you admit that I have deliberately elected the sovereign of my affections ; till you feel—yes, *feel*, that my devotion to you can never abate." He hesitated, and his voice faltered ; but he resolutely proceeded : "other shackles has your power over woman's weakness enabled you to cast off."

"Oh, no—no ; do not commend me for that—they fell off."

"Be it so : they could not fetter you : that is enough."

"Then," said Isabella, somewhat mischievously, "I think you like me for, what most men like not at all—my love of freedom and independence of control."

"Yes, I do ; for I think they are essential to the highest and most progressive nature ; but I should not love it if it were not blended with all the tenderness and softness of your sex. The fire, that mounts to Heaven from the altar, diffuses its gentle warmth at the fireside. Think you, that, while you have been tending my sister, I have been unmindful of your kindly domestic qualities, or blind to the thousand womanly inventions by which I see you ministering to the happiness of these unfortunate children ! Have you thought me insensible to your intervention for my poor boy, Kisel, though God, in much mercy to him, willed it should be bootless ! I do homage to your genius, talent, and accomplishment, but I love your gracious, domestic, home-felt virtues : I am exhausting your patience."

Isabella had covered her face ; overpowered with

the accumulated proof that Eliot had watched her with a fond lover's eye. After a slight hesitation, he proceeded to obey a most natural, if it be a weak, longing. "Allow me, if you can, one solace —one blessed thought to cheer a long life or loneliness and devotion. I am bold in asking it ; but, tell me, had I known you earlier, had no predilection forestalled me, had no rival intervened, do you think it possible that you should have returned my love ?"

Some one says that all women are reared hypocrites—trained to veil their natures ; Isabella Linwood, at least, was not. She replied, impulsively and frankly, "Most certainly I should."

Eliot again fell at her feet. He ventured to take her hand, to press it to his lips, to wet it with his tears. "I am satisfied," he said ; "now I can go ; and the thought that I might, under a happier star, have been loved by Isabella Linwood, shall elevate, guide, and soothe me, in all the chances and changes of life."

While Eliot was uttering these last words, and while Isabella was absorbed in the emotions they excited, the door was softly opened, and Lizzy Archer, flitting across the room, said in a low voice, "Oh, Captain Lee ! what shall we do ?—there are horrid soldiers watching at both our doors for you — mama is out, and I could not sleep—I never sleep when you are here, for fear something will happen—I heard their voices at the side door ; and when I came through the hall, I heard others through the street door—what shall we do ?—Cousin Belle, pray think—you can always think in a minute."

But "Cousin Belle's" presence of mind had suddenly forsaken her ; and as Eliot's eye glanced towards her, he saw she was pale and trembling. A hope shot into his mind, a thought of the possibility that if he were not now severed from her, that which she had generously admitted might have been, might still be. To exclude this new-born hope seemed to him like the extinction of life. He rapidly revolved the circumstances in which he was placed. He had done, in the affair intrusted to him, all, and even more than his commander expected ; it had failed of consummation through no fault of his ; he was in the American uniform, and thus captured, he might claim the rights of a prisoner of war ; the temporary loss of his presence in camp would be unimportant to the cause ; and remaining for a time within reach of Isabella Linwood might result in good, infinite good, and happiness to himself. He wavered ; but the fixed habit of rectitude prevailed, the duty of the soldier over the almost irresistible inclinations of the man : he shut out the temptation, and only considered the means of escape. "Dear Lizzy," he said, "if I could find my way to your skylight—I have observed the descent would not be dangerous from there to the back building, and so down on the roofs of the other offices."

"But," said Lizzy, for the little creature seemed to have considered the whole ground, "if there should be soldiers too at the back gate ?"

"I will avoid them, Lizzy, by going into the next yard to yours, then over two or three walls, till I find it safe to emerge into the street."

"I can lead you to the skylight. I am very glad I am blind, so I shall not need any light ; for that would show you to the soldiers, who are standing by the side windows of the hall-door. Oh, dear, I hope they won't hear my heart beat ; but it does beat so !"

There were other hearts there that beat almost audibly besides poor Lizzy's ; but there was no time to indulge emotions. Eliot kissed his unconscious sister ; and then grasping the hand Isabella extended to him, he would have said, "Farewell for ever !" but his voice was choked, and the last ominous word was unpronounced. His little guide led him noiselessly up the stairs, through the entries, and to the skylight ; and then fondly embracing him and promising to give his farewells to "mother and Ned," she parted from him, and stood fixed and breathless, listening till she believed he had eluded those who were lying in wait for him, when she returned to give full vent to her feelings on Isabella's bosom, and to find more sympathy there than she wotted of.

We shall not follow our hero through his "imminent dangers and hair-breadth 'scapes." Suffice it to say, he did escape ; and having passed the Hudson in the same little boat that brought "Harmann Van Zandt" to the city, he eluded the British station at Powles Hook, passed their redoubts, and at dawn of day received at the camp at Morristown the warm thanks of Washington, who estimated conduct by its intrinsic merit, and not, according to the common and false standard, by its results.

CHAPTER XXXVII.

Good sir, good sir, you are deceived ; it is no man at all !

At any other juncture, Mr. Linwood would have been restless and unappeasable under the privation of Isabella's society ; but now, in his interest and sympathy in Herbert's affairs, and in his fondness for Lady Anne, he found full employment for his thoughts and feelings. Lady Anne persisted in considering herself Herbert's betrothed ; and in spite of her aunt, who, as her niece affirmed, had become insupportably cross and teasing, she persevered in spending all her evenings with the Linwoods. The charm that love imparts to those who are connected with the object of a concentrated affection, was attached to Herbert's father and mother. Lady Anne felt the most tender anxieties for her lover ; but, sustained by the buoyancy of youth, and a most cheerful and sanguine disposition, she was uniformly bright and animated. Her sparkling eye and dimpled cheek were happiness to Mr. Linwood ; the old love cheerfulness as the dim eye delights in brilliant colours.

Mrs. Archer, who was always, in Mr. Linwood's estimation, the *next best* to Isabella, devoted her evenings to him. She saw, or fancied she saw, that Bessie's countenance expressed a pleased consciousness of Isabella's presence : at any rate, she knew that there was another countenance always lighted up by it. Accordingly, she repaired every evening to Mr. Linwood, and played rubber after rubber, performing her tiresome duty with such zest and zeal, that Mr. Linwood pronounced her a comfortable partner and respectable antagonist—"a deal more than he could say for any other woman."

While the surface of this little society remained as usual, there was a strong under-current at work. Herbert, after his explanation with Lady Anne, was resolved to leave no effort unmade to effect his escape from durance, and put himself in the way of those brighter hours that youth and health whispered might come. His first step was taken the morning after his parting with Lady Anne. He enclosed the permit for his visits at home, sent to him by Sir Henry Clinton, to that gentleman, with an acknowledgment of his kindness, but without assigning any reason for declining to avail himself of it farther. He was careful not to involve his honour by any pretences in relation to that obligation ; it was off his hands, and he thanked Heaven he was now free to use whatever stratagem would avail him. He feigned illness. He knew Rose would be sent to inquire after him ; and he also knew that, when told that he was ill, she would, by force or favour, obtain access to him. Fortunately, she was admitted without hesitation ; for Cunningham, conscious of the bad odour he was in on account of his ill-treatment of the American prisoners, deemed it his best policy to inflict no gratuitous hardship on the son of Mr. Linwood. Rose, once admitted, became first counsellor and coadjutor ; and with the aid of the young ladies at home, a project was contrived, of which this noble creature was to be the main executor. Herbert's illness, of course, continued unabated ; and Rose repeated her visits daily, and made her last, as she hoped, the evening succeeding Eliot's escape. "Lock me in," she said to the turnkey, "and leave me a quarter of an hour or so. I want to coax Mr. Herbert to take a biscuit ; he'd die on your dum stuff." Rose had, in fact, brought to Linwood, daily, more substantial rations than biscuit, and thus enabled him to gratify his appetite without endangering his reputation as an invalid. He was in bed when Rose entered, and out of it the moment the turnkey closed the door—"Oh, Rose, God bless you ! Is all arranged ?" he asked.

"Everything, Mr. Herbert, snug as a bug in a rug. The young ladies came with me to Mrs. Lizzy's, and she is to be at Smith's house with them precisely at seven. It is now half-past six. Mrs. Lizzy's boat, with the muffled oars, that's got off many a prisoner before you, is now waiting for you."

"And are my sister and Lady Anne going to Smith's house without any male attendant ?"

"Dear, yes ! they are wrapped in cloaks—nobody will know them ; and Mrs. Lizzy is as good a guard as horse, foot, and dragoon ; there's not a thimbleful of danger, Mr. Herbert, and they fear none, bless their hearts ! To be sure, Miss Belle is no great of a soldier in common, and Lady Anne will scream like all natur' at a mouse ; but love is a great help to courage in young parsons !"

While Rose was making these communications, to which Herbert eagerly listened, she was doffing an extra set of *linsey-woolsey* garments, and transferring them to her young master, who somewhat delayed their adjustment, by putting his feet first into the "cursed petticoat," as he profanely termed it. That most respectable feminine article arranged to Rose's satisfaction, she put over it a short gown, and a checked handkerchief over all. "Now for the beauties," she said, drawing from her pocket a wig and mask, and holding them up in either hand : "Miss Belle made one, and Lady Anne t'other."

The mask, if it might be so called, was well coloured, and bore a tolerable likeness to Rose. Linwood was enchanted. "Which," he exclaimed, "which did Lady Anne make, Rose ?"

"The mask."

Linwood seized it, kissed it, and exclaimed, "Admirably, admirably done !"

"It was not half the trouble the wig was," said Rose.

"Oh, that is capital too, Rose."

"But you don't carry on so about it. Laud's sake ! However, I suppose you love Miss Belle as well, only it an't a kind of love that breeds antics."

"True, Rose ; you may be sure I shall never love anybody better than I do my sister."

Rose was satisfied, and proceeded to tie on the mask, and adjust the fleecy locks. "It's a main pity," she said, "to cover your pretty shining hair with what looks like *nigger's wool*, as they call it."

"Not a bit—not a bit, Rose. I know some *wool* that covers a far better head than mine—more capable, more discerning ; and God never created a nobler heart than beats under one black skin."

"Pooh ! Mr. Herbert." Rose's "pooh" was a disclaimer ; but as she put it in, she brushed a tear from her eye ; then tying a mob-cap and black silk bonnet over the wig, and throwing over his shoulders her short blue broadcloth cloak, and hiding his white hands in her mittens, she laughed exultingly, declaring she "should not herself know him from herself." "Now you're *readied*," she said, "settle down as you walk—be prudent, Mr. Herbert—look before you leap. Don't answer them dumb fellows, when you get out, a word more than yes or no—I never do. Do your *endeavours* and the Lord will help you. He helps them as helps themselves—hark ! there comes the fellow."

Before the turnkey opened the door, she was in bed, her head enveloped in the bedclothes ; and Herbert stood, her basket on his arm, apparently waiting. No suspicion was excited, nor questions asked. They went out, and the door was re-locked. Rose raised her head to listen to their receding footsteps. The footsteps ceased, and she heard Cunningham's (the provost marshal's) voice : "Well, wench," he said, addressing, as she knew, her counterfeit, "how goes it with your young master ?"

"Now the Lord o' mercy help him !" she exclaimed ; "he used to mimic Jupe—if he only can me."

She did not hear Herbert's reply ; but she heard Cunningham say, as if responding to it—"Poorlier, hey ! I've got something here that will bring back his stomach—respects to your master—mind, wench." Again she heard Herbert's footsteps recede, and Cunningham enter her cell, and shut and lock the door.

Cunningham's name was a terror to the whigs, and to all that cared for them. The man's excessive cruelty and meanness may be inferred from the extravagant allegations current at the time ; that he was in the habit of putting the American prisoners of war to death, in order to sequester the rations allowed them. He had recently reason for apprehensions that an inquiry would be instituted into his conduct by the commander-in-chief, who certainly did not authorise unnecessary cruelties, if he neglected to take cognisance of them.

Rose's head was well muffled in the bed-clothes, when Cunningham, coming up to the bed, said, " How goes it Mr. Linwood ! bile uppermost yet ! Come, lift up your head, and speak, man—can't you give an answer to a civil word ! Come, come, I'm not Tom nor Sam to be put off this way— next thing you'll bolt, and I shall have it to answer for ; but they sha'n't say I did not do the good Samaritan by you. You won't eat—you won't hear to the doctor—the d—l is in you, man ; why don't you rise up ! Here's a dose you must take, anyhow—it's what they give in all cases, calomel and jalap—come, man, if fair means won't do, foul must."

The patient continued obstinate, and Cunningham set down the dose, which was mixed in a huge coffee-bowl, beside a basket of vials, containing sundry nauseous medicines, designed for the poor prisoners, as if bad food were not poison and torture enough for them. A contest began, in which Cunningham had reason to be astonished at the strength of the invalid. In the scramble, Rose's head was disengaged from the bed-clothes; the truth was revealed, and she sprang on him like a tiger on its prey. The cowardly wretch shrank back, and drew a knife, crying out, " You d—d nigger ! "

Rose wrested it from him, and her spirit disdaining the assassin's weapon, she thrust it into the wall, exclaiming—" Now we're even ! "

He sprang towards the door—she pulled him back, threw him down, put her knee on his breast, and by the time he had made one ineffectual struggle, and once bellowed for help, she had added laudanum, castor-oil, and ipecacuanha to the calomel and jalap ; and holding his nose between the thumb and finger of one hand, she presented the overflowing bowl to his lips with the other. When she had convinced him of her potentiality, by making him gulp down one swallow, she mercifully withdrew the draught, saying, " If you offer to move one inch, or make a sound, I'll pour it down your throat to the last drop."

She then released him from her grasp, and while he was panting and shuddering, she turned her back, muttering something of stringing him up in her *clothes*. The " clothes," which she quickly disengaged from their natural office, proved to be her garters. As she stretched them out, trying their strength, " My own spinning, twisting, and knitting," said she ; " they'll bear the weight of twenty such slim pieces as you."

" Are you going to hang me ! " gasped out Cunningham.

" Hang you ! Yes ; but not harm you, if you're quiet, mind. But I'd choke you twice over to give Mr. Herbert time : so mind and keep your breath to cool your porridge."

She then turned him over, bound his hands behind him with one garter, and made a slip-noose

with the other, while he, like a reptile in the talons of a vulture, crawled and squirmed with a hopeless resistance.

" There's no use ;" said Rose, " you're but a baby in my hands—it's the strong heart makes the strong arm."

She then set him upright on Herbert's bed, put the noose round his neck, and made the other end fast to an iron hook in the wall. This was just achieved, when a hurried footstep was heard, followed by a clattering at the door, and a call for " Master Cunningham !—Master Cunningham ! " Rose placed her foot against the foot of the bedstead ; Cunningham understood the menace, and suppressed the cry on his lips. The calls were reiterated. Cunningham cast one glance at Rose ; her foot was fixed, her lips compressed, and her eyes glaring with a resolution stern as fate. Cunningham felt that the alternative was silence or death, and his face became convulsed between the impulse to respond and the effort to keep quiet. The knocking and screaming were repeated ; and then finding them ineffectual, the person went off to seek his master elsewhere. Other sounds now roused Rose's generous spirit, and tempted her to inflict the vengeance so well deserved ; but hers was not the mind to be swayed by opportunity— " convenience snug."

The apartment adjoining Linwood's was spacious, and crammed with American prisoners. There was a communicating door between them, through which could be distinctly heard any sound or movement louder than usual. Loring, in his customary evening round, had entered this apartment. Loring was Cunningham's coadjutor, and is described by Ethan Allen, who had himself notable experience in that prison, as " the most mean-spirited, cowardly, deceitful, and destructive animal in God's creation." Rose heard Loring command the prisoners to get to their beds, in his customary phrase (we retrench a portion of its vulgarity and profanity) ; " Kennel, d—n ye— kennel, ye sons of Belial ! "

At this brutal address to persons whom Rose honoured as a Catholic honours the Saints, her blood boiled within her. She hastily withdrew her foot from the bedpost, and strode to the extremity of the narrow apartment ; then turning and stretching her arm towards Cunningham, she said, with an energy that made his blood curdle, " It is not for me to 'venge them, but God will. Their children shall be lords in the land, and sound out their fathers' names with ringing of bells and firing of cannon, when you, and Loring, and all such car'on, have died and rotted like dogs, as ye are."

The sounds in the adjoining apartment after a while subsided, and with them Rose's ire. She seated herself to await the latest hour when she could retire from the prison, and elude the suspicion of the sentinel, the only person whose vigilance she had to encounter.

The footsteps had ceased from the passages, and sleep seemed, like rain, to have fallen on the just and the unjust—the keepers and their prisoners. Cunningham, seeing Rose preparing to take her departure, begged her in the most abject manner, before she went, to release him from his frightful position.

" No, no," she obstinately replied to his supplications, " ye shall hang in *iffigy*, to be seen and scorned by your own people ; but one marcy I'll do you : if you'll hold your tongue, I'll not let out, while the war lasts—while the war lasts, remember, that you were strung up there by a ' d——n *nigger* '—a nigger *woman* ! "

It appeared that Cunningham was glad to accept this very small mercy, by the report which afterwards prevailed, that he had only escaped a fitting end through the forbearance of Mr. Herbert Linwood.

Rose passed unmolested through the passage and the outer door, which, being locked on the inside, and the key in the wards, opposed no obstacle to her retreat. The sentinel in the yard saw and recognised her ; but not being the same who was on guard when the first Dromio passed, he merely inferred that Rose had been permitted to remain longer than usual ; and kindly opening the gate, he responded civilly to her civil " good-night."

Rose went home, not however to enjoy the quiet sleep which should have followed so good a piece of work as she had achieved, but to suffer, and see others suffer, the most distressful apprehensions.

CHAPTER XXXVIII.

Let the great gods
That keep this dreadful pother o'er our heads
Find out their enemies now.

ISABELLA and Lady Anne, cloaked and hooded, repaired to Dame Bengin's some half-hour, as may be remembered, before the time appointed for their meeting with Linwood. This forerunning of the hour was to allow them to take advantage of Rose's escort. It did not pass without a censure from their wary coadjutor. " You lack discretion, young ladies," she said ; " and I lacked it too when I let you in partners in this business. My father used to say, ' If you want to go safe over a tottering plank, always go alone.' However, we must make the best of it now : so just take this box of ribands, and stand at the farther end of the counter, and seem to be finding a match. It is nothing strange for ladies to be tedious at that."

The young ladies obeyed, but Lady Anne fretted in an under voice at the delay ; and Isabella ventured a remonstrance, to which Dame Bengin, an autocrat in her own domain, replied, " she must go her own way ; that full twenty minutes were left to the time appointed for the meeting at Smith's house, and time was money to her."

" I wish to Heaven I could wring the parrot's neck," whispered Lady Anne ; " I do believe the people answer to its call." The parrot kept up a continuous scream of " Come in—come in ! " that might have tormented nerves less excitable than our friends' were at this moment.

" I surmise we are going to have a storm," said an old woman, who had stepped in for a pennyworth of *cochinia* for her grandchildren ; " it's always a sign of a storm when Sylvy keeps up such a chattering at night-fall." Lizzy Bengin went to the door, and looked anxiously at the gathering clouds.

" Come in—come in ! " cried Sylvy ; and, as if obedient to her summons, trotted in, one after another, half a dozen urchins. One wanted " a skein of sky-blue silk for aunt Polly : not too light nor too dark : considerably fine and very strong ; not too slack nor too hard twisted." Lizzy Bengin looked over half a dozen papers before she could meet the order of her customer.

" Pray send the whole to aunt Polly," cried Lady Anne ; " I will pay you, Bengin." The boy stared, the dame seemed not to hear her, and bade the boy run home and tell aunt Polly she hoped the skein would suit.

" Twopence worth of button-moulds—just this size, ma'am." The indefatigable Mrs. Bengin explored the button-mould box.

" Mammy wants a nail of silk, a shade lighter than the sample." Mrs. Bengin looked over her pile of silks.

" Come in—come in ! " still cried Sylvy, certainly not the silent partner of the house.

" Aunty wants a dust of snuff, and she'll pay you to-morrow."

" How much is a drawing of your best bohea, Mrs. Bengin ? "

" Mrs. Lizzy, uncle John wants to know if you've got any shoes about little Johnny's size ! " While Mrs. Bengin, who was quite in the habit of securing the mint, anise, and cummin of her little trade, was with the utmost composure satisfying these multifarious demands, the minutes seemed ages to our impatient friends ; Isabella took out her watch. The dame perceived the movement, and seemed to receive the impulse from it, for she was dismissing the shoe-inquirer with a simple negative, when in came a black girl, with a demand for " spirits of *camphire*."

" What's the matter, Phillis ! "

" Madam Meredith has got the *hystrikes*."

" Then she has my note," whispered Lady Anne.

While the camphire was pouring out, a sturdy sailor-boy entered. " Ah, is that you, Tom Smith ! A hand of tobacco you're wanting ! Well, first come first served—just be taking in Sylvy, while I'm getting a cork to suit the vial." Mrs. Bengin seemed suddenly fluttered by a look from Tom, and she bade the servant run home *sans* cork. The moment Phillis had passed the threshold, Lizzy said, " Speak out, Tom, there are none but friends here ! "

" It's too late, Lizzy Bengin, you're lost ! "

The inquiries and replies that followed were rapid. The amount of Tom's intelligence was, that some combustibles had been discovered near the magazine, and that, as strange persons had recently been observed going to and coming from Lizzy's shop, it was believed that a plot had been there contrived ; the commandant had issued an order for her apprehension, and men were by this time on their way to seize her.

Lizzy Bengin had so often been suspected, and threatened, and eluded detection, that she did not now believe her good fortune had deserted her. She heard Tom through, and then said, " My boat is ready and I'll dodge them yet."

Isabella ventured to ask, with scarcely a ray of hope, " if they might still go with her ! "

" Yes, if you're not afeard, and will be prudent. Shut the shutters, Tom—lock the door after us, and keep them out as long as possible, that we may gain time. Throw my books into the loft—don't let 'em rummage and muss my things, and look to Sylvy." Her voice was slightly tremulous as she added, " If anything happens to me, Tom, be kind to Sylvy !"

By this time her cloak and hood were on, and they sallied forth. Dame Lizzy's valour was too well tempered by discretion to have permitted her to consent to the attendance of the young ladies, if she had not, after calculating the chances, been quite sure that no danger would be thereby incurred. She believed that her pursuers, after being kept at bay by her faithful ally Tom, would be at a loss where next to seek her. The place appointed for meeting Linwood was a little untenanted dwelling, near the water's edge, called " Smith's House." There he was to doff his disguise, and there, should there be any uproar in the streets, the young ladies could remain till all was quiet. Isabella and Lady Anne were in no temper to consider risks and chances. Life, to the latter, seemed to be set on the die of seeing Herbert once more. Isabella felt a full sympathy with this most natural desire, and an intense eagerness to be immediately assured of her brother's escape ; so, clinging close to their sturdy friend, they hastened forward.

The old woman's interpretation of Sylvy's cries proved a true one. A storm was gathering rapidly. Large drops of rain pattered on the pavement, and the lightning flashed at intervals. But the distance to the boat, lying in a nook just above Whitehall, was short, and the moon, some seven nights old, was still unclouded. They soon reached " Smith's House," and heard the joyful signal-whistle previously agreed on.

" He is here !" exclaimed Isabella.

Lady Anne's fluttering heart was on her lips, but she did not speak. Herbert joined them.

" Now kiss and part," cried Lizzy Bengin. The first command was superfluous ; the second it seemed impossible to obey. It was no time for words, and few did they mingle with the choking sighs of parting ; but these few were of the marvellous coinage of the heart, and the heart was stamped upon them. The storm increased, and the darkness thickened. " Come, come ! this won't do, young folks," cried their impatient leader ; " we must be off—we've foul weather to cross the river, and then to pass the enemy's stations before day-light—the hounds may be on our heels too—we must go."

All felt the propriety, the necessity of this movement. Lady Anne only begged that they might go to the water's edge, and see the boat off. Dame Bengin interposed no objection ; that would only have caused fresh entreaties and longer delay, and they set forward. The distance to the boat was not above a hundred yards ; they had reached the shore, Mrs. Bengin was already in the boat, and Herbert speaking his last word, when they heard the voices of pursuers, and the next flash of lightning revealed a file of soldiers rushing towards them. Lady Anne shrieked ; Lizzy Bengin screamed, " Jump in, sir, or I'll push off without you."

" Go," cried Isabella, " dear Herbert, go."

" I will not—I cannot, and leave you in the hands of these wretches."

" Oh, no ! do not—do not, Herbert," entreated Lady Anne ; " take me with you." This was enough and irresistible. Herbert clasped his arm around her and leaped into the boat.

" Come with us, Isabella," screamed Lady Anne.

" For God's sake, come, Belle," shouted Herbert. Isabella wavered for an instant. Another glare of lightning showed the soldiers within a few feet of her, looking, in that lurid light, fierce and terrible beyond expression ; Isabella obeyed the impulse of her worst fears and leaped into the boat ; and Lizzy, who stood with her oar fixed, instantly pushed from the shore. Curses burst from the lips of their balked pursuers.

" We'll have them yet," exclaimed their leader. " To the Whitehall Dock, boys, and get out a boat !"

Our boat's company was silent. Herbert, amid a host of other anxieties, was, as he felt Lady Anne's tremulous grasp, bitterly repenting this last act of a rashness which he flattered himself experience had cured, and Isabella was thinking of the beating hearts at home.

Dame Bengin, composed, and alone wholly intent on the present necessity, was the first to speak. " Don't be scared, little lady," she said ; " sit down quiet—don't touch his arm—he'll need all its strength. Do you take the tiller, Miss Linwood—mind exactly what I tell you—I know every turn in the current—don't lay out so much strength on your oars, Captain Linwood—keep time to the dip of mine—that will do !"

Dame Bengin, with good reason, plumed herself on her nautical skill. Her father had been a pilot, and Lizzy being his only child, he had repaired, as far as possible, what he considered the calamity of her sex, by giving her the habits of a boy. Her childhood was spent on the water, and nature and early training had endowed her with the masculine spirit and skill that now did her such good service. The courage and cowardice of impulse are too much the result of physical condition to be the occasion of either pride or shame.

The wind was rising, the lightning becoming more vivid and continuous, and the pelting cold rain driving in the faces of our poor fugitives. The lightning gloriously lit up a wild scene : the bay, a " phosphoric sea ;" the little islands, that seemed in the hurly-burly to be dancing on the crested waves ; and the shores, that looked like the pale regions of some ghostly land. Still the little boat leaped the waves cheeringly, and still no sound of fear was heard within it. There is something in the sublime manifestations of power in the battling elements, that either stimulates the mind of man, "stirs the feeling infinite," and exalts it above a consciousness of the mortality that invests it, or crushes it under a sense of its own impotence. Our little boat's company were a group for a painter, if a painter could kindle his picture with electric light. Lizzy Bengin, her short muscular arms bared, and every nerve of body and mind strained, plied her oars, at each stroke giving a new order to her unskilled but most obedient coadjutors. Isabella's head was bare, her dark hair hanging in masses on each side her face, her poetic eye turning from " heaven to earth and earth to heaven," her face in the lurid light as pale as marble, and like that marble on which the sculptor has expressed his own divine imaginings in the soft forms of feminine beauty. Lady Anne sat at Herbert's feet, her eye fixed on his face, passively and quietly awaiting her fate, not doubting that fate would be to go to the bottom, but feeling that such a destiny would be far more tolerable with her lover, than any other without him. This dependence, "love overcoming the fear of death," inspired Herbert with preternatural strength. His fine frank face beamed with hope and resolution, and his eye, as ever and anon it fell on the loving creature at his feet, was suffused with a mother's tenderness.

In the intervals of darkness they guided the boat by the lights on the shores, and towards a light that, kindled by a confederate of Lizzy Bengin's for Herbert's benefit, blazed steadily, in spite of the rain, a mile below Powles Hook.

They were making fair headway, when they perceived a sail-boat put off from Whitehall. They were pursued, and their hearts sunk within them; but Lizzy Bengin soon rallied, and her inspiring voice was heard, calculating the chances of escape. "The storm," she said, "is in our favour—no prudent sailor would spread a sail in such a gusty night. The wind is flawy, too, and we can manage our boat, running first for one point and then for another, so as to puzzle them; and in some of their turns, if they have not more skill than any man has shown since my father's day, they'll capsize their boat."

We dare not attempt to describe the chase that followed; the dexterous manœuvring of the little boat, now setting towards Long Island, now back to the city, now for Governor's Island, now up, and then down the river. We dare not attempt it. Heaven seems to have endowed a single genius of our land with a chartered right to all the *water privileges* for the species of manufacture in which we are engaged, and his power but serves to set in desperate relief the weakness of his inferiors. The water is not our element, and we should be sure to show an "alacrity in sinking."

Suffice it to say, it seemed that the efforts of our little boat's crew must prove unavailing; that after Dame Bengin's sturdy spirit had yielded to her woman's nature, and she had dropped her oars, and given the common signals of her sex's weakness in streaming tears and wringing hands, Herbert continued laboriously to row, till Lady Anne, fainting, dropped her head on his knee, and Isabella entreated him to submit at once to their inevitable fate. Nothing indeed now remained but to run the boat ashore, to surrender themselves to their pursuers, to obtain aid for Lady Anne, and secure protection to her and Isabella. The resolution taken, the boat was suddenly turned; the sail-boat turned also, but too suddenly; the wind struck and capsized it. The bay was in a blaze of light when the sail dipped to the water—intense darkness followed—no shriek was heard.

After the first exclamations burst from the lips of our friends, not a sound proceeded from them, not a breath of exultation at a deliverance that involved their fellow-beings in destruction. The stroke of Herbert's oars ceased, and the fugitives awaited breathlessly the next flash of lightning, to enable them to extend their aid, if aid could be given. The lightning came and was repeated, but nothing was to be seen but the boat drifting away at the mercy of the waves.

A few moments more brought them to land, where, beside their beacon-light, stood an untenanted fisherman's hut, in which they found awaiting them a comfortable fire and substantial food. These "creature comforts," with rest and rekindled hope, soon did their work of restoration. And the clouds clearing away, and the stars shining out cheerily, Lizzy Bengin, aware that her presence rather encumbered and endangered the companions of her flight than benefited them, bade them a kind good-night, and sought refuge among some of her Jersey acquaintance, truehearted to her, and to all her country's friends.

CHAPTER XXXIX.

Good to begin well, better to end well.

WHAT was next to be done was as puzzling to our friends as the passage of that classic trio, the fox, the goose, and the corn, was to our childish ingenuity. Duty and safety were involved in Linwood's return to the American camp with all possible expedition. General Washington was at Morristown, and the American army was going into winter quarters in its immediate vicinity. Thither Linwood must go, and so thought Lady Anne must she. "Fate," she said, "had seconded her inclinations, and to contend against their united force was impossible; why should she not give her hand to Herbert at once and be happy, instead of returning to vex and be vexed by her disappointed aunt! After they had made sure of happiness and Heaven's favour, for Heaven would smile on the union of true and loving hearts, let the world gossip to its heart's content about Linwood running off with an heiress; he who was so far above a motive so degrading and soulsacrificing, could afford the imputation of it, and would soon outlive it." There was both nature and truth in her reasoning, and it met with her lover's full and irrepressible sympathy; with Isabella's too, but not with her acquiescence.

Poor Isabella! it was hard for one who had her keen participation in the happiness of others to oppose it, and to hazard by delay the loss of its richest materials. There was an earnest seconding of their entreaties, too, from a voice in the secret depths of her heart, which whispered that Eliot Lee was at Morristown; but what of that? ay, Isabella, *what of that?* Once at Morristown, her return to the city might be indefinitely delayed; innumerable obstacles might interpose, and to return to her father was an imperative and undeferable duty. To permit Lady Anne to proceed without her, would be to expose her to gossip and calumny. Isabella's was the ruling spirit; and after arguments, entreaties, and many tears on the lady's part, the lovers deferred to the laws of propriety as expounded by her; and it was agreed that Linwood should escort the ladies to the outskirts of the Dutch village of Bergen, which could not be more than two or three miles distant; that there they should part, and thence the means of returning to the city without an hour's delay might easily be compassed.

Accordingly, two hours before daylight, they set forth, following, through obscure and devious footpaths, the general direction of Bergen. Miranda truly says, "it is the good-will to the labour that makes the task easy." Lady Anne had no good-will to hers, and her footsteps were feeble and faltering. The day dawned, the sun rose, and as yet they saw no landmarks to indicate the vicinity of Bergen. Herbert feared they had missed their way; but without communicating his apprehensions, he proposed the ladies should take shelter in a log-hut they had reached, and which he thought indicated the proximity of a road, while he went to reconnoitre.

He had been gone half an hour, when Isabella and Lady Anne were startled by the firing of guns. They listened breathlessly. The firing was repeated, but unaccompanied by the sound of voices, footsteps, or the trampling of horses.

"It is not near," said Isabella to her little friend, who had clasped her hands in terror; "Herbert will hear it and return to us, and we are quite safe here."

"Yes; but if he is taken—murdered, Isabella! Oh, let us go and know the worst."

"It would be folly," replied Isabella, "to expose ourselves, and risk the possibility of missing Herbert; but if you will be quiet, we will creep up to that eminence," pointing to a hill before them; "if it is cleared on the other side, we may see without being seen."

They forthwith mounted the hill, which presented a view of an open country, traversed by several cross-roads. The point where they intersected, a quarter of a mile distant, at once fixed their gaze. A party of some thirty Americans, part mounted and part on foot, were engaged in a hot contest with more than an equal number of the enemy. Lady Anne grasped Isabella's arm, both were silent for a moment, when a cry burst from Lady Anne's lips, "It is—it is he!"

"Who! where—what mean you!"

"Your brother, Isabella!—there, the foremost! on the black horse!"

"It is he! God have mercy on us!—and there is Eliot Lee!"

Lady Anne's eye was riveted to Linwood.

"There are three upon him," she screamed; "fly, fly!—Oh, why does he not fly!"

"He fights bravely," cried Isabella, covering her eyes. "Heaven aid you, my brother!"

"It's all over," shrieked Lady Anne.

Isabella looked again. Herbert's horse had fallen under him. "No, no," she cried; "he lives! he is rising!"

"But they are rushing on him—they will cut him to pieces!"

Isabella sprang forward, as if she would herself have gone to his rescue, exclaiming—"My brother, Herbert—Oh, Eliot has come to his aid! God be praised!—See, Anne!—look up. Now they fight side by side!—Courage, courage, Anne! Mercy upon us, why does Eliot Lee turn back!"

"Oh, why does not Herbert turn too! if he would but fly while he can!"

"Ah, there he comes!" exclaimed Isabella, without heeding her companion's womanly wish, "urging forward those men from behind the wagons—On, on, good fellows! Ah, that movement is working well—see, see; the enemy is disconcerted! they are falling back! thank God, thank God! See what confusion they are in;

they are running, poor wretches; they are falling under that back fire!"

The flying party had taken a road which led to an inclosed meadow, and they were soon stopped by a fence. This opposed a slight obstacle, but it occasioned delay. The Americans were close upon them; they turned, threw down their arms, and surrendered themselves prisoners.

Shortly after, Eliot Lee, his face radiant with a joy that fifty victories could not have inspired, stood at the entrance of the log-hut, informing the ladies that Linwood had confided them to his care; Linwood himself having received a wound, which, though slight, unfitted him for that office, and rendered immediate surgical aid desirable to him. His friend had bidden him say to Miss Linwood that they had wandered far from Bergen; and that as they could not now get there without the danger of encountering parties of the enemy, nothing remained but to accept Captain Lee's protection to Morristown.

"Do you hesitate now, Isabella?" asked Lady Anne, impatiently.

"No, my dear girl, there is now no choice for us."

"Thank Heaven for that. Nothing but necessity would conquer you, Isabella." The necessity met a very willing submission from Isabella; and she was half inclined to acquiesce in a whispered intimation from Lady Anne, "that it was undoubtedly the will of Heaven they should go to Morristown." They were soon seated in a wagon, and proceeding forward, escorted by Eliot and a guard, and hearing from him the following explanation of his most fortunate meeting with Linwood.

Eliot Lee had been sent by Washington, with wagons, and a detachment of chosen men, to afford a safe convoy for some important winter-stores that had been run across from New York to the Jersey shore for the use of the officers' families at Morristown. In the mean time, a vigilant enemy had sent an intimation of the landing of these stores, and of their destination, to the British station at Powles Hook, and a detachment of men had been thence despatched with the purpose of anticipating the rightful proprietors.

Eliot, on his route, encountered one of the enemy's videttes, whom he took prisoner, and who, to baffle him, told him the stores were already at Powles Hook. Eliot, warily distrusting the information, proceeded, and directly after, and just as he came in view of the enemy's party, he met Herbert issuing from the wood. A half moment's explanation was enough. The vidette was dismounted, Herbert put in his place, armed with his arms, and a golden opportunity afforded (to which the brave fellow did full justice), to win fresh laurels wherewith to grace his return to the dreaded, and yet most desired presence of his commander.

CHAPTER XL.

Our profession is the chastest of all. The shadow of a fault tarnishes our most brilliant actions. The least inadvertence may cause us to lose that public favour which is so hard to gain.

THE quotation from a public reprimand of Washington to a general officer, which forms the motto to this chapter, contains the amount of his reproof to Linwood in their first and private interview. Even this reproof was softened by the generous approbation his general expressed of the manliness and respectful submission with which he had endured the penalty of his rashness. Linwood's heart was touched; and, obeying the impulse of his frank nature, he communicated the circumstances that had mitigated his captivity, and gave a sort of dot-and-line sketch of his love-tale to the awe-inspiring Washington. Oh the miracles of love! But let not too much power be ascribed to the blind god. Linwood's false impressions of Washington's impenetrable sternness were effaced by his own experience, the most satisfactory of all evidence. He found that this great man, like Him whom he imitated, was not strict to mark iniquity, and was, whenever he could be so without the sacrifice of higher duties, alive to social virtues and affections.

"Well, my young friend," he said, as Linwood concluded, "you certainly have made the most of your season of affliction, and now we must take care of these generous companions of your flight. Our quarters are stinted; but Mrs. Washington has yet a spare room, which they must occupy till they can return with safety to the city, and choose to do so."

Linwood thought himself, and with good reason, requited a thousand-fold for all his trials. His only embarrassment was relieved, and he had soon after the happiness of presenting his sister and Lady Anne Seton to Mrs. Washington, a most benign and excellent woman, and of confiding them to the hospitalities of her household. Eliot and Linwood's gallantry, in their rencounter with the enemy, was marked, and advanced them in the opinion of their fellow-officers; but the signal favour it obtained from the ladies of Morristown, must have been in part a collateral consequence of the immense importance, to their domestic comfort, of those precious stores which our friends had secured for them.

Their sympathy in the romantic adventures of the young ladies was manifested in the usual feminine mode, by a round of little parties: from stern necessity, frugal entertainments, but abounding in one luxury, so rare where all others now abound, that it might be thought unattainable; the highest luxury of social life—what is it?

With the luggage of our heroines came encouraging accounts from Mrs. Archer of Bessie Lee's progress, assurances of Mr. Linwood's unwonted patience, and hints that it would be most prudent for her young friends to remain where they were, till the excitement, occasioned by their departure, had subsided. Still Isabella was so thoroughly impressed with the filial duty of returning without any voluntary delay, that, at her urgent request, measures were immediately taken to effect it; but obstacle after obstacle intervened. Sir Henry Clinton was about taking his departure for the south, and he put off from time to time giving an official assurance of an act of oblivion in favour of our romantic offenders. The rigours of that horrible winter of 1780, still unparalleled in the annals of our hard seasons, set in and embarrassed all intercommunication.

It must be confessed, that Isabella bore these trials with such gracious patience, that it hardly seemed to be the result of difficult effort. It was quite natural that she should participate in the overflowing happiness of her brother and friend; and it was natural that, being now an eye-witness of the struggles, efforts, endurance, and entire self-sacrifice of the great men that surrounded her, her mind, acute in perception, and vigorous in reflection, should be excited and gratified. There are those who deem political subjects beyond the sphere of a woman's, certainly of a young woman's mind; but if our young ladies were to give a portion of the time and interest they expend on dress, gossip, and light reading, to the comprehension of the constitution of their country, and its political institutions, would they be less interesting companions, less qualified mothers, or less amiable women? "But there are dangers in a woman's adventuring beyond her customary path." There are; and better the chance of shipwreck on a voyage of high purpose, than to expend life in paddling hither and thither on a shallow stream, to no purpose at all.

Isabella's mind was not regularly trained; and, like that of most of her sex, the access to it was through the medium of her feelings. Her sympathies were not limited to the few, the "bright, the immortal names" that are now familiar as household words to us all. She saw the same virtues, that illustrated them, conspicuous in the poor soldiers; in that class of men that have been left out in the world's estimate, and whose existence is scarcely recognised in its past history. The winter of 1780 was characterised by Washington as "the decisive moment, the most important America had seen!" The financial affairs of the country were in the utmost disorder. The currency had so depreciated, that a captain's pay would scarcely furnish the shoes in which he marched to battle. The soldiers were without clothes or blankets, and this in our coldest winter. They had been but a few days in their winter quarters before the flour and meat were exhausted; and yet, as Washington said in a letter to Congress, after speaking of the patient and uncomplaining fortitude with which the army bore their sufferings, "though there had been frequent desertions—not one mutiny." Happy was it for America that, in the beginning of her national existence, she thus tested the virtue of the people, and, profiting by her experience, was confirmed in her resolution to confide her destinies to them!

Something above the ordinary standard has been claimed for our heroine; but it must be confessed, after all, that she was a mere woman, and that the main-spring of her mind's movements was in her heart. How much of Isabella's enthusiasm in the American cause was to be attributed to her intercourse with Eliot Lee, we leave to be determined by her peers. That intercourse had never been disturbed by the cross-purposes, jarring sentiments, clashing opinions, and ever-annoying disparities, that had so long made her life resemble a troubled dream. Eliot's world was her world; his spirit answered to hers. During that swift month that had flown away at Morristown, how often had she secretly rejoiced in the complete severance of the chain that had so long bound her to an "alternate slave of vanity and love!"—how she exulted in her freedom—freedom! the voluntary service of the heart is better than freedom.

There were no longer any barriers to Isabella and Lady Anne's return to the city. The day was fixed ; it came ; and while they were packing their trunks, and thinking of the partings that awaited them, Lady Anne's eyes streaming, and Isabella's changing cheek betraying a troubled heart, a letter was handed to Lady Anne. She looked at the superscription, threw it down, then resumed it, broke the seal, and read it. Without speaking, she mused over it for a moment, then suddenly disappeared, leaving her affairs unarranged, and did not return till Isabella's trunk was locked, and she was about wrapping herself in her travelling furs. She reproved her little friend's delay, urged haste, suggested consolation, and offered assistance. Lady Anne made no reply, but bent over her trunk, where, instead of arrangement, she seemed to produce hopeless confusion. " How strange," she exclaimed, " that Thérèse should have sent me this fresh white silk dress ! "

" Very strange ; but pray do not stay to examine it now."

" Bless Thérèse ! Here is my Brussels veil too ! "

" My dear child, are you out of your senses ! Our escort will be waiting—pray, pray make haste."

" And pray, dear Belle, don't stand looking at me—you fidget me so. Oh, I forgot to tell you Captain Lee asked for you—he is in the drawing-room—go down to him, please, dear Belle." As Lady Anne looked up, Isabella was struck with the changed expression of her countenance ; it was bright and smiling, the sadness completely gone. But she did not stay to speculate on the change, nor did she, it must be confessed, advert to Lady Anne for the next fifteen minutes. Many thoughts rushed through her mind as she descended the stairs. She wondered, painfully wondered, if Eliot would allude to their memorable parting at Mrs. Archer's ; " if he should repeat what he then said, what could she say in reply ! " When she reached the drawing-room door, she was obliged to pause to gain self-command ; and when she opened it, she was as pale as marble, and her features had a stern composure that would have betrayed her effort to any eye but Eliot's ; to his they did not.

Eliot attempted to speak the common-places of such occasions, and she to answer them ; but his sentences were lame, and her replies monosyllables ; and they both soon sunk into a silence more expressive of their mutual feelings.

" Lady Anne said he asked for me—well, it was but to tell me the cold had abated ! and the sleighing is fine ! and he trusts I shall reach the city without inconvenience ! What a poor simpleton I was, to fancy that such sudden and romantic devotion could be lasting ! A very little reality—a little every-day intercourse, has put the actual in the place of the ideal ! "

If Isabella had ventured to lift her eye to Eliot's face at this moment, she would have read in the conflict it expressed, the contradiction of her false surmises : and if her eye had met his, the conflict might have ceased, for it takes but a spark to explode a magazine. But Eliot had come into her presence resolved to resist the impulses of his heart, however strong they might be. He thought he should but afflict her generous nature by a second expression of his love, and his grief at parting. There had been moments when a glance of Isabella's eye, a tone of her voice—a certain indescribable something, which those alone who have heard and seen such can conceive, had flashed athwart his mind like a sunbeam, and visions of bliss in years to come had passed before him ; but clouds and darkness followed, and he remembered that Miss Linwood was unattainable to him—that if it were possible by the devotion of years to win her, how should he render that devotion, pledged as he was to his country for a service of uncertain length, and severed, as he must be, from her by an impassable barrier of circumstances ! As he had said to Isabella, he had been trained in the school of self-subjection, and never had he given such a proof of it as in these last few moments— the last he expected ever to enjoy or suffer with her. Both were so absorbed in their own emotions, that they did not notice the various entrances and exits of the servants, who were bustling in and out, and arranging cake and wine on a sideboard, with a deal of significance that would have amused unconcerned spectators. A louder, more portentous bustle followed—the door was thrown wide open, and both Eliot and Isabella were startled from their reveries by the entrance of Mrs. Washington, attended by a gentleman in clerical robes, and followed by Linwood and Lady Anne, in the bridal silk and veil that Thérèse, with inspiration worthy a French chambermaid, had forwarded.

" One word with you, Miss Linwood," said Mrs. Washington, taking Isabella apart. " This dear little girl, it seems, was left independent of all control by her fond father. The honourable scruples of your family have alone prevented her surrendering her independence into your brother's hands. She has this morning received a letter from her aunt, written in a transport of rage at her son's unexpected marriage with a Miss Ruthven. I fancy it is a Miss Ruthven of the Virginia family— Grenville Ruthven's eldest daughter ! "

" Yes—yes—it is, Madam," replied Isabella, with a faltering voice. The emotion passed with the words.

" Lady Anne's aunt," resumed Mrs. Washington, " declares her intention of immediately returning to England, and renounces her niece for ever. Lady Anne and your brother have referred their case to me ; she saying, with her usual playfulness, that she has turned rebel, and put herself under the orders of the commander-in-chief, or rather, he being this morning absent, under mine. I have decided according to my best judgment. There seems to be no sufficient reason why they should defer their nuptials, and endure the torments and perils of a protracted separation. So, my dear Miss Linwood, you have nothing to do but submit to my decision—take your place there as bridemaid—you see your brother has already stationed his friend, Captain Lee, beside him, as groom's-man—Colonel Hamilton is waiting our summons to give away the bride."

At a signal from his mistress, a servant opened the door to the adjoining room, and Hamilton entered, his face glowing with the sympathies and chivalric sentiment always ready to gush from his heart when its social spring was touched. Isabella had but time to whisper to Lady Anne.

"Just what I would have prayed for, had I dared to hope it," when the clergyman opened his book, and performed his office. That over, Mrs. Washington, as the representative of the parents, pronounced a blessing on the bridal pair ; and that no due ceremonial should be omitted, the bridal cake was cut and distributed according to established usage ; accompanied by a remark from Mrs. Washington, that it must have been compounded by some good hymeneal genius, as it was the only orthodox plum-cake that had been, or was like to be seen in Morristown, during that hard winter.

Now came partings, and tears, and last kind words, and messages, that were sure to find their way to Mr. Linwood's heart, and a bit of weddingcake for mama, who would scarcely have believed her son lawfully married, unless she had tasted it ; and, last of all, an order for a fine new suit for Rose, in compensation for that so unceremoniously dropped at " Smith's house."

At last, Isabella, in a covered sleigh, escorted by a guard, and attended by her brother and Eliot Lee, on horseback, set off for the place appointed for her British friends to meet her, and there she was transferred to their protection.

What Eliot endured, as he lingered for a moment at Isabella's side, cannot be expressed. She felt her heart rising to her eyes and cheeks, and by an effort of that fortitude, or pride, or resolution, which is woman's strength, by whatever name it may be called, she firmly said, " Farewell ! "

Eliot's voice was choked. He turned away without speaking ;—he impulsively returned, and withdrew the curtain that hung before Isabella. She was in a paroxysm of grief, her head thrown back, her hands clasped, and tears streaming from her eyes. What a spectacle — what a blessed spectacle for a self-distrusting, hopeless lover !

" Isabella ! " he exclaimed, " we do not then part for ever ? "

" I hope not," she replied.

The driver, unconscious of Eliot's returning movement, cracked his whip, the horses started on their course, and the road making a sudden turn, the sleigh instantly disappeared, leaving Eliot feeling as if he had been translated to another world—a world of illimitable hope, immeasurable joy.

" ' I hope not.' " Could Isabella have uttered a more common-place reply ? and yet these words, with the emotion that preceded them, were a key to volumes—were pondered on and brooded over, through summer and winter — ay, for years.

" Ah, n'en doutons pas ! à travers les temps et les espaces, les âmes ont quelquefois des correspondances mystérieuses. En vain le monde réel élève ses barrières entre deux êtres qui s'aiment ; habitans de la vie idéale, ils s'apparaissent dans l'absence, ils s'unissent dans la mort."

CHAPTER XLI.

Boy, fill me a bumper—now join in the chorus,
There's happiness still in the prospect before us ;
In this sparkling glass all hostility ends,
And Britons and we will for ever be friends.
        Derry down, derry down.—OLD SONG.

MORE than three years from the date of our last chapter had passed away. The European statesmen were tired of the silly effort to keep grown-up men in leading-strings, and their soldiers were wearied of combating in fields where no laurels grew for them. The Americans were eager—the old to rest from their labours, and the young to reap the fruit of their toils ; and all good and wise men contemplated, with joy, the reunion of two nations who were of one blood and one faith. King George, firm or obstinate to the last, had yielded his reluctant consent to the independence of his American colonies ; and the peace was signed, which was welcomed by all parties, save the few American royalists who were now to suffer the consequences that are well deserved by those who learn, unwillingly, and too late, that their own honour and interest are identified with their country's.

The 25th of November, 1783, was, as we are annually reminded, by the ringing of bells and firing of cannon, a momentous day in this city of New York. It was the time appointed for the evacuation of the city by the British forces, and the entrance of the American commander-in-chief with his army. To the royalists who had remained in the garrisoned city, attached from principle, and fettered by early association, to the original government, this was a day of darkness and mourning. With their foreign friends went, as they fancied, all their distinction, happiness, and glory. We may smile at their weakness, but cannot deny them our sympathy. Such men as Sir Guy Carleton (Sir Henry Clinton's successor), who made even his enemies love him, had a fair claim to the tears of his friends ; and others were there whose names grace the history of our parent land, and names not mentioned that were written on living hearts, and which made partings that day—

Such as press the life from out young hearts.

Though on the verge of winter, the day was bright and soft. The very elements were at peace. At the rising of the sun, the British flag on the Battery was struck. Boats were in readiness at the wharves to convey the troops, and such of the inhabitants as were to accompany them, down to Staten Island, where the British ships were awaiting them. At an early hour, and before the general embarkation, a gentleman much muffled, and evidently sedulously avoiding observation, was seen stealing through the by-streets to a boat, to which his luggage had already been conveyed, and which, as soon as he entered it, put off towards the fleet. He looked soured and abstracted, eager to depart, and yet not joyful in going. His attitude was dejected, and his eyes downcast, till some sound that betokened an approach to the ship roused him, when suddenly looking up, he beheld, leaning over the side of the vessel, an apparition that called the blood and the spirit to his face. This apparition was his wife—Mrs.

Jasper Meredith. There she stood, bowing to him, and smiling, and replying adroitly to such congratulations from the officers of the ship, as, "Upon my word, Mrs. Meredith, you leave the country with spirit—your husband should take a leaf out of your book."

Meredith entered the ship. His wife took him by the arm and led him aside. "One word to you, my dear love," she said, "before that cloud on your brow bursts. I have known, from the first, your secret intention, and your secret preparations to go off with the fleet, and leave me here to get on as I could. I took my measures to defeat yours. You should know before this time of day, that I am never foiled in what I undertake — "

"No, by Heaven, never."

"There's no use in swearing about it, my love; nor will there be any use," she added, changing her tone of irony to a cutting energy, "in doing what, as my husband—my lord and master—you may do, in raising a storm here, refusing to pay my passage, and sending me back to the city. Officers—gentlemen, you know, all take the part of an oppressed wife—you would be put to Coventry, and make your *début* in England to great disadvantage. So, my dear, make the best of it; let our plans appear to be in agreement. It is in bad taste to quarrel before spectators—we will reserve that to enliven domestic scenes in England."

"In England! my mother declares she will never receive you there; and I am now utterly dependent on my mother."

"I know all that; I have seen your mother's letters." Meredith stared. "Yes, all of them, and, in them all, she reiterates her governing principle, that 'appearances must be managed.' I shall convince her that I am one of the managers, and the *prima donna* in this drama of appearances."

Meredith made no reply. He saw no eligible way of escape, and he was, like a captive insect, paralysed in the web that enclosed him. "You are convinced, I perceive, my dear," continued his loving wife, "be kind enough to give me a few guineas; I paid my last to the boatmen, and it is awkward being without money."

Meredith turned from her and walked hurriedly up and down the deck; then stopped, and took out his pocket-book to satisfy her demand; but his purpose was suspended by his eye falling accidentally on the card, on which, ten years before, he had recorded Effie's prediction. The card was yellow and defaced; but like a talisman, it recalled with the freshness of actual presence the long, but not forgotten, past—the time when Isabella Linwood's untamed pulses answered to his—when Bessie Lee's soft eye fell tenderly upon him—when he was linked in friendship with Herbert—when the lights of nature still burned in his soul—while as yet his spirit had not passed under the world's yoke, and crouched under its burden of vanity, heartlessness, and sordid ambition. His eye glanced towards his wife, he tore the card in pieces, and honest, bitter tears flowed down his cheeks.

Bessie Lee, thou wert then avenged! Avenged! Sweet Spirit of Christian forgiveness and celestial love, we crave thy pardon! Bessie Lee, restored to her excellent mother, and to her peaceful and now most happy home at Westbrook, was enjoying her renovated health and "rectified spirit." The vigorous mind of Mrs. Archer, and Isabella's frank communication of her own malady and its cure, had aided in the entire dissipation of Bessie's illusions, and no shadow of them remained but a sort of nun-like shrinking from the admiration and devotion of the other sex. She lived for others, and chiefly to administer to the sick and sorrowful. She no longer suffered herself; but the cord of suffering had been so strained that it was weakened, and vibrated at the least touch of the miseries of others. The satirist who scoffs at the common fact of devotion succeeding love in a woman's heart, is superficial in the philosophy of our nature. He knows not that woman's love implies a craving for happiness, a dream of bliss that human character and human circumstances rarely realise, and a devotedness and self-negation due only to the Supreme. The idol falls, and the heart passes to the true God.

All things on earth shall wholly pass away,
Except the love of God, which shall live and last for aye.

That love of God, that sustaining, life-giving principle, waxed stronger and stronger in Bessie Lee as she went on in her pilgrimage. Her pilgrimage was not a long one; and when it ended, the transition was gentle from the heaven she made on earth to that which awaited her in the bosom of the Father.

We return to the shifting scenes in New York. The morning was allotted to the departure of the British. "Rose," said Mr. Linwood, "give me my cloak and fur shoes, and I will go through the garden to Broadway, and see the last of them—God bless them!"

"And my cloak and calêche, Rose," said Mrs. Linwood; "it is a proper respect to show our friends that our hearts are with them to the last—it should be a family thing. Come, Belle; and you, Lady Anne, come too."

"With all my heart, dear mama; but pray—pray do not call me *Lady* Anne. I have told you, again and again, that I have renounced my title, and will have no distinction but that which suits the country of my adoption—that which I may derive from being a good wife and mother—the true '*American order of merit.*'"

"As you please, my dear child; but it is a singular taste."

"Singular to prefer Mrs. Linwood to Lady Anne! Oh, no, mama."

Mrs. Linwood received the tribute with a grateful smile, and afterwards less frequently forgot her daughter-in-law's injunction. Her affections always got the better of her vanity—after a slight contest. "Rose," continued Lady Anne, "please put on little Herbert's fur cap, and take him out to see the show too. Is not that a pretty cap, mama! I bought it at Lizzy Bengin's."

"Lizzy Bengin's! Has Lizzy returned?"

"Yes, indeed; and re-opened her shop in the same place, and hung up her little household deity Sylvy again, who is screaming out as zealously as ever—'Come in—come in.' Lizzy, they say, is to have a pension from Congress *."

"The d——l she is!" exclaimed Mr. Linwood;

---

* Lizzy Bengin actually received the pension.